The Political Economy of South Africa Revisited:
Tracking and Debating the Minerals-Energy and Financial Complex

Studies in Critical Social Sciences

VOLUME 350

The titles published in this series are listed at *brill.com/scss*

The Political Economy of South Africa Revisited: Tracking and Debating the Minerals-Energy and Financial Complex

Critical Reconstructions of Political Economy

VOLUME 9

By

Ben Fine

BRILL

LEIDEN | BOSTON

The Library of Congress Cataloging-in-Publication Data is available online at https://catalog.loc.gov
LC record available at https://lccn.loc.gov/2025948546

Typeface for the Latin, Greek, and Cyrillic scripts: "Brill". See and download: brill.com/brill-typeface.

ISSN 1573-4234
ISBN 978-90-04-74832-3 (hardback)
ISBN 978-90-04-74833-0 (e-book)
DOI 10.1163/9789004748330

This book is printed on acid-free paper and produced in a sustainable manner.

Contents

List of Figures and Tables IX

1 Locating the Minerals-Energy Complex 1
- 1 Introduction 1
- 2 The Post-apartheid Conundrum 6
- 3 Whither or Wither the MEC? 15
- 4 Brief Overview 21

2 Total Factor Productivity vs. Realism: The South African Coal Mining Industry 22
- Postscript as Personal Preamble 22
- 1 Introduction 23
- 2 Measuring Total Factor Productivity 26
- 3 The Measurement of Output 29
- 4 Competition in the Markets for Coal 32
- 5 The Supply Side 33
- 6 Coal and the State 34
- 7 The Labour Market 35
- 8 Concluding Remarks 36

3 "The Rise in African Wages: 1975–1985": A Dissenting and Wide-Ranging Commentary 39
- Postscript as Personal Preamble 39
- 1 Introduction 40
- 2 The Orthodoxy We Inherit 42
- 3 Modelling Labour Markets? 49
- 4 Does Segmented Labour Market Theory Offer an Alternative? 54
- 5 Towards an Alternative 61
- 6 Concluding Remarks 67
- Appendix 70
  - *CLPT as Critical Point of Departure* 70

4 Debating the South African Minerals-Energy Complex 78
- Postscript as Personal Preamble 78
- 1 Introduction 79
- 2 The MEC Core 83

3 On Import-Substituting Industrialisation 85
4 The MEC as a System of Accumulation 87
5 Future Prospects 89
Appendix 91
Postscript 91
Opportunity for Opportunism Missed 92

5 **Engaging the MEC: Or a Lot of My Views on a Lot of Things** 93
Postscript as Personal Preamble 93
1 Introduction 95
2 The History of the 'MEC' 98
3 The Reception of the MEC 106
4 Post-apartheid Economy 109
5 From History of "MEC" to History of MEC 120
6 Concluding Remarks 125
Appendix 126
Historic Compromise or Own Goal? 126

6 **Political Economy for the Rainbow Nation: Dividing the Spectrum?** 137
Postscript as Personal Preamble 137
1 Introduction 138
2 Identifying Identity 142
3 Is Neoliberalism Dead (Was It Ever Alive) – Long Live Neoliberalism? 143
4 From Neoliberalism to the MEC 148
5 Neoliberalism Changes Gear? 148

7 **Amnesty International?: The Nature, Scale and Impact of Capital Flight from South Africa** 154
Postscript as Personal Preamble 154
1 Introduction 156
2 Capital Flight and the Political Economy of South Africa 160
3 Capital Flight and Economic Development 166
4 Calculations for Capital Flight from South Africa 167
5 Capital Controls, Wealth Repatriation and the Prevailing Policy Framework 172

6 Conclusions 174
Appendix 1 176
Appendix 2 177
Technical Details 177

8 **Neoliberalism, Varieties of Capitalism, and the Shifting Contours of South Africa's Financial System** 179
Postscript as Personal Preamble 179
1 Introduction 181
2 Varieties of Capitalism 183
3 From EMH to IEMH 188
4 From IEMH to Financialisation 193
5 From Apartheid to Post-apartheid Economy and Financial System 194
6 The 1980s Onwards: Deregulation, Internationalisation and Renewed Concentration 200
7 Conclusions 207

9 **The Meaning of Marikana** 210
Postscript as Personal Preamble 210
1 Some Underlying Determinants 210
2 The Present Crisis 218

10 **Across Developmental State and Social Compacting: The Peculiar Case of South Africa** 219
Postscript as Personal Preamble 219
1 Introduction 220
2 The Developmental State Paradigm 222
3 The DSP in the Age of Financialisation 231
4 From Developmental State to Social Compacting 234
5 South African DSP and SCP: 'Twixt a Rock and a Hard Place? 242
6 Concluding Remarks 250

11 **Vishnu Padayachee as Engaged Political Economist: A Personal Journey** 252
Postscript as Personal Preamble 252
1 Introduction 252
2 Neoliberalism Is as Neoliberalism Does 253
3 From Mainstream to … 259

4 … Heterodoxy 265
5 The Post-apartheid Context 269
6 Post-apartheid Economics: From Unravelling to Disempowered 277
7 Locating Vishnu 283

References 287
Index 319

Figures and Tables

Figures

7.1 Capital flight as a percentage of GDP 1986–2009 168
7.2 Breakdown of capital flight into components of unrecorded capital flows as a percentage of GDP 169
8.1 Number of registered South African banks 203
8.2 Market share of assets for selected years: South African banks 203
8.3 Market share of assets of South African banks 205
8.4 Return on assets – South African banks 205

Tables

2.1 Output and input indices, 1950–80 24
2.2 Average annual growth in productivity variables 25
7.1 Breakdown of components of capital flight as percentages of GDP 169
7.2 Trade mis-invoicing by sectors 1995–2006 (USD millions) 171
7.3 List of data and sources 176
8.1 South African Banks: assets and market shares in 2010 202

CHAPTER 1

Locating the Minerals-Energy Complex

1 Introduction[1]

This is the last of what has turned out to be three Volumes on South Africa, and the ninth in the series of Volumes as a whole.[2] It may also be the last in the series. I have not made up my mind yet. When I set out, I had planned for the South African Volume(s) to be the last for reasons that I will revisit later. I have though brought the theme of South Africa forward and, as a result of the coverage within the other six Volumes as well, the contributions available for inclusion going further forward have inevitably diminished, not least as many of the already published contributions cover more than one topic/theme.[3] Prospectively, I had planned (one or more) further Volumes on each of mainstream economics, heterodox economics, Marxist political economy, and policy. Apart from my own energies, I will have to investigate whether these remain viable in and of themselves, bearing in mind I have generally confined myself to inclusion of journal articles or previously unpublished pieces, and some of the topics will already be covered at length in my own books, edited collections, or Chapters within the latter (all of which have generally been excluded from these Volumes).

What might be the last Volume prompts me to reflect back upon the series as a whole, bearing in mind it was intended in part to be personal and autobiographical in passing, allowing for some insight into how the intellectual scene has changed over time and how this relates to material circumstances. In retrospect, having worked over the contributions to prepare them for publication from old versions and printed versions, I am struck by how they remain timely and of interest even though they range back for forty years or more (but no doubt I am biased in assessing my own work, even from a distance). At the very least, the pieces are markers in the history of economic thought. At the time of writing, they would have been of interest to me and to those willing to

1 Throughout this Chapter, I take considerable liberties with the presumed knowledge of the reader, to avoid repetition with what is contained within the following Chapters.

2 See Fine (2024a–d and 2025a and b and d and e).

3 As a result of reproducing articles and commenting upon them, there is liable to be understandable repetition across and within Volumes as the same material is revisited across topic and context for which I apologise profusely. This is especially so for the South African Volumes for which I was on a mission to have an impact in scholarship, policy and activism.

 | DOI:10.1163/9789004748330_002

publish them. This does mean the pieces are dated to some degree, failing to keep up with the passage of scholarship and events but, taken together and in light of the Volume introductions and Chapter preambles that occasionally situate the past contributions in relation to the contemporary, they do offer some insight into the chronology of my own scholarship and, through that prism, of scholarship more generally. The value of this is not to be underestimated in a discipline, economics, which tends to be unduly negligent even of its own history and influences. This is especially important across an intellectual scene in which even grand postures around the meanings of Keynesianism, monetarism, neoclassical economics, let alone globalisation and, as a relatively new arrival on the scene, financialisation, are both shifting and subject to disputes that readily fall to the fate of myopia. I was a child of a discipline, for example, in which even to question the IS/LM interpretation of Keynesianism was considered heretical both intellectually and as providing the analytical foundations for policy that underpinned the post-war boom. How things have changed but how, why and with what consequences?

Here my contributions on economics imperialism (EI) are vital, forming the leading focus of at least the first three Volumes, and heavily present in Volumes 5 and 6 on development and 'development' (as well as Chapter 6 in Volume 4). It is a bitter disappointment to me that after the noughties, attention to EI was heavily eroded, what I call the watershed, even though it accelerated with the increasing prominence of market imperfections economics (giving rise to the second, new phase of EI, as opposed to the old, initial phase based on the economic and social as if perfectly working markets). Perversely, heterodox economics and, especially, other disciplines have continued to remark the sore inadequacies of economics whether it is addressing the 'economic' or the non-economic. And they frequently do so by critiques that are pointing to its imperialism (although critiques of economics from outside often work with a model of it that is well out of date and as if every mainstream economist is a headbanging neoliberal, wedded to an undiluted methodological individualism based on utility maximisation, etc.). But these critiques most rarely acknowledge economics imperialism explicitly and, in their singular applications, seem unaware of what is happening within economics and across the social sciences more generally into which these critiques form an integral part.

But this bigger picture is neither simple nor unchanging. As is charted throughout the Volumes, and the periods of my writing that are covered, this is the era of neoliberalism (NL). Alongside its evolution, I successively identify three phases of neoliberalism both logically and, generally, chronologically: the initial shock phase (privatisation and the like); followed by Third Wayism (ameliorating the impact of the policies attached to the shock phase but allowing them to be continued albeit in new forms); and, as currently, increasingly close collaboration between the state, capital and finance to seek to promote renewed accumulation. Common to all three phases is continued and extensive state intervention (neoliberal ideology to the contrary) and connections but dissonances across such ideology and the worlds of scholarship and policymaking (and world vision in their combination). In particular, the three phases of neoliberalism are shown to have a correspondence with the three phases of EI – the old and the new, already specified above, and the newer in which mainstream principles (around optimisation, equilibrium, etc.) are 'suspended' (both there but supplemented by whatever considerations are brought in from across the social sciences). And, by the same token, development economics (and its imperialistic designs on development studies) has gone through the three phases of the new (Washington Consensus, the newer (Post-Washington Consensus) and newest (PWC plus suspension to incorporate anything else to suit willy-nilly).

This is a drastic summary of a body of work that began in the 1990s, with major impetus from a two-year professorial fellowship from the UK's ESRC around the turn of the millennium (i.e. before the watershed when notice was taken of EI). It spawned, linked and added value to or simply complemented other major themes in my continuing research. These include economic history as cliometrics (and its new, newer and newest forms), development economics and studies (ditto), obsessive attention to social capital over a couple of decades, the material culture of consumption over even longer, and labour market theory. Each of these also tended to address narrower, if far from narrow, topics – food (and clothing and advertising) in case of consumption and minimum wages and equal pay for labour markets, for example. This is indicative of how much these contributions went well beyond the theory involved to be both empirically grounded and engaged with activism and policymaking. In addition, this work is always marked by an explicit and ruthless critique and exposure of orthodoxy for its narrowness in methodology, methods, theory, conceptualisation and scope, with one goal of offering alternatives and another implicit goal, against the odds, of keeping alive the ruthlessly critical command of orthodoxy.[4]

4 I have long argued that, from the perspectives of both realism and the other social sciences, economics is so impoverished, so intolerant of alternatives and so technically demanding, that it discourages attempts to engage with it from alternative perspectives. What's the point? The answer is both to keep alternatives alive and not to let it get away with it unanswered.

I have also become increasingly aware of two further features of my work. On the one hand, over and above where I have made major, continuing assaults on, and contributions to, the literature (economics imperialism, social capital, consumption, World Bank economics, etc.), there are also occasional, targeted, one-off detailed literature surveys on specific issues, usually prompted by their relevance to policy or activist engagement. One that stands out, for example, is the consideration of dumping in seeking to address the issue of international pricing of steel (Fine, 2025e, Ch. 7). But there are others such as equal pay. On the other hand, with these ventures and more generally, unless going for a quick fix and even then to some degree, my approach has always been to locate analysis contextually, in the history of thought and with close attention to interdisciplinarity (not privileging the economic and economic analysis, as it were even, if this is central).[5] Even in dealing with the contemporary (in thought and deed) it is instructive to be fully aware from where material conditions and discourses have derived – what have been the influences as well as what might have been discarded (and might be restored and/or reconstructed rather than overlooked).[6]

The issues and fields listed in the previous paragraphs have dovetailed with attention to major framing devices, or on topics residing somewhere in-between the two such as social policy or financialisation. Each of the latter, for example, played major roles in understanding the nature of neoliberalism (and its three phases) alongside increasing attention to economic as embedded within social reproduction.[7] In specifying neoliberalism as a stage of capitalism distinguished by, but not reducible to, financialisation, contributions and themes from across other work have been drawn together alongside what has already been mentioned. In particular, the system of provision approach

5 This has also allowed me to draw upon but also to be sceptical of all forms of economics and political economy that depend upon a distinction between micro and macro as traditionally conceived – although they can be deployed to make progressive arguments (in teaching and more widely) and to promote progressive policy. See Fine (2016b and 2025e, Ch. 8) and Fine and Dimakou (2016).

6 This is so much easier said than done and, I do not doubt, that I have failed miserably to meet these goals in part out of my own abilities, my starting point within economics (with the purest of mathematical backgrounds prior to this although this has its compensation in capacity for commanding the mainstream), and the disciplinary imperatives to take the economy and mainstream economics as initial critical point of departure. Who is to be persuaded of what?

7 It goes without saying that the approach holding all of this work together were the insights gained from Marxist political economy, even if this is less apparent in contributions to (the mathematical measurement of) inequality, the nature of identity, ethics, and so on.

(SoP) to public and private consumption (Bayliss and Fine, 2021a), and its corresponding material cultures, have figured strongly together with longstanding attention to how economic (and social reproduction) is contingent upon economic (and industrial) restructuring. In general, this led to the formulaic summary laid out and addressed in detail in Fine (2024d, p. 4 fwd):[8]

Glob, NL, finn, CCFCC, (PS)SoPs, Norms, MC as 10Cs, ER&SR and V^3

Such is a drastic shorthand for a layered and multidimensional framing of what has become an increasing focus upon the nature of neoliberalism and how its complexities and differentiations have evolved – as opposed to a tendency to see it in much more simplistic and general economic, political and ideological terms (in favour of free markets, state minimalism, working class oppression and increasing authoritarianism, Fine, 2024d). With a starting point of the distinctive role played by financialisation in defining neoliberalism as the contemporary stage of capitalism, economic has increasingly underpinned social analysis. Emphasis has been placed upon, first and foremost, not the withdrawal of state intervention (quite the opposite) but the weakening, hollowing out and marginalisation of the labour movement, progressive forces (and ideas) and institutions in the making of, and influence over, policymaking. This has been complemented by increasing centralisation and authoritarianism in the exercise of state power with increasing influence of financial and global imperatives. Electorally, the result has been a decline in active participation and the rise of various forms of populism, heavily influenced by the loss of means of collective participation other than through social media and the like, and spontaneous, volatile and uncertain eruptions of dissent, alongside the emergence of iconic issues or leaders as more or less temporary focal points. This can on occasion favour progressive forces but the overall balance is to swing heavily to the right, with politics conducted horizontally across elites with corresponding revolving doors and networks, dragging more progressive potential with it, and precipitating ever more (global) crises (economic, political, military, environmental) and pre-empting solutions to them.

8 Respectively: globalisation; neoliberalism; financialisation; commodification, commodity form and commodity calculation; (Public Sector) Systems of Provision; Social Norms (of who gets what and how); Material Cultures as Constructed, Construed, Conforming, Commodified, Contextual, Contradictory, Closed, Contested, Collective and Chaotic; Economic within Social Reproduction; and all subject to variegations, volatilities and vulnerabilities.

2 The Post-apartheid Conundrum

Previously, in this Chapter and earlier Volumes, I have reported that I had intended to leave the contributions on South Africa to the end of my endeavours across the series as a whole. Having gone through nine Volumes, with the last three on South Africa, I can now explain why, not least as I have a better understanding of what was previously an uneasy intuition that could only be set aside as the series progressed. The obstacle as I felt it was that I had some understanding of the nature of contemporary capitalism, not least as neoliberalism as its current stage. I also had a longstanding knowledge of the political economy of South Africa, and its implications for economic and social reproduction. I have, however, always felt this to be partial, not least because, as an outsider and frequent visitor of only short durations, the complexities and diversities of the society inevitably escaped my knowledge and understanding. South Africa is a place, much more so than elsewhere, where a drive around with informed or even just local commentary, is a major source of knowledge and insight which is difficult if not impossible to garner from most forms of scholarship (at a distance, although close proximity can be a source of blinkered blindness to the bigger picture).

As a result, the challenge for scholarship on South Africa (and more generally) is how to wed, attach, connect grand, abstract theory to its more complex and concrete manifestations. I certainly felt this had been achieved and only required filling in and joining the dots as far as the political economy of apartheid is concerned. The major concept for doing so had been the Minerals-Energy Complex. The problem with the post-apartheid period is, first, that the MEC plays a different and even more subsidiary role – if ever it was previously, developments could not now be read off from its supposed interests and dynamics, pervasive though these may be. Second, change within the post-apartheid condition has been fast but also extremely diverse in ways that appear to defy even a multi-layered, hierarchical explanation of underlying causal factors, however neatly arranged. How do we account for the bewilderingly different levels of attention to, and nature of, policy, for example, within and across state provision and over time (such as electricity, water, education, health and social security)? And the same applies to industrial policy with some sectors favoured for extensive intervention and support as opposed to others.

In short, my problem was that I could not fully fit the jigsaw of abstract theory and underlying determinants to the multi-dimensional diversity of concrete outcomes and developments. Most sharply, for example, how can you both appeal to the MEC as central to post-apartheid but also as being failed miserably by the state, not least in economic and social infrastructure with electricity power cuts to the fore on which the MEC is so dependent? Why is overt industrial policy so pronounced for cars and textiles and clothing but so much less so for other sectors? Why has privatisation been present but so limited? Why was a national minimum wage introduced against much business and media opposition? Are social security payments (comparatively) unduly generous and widely applicable, or not? And so the list could run on.

Eventually, I have found it appealing, if a little too self-serving, to suggest that the lack of fit between deep underlying determinants and the diversities of outcomes to be less the problem than the answer itself to the problem. The huge complexities and incoherencies of the post-apartheid condition are the consequence of these determinants rather than the latter rigidly giving rise to outcomes by virtue of preordained laws of (lack of) development or the direct and full serving of singular class interests. After all, each of the determinants that has been identified is not homogenising by its nature, precipitating tendencies and reactions against them, whether it be globalisation, neoliberalisation or financialisation and their impacts upon economic and social reproduction. Variegation is the name of the game. This is reinforced once contextualised within the post-apartheid trajectory. Here, at the economic level, the key features are the restructuring of the MEC through conglomerate unbundling and integration into global production networks, (illegal) capital flight, Black Economic Empowerment (BEE, as the creation of a new elite) and the consequential 'five lows' nature of the South African economy – low (real domestic) investment, productivity, employment, wages and public provision (Mohamed and Fine, 2025),[9] alongside reproduction of the deepest multidimensional levels of inequalities and deprivations.

In these and other respects to be considered, the post-apartheid period has been characteristically neoliberal, properly understood (as highly interventionist to promote financialisation and manage its consequences). This has involved particular political, institutional and policy processes. First has been the centralised, authoritarian exercise of power through the Presidency and Treasury, not least with the adoption of the neoliberal GEAR as token of control over the Tripartite Alliance by the ANC as party of government, and from the ANC as government to its top leadership. Second, this has been part and parcel of a much more general erosion of the strength and presence of progressive forces and institutions in determining policy. Third has been a total lack of coherence, and bewildering shifts and changes, in the making and

9 And, for a more detailed account, Adelzadeh (2023).

implementing of economic and social policy, with uneven and conjunctural developments contingent upon the purchase exercised outside or through core, centralised leadership. Sixth, the Mandela/Mbeki period involved total distrust, marginalisation and/or incorporation of progressive forces deploying both loyalty to leadership and political or other rewards as the means to contain dissent. Seventh, irrespective of the view taken of this period (disastrous neoliberalism, yes, versus laying the secure fiscal foundations for future growth, no), Zuma assumed power as a symbol of a popular progressive antidote. As a result, these processes of centralisation and incoherence were taken to extreme in what has been termed 'state capture', with corruption, institutional degeneration and dysfunction at levels that no one could have anticipated. But, as it were, state capture was already in place as part and parcel of the neoliberal condition, if less extreme and differently directed. Eighth, it is not only that progressive forces have been weakened and marginalised, but they have also themselves, most obviously across the Tripartite Alliance, both collectively and within its constituent elements unravelled and dissipated not least through jockeying for position around loyalties, rewards and other motivations and ideologies. As a result, loyalty to, and popularity of, the ANC, in light of its role in leading the struggle against apartheid, is evaporating with both the passage of time (formally, apartheid ended over thirty years ago) and the failings across developmental achievements. Where previously, the ANC leadership justified neoliberal policies on the grounds of stabilising for future gains in what was initially a chosen Government of National Unity, now it is a matter of GNU as an enforced coalition, with neoliberal restraints considered essential until corruption can be brought under control.

As chance would have it, I began to think about this Chapter just as the final proofs of the first of my Volumes on South Africa became available, the first proofs of the second Volume arrived, and I was also putting together this, the third Volume. It came as a (un)pleasant surprise (depending on whether emphasising what was already there as opposed to what it was) to find that, over the contributions taken together all more or less at the same time, all of these points are found to be present, whether in detail or in passing, at an early or late stage, developed or embryonic – although the earlier contributions remain marked by the hope that certain policies might be actively pursued and even adopted, despite the MERG experience. Patient advice has given way to cynicism/realism depending upon how you look at it. With the benefit of hindsight, or a better memory in the first place, I might not have been so troubled over the prospects of coming to terms with the post-apartheid condition. It has simply been a matter of putting varieties of insights together in framings that respect both continuing overall grand narratives and the contextual diversities of outcomes which they or, more exactly, the realities they represent, allow.

Unsurprisingly, there is plenty of scholarship to support these prognoses.[10] I will offer a selective account from what has come my way, especially most recently. Most prominent have been contributions on a just energy transition, vital given South Africa's uniquely energy- and coal-intensive dependence. To some degree, as globally, this entails inertia in face of the interests and power of 'fossil fuel' capitalism. Within a South African context, this leads to frequent references to the MEC and its role as a deadweight against renewables (Bookbinder, 2024 for example). For Montmasson-Clair (2024), and inevitably across the literature as renewables have increasingly offered economic and political rewards against business as usual,[11] the South African transition has been marked by lots of (potential) capacity, insufficiently coordinated state support, burst and bust in provision, and imports as default option rather than building and coordinating domestic capacity. Similarly, Morris et al. (2022, p. 490) see wind value chain "governance as dependent on system integration dynamics, with lead firms operating as system integrators. The empirical analysis focuses on the interplay between energy and industrial policy showing how policy failure, driven by coal based vested interests, disrupted system integration and undermined the renewable energy programme."

More generally, for the South African energy transition, Andreoni and Roberts (2024, Abstract) point to what conditions are required for it to be successful, with an at least implicit presumption that they are simply not present:

> Climate change requires rapid, major, and systemic economic changes at the local, national, regional, and global levels … Upstream and

10 As is apparent, I draw heavily on Andreoni et al. (eds) (2021) and Mohamed et al. (eds) (2023). Invaluable though these volumes are, they tend unevenly and with exceptions to suffer from a double schizophrenia. On the one hand, they both draw upon and ignore MEC framings. On the other hand, they point to sore deficiencies in policy and policy-making, suggesting what is otherwise required without tending to question why this has not already occurred in light of configurations of economic, political and ideological factors. The issues are, however, occasionally acknowledged in passing (Andreoni et al. 2021a, p. 75, for example) but much more so in the other volume.

11 Most notably with the launch of the Just Energy Transition Investment Plan (JET-IP), a $8.5bn deal to support decarbonisation of the South African economy, negotiated at COP26 in 2021, involving cooperation with France, Germany, the UK, the USA and the EU. For critical commentary, see IEJ and CliFT (2023) and COSATU and IEJ (2023) not least around JET-IP running the risk of imposition of broader conditionalities to prioritise donor and private over public interests.

> downstream linkages running vertically and horizontally between energy, minerals and industrial sectors can be leveraged to drive domestic industrialisation, create new employment and spur diffusion of green technologies. Countries in Southern Africa could leverage mineral endowments, given the global demand pull, to establish a new developmental energy-mineral complex. Development opportunities can however turn into development traps if such green transitions are not governed and regulated through a strategic approach aligned to industrial policy and regulatory reforms. Building on ongoing fieldwork and research, in this paper we focus on the employment implications of such green transitions depending on the approach to: developing linkages from renewable energy, upstream and downstream; key challenges in locating the transition in the context of structural transformation; and, the implications for rethinking the role of the state.

Similar considerations apply again and again to industrial performance and policy which has been abysmal if uneven. Andreoni et al. (2021, p. 338) report:

> Minerals, along with basic metals and basic chemicals, remained almost as important in the country's goods exports in 2019 as they did twenty-five years earlier. There are, however, a few counter-examples, led by high-value fruit exports and niches within machinery and equipment, which demonstrate a possible alternative path.

And for Zalk (2021, p. 36):[12]

> Three main diversified manufacturing sectors recorded meaningful real value-added growth: motor vehicles and parts [subsidies but limited value added], food and beverages [import protection and retail], and machinery [for mining], with the remainder collectively little larger in real terms than they were in 1994.

And this 'deindustrialisation' (Andreoni and Tregenna, 2021) is explained by Zalk as follows, p. 39:[13]

---

12 Nimrod has been a longstanding, leading researcher at the Department of Trade and Industry. He also completed his PhD at SOAS on the steel and engineering industries, although choosing not to be supervised by me (Zalk, 2017).

13 As reported in Newman (2019, p. 14), citing Zalk (2017), "leveraging industrial development through public procurement was only introduced in 2012 in the 'Preferential

> In the absence of any overarching manufacturing strategy, particularly for underdeveloped diversified sectors outside heavy-industry, industrial policy was relegated to a set of dispersed incentives supposed to assist firms adjust to trade liberalization. Only two sector-specific programmes were formalized: the Motor Industry Development Programme (MIDP) (Chapter 5 [Barnes et al. 2021]) and a Duty Credit Certificate Scheme (DCCS) for clothing and textiles. In parallel, and stark contradiction with their disavowal of state intervention, private conglomerates secured extensive public support for heavy-industry expansions throughout the 1990s, supported by tax incentives, co-funding by the Industrial Development Corporation (IDC), and cheap electricity (Zalk, 2012 and 2014).

Accordingly, evolving and detailed long-term plans for industrial policy (Industrial Policy Action Plans, IPAP) have been observed in the breach with lack of adoption across most sectors and heavily diluted and ineffective where adopted (cars and clothing and textiles).

To some degree, as already implied, this reflects the continuing presence of the MEC. Here, it is worth quoting from Andreoni et al. (2021a, p. 59) at length:

> The downstream industries have not had a major coordinated industrial policy programme of support and services, including targeted skills and technology support through institutions of industrial policy. Instead, there has been an evolving mix of ineffective incentives and initiatives. These include investment incentives in the 1990s, the bulk of which went to the basic metals producers rather than diversified downstream and labour-absorbing producers (Roberts and Rustomjee, 2009). There were also technology support measures under the Integrated Manufacturing Strategy and the Advanced Manufacturing Technology Strategy (Machaka and Roberts, 2003). Cluster developments were championed by the South African Capital Equipment Export Council (SACEEC), estab lished in 2000 as a public-private partnership between the industry and the Department of Trade, Industry, and Competition (DTIC), but the emphasis was on driving market access through public procurement, export promotion, and marketing initiatives, such as international trade fairs. In fact two separate developments worked against diversifying the

---

Procurement Policy Framework Act'. In reality, there has been little evidence of compliance with designations for local content and reportedly corrupt deals struck with foreign suppliers ... In 2017, there were 115,000 fewer jobs in textiles and clothing than there had been in 1993."

> industrial base. First, substantial engineering capabilities in subsidiaries of the major conglomerates, led by Anglo American and including its Dorbyl business, were eroded when the conglomerates unbundled and a short-term asset stripping took place (Zalk, 2017; and Rustomjee et al. 2018). Second, the procurement policies, including under black economic empowerment (BEE) provisions in the 2000s to favour black suppliers, did not measure local value added and led to black entrepreneurs setting up as local suppliers for multinational producers importing into South Africa (Vilakazi and Bosiu, 2021).

And they continue, p. 73:

> As the 'big steel' case highlights, the entrenched power of the upstream firms continued to drive the agenda and shape the overall development of the industries. Downstream in the value chain, as is evident in the mining machinery and equipment industry, there was extensive international integration, in terms of ownership, technology, and trade. However, this was accompanied by increasing import penetration, persistent industry fragmentation, and ineffective and poorly coordinated policy and institutional support.

In short, we are witnessing, albeit in different circumstances and for different reasons, a continued experience of the longstanding MEC syndrome of failure to diversify out of its core strengths – albeit accompanied by failure to expand and support successfully the core of the MEC itself.

But there are exceptions that prove the rule. And these arise out of globalisation, financialisation and BEE. Consider each in turn. For globalisation, we have the unbundling of conglomerates into sectoral monopolies without due regard to domestic goals.[14] For Vilakazi and Bosiu (2023), unbundling is the form being taken by MEC restructuring. But it leads to investment by the largest (foreign) firms for mergers and acquisitions as opposed to new investments with uneven outcomes across sectors. Further, the process of "internationalisation for South Africa is that lead firms raise capital from the domestic economy to largely fund international investments rather than local productive investments. Moreover, firms have invested heavily in short-term, non-fixed assets and/or paid out dividends to shareholders", p. 173. There has been a massive

14 But note, as previously emphasised, such restructuring is variegated as illustrated by the contrast between SASOL which remains vertically integrated and even spread horizontally, whereas ISCOR has been vertically disintegrated (Goga and Mondliwa, 2021, p. 172).

increase in concentrated foreign and institutional ownership, even if with a shift from total dominance of mining-related firms in the 1990s to finance, telecom, property, retail and consumer credit and services.

For financialisation, and the oft-overlooked (illegal) capital flight, the issue is covered elsewhere across my three Volumes on South Africa, not least as the "elephant in the room" that underpins the previously designated five lows with knock-on effects to macroeconomic policy, policymaking institutions and the exercise of power through and on them. Focusing on a case study of SASOL and Shoprite, Andreoni et al. (2021c, p. 231) report:

> The core findings illustrate an increase in financial activity relative to productive activity, indicated by an increasing reallocation of precious firm resources away from productive investment and toward financial interests, paying high returns to property in shareholdings and to creditors. It is also clear that while companies operating in different sectors and stages of the value chain are all affected by financialization, there is heterogeneity in the ways in which financialization operates across NFCs [non-financial corporations]. So, to the extent that financialization can manifest differently, it also hampers structural transformation in different ways.

They suggest, "Aggregate evidence of the coexistence of high profitability, deep financial markets, and sluggish productive investment is provided. This is borne out further by the focus on two large, publicly listed corporations operating across different economic sectors – Sasol in heavy manufacturing industry, and Shoprite in supermarket retail", p. 213, neatly overlapping with and complementing the study by King (2021) of financialisation of Anglo, Shoprite and South African Breweries.[15]

As for BEE, despite or because of its continual redefinitions, it is the ineffectual tail that shakes the policy body, or possibly parasitical fleas offers a

15 For such financialisations, Andreoni et al. (2021c, p. 226) emphasise, "It is worthwhile recapping the six major interlinked factors ... (1) sectoral heterogeneity (at firm, industry, and value chain levels); (2) value chain positioning and opportunities for rents; (3) financialization pressures on firms due to endogenous asymmetries in GVCs; (4) ownership structure, especially in regard to foreign institutional investors; (5) risks associated with reliance on international financial markets for relatively cheap credit and foreign exchange needs; and (6) the impact on domestic enterprises of the need to provide foreign investors with high risk-adjusted returns due to middle-income countries' subordinate position in global financial hierarchies". In other words, as deployed by King, financialisation is variegated in scale, incidence, forms and effects.

more apposite metaphor. For BEE, Bowman (2019, p. 240) offers a compelling account for mining:

> the relatively coherent empowerment alliance … has given way to a much more complex fragmentation of competing interests and ideological positions. This fragmentation corresponds with the emergence of intense factional contest within the Tripartite Alliance and increased differentiation within the black business class, and mounting dissatisfaction over the pace and extent of economic transformation. As has been argued above, this is in part a consequence of the shortcomings of conventional BEE policies as a form of financialised redistribution and the changing forms of inequality and exclusion it created. Rather than the envisaged 'patriotic bourgeoisie' aligning political and economic power, this has, despite ostensibly large transfers of wealth, predominantly created a fragile patchwork of black business interests in mining, holding highly leveraged minority stakes in established enterprises, with ultimate redistributive outcomes hinging on volatile equity market returns. This generated a relatively small group of wealthy politically connected individuals among those benefiting from opportune timing in the commodity cycle for entry and exit from investments. However, in many instances inclusion of BEE partners has not translated into meaningful economic empowerment, either in terms of income streams or the ability to exert strategic control of the industry's trajectory.

This begs the question of economic empowerment and strategic control for whom as opposed to individuals seeking to belong as high as possible within the elites at global, national and local levels. But, and here there is a telling contrast of context and process with the creation of the Afrikaner elite business class under apartheid,[16] precisely because of globalisation and financialisation, it is not just that BEE is about redistributing or appropriating, rather than creating, wealth. It also is subject to uncertainties, volatilities and the powers of global 'markets' and elites that can be impoverished as quickly as they are enriched. Vilakazi and Bosiu (2023, p. 176, Table 6.1) strikingly reveal for the Johannesburg Stock Exchange the massive increase in foreign and institutional ownership, but the decline of black ownership from 7.15% to 0.88%

16 For a wide-ranging contrast between the two periods of elite wealth redistribution, see Chatterjee et al. (2025).

from 1998/9 to 2015/9.[17] In contrast to Afrikaner conglomerate and elite success within the domestic (and hence, increasingly, the global) economy, there is a sense in which BEE is chasing a moving target so that it will always be there but never succeed – at least until it is developmental as opposed to parasitical – seeking to join the (global, financialised) elite but always remaining dependent upon it, with corresponding disposition towards policies that redistribute wealth for the few rather than create genuine economic empowerment for the many through five highs rather than lows.[18]

3 Whither or Wither the MEC?

So, where does this leave the MEC as a way of framing our understanding of the post-apartheid condition? As increasingly acknowledged, often implicitly, reference to the MEC across scholarly, policy and popular discourses has become commonplace. Such recognition is not always accompanied by depth of understanding. And it is often accepting but begrudging, possibly because of dissatisfaction with one or other aspect of the analytical or policy conclusions drawn from those who have taken the lead in promoting the MEC, and who have also willingly accepted that it should acknowledge the significance of the financialisation of the South African economy by now referring to the Minerals-Energy and Financial Complex (MEFC). Consider, for example, the commentary of Michael Sachs (2024) in his review of Mohamed et al. (eds) (2023)[19] that is heavily referenced above and is notable for heavy reliance upon ME(F)C framings.[20]

17 It would be worth investigating the extent to which BEE (and the South African economy more generally) rode the commodities super cycle of the noughties through appropriating rather than reinvesting the corresponding surpluses with inevitable consequences for continuing growth as commodity prices fell.

18 Zalk (2021, p. 41) offers telling statistics for an economy running investment levels at half of what is needed, "the net value transferred to beneficiaries of BEE deals from the one hundred largest JSE-listed firms between 2000 and 2014 was equivalent to 8 per cent of total GFCF and 29 per cent of manufacturing GFCF over the same period".

19 A volume to which I contributed (Fine and Mohamed, 2023), as did the praised Netshitenzhe (2023) who hails from MISTRA, following an illustrious political career and more (including touching base as his teacher when taking a distance-learning MSc from SOAS). MISTRA commissioned the volume.

20 Sachs was an MSc student of mine whilst at SOAS but our contact subsequently has been minimal, suggesting lack of interest in MEC framings. He worked for Treasury and rose to become head of its budget office before resigning in November 2017 ostensibly in protest

Sachs' starting point is to cite Bill Freund to the effect that the MEC has failed to offer policy perspectives, p. 1:

> As historian Bill Fruend [sic] pointed out, the MEC lens, notwithstanding its defining contribution to the historiography of South Africa's industrial development, has always struggled to define clear policy implications. In Fruend's words, Fine and Rustomjee [1996] "is an impressive assessment but what to do with it? The final section of the book that tries to look ahead to policy is in my view much less incisive and clear. This is one reason why … the MEC has seemingly had so little impact on policy".

Now Bill was a great admirer of the MEC analysis, so much so that he applied it to his own work on what might be termed the Afrikaner developmental state (Freund, 2010, 2011, 2013 and 2018). He might be excused for failing to acknowledge the policy implications of the MEC at the time of the book's publication in 1996, even though MERG (1993) had already happened and extensive debates over policy had already been engaged. But for Sachs to suggest no policy implications looking back nearly thirty years later is simply incomprehensible. Within the book itself, the clear and enduring policy implication is that the failure to diversify out of the MEC core had to be remedied. More generally, though, and in retrospect, as could not be more apparent across the two Volumes of mine already published on South Africa, quite apart from this one as well, the MEC has always been overflowing with policy implications, with the first Volume organised around 'there were alternatives' from GEAR onwards, and the second on policy debates themselves. And, crucially, the precondition for successful policy has been highlighted by MEC analysis of (illegal) capital flight, something that surely ought to have been highlighted and addressed by the budget office to which Sachs was long attached.

In short, it has to be concluded that the suggestion that the MEC has limited policy conclusions is a veil over wishing to reject the extensive policy proposals that have been put forward but without addressing them (just like MERG previously and from before the ANC came to power). And the acceptance of the MEC as a defining contribution to historiography is a way, like the supposed lack of policy, of confining it both to the past and to the ivory towers. Sachs continues by making numbers of claims about the MEC that are only mildly less incomprehensible than those for policy. They include that: it waves

against excessive expenditure plans under Zuma (to support university students). He subsequently joined the Southern Centre for Inequality Studies (SCIS) at Wits.

neoliberalism as a vague causal factor; it does not see the state as a problem;[21] nor that social relations need to be reconstructed; and, "on the path to academic hegemony that it now commands, the idea of the MEC displaced these and other South African approaches to political economy that were better able to frame these questions about the state and its politics, social transformation, and the economy", p. 2. These other approaches derive from Gelb, Netshitenzhe, and Seekings and Nattrass, all of which have been critically assessed at one time or another throughout the course of my Volumes on South Africa. Sachs, however, exaggerates what influence any of these approaches had on thinking let alone policy and practice, and there is no evidence that the MEC crowded out alternative thinking (and its influence on policy) – this is surely to blame the victim for raising its voice not drowning out others.

Although not even beginning to come to terms with MEFC analyses and their implications for policy, Sachs does explicitly raise one key issue whilst neglecting another. The first concerns the implications of the economic analysis of the MEFC for social reproduction more generally than for economic reproduction, not least the role of the state and the influences upon it. Here his claim of MEC neglect is only partially and mildly correct. Understandably, MEC analysis began with and presented first its account in economic terms. But, from an early stage, broader considerations and topics were brought into play, not least with the MERG's (1993) account of housing, education, health and electrification. It has ultimately been wedded to the formula reproduced from above, to which specific South African aspects have been incorporated, as also previously discussed, and especially globalised corporate unbundling, (illegal) capital flight and BEE.

Glob, NL, finn, CCFCC, (PS)SoPs, Norms, MC as 10Cs, ER&SR and V^3

The second issue, overlooked by Sachs, in the haste both to praise the historiography of the MEC but also to dismiss its policy (and continuing) relevance, is to question whether the MEC still exists or whether it simply reflects a passing, or passed, moment or two. Precisely because of the form take by post-apartheid developments, the MEC has at the very least been significantly transformed if not substantially eroded. Clearly, the domestic conglomerate structure has gone with globalisation and unbundling, and financialisation (and the growth of services) has decreased the weight of MEC core and related sectors (as well as witnessing the decline of gold and rise of platinum alongside, hopefully,

21 Presumably, for Sachs, the state becomes a problem with Zuma.

the prospect of decreases in coal and energy-intensity). To some degree, the reinvention of the MEC as MEFC is self-serving if incorporating finance in measures of its weight (whatever grows gets counted as MEC?).

Nonetheless, continuing work has shown that the MEC remains a remarkably important and self-integrated aspect of the South African economy (Newman, 2019). Yet, the MEC has never been defined simply in terms of input-output tables nor even conglomerate structure but also in terms of how these co-evolve with both the evolution of (fractions of) classes and their economic and political relations with one another, with corresponding leverage on and through the state. Like the narrow economic analysis (lesser weight of the MEC core, do we include finance), this also presents conundrums – not least with the increasing influence of the global and the financial, and the rise of a new black elite and the unravelling of progressive political formations. And, indeed, the MEC, if it still exists, has been poorly served by the state.

I do not doubt that the MEC is being restructured nor even that it could be restructured out of existence. But, if so, it still has a long way to go. More important is that the current restructuring of the South African economy (and the corresponding impact upon its society) remains tightly bound to the restructuring of the MEC. It is hardly accidental that MEC analyses of globalisation, corporate unbundling, financialisation, (illegal) capital flight have been to the fore. It would be ironic for the MEC approach to be dismissed on the grounds of its own insights.

The value added of the MEC approach is not necessarily to displace but to enrich other approaches.[22] Thus, for example, Reboredo and Carmody (2024, p. 3) see developments in infrastructure "in simple terms, a combination of top-down neoliberalism and state capture". Drawing on Hart (2002, 2014 and 2015), they correctly point to, p. 6:

> four major political tendencies that have intensified since the mid-2000s: (1) proliferating expressions of discontent manifesting as protests (often directly related to infrastructure and service provision), (2) growing tensions and splintering within the African National Congress (ANC) (South Africa's governing party), (3) increasingly visible populist politics across scales, and (4) increasingly fruitless efforts to manage growing inequality and rising government expenditures at all levels.

22 As is implicitly acknowledged by its having become deployed as contextually descriptive.

But how are we to explain these tendencies and the diversities to which they are attached? And do they or do they not have deep roots in the MEC as a system of accumulation. Extremely common are explanations for South Africa's malaise in terms of institutional failings (leading to poor policy) but then why do some institutions fail and others not, why are institutions not put right, and why do they adopt the policies that they do?[23] An answer might be given in terms of the political settlement approach in which rents are pivotal and secured through power. For Mondliwa and Roberts (2021, p. 315), the sources of holding power include economic structure, violence rights, rents and ideology, but how do these translate into particular outcomes, and how do the sources emerge and mutually evolve? Unfortunately, and surprisingly, their account makes little or no reference to the MEC, neoliberalism and financialisation.[24]

With the launch of GEAR (through the prior centralised political leadership that preceded it), three major strategies were adopted:[25] to embrace what was perceived to be economic (policy) orthodoxy; to promote a class of black business; and, third and foremost, to contain sources of dissent to the other two and their implications for developmental progress (i.e. a strategy to limit and manage what were deemed to be unreasonable and destabilising aspirations).[26] As argued throughout my Volumes on South Africa, in forging bits and pieces together over time into a fuller picture, the conditions of the globalised, neoliberalised restructuring of the MEC has resulted in the failure to create institutional capacity to implement and coordinate policy even at the expense of the three delineated main strategies themselves let alone to be able to serve

23 Interestingly, Mazzucato and Gasperin (2023) propose the institution of a state holding company to coordinate public enterprises, without questioning why this coordination is not already in place. More than twenty-five years previously, I suggested the same just for steel (Fine, 1998c). Just blowing in the wind.

24 Similar neglect occurs for neoliberalism in Andreoni et al. (eds) (2021) but not for the MEC and financialisation. But these are all vital in combination for understanding the holding of power through the sources they identify (and otherwise).

25 I hesitate to deploy, and even reject, what might be termed the continuity thesis that post-apartheid sustained the apartheid project under the guise of democracy (insightful though it may be in highlighting persisting inequalities, etc). But Soer (2025) offers an account of neoliberalism under late apartheid revealing that its priorities were to establish the preconditions for some mythical free market nirvana, brought about, inconsistently, through both state support and marginalisation of those who would seek more from the state and so jeopardise the endeavour. There are striking parallels with the post-apartheid imperatives of the first Government of National Unity, driven by Mbeki.

26 It might be thought that Mbeki's (2024) recent if belated rant over what went wrong – an unnamed but successful conspiracy to sabotage his "revolutionary" path – is not so crazy after all if any opposition to it is seen as counter-revolutionary dissent.

the MEFC[27] and build development success by drawing upon, and diversifying, out of it. By the same token, the centralisation of authoritarian power over policy has given limited scope for the presence of checks and balances on the exercise of that power, and to steer it in coherent and effective directions.[28] Further, there has been what I have termed the unravelling of the Tripartite Alliance and its constituent elements,[29] the loss of ANC electoral popularity, and variegated initiatives and outcomes across time, place and issue albeit with the persistent theme of the five lows, deeply entrenching inequalities and impoverishments.

From all of this, it follows, controversially, that there are far from major differences between the three Presidencies of Mbeki, Zuma and Ramaphosa other than in the forms in which these complex set of determinants are realised and, admittedly, have effects. Power was centralised under Mbeki's regime, it was deployed through 'state capture' under Zuma, with Ramaphosa at most seeking to roll back the latter's excesses. From within the Department of Trade and Industry, there is a sense in which Zalk (2021) agrees. He points to three phases for industrial policy: the first as "Core Bargains, Liberalization, and Stabilization"; the second as "The Illusion of Progress, the Ostensible Shift to a 'Developmental State', and the Introduction of Industrial Policy"; and the third for which "Industrial Policy – Formally Embraced, Undermined in Practice". He concludes that industrial policy has been obstructed by macroeconomic policy, the management of state-owned enterprises, corruption and the maladministration of BEE. Seen from a different perspective, the same applies to Andreoni et al. (2021a, p. 75) in bemoaning who makes policy and how:

27 Although finance has done incredibly well, as I lampoon, it takes 25% of GDP as reward for failing to generate sufficient investment by a half of what is needed, and has the cheek to suggest it has increased GDP by 25% by doing so, meaning its contribution is a mere 20% to GDP (25% out of 125%).

28 As it were, better a corrupt black elite than an over-aspirational trade union movement?

29 Note that Levenson and Paret (2025) make the case that the MDM facilitated the post-apartheid transition as a (Gramscian) passive revolution, through a "Goldilocks syndrome", essentially being accommodated but ineffective through leadership tolerance. Whatever the merits of their case (as it conforms with all evidence to the contrary as it potentially counts as supportive), they take a further step, without discussion, emphasis added: "Some hoped for a radical path, others for moderation. What was clear, however, was that the ANC now had a popular mandate to lead South Africa's transition to a liberal democracy *and, ultimately, neoliberal capitalism*", pp. 16–17. The latter emphasis (added) can neither be taken for granted nor can it blame be placed upon the MDM which, as part of the UDF, as is observed in their previous paragraph, self-liquidated in August, 1991 – unless this is itself seen as an unconscious Goldilocks action in support of neoliberalism.

> While policy instrument design and governance frameworks are critical, the effective implementation and enforcement of any industrial policy will depend on the extent to which the policy is able to promote the emergence of a new coalition of productive interests, or offer the existing powerful groups alternative and more productive ways to operate in the economy. This is the ultimate 'feasibility' test for the policy.

It is a test that is now not only absent from the policy(making) agenda but, most depressing of all after thirty years of post-apartheid, also difficult to envisage how it will be restored let alone passed with flying colours and distinction.

4 Brief Overview

The Chapters in this book tend to appear in chronological order of being written and subject matter covered. They are all about the ME(F)C, either closely focused or contextualised with broader implications attached. All engage heavily and critically with other literature. Thus, Chapter 2 covers the coal industry (and the fallacy and lessons to be drawn from deploying total factor productivity, TFP). Chapter 3 re-examines South African labour markets in light of critique of mainstream labour economics and its application to South Africa (with the post-apartheid putative abolition of labour market 'discrimination'). Chapters 4 and 5 focus on laying out, and defending, the MEC as a system of accumulation. Chapters 8 and 10 do so relative to the Developmental State, Varieties of Capitalism and Social Compacting Paradigms. Meaning is, in a sense, the topic of Chapters 6, 7 and 9. The first interrogates the nature of identity for the Rainbow Nation under the shadow of the MEC. What is it to be a post-apartheid South African? One aspect, laid out in Chapter 7, is to be subject to condoned (illegal) capital flight; another is to be subject to (state) violence as illustrated by Chapter 9 on Marikana. Finally, Chapter 11 is a long meandering update on a variety of related topics, drafted in honour and memory of Vishnu Padayachee, in the wake of his sudden death. It offers sketches of the post-apartheid economy, its political economy and the broader material and ideological context in which they are evolving.

CHAPTER 2

Total Factor Productivity vs. Realism: The South African Coal Mining Industry

Postscript as Personal Preamble

From the mid-1980s, at the request of the ANC, I began to work on South Africa in earnest, with mining and all related to it serving as an important starting point. I devoured all available literature voraciously and, unsurprisingly, came across the piece by Jones (1983) that is critically assessed in the Chapter that follows. Publication from the time of the initial draft was extremely slow. Mindful of an academic boycott against South Africa, I initially submitted to the *Zimbabwean Journal of Economics* where it seemed to get lost without trace (of outcome). Eventually, I must have made up my mind it was ok to sanction bust by submitting to the *South African Journal of Economics*, something I saw as an act of provocation given that it was compromised by its limited critical commentary on apartheid and being generally committed to mainstream economics, and especially in favour of free markets (although with a bit of a streak of neo-Austrianism within the establishment – begging the question of how you can both favour free markets and be complicit with apartheid).

To my surprise and delight, my piece was accepted to be published. It had been written in a particular way to make this more rather than less likely. Specifically, Jones had calculated total factor productivity (TFP) for the South African coal industry and had sought to explain its empirical trajectory in terms of ups and downs deriving from the introduction of new technology. My strategy was to ask the simple question – do the conditions of the South African coal industry satisfy those that are necessary to justify the calculation of TFP. These include no economies of scale, perfect competition in input and output markets, no excess capacity, and an economy with only one sector (otherwise TFP measures shifts in demand as shifts in supply, one way of interpreting the Cambridge Capital Critique, see below). For reasons laid out in detail in the Chapter, these conditions are only observed in the breach. Indeed, one way of interpreting the measurement of TFP is as a measure of productivity together or jumbled up with the impact of all of the deviations from perfect competition (and a one-good economy).

My contribution allowed for two motivations. One was to put the Cambridge Critique on the map in empirical work, something that has been relatively rare.

 DOI:10.1163/9789004748330_003

Instead, the Critique has been deployed to argue against the one sector neoclassical production function in theoretical work and, in particular, that the rate of profit can be determined by the marginal product of (aggregate) capital (and all the implications that follow from this).[1] The other motivation was to put the Minerals-Energy Complex on the map if not explicitly as it happens.[2] In the specific context of South African coal, measuring deviations from the conditions necessary for TFP to be valid means pointing to the conglomerate structures around the MEC, including the mining houses, the linkages to other sectors, the close collaboration with the state (and its enterprises and market quotas) as well as the migrant labour system. As measurement of TFP is commonplace across any number of applications by sector, countries and even regions, I have always advised a good starting point for initiating and promoting alternative research is to take the conditions necessary for them to be valid as critical point of departure for presenting how realities are entirely different whether it be competitiveness, increasing returns to scale and scope (and externalities) and full employment. I have had at most limited success.[3]

1 Introduction[4]

The purpose of this Chapter is to examine the position that the coal industry has occupied in the South African economy. However, we do this indirectly by consideration of an earlier attempt to look at the South African coal industry by Jones (1983). He adopts the conventional method of measuring total factor productivity (TFP) but he does not question whether the economic conditions within South Africa justify the application of the neoclassical paradigm in this respect.

1 For my own accounts, see Fine (1980 and 2016b) but there is a massive heterodox literature patiently laying out the critique, which has been accepted by its opponents. And there is a minority heterodox sport questioning why the mainstream persists as if the critique does not exist and has been accepted as valid.

2 In the text, the term energy minerals complex is deployed suggesting, at initial time of drafting, I had yet to fix upon the MEC as such. Yet, at time of publication, an ESRC-funded research project on the MEC had already been in place for two years (on top of the time for it to be submitted and funded).

3 But see Sato (2005), this forming part of his PhD under my supervision, not least dealing with the idea that South Korean steel had no scale economies, a vignette in the denial that the East Asian NICs had no productivity miracle.

4 First published as Fine (1992a). Department of Economics, Birkbeck College, London. Financial support of the Economic and Social Research Council (UK) is gratefully acknowledged.

TABLE 2.1 Output and input indices, 1950–80

Year	Output	Labour	Capital	Raw materials
1950	100	100	100	100
1960	148.2	121.0	122.2	190.5
1970	206.3	136.3	201.0	369.0
1980	406.6	165.5	436.3	1007.8

SOURCE: SEE TEXT, AMENDED FROM JONES (1983)

Of course, it could be said at the outset that the methodology of calculating TFP has long been known to be invalid.[5] Relying upon a model of the economy which treats it as if it can be reduced to a one good world in which marginal productivities of factor inputs correctly measure contribution to output, it necessarily conflates changing production conditions (such as improved availability of techniques) with other changes in the economy (such as demand conditions). We are not concerned here to repeat these criticisms, devastating though they may be. Rather, we will, as far as our discussion will allow, accept that for our purposes, South African coal mining is equivalent to a one good world, in which coal is not only the single produced good but, equivalently, also the capital input and the wage-consumption commodity. We are more concerned to examine whether, within this ideal conception of the economy, the conditions for measuring total factor productivity hold. By showing that they do not, we will have uncovered some of the major characteristics of the industry together with an understanding of its place in the economy.

We begin in this introduction by giving a summary of Jones' results. He has estimated total factor productivity for the South African coal mining industry between 1950 and 1980. His results and methodology are considered sufficiently sound that the International Energy Authority extends his calculations to 1983 (IEA, 1986). Jones' analysis reveals some remarkable achievements. Table 2.1, which is reproduced from his own table for an annual series, shows that output expanded four times over the thirty years, labour productivity having

5 This fallacy of one-sector growth models is usually associated with the theory of distribution and with Joan Robinson and the Cambridge Capital Controversy. But the criticisms carry over into statistical estimation of production functions. For a comprehensive review of the issues involved, see Harcourt (1972) and for a specific treatment of the potential errors of estimating the economy as if it only had one good, see Fine (1980).

TABLE 2.2 Average annual growth in productivity variables

Period	Output	Total input factor	Labour	Capital	Materials	Spares and repairs
1950–58	4.3	3.1	2.3	2.0	6.0	11.1
1959–67	3.2	4.3	2.0	4.3	7.7	12.4
1968–74	4.2	2.0	−0.8	4.2	3.9	9.4
1975–78	7.4	12.1	5.8	12.6	21.0	29.2
1978–80	10.4	4.5	−1.2	8.5	7.5	9.8

SOURCE: SEE TEXT, AMENDED FROM JONES (1983)

increased almost two and a half times. Growth of capital stock, however, has more than kept pace with output whilst raw material inputs have increased by two and a half times output. It can be seen that the changes that took place over the first twenty years of the period under consideration were more or less duplicated over the following ten years, so that the pace of growth and change doubled.

Jones, however, finds that the overall trend in TFP has been far from satisfactory. For the level of TFP has scarcely changed over the period, exhibiting a distinct cyclical pattern with TFP never rising more than twenty per cent above its original 1950 level even if rarely falling below this level. Jones suggests that this is due to alternating periods of learning and familiarity as new techniques are introduced into the coalfields. Between 1959 and 1967, hand-got mining gives way to conventional load-haul-dump methods and, between 1975 and 1978, in turn, this makes way for sophisticated capital-intensive mining (continuous miners, long walling and open cast). This cycle of learning and familiarity is deemed to be illustrated in Table 2.2, again adapted from his own table.

In the second and fourth periods, output growth is below total factor input growth with the implication that productivity has fallen. An unusual aspect of Jones' method is the inclusion of raw materials in the group of inputs (shown in column 5) of which spares and repairs form a part (column 6). He argues that the exceptional rate of growth of raw materials, and especially of spares and repairs, during periods of learning is the proximate cause of the falls in productivity as familiarity is gained rather than being exploited. We question this claim in the following section, partly by amending Jones' calculations and partly by reinterpreting them. The focus is upon whether rapid growth in use of raw materials (and spares and repairs) is indicative of productivity decrease (due to learning as for Jones) or of productivity increase (due to more intensive production as argued here). In addition, before arguing this, it is shown that even if the residual approach to measuring TFP is (erroneously) accepted, Jones' measurements of the contribution of raw materials biases the calculations downwards.

In the following sections, we examine whether the conditions of perfect competition necessary to justify the measurement of TFP have been characteristic of the South African coal industry. In finding that they do not, we draw opposite conclusions to those of Jones. The industry is seen to have gone through a remarkable transformation as capital-intensive methods of production have increasingly been adopted on large-scale mines. This process has quickened over recent years, and Jones' (cyclical) periods of TFP decline are more likely to have represented an acceleration of what are secular trends in the development of the South African coal industry. This is argued in the concluding remarks.

2 Measuring Total Factor Productivity

In measuring TFP, Jones has used a formula of the type:

$$g\langle Y\rangle = g\langle A\rangle + ag\langle K\rangle + bg\langle L\rangle + cg\langle R\rangle$$

where $g\langle\cdots\rangle$ is rate of growth, Y is output, A is level of TFP, K is capital stock, L is labour and R is raw materials and a, b and c are the shares of inputs in output. The use of R as though it were an input with the same status as K and L is, however, problematic, as we shall see. For unlike capital and labour in which their measurements as inputs are in principle separate from their factor rewards or shares as profits and wages, raw materials have a factor cost which is identical to their share in output. There is no separate measurement of their contribution to output by the use of marginal products.

In short, $c = 1$. Now presumably, the formula above is derived from a production function, $Y = f(K, L, R, t)$, where t is time. Differentiating and manipulating:

$$G\langle Y\rangle = f_t/f + (f_K K/Y)g\langle K\rangle + (f_L L/Y)g\langle L\rangle + (f_R R/Y)g\langle R\rangle$$

By comparison of the two formulae, it follows from the coefficients of $g\langle R\rangle$ that $f_R = 1$. Hence, integrating:

$$Y = f(K, L, R, t) = F(K, L, t) + R$$

This means that raw materials simply pass their value onto output. This result is a consequence of the use of raw material inputs as though they obtain a factor reward equal to their actual share in revenue. Differentiating, we obtain:

$$G<Y> = F_t/F + (F_K K/Y)g<K> + (F_L L/Y)g<L> + (R/Y)g<R>$$

Now a shift in the production function (representing a change in TFP) is given by F_t/F. Consequently, it is being undermeasured by the formula implicit in Jones' calculation. The ratio of the two measures is $F/(F + R)$ which equals $1 - R/Y$ or the share of non-raw materials in output. Now it appears from Jones' account as though this falls from 83 per cent to 67 per cent (as the share of raw materials rises from 17 per cent to 33 per cent). In other words, change in productivity has been underestimated by 23.8 per cent (given by 83/67).

Of course, the formula we have derived above could be rewritten as a production function for *net* output:

$$Y - R = f(K, L, t)$$

This raises the question of what economies of scale to assume for the function F. Jones calculates factor shares by subtracting the wage and raw material shares from unity to obtain the profit share as a residual. Whilst this appears to involve constant returns to scale, in the case of the function F there are decreasing returns given by the sum of profit and wage shares (in fact varying between 0.67 and 0.83, as given above).

It must be recognised, however, that there have been considerable increasing returns to scale in coal mining and, in South Africa over the eighties, these have been especially important.[6] Whereas previously mines were of the size of an annual output of at most a few million tonnes, the latest mines tied to power stations have output levels exceeding ten mpta (million tonnes per annum). The Bosjesspruit colliery, serving the coal to oil conversion plant (SASOL) through the Secunda complex, has a capacity of around thirty mpta. For export markets, opencast production is the norm with capacity around four mpta. Unfortunately, for the TFP method of measuring technical change, the existence of economies of scale is entirely destructive since it does not allow the contributions of factor inputs to be measured by their factor shares.

6 In the eighties, the expansion of output is geared towards a very small number of mines considerably larger than even the largest ones of the seventies. See Pardoe and Pedroncelli (1982) who also give details of the relative costs of the different mining methods.

In the absence of economies of scale as causal, Jones explains the pattern of TFP over time by the adoption and learning of new techniques up to the point of familiarity. Learning is associated with the excessive use of raw materials, particularly spares and repairs. Not only do the latter grow most rapidly during the periods of supposed learning (Table 2.2) but they ultimately reach a weight of 43 per cent in raw materials. It is suggested that use of spares and repairs during learning are running out of control.

We would suggest an alternative explanation. First, as Table 2.2 reveals the growth of spares and repairs over the entire period from 1950 to 1980 is higher than for any other variable. If it were simply a matter of the cycle of learning and familiarity, then the growth of repairs and spares could be expected to fall below the growth of other inputs during the familiarity stage. In other words, the growing share of raw materials, and of spares and repairs within it, is a secular trend even if it does have a cyclical rhythm around its trend (like all variables to some degree).

Second, as we have seen above, if raw material use accelerates for whatever reason, it will tend to bias down the measurement of TFP. This suggests that the periods of learning are in fact correctly perceived to be times when there is an increase in the pace of movement towards the use of new techniques but, because these use more capital-intensive methods and a higher ratio of raw materials (and an even higher ratio of spares and repairs), they are falsely associated by Jones with lower TFP.

Third, if we examine the major items of expenditure associated with spares and repairs, we find that for the last twenty years this has consistently comprised scrapers, haulages, loaders and winches, vehicles, conveyors, coal cutting machinery and other electrical and non-electrical machinery. Some of these obviously have very little to do with learning and breakdown, and the rest could easily be wearing out as a simple result of their more intensive use or through establishment of new opencast sites or new pits at deeper levels. In short, the association of the increased use of spares and repairs over the learning period cannot be taken as an indication of breakdown or poor performance. Indeed, it suggests that the workforce may be using capital equipment more intensively than previously.

Fourth, if breakdown were responsible for the supposedly poor levels of TFP, then we would expect non-operating time of machinery to be a major explanation of the differences in the levels of productivity between mines. But a detailed study of the use of continuous miners shows that this is not important and that the major source of productivity differences is derived from the levels of output achieved whilst machinery is in use (Hardman and Oberholzer, 1987).[7]

Fifth, the massive investments in the seventies would only begin to give returns after a time and this should not be confused with learning. Far from being slow at bringing its investments to maturity, the South African industry has been remarkably proficient in recent times – Bosjesspruit colliery for Sasol yielding 27.5 million tonnes within an eight-year period, when a decade is a normal gestation period for a colliery (van Garderen, p. 282). Moreover, it seems anomalous to have taken eight years to learn load-haul-dump methods but a mere three years to familiarise with continuous, longwall and open-cast mining, particularly when this is a period shorter than that often required to construct the mines that embody the new techniques!

Close scrutiny, then, of Jones' results for 1950 to 1980 suggests that they systematically underestimate productivity increase. There are good reasons to believe in economies of scale in the South African coal industry, and this is associated with increasing capital intensity and hence increasing intensity of labour as labour productivity has grown two and a half times. The increase in labour productivity is linked to its working up six times more raw materials per head (and a staggering thirty times more in spares and repairs). Moreover, these changes have accelerated over the last decade under consideration, with this period achieving as much as the previous twenty years. In the following sections, by questioning the assumptions necessary for TFP to be measured, we reveal the structure of economic and industrial organisation that has made this all possible.

3 The Measurement of Output

Since factor shares are, by marginal productivity theory, to measure factor contribution to output, it is necessary to assume that the economy is perfectly competitive, for otherwise TFP will be measuring the monopoly position within particular markets, rather than real contribution to output, and/or TFP will be measuring changes in the level of capacity utilisation in the absence of

7 The research in this paper has been for the Chamber of Mines and is based on approximately 6,000 machine months of information for the period 1978 to 1986.

full employment.[8] We leave these issues aside together with those associated with the trade cycle for which, during recession, the potential output of factor inputs is understated by idle capacity.

Instead, let us begin our discussion with the measurement of output. Here there would appear to be little problem. To paraphrase Gertrude Stein, a tonne of coal is a tonne of coal ... Output can be measured in physical terms, and this has the advantage of appearing to sustain consistency with the neoclassical motivation of estimating the production function as a simple physical technical relation between inputs and outputs.[9] But there are as many varieties of coal as there are of roses. Coal is far from being a homogeneous commodity because of its variable chemical properties. Nor is this a matter which is fixed by the naturally given geological conditions, although this is extremely important. Methods of extraction as well as treatment of the coal after extraction affect its quality. Both of these in turn depend upon the demand for coal. Coal-fired power stations, for example, have been able to employ coal of inferior quality through improvement in furnace technology. More important for our purposes is that export coal tends to be of the highest quality. There is not much point incurring transport costs of about half of mining costs in order to send coal abroad which is heavily mixed with dirt.

By 1980 coal exports had reached almost thirty million tonnes (out of a total output of 115 million tonnes) from a negligible figure less than a decade before (when total production was 63 million tonnes). Whilst half of output has been used by pithead power stations and coal to oil conversion plants without washing, the remainder is cleaned prior to transportation. In 1980, there were washing facilities at 51 of the 87 collieries, (Murray and Granville, 1982). These constitute a heavy burden on capital expenditure so that the measurement of capital stock is in a sense divided between two separate industries – the mining of coal and the preparation of coal – whilst TFP is measured by Jones as if it were responsible for the capital (and other expenditure) of both of these activities. Stretching a point, it would be just as appropriate to include the costs of

8 These two influences, of distortion of market rewards and of less than full employment, can dovetail with each other. According to one theory of oligopoly, firms may maintain a monopoly by keeping capacity idle as a barrier to the entry of other firms through the threat of flooding the market. For a recent discussion, see Cowling (1982) but for a critique of its overall significance for the economy as a whole, see Fine and Murfin (1984).

9 Jones comments on "the purity of a physical-units measure and a true technological relationship is, therefore, preserved," p. 511. Such purity is questionable given that the conceptual basis for the technological relationship is invalid. It is perhaps a bit like administering an anaesthetic for a post mortem investigation.

transportation in the factor inputs of the industry (which, by the way, have been increased enormously to provide a 300 km railway from the coalfields to the expanded and modernised port at Richards Bay).

Nor is this a minor debating point. The Grootgeluk colliery planned to strip fifteen mpta, was expected to incur a total investment cost of R8280 million for mining equipment, housing and railway links. Of this, as much as R8120 million was required for the washery, the largest in the world and capable of handling 3000 tonnes per hour (Murray and Granville, 1982). It alone involves an investment cost of R20 per tonne per annum which is close to the price of coal on the domestic market.

In a discussion of approach and methodology at the outset, Jones does make clear that he is setting aside considerations of quality of inputs and outputs, although his discussion is confined to inputs. The idea is that changes in quality should be part of the residual, which is to be explained after taking account of the basic use of capital and labour inputs. Whilst he does not discuss coal quality in explaining the movement of TFP, this might be thought to be subject to remedy in principle. But the conclusion would be rather perverse. The productivity performance of the industry is poor because it has devoted large resources to improving quality. But this is precisely one essential factor in the success of the astonishing export drive.

There is, however, a way of dealing with this problem whilst remaining in the one-sector world of TFP. This is to remeasure output taking account of quality change, treating one tonne of better coal as more than one tonne of poorer coal. This could be done on a physical basis by constructing a quality index according to the various chemical properties of the coal. Apart from the index number problem itself – how do we weigh differing ash content against calorific value, for example? – the quality of the coal is not an intrinsic property of the coal itself but reflects the changing technologies in the use of coal.

This tends to put us back into the critique we are trying to avoid, the problems of treating the world as though it were governed by a single commodity. Even if we accept this in principle, when putting it into practice when constructing the data, we need to recognise and reconcile the more complex economy of many commodities. But, within the method already adopted for the measurement of the heterogeneous capital stock, there is the obvious solution of measuring output in value rather than physical quantities. This should then take account of quality differences in output (and we set aside the Cambridge critique problem of using prices to construct what are supposed to be our theoretically prior physical quantities of inputs and, in this case, outputs). Indeed, the value rather than the volume of output was used by Jones to obtain input factor shares.

4 Competition in the Markets for Coal

There would still remain one problem, which also exists for the capital stock, the need to deflate the level of the value of output index according to the level of inflation (and, given exports, to choose an appropriate of the exchange rate). Again, caught in a theoretical world of one commodity and a statistical world of many, we are faced with choosing an appropriate index of inflation. A natural one might be an international or domestic index of coal prices or of energy prices more generally. But the validity of this, even within a world equivalent to a one good economy, to return to an earlier theme, is that all markets should be perfectly competitive. For otherwise, our index of inflation will be distorted by the changing strengths or weaknesses of the producers and/or consumers in the market place and this will be measured rather than, or as contributing to, TFP.

The purpose of the previous paragraphs has not been to establish the preliminaries for improving the measurement of output, the better to measure TFP. It has shown that, even within the one good economy, the measurement of output in physical terms without a price evaluation still requires, in principle, perfect competition in the sector concerned. Thus, it is legitimate to examine competition in the production of output as well as in the purchase of factor inputs. We do this by examining competition between the industry and other sectors and competition within the sector, linking the two by a brief account of the institutional context.

Coal is in competition with other fuels, most obviously electricity for which it is the major input in South Africa, and with oil as a primary fuel. But it cannot be contended that the price of any of these fuels reproduces the market value associated with perfect competition. The price as well as the supply of each is heavily regulated by government. In the case of electricity, its price has been increased in recent years to support the financing of a massive investment programme in the face of decline in other sources of funds. The contribution of tariffs to capital expenditure rose from 22 per cent in 1975 to almost 50 per cent in 1979 (ESCOM, 1985, p. 5). In the case of oil, South Africa is, in principle, heavily constrained by sanctions. This means that it has to pay a premium on imports which has been estimated at $3 per barrel (EIU, 1985). As a result of the policy to be independent as far as possible from imported oil, the Sasol coal to oil conversion plants are responsible for as much as fifty per cent of domestic oil requirements.

Although presumed by some to be economic at $15 per barrel (EIU, 1982), it would be hard to argue that the Sasol complex is the outcome that would have resulted from market forces. Moreover, it relies upon its own collieries,

Sigma (six million tonnes per annum) and Bosjesspruit (28 million tonnes by 1984) which would force up the domestic demand for, and supply of, coal independently of the sole interplay of market forces (Murray and Granville, 1982). On the other hand, it is estimated that coal exports are sold at a discount of $2 per tonne on export markets to compensate for presumed instability and/or political distaste associated with trade with South Africa (EIU, 1985).

In domestic markets, the major consumer of coal has been electricity, accounting for over sixty per cent of domestic consumption. Although privately owned and run, the collieries serving power stations are tied to them on site with at least forty years reserves when set up, and the price of their output is regulated to guarantee profitability (EIU, 1982). Together, just three customers – ESCOM (the state-run electricity utility), SASOL and the previously state-run iron and steel utility, ISCOR – have accounted for 90 per cent of domestic coal consumption.

5 The Supply Side

Looking at the demand for coal, it appears then that it diverges from the conditions associated with perfect competition as a few major users dominate sales and, as we shall see, there has been a premium on export markets. The evidence is then that market prices do not reflect the conditions required for the validity of calculating TFP. This is confirmed if we examine the conditions of entry into the industry. The sector has been highly concentrated, with the two largest companies accounting for sixty per cent of output, and the next three largest companies taking up a further thirty per cent (Murray and Granville, 1982). The frustrated desire to enter the industry is illustrated by the government-controlled export permit allocation system which was entering its fourth phase in the mid-eighties. Applications for export quotas, for which a tonnage is assigned to individual mines and companies for a period of thirty years, totalled two hundred million tonnes per annum but only forty million tonnes were allocated (King, 1985). One of the factors involved in making the allocations was "the contribution the various companies made to domestic energy supplies".[10] The ability to fulfill export quotas is, in addition, heavily constrained by the capacity of, and the access to, the Richards Bay harbour

10 See Financial Mail (1985). The reluctance to some degree to engage foreign companies in the coal industry is illustrated by the Anglovaal acquisition of a thirty per cent stake in the one billion tonnes of reserves of the Eloff Mining company owned by Utah International (itself a subsidiary of BHP of Australia) in anticipation of an ESCOM power station

facilities. In 1985, the Independent Coal Producers Association was refused access to the dock facilities despite an excess capacity which was reserved for the major producers (EIU, 1985, p. 2).

6 Coal and the State

In the narrow economic terms of the market, the South African coal industry has not conformed to the laissez-faire model essential to support the use of TFP methods. Further the absence of perfect competition is confirmed by the institutional structure within which the industry operates. The three main coal mining companies formed half of the members of the group system, the six major corporations which run most of South Africa's mining companies across a range of minerals of which gold is the most important. Formally, the group system is embodied in the Chamber of Mines (1984) which, in its own words, is:[11]

> A private enterprise employers' organisation funded and controlled by its member mines and the mining houses ... on a budget of more than R8300 million a year and its governing body is a council comprising two representatives of each of the six mining houses with day-to-day policy being determined by an executive committee comprising one representative from each of the six mining groups.

with the result that:

> The main characteristic of the South African mining industry is its strong cohesiveness which has facilitated a degree of co-operation *probably unmatched in the private sector anywhere in the* world. (emphasis added)

This cohesiveness and co-operation have been encouraged and reinforced both by the economic structure of South African industry and by government policy and institutions. Recall that the vast majority of coal has been produced by members of the group system for the purposes of tied sales to ESCOM for electricity generation which lies at the core of the energy needs of South African industry. But one of the major users of electricity is the (group system's) gold

contract and the "open secret" of its unwillingness to give the contract to a non-South African company (EIU,1984 p. 4).

11 Unable to find original for page citation.

industry – with roughly an equal third share with each of industry and domestic consumption. Indeed, the nineteen largest electricity consumers in 1983, excluding municipalities, were responsible for twenty-five per cent of electricity consumption. Of these, as many as nine were individual gold mines and the others were almost all related to the energy-mineral complex surrounding the group system (ESCOM, 1985, p. 69).

As seen, over the period under consideration, the coal industry has been subject directly to government policy through price regulation and export quotas and, indirectly, through the policies of ESCOM and other state enterprises such as ISCOR, SASOL and South African Transport Services. Formally, making proposals for policy was in the hands of the Energy Policy Committee (EPC) of the Department of Mineral and Energy Affairs. The Department was itself created in 1980 as "the combination of the energy and minerals functions is of great importance for effective determination of policy by the Government on a co-ordinated basis" (DMEA, 1980, p. 72). Whilst the group was not represented on the EPC, it appears that it serves to supplement the co-ordination already provided by the Chamber of Mines.

7 The Labour Market

One of the major functions undertaken by the Chamber is the recruitment and training of labour. It is here perhaps that the perfectly competitive conditions necessary for the measurement of TFP have been furthest from being met, given the compound system of labour. Jones makes no distinction between black and white labour, simply aggregating the two together to give total number of employees – for which marginal productivity is putatively measured through the factor share occupied by wages. But, if we consider the black labour force we find for coal and gold mining taken together that employment has expanded by a quarter in the seventies, despite the loss of a third of the workforce through the displacement of foreign migrant workers.[12] This suggests that the labour market cannot have been in any sort of persistent equilibrium, given the decline of foreign migrant workers from over fifty per cent to under fifteen per cent.

This conclusion is confirmed if we examine the movement of relative wages over the period. Between 1970 and 1979 the white/black pay differential in coal

12 See Malan (1985). The substitution was partly enforced by the withdrawal of labour from South Africa and partly by a deliberate policy to minimise the potential disruptive effects of such a withdrawal in the future.

mining narrowed from 19.8 to 6.7 whilst that in manufacturing declined from 5.8 to 4.3 (Spandau, 1980). This reflects both a dramatic increase in real wages in the mining sector (which had remained constant in real terms over the previous fifty years) and a narrowing but continuing relative advantage for black workers in manufacturing. Whether these changes reflect a shift in the balance of the labour market following the withdrawal of foreign labour and/or the rise of black trade unions in mining is beside the point. The real wage cannot have equalled marginal productivity consistently or even closely throughout the period, as is required for the measurement of TFP.

There are also problems of lumping black and white labour together and treating them as competitive, quite apart from aggregation problems in calculating marginal productivity when one group of workers earns between seven and twenty times as much as the other. In mining, training to the most skilled jobs has been reserved for whites and has been fiercely defended by white trade unions even against the opposition of the employers.[13]

In short, as one might expect, there is little evidence to suggest that the apartheid system is conducive to a freely operating labour market nor, as some might suggest in other circumstances such as in discussing the power of trade unions, that the pressure of the market overcomes obstacles in its way. Neither in principle nor in practice can the labour market in the South African mining industry be considered fertile ground for the application of marginal productivity theory to measure TFP.

8 Concluding Remarks

In his approach, Jones calculates TFP on the basis of the barest collection of factor inputs. The trend of TFP that then results becomes a central statistical artefact which has to be explained by reference to other considerations, some of which might, if so desired, have been included in the original TFP calculations – as in our discussion of coal quality leading to a change in the measurement of output. Whether this can be done or not is more a matter of available data (or its construction) for some factors are not readily quantifiable – such as the general level of education of the workforce – and these might be best left as explanations of the change in TFP rather than used in its calculation.

In addition, there are those factors previously unconsidered in the calculation of TFP which tend to undermine the exercise in the first place.

13 See Wiehahn (1979/80). Its recommendations to end job reservation were only finally legislated for towards the end of 1987.

Paradoxically, these can also be used to explain the movement in TFP even though their presence invalidates the exercise. For example, the distributional gains of black workers in the middle seventies, because of the growth in employment (up 20 per cent in the seventies) and the massive increase in (gestating) capital (more than doubling), could be argued to bias the measure of TFP down in Jones' learning period from 1975 to 1978.[14]

One conclusion to be drawn, then, is that the measurement and explanation of TFP is not a worthwhile exercise in the case of the South African coal industry, although it has thrown up some important features, most notably the increasing intensity of capital and raw material use in production and the accompanying rise in labour productivity. A more important conclusion, however, has emerged from this initial rejection of TFP. We have shown that the transformation of coal mining has been the consequence of a particular form of economic organisation.

First, apartheid's system of compound labour has made available a cheap workforce. Second, there has been dependence upon a close-knit mineral-energy complex that has coordinated developments across industries (coal, electricity, gold, oil and transport, etc.) and between industry and the state (the group system, the Chamber of Mines, the Department of Mineral and Energy Affairs, etc.). Coal has been privately produced for state-run power stations that have generated electricity for the extraction and processing of gold ore by the very same mining companies that produce the coal and which make up the Chamber of Mines. Export markets have been allocated through state quotas and are served by a specially enhanced state-owned (electrified) railway that runs coal three hundred miles from the inland mines to the docks. The production of oil from coal has been a political response to the threat of sanctions.

This close co-ordination between state and industry and, the exploitation of apartheid labour, has been the source of the coal industry's success, and its accelerated development over the last decade under consideration has been a product of the boost to both gold and coal following the breakdown of both monetary and energy international markets in the seventies. These conditions of success are, however, being eroded. The South African economy has stagnated throughout the eighties and into the nineties, and the gold price has long since ended its meteoric rise; net foreign investment has become negative

14 The use of factors to explain TFP, whose presence would invalidate the calculation of that TFP in the first place, is to be found in the most prestigious work. See Matthews et al. (1982), the classic examination of British economic growth, where movements in TFP are variously explained by an increase in workers' bargaining strength and the presence of excess capacity.

through divestment and in response to a debt repayment freeze; the internal economic and political situation remains uncertain as the struggle against apartheid and to establish a constitutional settlement intensifies. Clearly, these developments strongly impinge upon the future prospects of the coal industry – as demand for coal at home and abroad falls, as trade unionists press for higher wages and better working conditions, as sources of finance for investment become scarcer, as the demands for more skilled black workers confront the traditionally reserved occupations of white workers. These sorts of influences and the conflicts around them, rather than TFP, must surely determine the future course of the industry.

CHAPTER 3

"The Rise in African Wages: 1975–1985": A Dissenting and Wide-Ranging Commentary

Postscript as Personal Preamble

This Chapter was drafted as part of the MERG initiative but never appeared as such in the published report.[1] But it has a longer history. From electronic files still available, first drafts and interest go back at least as far as 1992, and I have copies of correspondence with Julian Hofmeyr but no record of his responses, if any – I do not recall. I also found, also having slipped my memory, a covering letter of submission to the *South African Journal of Economics*. Once again, I have no record of response but the piece must have been rejected. I seem to recall with this nudge to have received no feedback nor rationale for the rejection.

Less immediately, my discussion of South African labour markets fitted neatly into what was a continuing programme of work on labour markets more generally. Concerted attention had first been focused upon labour markets in the mid-1980s when I reviewed the literature on segmented labour markets, in part stimulated by preparing evidence for a (UK) NUM equal pay claim for female canteen and surface workers (Fine, 2023 for an account, but see also O'Donnell, 2023). Subsequently, study of labour markets dovetailed with a Leverhulme-funded research project on the relationship between consumer durables and female labour market participation, leading to a book on the latter (Fine, 1992b). Different topics were broached in contributions to the Presidential Labour Market Commission, including minimum wages, and have been reported upon in the previous Volume (Fine, 2025e), And, subsequently, this work and much more besides was put together for both a general critique of (mainstream) labour market theory and its reconstruction (Fine, 1998a). Even more recently, I have puzzled over how to understand the value of labour

1 I have always been mindfully self-critical that the MEC approach has heavily leaned towards investigating what capital, rather than labour or others, did. Even so, what was done on labour has tended to be overlooked, understandably as it rarely made its way into publication. Significantly, a close MEC collaborator suggests, "the labour regime is given insufficient emphasis in the original 1996 formulation of the MEC thesis" (Ashman, 2023, p. 64).

 | DOI:10.1163/9789004748330_004

power and its relationship to economic and social reproduction (Fine, 2008f and 2020 most recently, but see also Appendix to this Chapter).

Throughout all of this work, the single most important question has always been around what differentiates one labour market from one another as well as what do they have in common – particularly in a South African context, female domestics are very different from male migrant miners, not only by virtue of wages and working conditions but also by being attached to different structures, relations, processes and relations. How are we to analyse this? Alongside such issues has also been detailed critique of the evolving nature of mainstream labour economics – not least the dismissal of segmented labour market theory for being descriptive, atheoretical and sociological as prelude to its stunning transformation into an exercise in (asymmetric information) market imperfection economics – especially as illustrative of economics imperialism (Fine, 2024a and b).

The abstract drafted for the submission offers an appropriate overview of its content which now follows:

> A critical assessment is made of Hofmeyr's analysis of the sources of changes in African wage levels over the period 1975 to 1985. Particular attention is paid to the weak modelling underlying the econometric estimation, to the limited range of factors considered and to the conceptualisation of what constitutes a structure within a labour market. An alternative approach both to neoclassical and radical theories of labour markets is offered in which it is argued that different labour market segments have to be analysed as structured differently and, thereby, not amenable to a common model or theory.

1 Introduction[2]

The study of labour markets is in some respects in its infancy in South Africa.[3] We have had very few studies that are standard for other countries, especially

2 Previously unpublished but thanks to John Sender for comments on an early draft. The support of the Economic and Social Research Council (ESRC) of the UK is gratefully acknowledged. The work was funded by ESRC award number R000232411 for a grant to study the South African minerals-energy complex. Some research on labour markets was also undertaken whilst assisting in the preparation of MERG (1993).

3 For a recent text, see Barker (1992). For further empirical detail, see Viljoen (1991), Hindson (1991), Hindson and Crankshaw (1990) and various issues of the annual report of the South African Institute of Race Relations.

those in the advanced capitalist economies. Do trade unions cause inflation; is there a union/non-union wage differential; do workers share in the rents derived from monopoly profits; what is the impact of the benefit-wage ratio on unemployment; what are the extent and causes of wage differentials by race, gender, occupation, sector, public or private employment; what is the relationship between the functioning of labour markets and productivity change, etc.? No doubt, part of the reason for this paucity of literature flows from the rigidities that have apparently characterised the functioning and institutional context within which South African labour markets have operated. Such questions as those listed above have seemed inappropriate, and labour market studies have been more pre-occupied with the shifting relationship between apartheid and capitalism.[4] Whether this has indeed justified a lack of attention to the more traditional concerns of labour economics is now a matter of academic and historical interest. For, South Africa has formally abandoned the labour market restrictions attached to apartheid, reflecting two decades of an increasing "liberalisation" of labour markets – although this has been far from a unilinear and even process.

As the discipline of labour economics develops in South Africa, there is the potential to derive latecomer benefits. Theories, studies and hypotheses that have already been applied in other countries can be replicated for South Africa, and even be given their own local twists and angles. But there is also a corresponding danger. It is necessary to be convinced of the validity of the analyses that others have used. Its confrontation with South African conditions offers the opportunity not only to question their applicability on this new terrain but also to reflect back upon their intellectual origins. Just how good are the various components of labour market economics and how appropriate are they to an economy in transition and with South Africa's peculiar history?

In this light, Hofmeyr's (1994) analysis of the changing patterns of African wages is to be welcomed for at least putting this issue squarely on the agenda. It is one amongst a number approaching South African labour markets from a neoclassical perspective. As such, it is all the more important that it should be fully and critically assessed for the direction in which it takes the fledgling discipline of South African labour market analysis. The purpose of this commentary is to reveal the considerable inadequacies of Hofmeyr's paper. It also offers the opportunity to assess some of the related literature more generally, although no claims are made in what follows even for a partial survey. In the first section, an account is given of the intellectual tradition to which

4 See Posel (1991).

Hofmeyr's contribution belongs, as it has been applied to South Africa. The second section highlights problems which arise out of the limited application of Hofmeyr's own methodology. The third section considers the approach offered by segmented labour market theory. The fourth section seeks an alternative to both of these other approaches, arguing that labour market structures need to be examined differently from segment to segment. This is illustrated by a brief overview of developments within mining. The concluding remarks return to Hofmeyr's paper, rejecting the commonly held view that the apartheid system is appropriately understood as a form of (labour) market restrictions that are now being dismantled.

2 The Orthodoxy We Inherit

Hofmeyr is concerned to investigate the extent to which wage differentials have narrowed between different categories of the workforce. This begs the question of what is meant by segmentation or labour market structures. The answer within neoclassical economics takes as its starting point the treatment of labour as subject to the laws of supply and demand, just like any other commodity, although labour is perceived to have certain special features.[5] In a partial equilibrium context, supply and demand depend in the normal way upon the real wage as the price of labour, with supply increasing, and demand falling, with rising real wages.[6] In a general equilibrium context, labour decisions and outcomes are made in conjunction with decisions over consumption, saving and investment (how capital-intensive should production be).

In either case, wage levels and differentials are presumed to reflect differences in the individual attributes of workers, what is known as human capital, whether the latter is acquired prior to, or after, entering the labour market. Education, for example, is seen as a pre-entry labour market factor that enhances worker productivity and hence wage levels. On the job training, on the other hand, usually measured by length of (continuous) employment, is a post-entry factor with the same effect. Women who take breaks from work to bear children are presumed to lose some productivity as a consequence, purportedly one reason for them being paid less than men.

On this basis, it is argued that a perfectly functioning labour market will grind out wages that accurately mirror the range of personal attributes, inherent or

5 See Fine (1982).

6 Although labour supply can become backward-bending as sufficient wages are earned and leisure becomes more important as a source of utility relative to the disutility of work.

acquired, that characterise the productive potential of individual workers (including their tastes for work as opposed to leisure or future consumption). However, it is equally recognised that labour markets do not work in such a perfect way in practice. Most obviously, a trade union, for example, would be perceived as an obstacle to the perfect functioning of the labour market, with levels of real wages being forced above their equilibrium level at the expense of the overall level of employment. More generally, there may be a host of labour market imperfections, each associated with an impact on wage and employment levels. These might include lack of, or slow, labour mobility between sectors, possibly distinguished by capital-intensity of production; monopolisation leading to the sharing of rewards of higher profitability between capital and labour; and there may be labour market discrimination or other forms of labour market hierarchies, whether imposed by workers or employers.

The net result of such analysis is to suggest that (relative) wages depend upon a host of factors, more or less loosely divided into those denominated as due to market forces as opposed to those that are not and which are perceived to be obstructing the pure operation of the market.[7] It is such impediments which constitute structures for neoclassical theory. Many have been concerned with migrant labour and with the specification and measurement of the push and pull factors that have induced urbanisation, for example. The origins of such models are to be found in the classic argument of W.A. Lewis in which the urban and the rural are distinguished from one another by suggesting one pays the marginal product of labour and the other the average product of labour, respectively. The two levels of remuneration are equalised with the result that surplus labour is inefficiently attached to the land, contributing a marginal, even negative, product – certainly below that of urban areas (although more cannot be earned there, given that the rural wage is, in effect, self-subsidised). In this view, there is a structural division between urban and rural, possibly relabelled as formal and informal, industrial and handicraft, or as modern and traditional, in which labour is artificially retained in one diode at the expense of the other.[8]

Quite the opposite view is taken by those models following on from the work of Todaro, since the problem is seen as one of explaining why there is excessive

7 This analytical division can be expressed in ways other than as a market/non-market dichotomy, although the market is usually seen as one side of the opposition, from which there is divergence. Popular is the idea that there are a variety of institutions other than the market, or that culture, custom, ideology or social relations play a role as opposed to the market.

8 If the division is interpreted as pre-capitalist and capitalist, the model can be interpreted as implicitly addressing the issue of the transition to capitalism through the creation of an urban proletariat.

urbanisation with correspondingly high numbers of unemployed even though they earn a zero wage. The answer is found in the artificial behaviour in the urban labour market, whereby trade unions or government intervention are perceived to lead to wage levels that are too high. The average expected wage in the urban labour market, taking the chances of unemployment, is equated to the level of rural subsistence.

These elementary models have the advantage of revealing the nature of the neoclassical argument around migrant labour in their simplest form. They require that at least two sectors of the economy be distinguished from one another, with at least one of them departing from reliance upon efficient labour market wage-setting. From this starting point, it is possible to build more complex models concerning the internal operation of the two (or more) labour markets and the relations between them.

In the context of apartheid, an excellent illustration is provided by Ault and Rutman (1992).[9] For them, the rural sector imposes certain obligations on (oscillating) migrant labourers who must return to rural areas to work at particular times over the agricultural season. In addition, migrants have been prohibited by apartheid from permanent urban residence and the ownership and operation of non-agricultural assets in white areas. Nonetheless, within these two-sided constraints, wages can be earned in mining, for example, and the revenue employed to enhance rural earnings through acquisition of land and investment upon it. A complex model results in which mineworkers are able to allocate time between the rural and the mining sector and to allocate revenue between consumption and investment. Moreover, the level of wages that can be earned depends upon human capital accumulated through education and work experience, and rural earnings depend upon access to land rights, leading to account being taken implicitly of differentiation within the black workforce – in earnings, accumulated assets and landownership.

Notably absent from the analysis is discussion of the wage-setting process in mining (other than greater rewards for greater human capital); wages are essentially taken as exogenous, even if the wage is large enough, relative to rural earnings, to ensure a labour supply. Nor are black wages set against the wage levels of white miners. The latter is the focus of other studies within the neoclassical tradition which have used human capital theory to examine the extent of discrimination within the South African labour market. What they have found without exception is that there has been a sharp reduction in discrimination from the 1970s onwards as the relativities between black and

9 They also review and reference earlier work, including their own.

white workers has narrowed considerably, especially in mining.[10] This leads to the idea that apartheid is being eroded or discrimination is on the decline. It is explained by reference either to institutional factors, such as foreign pressure, changing government and management attitudes, and working class action, or by market forces and labour shortages as a consequence of economic growth and development – although the two are not necessarily perceived as independent of one another.[11]

More generally, Lundahl (1989)[12] reviews the contribution that neoclassical models can make to the understanding of apartheid. He notes that different types of discrimination have been modelled, either singly or in combination, in a variety of ways in terms of what factors are taken as endogenous and exogenous and what divisions make up the structure of the economy and of the labour force. He identifies seven types of discrimination, p. 826:

> (1) alienation of African land; (2) "civilized labor policy", whereby a given proportion of all jobs are reserved for whites; (3) monopsonization of the African labor market; (4) reservation of skilled jobs; (5) control of the influx of Africans; (6) increases of white wages; and (7) decreases of black wages.

At the simplest level, neoclassical economics argues that discrimination is inefficient as it implies that resources are not allocated according to marginal productivities, and those that exercise a taste for discrimination (rather than their victims) are made worse-off because of the need to pay higher prices for what they buy (white, instead of black, labour for example). But, within this theoretical framework, even though the economy is inefficient, and all could be made better-off without any being made worse-off, it is possible for certain discriminating groups to benefit disproportionately (whether white workers or capitalists at the expense of black labour) – just as a monopolist in any market is a source of Pareto-inefficiency but benefits at the expense of consumers.

Lundahl translates such observations into a chronology of apartheid. Theoretically, he argues that its shifting parameters reflect the greater or lesser success of farmers, capitalists, and skilled and unskilled white workers in carving out restrictive practices on their own behalf – what he views as socially

10 See especially Knight and McGrath (1987), McGrath (1990) and, for coloured workers, Moll (1992). See also Fallon (1992) and, for a particularly crude exercise, Lachman and Bercuson (1992).

11 See Hofmeyr (1990a and b).

12 See also Lundahl (1992).

unproductive rent-seeking behaviour. As the economy develops, so it creates changing pressures on, and alliances between, the various interest groups. In this light, he concludes that neither the liberal nor the radical analysis of apartheid is correct – that capitalism must be seen as the victim or the beneficiary of apartheid, respectively. Rather, he seeks and poses his own analysis as a synthesis of these two stances – what he terms a "radic-lib" analysis – in which the relationship between apartheid and capital(ism) is contingent upon the positions of other interest groups in determining whether it is or is not functional for capitalists (as is generally argued by radicals and denied by liberals).

In short, and explicitly, within a neoclassical framework, Lundahl is able to comprehend apartheid as a material conflict between heterogeneous white groups whose economic interests are directly translated into discriminatory economic practices even if through resort to political alliances and compromises.[13] Consequently, taking the neoclassical arguments together, for migration as well as for discrimination, they incorporate a wide variety of factors, many of which can be interpreted as structural in the neoclassical sense and, as a result, are perceived to be open to reform.

Necessarily, what constitutes these structures is a matter of *a priori* judgements although, relative to other economies, there are those attached to race that stand out as distinguishing the South African labour market. But, as in other economies, housing, transport, fertility, financial institutions, education, etc., also have an impact upon the labour market and can do so according to their structural characteristics. As apartheid has had implications for each of these factors, then, it follows that the labour market is equally structured by them and that the seven-wise types of discrimination is too limited. Indeed, experience in other countries is precisely that the existence and level of labour market discrimination by race is highly dependent upon disadvantage in these and other areas. Precisely because the apartheid system has been endemic across all socioeconomic variables, and not just those unacceptable to western democracies, so what are market imperfections and discrimination within a neoclassical framework must be multiplied many times over with corresponding impacts upon labour market structures. It also follows that formal removal of the legal and political practices defining the apartheid system will not eliminate, or even significantly reduce, high levels of differentiation within and between labour markets, as is also evidenced by their presence in countries

13 Thus, "South Africa is a Western-type democracy as far as the white population is concerned ... government policy reflects the demands of the electorate on which the ruling party depends for support" (Lundahl, 1989, p. 829).

which are more developed than South Africa and which have never formally instigated such extreme overt racist practices.[14]

Recently, the World Bank has used neoclassical methods to assess the South African labour market. Fallon (1992) constructs a formal model and uses econometrics to estimate employment levels, decomposing the workforce into Africans (designated unskilled and in excess supply), whites (skilled and in short supply), and Asians and Coloureds (somewhere in-between). African employment is determined by an efficiency-wage argument in which employers choose, or are forced, to pay a wage above the market-clearing level (to avoid high turnover, poor work effort, and industrial action).[15] White wages, on the other hand, are perceived to be more responsive to 'market forces' or the level of overall demand so that they vary inversely with the level of employment. As whites have been close to being fully employed, their levels of employment are even taken as an index of capacity utilisation, p. 27:

> Until quite recently, full employment was maintained among whites, this thus suggests that the growth in white labor supply may have acted as a constraint both upon economic growth in general and the employment growth of blacks.

Four possible reasons – bottlenecks in white employment, excessive capital-labour ratios due to high wages and low user-costs of capital (interest rates), recession, and black wage increases – are investigated for their impact on the low levels of black employment. On this basis, it is concluded that, "the empirical results indicate that this can overwhelmingly be traced to upward movements in black wages".

This analysis might reasonably be considered to be thoroughly irresponsible. It is extremely casual and crude by academic standards, and it is riddled with arbitrary assumptions whether to handle technical tractability, data availability or, one suspects, to obtain meaningful and even qualitatively and quantitatively acceptable results. Although the model is concerned with macroeconomic relations, it is not a fully worked out macroeconomic model (having no international nor monetary sectors).[16] It is not intended here to

14 The same applies to the limited impact that legislation has had on racial discrimination in labour markets.

15 Strikes are used statistically, for example, as an index of wage pressure even though many have been for political purposes and not all have been successful.

16 Some monetary and international factors are introduced but merely in the unsystematic attempt to improve goodness of fit.

unpick this model and criticise it fully for the simple reason that this would not prove the most fruitful way of formulating an alternative understanding of how South African labour markets operate.

There are, however, two issues that are worth addressing with these purposes in mind. The first concerns excess capacity. Over the 1970s, investment in the South African economy was dominated by the public sector, ultimately giving rise to considerable excess capacity in the eighties, especially in electricity generation, for example. This was prompted by the expansion of mining especially, but not exclusively, gold. This excess capacity continues to persist. It suggests that aggregate production functions, and models based upon them, are at best only appropriate when taking account of extensive lags differentiated by sector (since such investments have long gestation periods). Thus, particularly in the South African context, capital-labour ratios have been heavily determined by a few sectors which can only respond slowly to price signals and, further, are in any case heavily influenced by other considerations such as strategic political decision making. Given the weight of such public investment in the seventies and the stagnation of both public and private investment in the eighties, whatever regular quantitative relations are discovered between capital-labour ratios and factor prices, they must be treated with considerable scepticism as the basis for forecasting or policymaking.

Second, analysis of (South African) labour markets must be sensitive to the variety of conditions that prevail across them, whether these be indirect as in differences in investment, technology and excess capacity, etc. or direct as in overt discrimination between different sections of the workforce. Indeed, if the hypotheses put forward by Fallon (1992) are re-examined at a disaggregated level, then it is found that they are inconsistent with the evidence – some of which is presented by Fallon himself. Thus, unemployment is highest amongst those sections of the workforce (women and youth) with the lowest levels of wages. In rural areas, unemployment is comparable to the level in urban areas even though wages are driven down to levels as little as five rands per day. And similar anomalies emerge for the sectoral and geographical distribution of wage rates and unemployment.

Of course, such evidence could be reinterpreted by incorporating further explanatory factors specific to the disaggregated labour markets concerned. But this merely serves to confirm the need to identify how a series of labour markets function, how they are structurally related to one another and the economy and society more generally. Fallon does distinguish labour markets by race (and occasionally by other socioeconomic factors such as gender, age, skill and education). However, these have not been adequately addressed in confronting the relationship between wages and employment and the other determinants of labour market outcomes.

3 Modelling Labour Markets?

Now Hofmeyr's contribution lies within the tradition just outlined. In some respects it is more sophisticated (in the range of variables included and their application to a household level data set). Yet, many of the factors concerned are omitted. Consider initially what Hofmeyr denotes as his methodology. This has two components, the second of which is simply a statistical device for decomposing the different effects within and between occupational structures. The first component is termed "the basic model". In fact no model is given at all. Rather, a single equation is offered relating the money wage rate to a variety of personal and other characteristics attached to the job. Now, this is little more than graph drawing by computer, or guilt by association. As we expect a number of variables such as work experience, education and gender to affect the level of an individual's wages, let us throw them into a simple, multiple regression.

This problem can be put in another way. What exactly is the equation being estimated even from an orthodox, neoclassical point of view? Is it the supply of labour or is it the demand for labour? Or is it some reduced form of the two? For human capital theory, which motivates Hofmeyr's estimation, the answer would appear to be the demand for labour, further warranted by the notion that there is general excess supply of labour (so that outcomes are always on the demand curve).[17] Further, this would also be legitimate in principle should it be assumed that supply-side effects are statistically independent of the demand-side, given the reliance upon cross-section household data. However, this would all need to be taken into account in deriving the form of, and restrictions on (signs of parameters), the equation to be estimated. Obviously, for some variables, the sign of parameters in the labour equation will be different (even of opposite sign) according to whether they reflect supply or demand.

17 This is confirmed by his discussion of the clustering, and hence potential sample bias, attached to taking more than one worker from a given household. This is set aside on the grounds that employers determine whom to employ on the basis of their individual characteristics. Necessarily, this implies the irrelevance of household labour supply strategies.

Workers might prefer not to live in hostels in opposition to their employers' wishes or requirements for example.[18]

The lack of a specific, or well-specified, theory is reflected in a number of different ways. First, there is no alternative hypothesis against which Hofmeyr tests his results, other than the trivial one of significance for his test-statistics. What is meant here is that he posits a particular way in which the labour market works. It is perceived to be more or less distant from an ideal, perfectly competitive labour market according to the extent to which unjustified wage differentials persist, and these are in turn 'explained' by a collective set of factors gathered under the umbrella of institutional structure. Now, even this account suggests that the labour market is structured (even if by ill-defined institutions). Consequently, this suggests that there ought to be some structure to the equations estimated. Thus, not only is there no structure to his analysis in the sense of carefully distinguishing supply and demand, but labour market structure is itself only identified with differences in parameter values as estimated in a single equation.

This leads to the conclusion that if men and women, say, with the same labour market characteristics are paid the same wage, then, there are no labour market structures. This is absurd, given that it is consistent with heavy, even total, occupational segmentation by sex. The purpose at this stage is less to observe how limited is Hofmeyr's notion of labour market unification, an extremely important point to be taken up later, than to highlight how limited is the theoretical and statistical extent to which he investigates the presence of labour market structures.

Second, although this is a corollary of the first point, Hofmeyr is theoretically deficient in failing to explore the potential connections between the variables that he takes to be independent of one another for the purposes of his single equation regression. To have done so would have given some structure to his 'model'. It surely can be argued that there are definite relations between gender, occupation and sector (and across the other variables employed by Hofmeyr).

18 More generally, Fine (1987) has shown that the same equations are often estimated to identify labour market structures even though they may be motivated by either the supply-side or the demand-side Thus, if differences across industrial sectors (capital-intensity, unionisation, degree of concentration, etc) are considered to determine (the demand for labour) and wages, corrections have still to be made for considerations attached to human capital theory On the other hand, if pre-entry supply-side factors are considered to be important (race, gender, education, location, etc), then corrections have to be made for the industrial characteristics of the jobs concerned.

Interestingly, this is cursorily investigated by Hofmeyr in the attempt to reduce the number of independent variables used in his regressions. He reports that a factor analysis gave results that, "were disappointing, as there were no clear groupings round a relatively small number of factors. This method was therefore abandoned", p. 203. Unfortunately, this can be considered a premature rejection of a promising line of enquiry. For, the failure of the factor analysis (a statistical method designed to find the most important common relations between a collection of variables) suggests that the relationship between the various variables is liable to be different, from one sector to another for example. This will not be picked up theoretically or statistically by an approach that sees the labour market as uniformly fluid across all employment, with wage levels finding higher or lower levels according to the additive impact of a series of common, but independent, factors.

A third peculiarity of Hofmeyr's 'model' is the tripartite division of variables into (1) those that are included in his regression, (2) those that are included in the analysis but outside his regression, and (3) those that are excluded altogether. Taking (1) and (2) together first, (1) is used to construct a set of statistics, decomposed changes in average wages, which are then explained by (2). The latter includes poorly specified institutional change[19] and labour market conditions such as relatively greater excess supply of unskilled labour. Thus, for example, the unskilled are expected to have improved their position less than the skilled, and the demise of apartheid is associated (without reason given) with the narrowing of differentials by gender, region and sector.

In short, the procedure is to derive, however satisfactorily, a set of statistics (the decomposed shifts in wages) from an ill-specified equation, and then to explain those statistics by an informally defined set of factors and, presumably, a complementary set of ill-specified theoretical propositions. This begs the questions of why the supplementary set of variables, (2), were not included in the initial regressions and whether the two sets of theoretical propositions are consistent with one another. There may be data reasons for the first issue – how are we to quantify institutional change, for example? On the other hand, it generally is possible to quantify differential demand pressure, for example, in the separate segments of the labour market. Indeed, how else do we know that unemployment has been greater for the unskilled?

The second issue of theoretical compatibility between (1) and (2) is equally serious. For, the estimates from (1) are based on a human capital theory in which the institutional factors of (2) are presumed to be absent (unless

19 Reference is made to an as yet unpublished paper. But see Kraak (1993).

inadvertently captured in the independent variables). As previously observed, the single equation estimation implies that labour markets are only structured by shifts in the parameter values. Consequently, to the extent that labour markets are more fundamentally structured by institutional change, there is an inconsistency between the way in which the estimates are made and the way in which they are explained. For, the estimates depend upon the absence of the institutional change which are then used to explain them![20]

Now consider (3), absent variables. Even standard, single equation labour market analysis is liable to include variables reflecting capital-intensity, industrial structure, level of profitability, etc. It is worthy of note that the two five-year periods discussed by Hofmeyr are very different even from a casual economic commentary. From 1975 to 1980, the low level of private investment was compensated for, to some extent, by high levels of public investment and the continuing impetus provided by the high prices of gold and energy. This contrasts with the second five-year period, characterised by stagnation in both private and public investment. It is inescapable, along with shifting and varied policies around reform and repression, that various labour markets should be affected very differently by these developments.[21]

Further, by far the most significant source of increase in employment for black workers has been in government service. Its share has grown from 7.8% in 1960 to 11.6% in 1980 and to 15.6% in 1990.[22] Whilst white employment by the state has also risen, it has been from a much higher initial base, the corresponding figures being 15.2%, 18.2%, and 19.7%, respectively. The only other major source of employment increase for whites has been in financial services, its share rising from 8.2% to 15.4% from 1960 to 1990 (the corresponding figures for blacks being 0.9% and 2.6%, respectively). It follows that the state is important not just in its labour market policies but also as an employee itself

---

20 There is often an analogous practice in the calculation and explanation of total factor productivity. This is constructed on the basis of full employment and perfect competition for factor inputs but then its changes over time are explained by factors such as excess capacity, strength of trade unionism, etc which contradict the initial basis on which TFP has been measured. See Chapter 2.

21 More generally, labour markets have been profoundly affected by the pattern of accumulation in the South African economy which was dominated in the 1970s by a heavily state-promoted commitment to mining, energy and related activities. For a detailed account of this in terms of the continuing influence of a minerals-energy complex, see Fine and Rustomjee (1996).

22 By way of comparison, domestic service has fallen from 19.4% to 14.1% over the same period.

(even more so if account is taken of, possibly former, state corporations such as ISCOR, ESKOM and TRANSNET, formerly SATS). It would, indeed, be paradoxical to suggest that the labour market has become more unified, i.e. more reliant upon unadulterated market forces, as a result of increases in employment generated by the state itself – together with its *interventions* to expand expenditure on black education and to recognise those apparently anti-market institutions, (black) trade unions. In short, the institutional changes on which Hofmeyr relies to suggest a closer move towards the free market are better seen as new forms of intervention favouring the black population.

Some omitted variables are openly mentioned by Hofmeyr – most notably the impact of trade unions and the non-African workforce. No justification is given for the exclusion of the latter in the sense of why interactions between the two sets of labour markets should be negligible or neutral within the African labour markets. This is especially perverse given that upward occupational mobility of Africans is explicitly associated with, "a penetration of Africans up the occupational ladder as jobs previously reserved for Whites were increasingly opened up", p. 199.

Finally, Hofmeyr's notion that there was an absence of labour market pressure from trade unions for most of this period is truly astonishing.[23] The second half of the 1970s witnessed the emergence of black trade unions, their enforced recognition, and extensive industrial action for both economic and political purposes. Now, it might be argued that trade union membership was limited across the 'modern sector' as opposed to mining, a sector included by Hofmeyr and surprisingly found by him to be a good payer (due to the arduous conditions!). But if so, Hofmeyr necessarily sets aside two important considerations – that the impact of trade unions, or of industrial relations more generally, is not exclusively measured by trade union membership and, in addition, the impact of wage increases won in unionised sectors is liable to be followed to some degree by copycat increases in other sectors even if they are not unionised. In any case, Moll (1993), using the same human capital methodology as Hofmeyr and *exactly the same data set*, has shown the importance of the trade union wage differential, estimating it at as much as 24% for black blue-collar workers.

23 In a separate paper, Hofmeyr (1993, p. 279) concludes that union pressure was the major force driving African wage levels in the second half of the 1980s, but that it was market forces in the first half of the decade.

4 Does Segmented Labour Market Theory Offer an Alternative?

Many of the preceding points of criticism are, in principle, open to be addressed within orthodox economic theory and econometric techniques. This would serve as a worthwhile extension of the results offered by Hofmeyr. What would appear to be less palatable is to take his results on the decomposed sources of wage increases, even if they are marginally modified, and treat them as if they were sensible statistics that had to be explained by reference to institutional change. The results he offers are best seen, not as a rough and ready first shot, but as an arbitrary exercise in imposing inflexible and questionable methods on a data set.

The purpose of the present section is, however, to examine an entirely different way of proceeding, that more attached to political economy, although there are some points of contact with the previous discussion. The central issue is to examine not only empirically but also conceptually what is meant by a labour market structure. This is clearly at least implicit in Hofmeyr's approach, in order for him to be able to argue around segmentation and for a tendency towards unification. Essentially, his view of labour market structures is one defined by outcomes – in which wage differentials remain, even after correcting for human capital and other factors.

This is profoundly unsatisfactory. First, it takes no account of labour market structuring attached to outcomes other than wage differentials. There may, for example, be other differences in wages and conditions, not least in occupational segregation, career prospects and security of employment over both the long and the short runs. Interestingly, with regard to the latter, Hofmeyr offers annual wages on the basis of calculations from weekly or daily rates, regretting that no account can be taken of actual hours of work. This, as he observes, is liable to introduce a further element of arbitrariness into the statistics. But he seems unaware of what is potentially an even more serious bias, that is the differential impact of spells of unemployment which obviously make jobs more or less attractive (and in ways that have always defied orthodox analysis that eschews structures since the most insecure jobs are generally the worst paid).

Second, then, it is possible for labour market structures to exist even where there are no wage (and other) differences – in case of occupational segregation or differences in security or prospects in employment, for example.[24]

---

24 A favourite example here is provided by employment and career structures within the US Catholic church. Women are subject to job reservation – they cannot become priests – but they are welcome, even as nuns, to be highly trained as administrators and educators. If they were paid accordingly, they might well earn more than their male counterparts.

And wage differences can persist in the apparent absence of labour market structures – if all appropriate wages and conditions are not included in the comparisons across workers. Thus, if differences in travel to work areas, presence and role of trade unions, availability of childcare, etc. are not included in the measurement of wage differentials, then these will be overlooked as potential sources of labour market structure. But, it does not necessarily follow that differences in these conditions, with or without compensating wage relativities, always signify the presence of labour market structures. Surely, there may be differences between workers, their jobs and their conditions without this always constituting a labour market structure?

Third, and at a deeper methodological level following on from the previous point, the unquestioning identification of (compensated) inequalities with structures suffers from what Connell (1987) has termed categoricism in the context of gender inequality. Essentially, if we discover an inequality, in wages, education, income, housing, or whatever, it can be categorised as a structure. This potentially renders structures ubiquitous, if not in Hofmeyr's case since his only category is wage differentials. Further, there is a danger of degenerating into tautology. Structures are identified with empirical inequalities and are then used analytically to explain them. Hofmeyr does tend to fall into this trap, although it is concealed by the intervening statistical analysis. For we are told that the erosion of labour market structures that were more strictly applied to women should lead to an erosion of their labour market disadvantage. Putting this all in another way, it is essential both to identify what constitutes a (labour market) structure and how it is reproduced or transformed.

Fourth, more specifically, and well-recognised by, if not confined to, labour market analysis from disciplines other than economics, labour market outcomes depend upon a combination of pre-entry and post-entry factors. The latter have been discussed to some extent already. The former is made up of education, housing, transport, and more general relations around gender and race, for example. Each of these has been profoundly affected by the shifting history of apartheid. Consequently, labour market structures in general, and especially those attached to the apartheid regime with its acute and unique forms of racial oppression as well as its peculiar dependence upon migrant labour, cannot be identified and understood on the basis of post-entry outcomes. It is almost impossible to do this, for example, for occupational segregation by gender even in the absence of overt racial oppression.

However, they also tend to be poorly paid in view of their religious commitment. See LaMagdeleine (1986), and Fine (1987) for a discussion of this case study for its implications for segmented labour market theory.

Now much of the above is compatible with the radical alternatives to orthodox labour market economics, especially segmented labour market theory.[25] It suggests that labour market imperfections are endemic, not contingent, so that the economy necessarily generates differentiation of the labour force into structurally, separated segments. The earliest version of this theory sought to explain what were thought to be dual labour markets, primary or core as opposed to secondary or peripheral, corresponding to the dualistic industrial structure of the United States, in which large-scale monopolies provided secure, careered, well-paid and unionised employment in contrast to the casualised, poorly paid jobs within the competitive small-scale sector. The most sophisticated and developed form of the analysis, however, is to be found in segmented labour market theory (slm).[26] Here, the idea is that there are supply- and demand-side factors but they are interpreted as reflecting underlying, dynamic and non-equilibrating structures and processes. These interact to give rise to a variety of definite but shifting labour market structures which mutually influence one another whilst, nonetheless, generating relative advantages and disadvantages in wages and conditions within and across the labour market segments. Typically, on the supply-side, the factors considered to be of importance are the presence or not of trade unions, and their strength, the role of the state, and the reproductive role of women and other influences associated with gender and racial inequality. On the demand-side, there is the nature of technology and work organisation, the structure of product markets, industrial organisation, and the imperatives of profitability.

Fine (1987) has argued that slm theory adopts what can be termed a middle-range methodology. At an intermediate conceptual level, the analysis abstractly derives the existence of labour market segments from what is essentially an unspecified, but grander, level of analysis. Sexism, racism, the imperatives of capitalist production, etc. create segments for men and women, black and whites, skilled and unskilled, etc. Subsequently, empirically observed structures in the labour market, with corresponding wages and conditions, are then explained by reference to the supply- and demand-side features that characterise them. The reasoning becomes circular with the identification of segments by criteria that simultaneously explain them. But the analysis is not thereby without content. For it depends upon the insight and pertinence with which segments are identified, much as for the neoclassical alternative, even if from a different perspective.

---

25 For a dispute over its relevance in the South African context, see Cassim (1982 and 1983a and b) and Truu (1983a and b). More recently, see Kraak (1991).

26 For a comprehensive survey and critical assessment, see Fine (1987).

It follows that the differences between the two theories lie less in the evidence that they present than in the way in which they interpret it.[27] For both are able to acknowledge that there are structures governing the operation of the labour market and to measure their quantitative impact. But the neoclassical approach sees these as externally given constraints which impede the attainment of an efficient labour market equilibrium, whereas the radical approach views them as the systemic outcome of underlying forces. To some extent, the affinity between the two approaches is apparent when the focus is shifted to studies of the labour market other than from within economics. For, in industrial relations, the sociology of labour and in labour history, it would be conventional to relate factors such as industrial organisation, strength of trade unionism and the gender of the workforce to the latter's pay and conditions without necessarily questioning whether these derived from deviation from, or absence of, a notional economic equilibrium.

The paradoxical affinity, between what are often fiercely contested interpretations of how labour markets operate,[28] is highlighted by the way in which empirical evidence is employed. For the neoclassical approach, equations can be investigated that include gender, race or whatever as dummies or which estimate their differential impact for different segments of the workforce. To the extent that these are found to have a significant effect, given that other factors, such as human capital, have been corrected for, then there is evidence of discrimination and a measure of how important it is. In this way, wage relativities can be explained by a combination of differences in labour market attributes and the differences in the impact of those attributes. A black worker, for example, may on average have less education than a white worker but also be paid less even with the same education as a particular white worker (and have a greater or lesser differential over a black worker with less education than a white worker does for an educational advantage over another white worker). Consequently, wage differentials can be arithmetically measured as a result of differences in labour market attributes together with a residual measure of discrimination due to differences in how these operate for different (racial) segments of the workforce.

27 There also tend to be differences in the way in which evidence is presented, with the orthodoxy relying upon econometric models and the radicals tending to use less formal statistical techniques.

28 More recently, radical labour economics has departed from slm theory and has forged closer links with neoclassical arguments, particularly those associated with efficiency wages. See Rebitzer (1993).

Elsewhere, this has been termed the simultaneity approach to the labour market.[29] The reason is that the various effects are measured against one another so that they can be mutually reinforcing or compensating. Trade union organisation might raise wages whilst lack of education might lower wages. In principle, the various factors whose effects are estimated simultaneously might be statistically and causally correlated (higher skills, trade unionism, male employment, capital intensity and monopolisation, for example) but account is rarely taken of such considerations – although this would be possible if a more complex model is specified and estimated. In this case, the labour market would have to be modelled both through the direct simultaneous effects of the various factors involved as well as through some structural equations specifying the relationships between those variables.

Slm theory has not appealed to different empirical evidence. As argued previously, it simply interprets the results differently – as evidence of deep-rooted socioeconomic inequalities rather than as market imperfections. This, rather than differences in the measure of discrimination, is what motivates the alternative approaches to labour market policy. Where neoclassical economics would seek to correct for, or remove, market imperfections, slm theorists would target more positive measures to support those who are socioeconomically disadvantaged.

Whilst analytical sympathy here lies more with the second approach, it does reflect certain weaknesses which are the result of the way in which the labour market is perceived to operate as a whole. Consider initially, however, the empirical methods for measuring discrimination. These are themselves, for both schools of thought, fundamentally flawed for two reasons which weaken the validity of policy conclusions that might be drawn from them. First, even if all explanatory variables are included in the estimated equations, there is what economists call an identification problem – what exactly is being estimated, a supply or a demand curve?[30] Now, in the South African and other contexts, it might be argued that the demand curve is being estimated given the very high levels of employment so that supply is always on the long side of the market. However valid this might be for an individual labour market, overall demand would be important in examining the functioning of the economy as a whole. Specifically, the equations estimated generally reflect a casual approach to use

29 See Fine (1992b).

30 For attempts to measure labour market discrimination on the basis of human capital theory, see the work of Hoskings (1992a–d), for example. Note that he refers to a different identification problem – that all relevant labour market variables be included and properly measured – rather than the market be fully modelled as suggested here.

of underlying theory. Further, the approach is usually insensitive to the level of employment at which the economy is operating, and it seems unreasonable to presume that the extent of discrimination is independent of the overall level of (un)employment.

Second, the measure of discrimination is given by the residual unexplained by the equations, the signs on the dummy variables for race or whatever, or the differences in sign for estimated parameters for human capital, etc. These then are precisely ways of measuring the incidence of discrimination but without explaining it.

Consequently, for both of these reasons, we have to be extremely wary about drawing implications or policy conclusions from such estimates. If for example, it is found that black workers have lower wages because they have lower education, it cannot be concluded that equalising or raising their education levels will have the measured effect on reducing discrimination. This is because the sorts of socioeconomic changes that would be necessary to bring about such educational changes are themselves liable to have a profound impact on the workings of the economy and the labour markets which are not incorporated within the model.[31] It is equally plausible to suggest that raising black workers skill levels will lead to other forms of compensating discrimination, as in the context of "floating" job reservation. Black workers may be moving up the job ladder but the extent of interpenetration with white workers remains open to question.

This raises again the issue of what constitutes separate labour market structures as opposed to differentiation within a segment. Do two groups of workers belong to the same segment because they share certain characteristics in common, even if they experience certain differences in wages and conditions, or does the latter imply they are structurally differentiated? Do workers, for example, who belong to a trade union also experience or create a different labour market structure than those who do not? The issue can be put in another, slightly different, way. We observe empirical differences in the wages and conditions of the workforce. There are also differences in their socioeconomic characteristics – gender, race, class, education, regional origin, housing, etc. Is it appropriate to translate any such combination of differences over

31 Thus, because women's wages are found to be lower than men's more because of occupational segregation (women are in low pay sectors) than because of pay differences within sectors, it is often argued that more attention should be given to breaking down occupational segregation than equal pay for equal work. This does not follow since dealing satisfactorily with the factors that cause intra-sector pay differences is also liable to have a major impact on occupational segregation also. In any case, there is no reason to address either one or the other policy issue. For further discussion, see Fine (1992b).

these factors into a series of structural determinants, both identifying and purporting to explain labour market segments?

Paradoxically, then, the problems with the slm approach are similar to those previously outlined for more mainstream analyses. Empirical studies almost inevitably identify labour market segments by the same factors that are deemed to cause them – women are low paid because they are structurally disadvantaged for example. Or, in the context of Hofmeyr's analysis, apartheid institutions disadvantage black workers.

By the same token, the issue of what determines a labour market structure, as opposed to a labour market difference, has been glossed over – in part through appeal to the notion that such structures are both dynamic and overlapping. Again, in this respect, the general theory (as opposed to the case study of particular labour market segments) shares a further feature with the orthodoxy, as also exemplified by Hofmeyr. This is the presumption that all labour markets are structured together by a common set of underlying factors. What distinguishes the two approaches is that the orthodoxy views such (re)structuring as a deviation from the structureless norm of perfectly competitive labour markets. Segmented labour market theory, arguably correctly from both a logical and empirical point of view, flatly denies this and views labour markets as always structured by their underlying determinants.

This latter observation can, however, be taken further. For there can be no presumption either that labour markets are mutually structured altogether in anything other than a tautologous sense or that each labour market is structured in the same way as any other, corresponding to a general theory of the outcome of underlying determinants. The latter's impact on labour market structures, and sufficient factors have already been listed previously, are liable to function in very different ways in one labour market as opposed to another. Thus, labour markets not only have different structures, as is evident even from casual empirical observation, but the way in which they are structured is different. Potentially, we need different theory for different labour markets, not an all-encompassing theory for them all whether it be human capital theory based on a simultaneity and balancing of factors or slm theory with its dynamic restructuring of segments in accordance to underlying social determinants. For example, to be discussed at greater length below, migrant mining labour, as opposed to permanently-urbanised labour, not only belongs to a different labour market structure, it is structured in an entirely different way. Similarly, whites and blacks, men and women, skilled and unskilled, farm as opposed to industrial workers, etc. are structured in the labour markets in very different ways.

5 Towards an Alternative

This implies that labour market structures, and their potential erosion, cannot be identified by the sort of analysis undertaken by Hofmeyr. Although results of the sort that he offers can be a suggestive basis for further investigation, they are unable to distinguish how one labour market structure is created rather than another since the differentiated interaction and effects of underlying determinants are not addressed. Nor, to return to an earlier theme, is it possible to identify what constitutes a labour market structure as opposed to a difference within a structure. The latter requires an explicit analysis of how underlying labour market determinants interact to give rise to an integral mode of operation of that labour market that is reproduced distinctly from others. Thus, differences in trade unionism, travel to work, fringe benefits, and even wages do not in and of themselves indicate the presence of a labour market structure unless they can be shown to reflect and create a sufficiently different mode of operation within that labour market from other labour markets. This is most apparent in explicit institutional arrangements for that purpose, as in job reservation, for example, but it is not necessarily dependent on this – as in the range of factors that, possibly more informally even if still systemically, structure occupational segregation irrespective of the formal institutions devoted to that purpose,[32] as in the gendering of education, the ideology of work, familial responsibilities, etc.[33]

To raise these same problems within slm or more mainstream theory does little to resolve them. Nor, however, is this to dismiss analyses based on either theory. For, however satisfactorily, they both investigate the processes and structures associated with labour market differentiation. But the contradictions and tensions between these processes and structures have to be comprehended in order to address the issue of change. To do this, three points of departure from slm theory are emphasised. First, the mechanisms connecting underlying social structures to labour market outcomes, including segmentation, have to be specified. They will be complex and, as a crucial second point, differentiated themselves from one labour market to the next. In other words, whilst labour markets do share certain underlying determinants in common, they are not simultaneously structured by these but each labour market is in part created and reproduced separately as a consequence of the conditions

32 For similar methodological considerations in constructing a theory of consumption from an interdisciplinary perspective, see Fine and Leopold (1993).

33 See Martin and Beittel (1987) and Murray (1989).

within which it alone operates. Thus, the impact of migrant labour, urbanisation, job reservation, education, childcare responsibility, access to land is common to the labour market as a whole, but influences each segment of employment quite differently both in manner and extent.

Third, to integrate these two aspects of our approach, we emphasise (differential) *access* to employment as a means of understanding the (re)structuring of labour markets – whether, how and in what way workers are able to obtain (waged) employment. This can be understood in the most abstract sense in terms of the generally specified conditions under which the labour market operates. But access to employment can also be specified at the more immediate levels through which different labour markets are structured and their wages and conditions determined.[34] Even in societies unrestricted by the constraints of apartheid, it is well-known that the housing market and transportation have an important impact on labour markets.[35] They also interact with other factors – so that women's responsibility for childcare, for example, will often mean that they can only work at convenient travelling distance from where they work. This depends on how childcare or, more generally, social reproduction of the workforce, is organised. In addition, access to employment is often dependent upon qualifications, whether due to formal education, work experience or apprenticeship. Management will also structure access to employment in order to exercise control over labour and the overall level of the wage bill. Accordingly, the notion of labour's access to employment covers the most abstract and the most complex factors as well as the processes with which they are associated. It implies not only that there are different labour market structures but that these are separate from one another in the ways in which they are created and function.

Understood in these terms, the specific features of the South African labour market are well-known and bear some repetition in the light of attention to access to employment.[36] First, and historically with few exceptions, blacks have been denied access to sufficient land to enable their basic reproduction without recourse to wage labour, whether as migrant labour or not, or whether employed by mining, agriculture, manufacturing or services. In addition, as a means of enhancing competitiveness of white farming, the latter has been the beneficiary of a range of supports that have not been available to black agriculture irrespective of its access to sufficient qualities and quantities of land.

---

34 Analysing labour markets in terms of access to means of production is laid out in greater detail in the context of women's employment in Fine (1992b).

35 On the role of housing in South Africa, for example, see Simkins (1990).

36 For an overview of developments in the South African labour market, see Kraak (1993).

Second, in South Africa, a major aspect in access to employment has been influx control. Apartheid ideology, as much as practice, has been caught on the contradiction between separate development and dependence upon black labour. Structurally, the labour force has been differentiated between those on the homelands (possibly employed on white farms), those oscillating between the homelands and white urban areas, and those permanently based in or around white urban areas. Legislation and policy have fluctuated around how to *define* and distinguish these segments and how to control them (and render them functional). In retrospect, the crisis of apartheid from the 1970s onwards, as repression became increasingly futile as a mechanism of control, led to a strategy focused upon the granting of rights to a permanent or commuting workforce whilst intensifying the oppression against those (the majority) excluded from such privileges.[37] Consequently, the distance between urban and rural conditions has widened as education, housing and employment conditions have diverged. The result has been even greater pressures for urbanisation. This has had an important effect, and one only partially captured in the analysis of Ault and Rutman in which migrants optimise in face of given constraints (rather than these being shifted to secure the continuing control over migrants and the more permanently-established). Because of its higher levels of productivity, capitalist agricultural development does tend to undermine the viability of small-scale, subsistence agriculture. But there are countertendencies; small-scale agriculture finds that markets are created for its products, cheaper inputs are made available, and other sources of revenue, most notably wage remittances, can be earned to finance them (including casual labour). For these reasons, we tend to observe both the growth of large-scale agriculture and the survival of small-scale farmers, the exact balance depending on how well their economic interests are represented.[38]

Characteristic of the apartheid system has been the extent to which the tendencies to small-scale, black agriculture have been undermined by apartheid policies, together with the economic viability of the homelands. It is a transparent outcome from the use of wage remittances to support homeland subsistence rather than further economic activity, although this can occur by way of exception. Significant is the lack of a vibrant 'informal' sector in South Africa,[39] the use of wage remittances to buy consumption goods produced by

37 See Hindson (1987).

38 See Fine (1994c).

39 See Nattrass (1990), for example.

the (external) capitalist sector[40] and, as an exception that proves the rule, the success of the taxi system for transport arising out of economic opportunities provided by the apartheid's system of segregation.[41]

In addition, dependence on wage remittances has given rise to a specifically sharp gender division of labour in which homeland agriculture has been increasingly the responsibility of women. The counterpart to such poor opportunities in agriculture has been women's availability as a cheap, often casualised, source of labour, especially in white agriculture and domestic service, the latter potentially magnified in current conditions of high unemployment and the relaxation of restrictions on urbanisation. In this light, it can be seen, as argued previously at the theoretical level, that there are some common determinants to male migrant mine labour and female domestic service, but the two labour markets are structured entirely differently from one another, something which cannot be captured by reference to differences in wages and conditions alone.

Further, job reservation has structured employment along racial lines, for which the state has played a major role both legislatively and as an employer itself. Such employment hierarchies are neither inflexible nor unchanging and, even to the extent that they are, this has to be explained against the processes and pressures associated with the 'dilution' of white labour by cheaper, or more readily available, black labour, and the recomposition and redefinition of skills as technology changes. The definition of skill, and corresponding grading and remuneration, is socially constructed in a number of ways, not least the technically determined requirements of the job, the need for management and control, the access to education and training whether to acquire formal qualifications or as a screen for socialisation into work habits, and the (ideological) labelling of jobs as more or less skilled according to trade union or other conflicts over grading (with what whites or males do as more readily recognised as skilled over what blacks or women do irrespective of the inherent skills required). Whilst there has been an upgrading of black skills in recent years, it has given rise to a 'floating' colour bar rather than a breach in the colour bar, as the white/black hierarchies have remained predominantly untouched.[42]

---

40 See Wilson and Ramphele (1989) and Lundahl and Petersson (1991), for example, for Lesotho's dependence both on wage remittances and on commodities 'imported' from South Africa.

41 See Khosa (1991).

42 Kaplan (1990, p. 32) shows, for the telecommunications industry, that job reservation was not always imposed. For Lewis (1984), white unions employed job reservation to preserve their designation as skilled workers in face of technological change and the threat of

Against this background, there can be no doubt that, over the 1970s, a major transformation took place in the way that labour markets operated within South Africa – as recognised from a variety of points of view in the previous discussion. The dependence of the mines on foreign migrant labour had declined from 80% to 40%; white: black wage ratios in mining had declined from 20:1 to 6:1 and were closely aligned to wage levels and ratios typical in manufacturing; black trade unions, it is now known in retrospect, had securely established themselves, were rapidly growing in membership and were actively engaged in both industrial and political activity. By the end of the decade, the Wiehahn and Riekert Commissions were, respectively, accepting the need for recognition of black trade unionism and greater rights of residence for blacks in secure urban employment. How are such changes to be understood?

In terms of labour's access to employment, the most startling change has been the decline in foreign migrant labour to the mines. As documented by Wilson (1972a and b), through all the vicissitudes of the previous fifty years, the ability of the mining companies to recruit such workers had enabled black wages to stagnate or even to decline in real terms. Consequently, they remained at levels which rendered them too low to attract or to make attractive a majority South African labour force. Undoubtedly, the liberation of the frontline states totally transformed the conditions of the mines' access to labour irrespective of the extent to which mutual economic dependence (the mines on labour supply, the frontline states on wage remittances) was used by one side or the other in political conflicts.[43] As Crush et al. (1991, p. 104) put it, the 1970s witnessed the "break-up of the mining industry's northern empire".

Obviously, the relative loss of foreign migrant labour strengthened the hand of their domestic counterparts. Similarly, the rising price of gold in the 1970s enhanced profitability on the mines and more readily enabled mining companies to pay higher wages.[44] Longer-run factors included the growing costs of the migrant system itself, in terms of transport and recruitment, and the need for a more stable workforce as the capital expenditure on the fabric of mines and on mechanisation dictated the need for skills derived from continuous work experience.[45] For the latter, foreign migrant workers often had accumulated higher levels of skills and experience so that the rapid adjustment to

"dilution", a strategy pursued by ISCOR, for example, Clark (1987). See also Webster (1985) and Cross (1993).

43 On the significance of foreign migrant labour, see Crush et al. (1991) and Freund (1991).

44 See Spandau (1980a).

45 See Spandau (1980b).

use of South African labour must have entailed the loss of much accumulated expertise.

It is also important to recognise, however, how certain structures have remained essentially unchanged, especially over the period covered by Hofmeyr. One significant example is the residential housing at the mines which has continued to be predominantly for whites. The legal limitation to 3% of the black labour force has been lifted (and was never a binding constraint) but with only token response in housing programmes. A second example is the skill hierarchy between whites and blacks which remains rigid, even if the latter are rising in the skill hierarchy and pushing up whites above them – and as black skills are increasingly recognised in practice through (re)grading. Indeed, job reservation on the mines was only lifted in the late 1980s, and training and skilled posts more fully made formally available to black miners.

Such factors, and changes in them, were not unique to the 1970s. The gold price had risen in the 1930s; the relative strength of white miners had been shattered in the 1920s; and labour markets had been tight in and after the second world war. What appears to have been decisive in restructuring the labour markets in the 1970s was the coincidence of these factors, together with the successful prosecution of struggle by the workforce. There was the growth of the National Union of Mineworkers in the context of broader industrial action, following on from the strikes in Durban in 1972/73; but equally if not more important, was a crisis of control within the mining compounds themselves, as both work and living conditions became a contested terrain.[46]

Developments within the mining industry have interacted with those external to it. During the 1970s, conditions in the homelands continued to deteriorate.[47] Although the proportion living below subsistence is estimated to have fallen from 99% to 81% between 1960 and 1980, the absolute numbers have risen from 13 to 15 million, creating pressure for migration, urbanisation and dependence on wage remittances. Alternative employment opportunities in agriculture have been eroded with an absolute decline in the workforce, as farms have increased in size and have relied heavily upon mechanisation.[48] There has also been a heavy increase in unemployment, estimated to have

46 See Horner and Kooy (1980), and Crush (1989) for argument that foreign migrants were no more difficult to organise on the mines. See also James (1992) who argues that divisions amongst corporations over industrial relations was an important factor in the rapid growth of the NUM.

47 For what follows, see especially Wilson and Ramphele (1989).

48 See May (1990).

doubled between the 1960s and the 1970s, and standing at a level of 40% or so depending on how it is defined and how reliably it is measured.[49]

In these circumstances, it is hardly surprising that the mines should have been able to recruit domestic labour in place of foreign migrants. Symptomatic of this was the erosion of conflict between different employers over labour supplies. By 1986, legal protection of black farm workers against recruitment for the mines was withdrawn and urban recruitment became less contentious.[50] However, it would be a mistake to conclude that the systemic structures within the labour market had, thereby, been removed. The 1970s does appear to have witnessed the erosion of some of the disadvantages confronted by the black mining workforce compared to those of manufacturing so that, for the black workforce, wages and conditions are determined in comparable fashions, subject to the variety of 'simultaneity' of factors that influence each differentially. The change has come about with the reduction in foreign migrant workers. But the same cannot be said of agriculture and female employment and of the racial hierarchies in employment more generally.

6 Concluding Remarks

The example of mining shows how its employment and employment conditions have been restructured in response to shifting conditions of access to employment. Its comparison with other sectors shows how it shares certain underlying and immediate determinants, but it also has a dynamic of its own. Now, what are the implications of this alternative theoretical approach for analysing changes in labour market structures? There are three different effects that potentially follow from changes in underlying determinants. First, individual labour market structures may be reorganised and function differently internally. This would almost certainly follow from the effective elimination of formal job reservation, for example, although it is not guaranteed. Second, the division between labour market structures may be reorganised – this might follow within the civil service, for example, from the incorporation of the homelands. Third, irrespective of the former, shifts in underlying determinants

49 See Lewis (1991).

50 See Crush et al. (1991) and especially Crush (1993) who shows how the conflict between mining and farming over access to labour has long and unevenly persisted – despite high levels of unemployment and increasing capital-intensity on the land. We would argue how this illustrates a common commitment to 'compete' for labour whilst keeping wages low. It also possibly represents the longest lasting disjuncture between Afrikaner and English interests.

may influence outcomes within labour market structures without modifying those structures – thus, for example, a strengthening of trade unionism within a sector may enhance its wages relative to other sectors without further fundamental change.

Hofmeyr has effectively only considered the last of these three possibilities. This, together with the other features of his contribution, is what makes it appear to him that, after 1975, segmentation for urban Africans along sectoral, regional and gender lines, "tended to lessen or disappear over the ensuing ten years", p. 213. Whilst it is Marxists who claim to study science as the divergence between appearance and reality, Hofmeyr's conclusion is remarkably out of tune with what must be the most strikingly obvious features of differentiation within South African labour markets, even to a casual observer. It is tempting to suggest that this is the consequence of his unthinking use of existing techniques for South Africa where they are even less appropriate than in other applications.

This also appears to have induced Hofmeyr to underestimate both the nature of apartheid and its continuing significance in the functioning of labour markets. At a general level, as previously observed, his view involves perfectly competitive labour markets as a norm from which institutional structures induce deviation. Stepping outside the metaphysical world of neoclassical general equilibrium theory into any other branch of economics, or any other discipline that confronts labour market structures and outcomes, can only lead to the rejection of this starting point. Labour markets are necessarily dependent upon, and structured by, a range of socioeconomic factors. Consequently, although it is recognised that "apartheid affected virtually all aspects of life in South Africa", it is entirely inappropriate to consider, along with many other analysts, that "the essence of the system was an attempt to defy the operation of the forces of the market", p. 198.[51] As in other countries, economic and political interests are served by a shifting and complex combination of state- and market-led policies.

A corollary of the notion of apartheid as defiance of the market is that once some idealised notion of market restrictions is removed, so the labour market is unified. Yet, labour markets are always structured and by factors in the South African context, such as housing, welfare, transport, intergenerational mobility, etc. that remain particularly acute, quite apart from race and gender. One must wonder whether Hofmeyr is conscious of the wealth of empirical

51 Nor is it clear why education and labour should be privileged as the most far reaching and pernicious aspects of the system – as opposed, for example, to political equality and the use of violence.

evidence, even with a human capital methodology, which points to the persistence of labour market 'discrimination' long after the realisation of the institutional changes to which he appeals. Measured as a residual after accounting for personal and other differences, wage differentials and other forms and consequences of labour structuring (such as occupational segregation by gender and race) remain endemic in advanced capitalist countries despite attempted moves towards greater equality in pre- and post-entry labour market conditions. Is it to be believed that these considerations have been rendered redundant in South Africa within a decade, despite the particularly severe extent to which they were previously entrenched?

Hofmeyr does, however, fleetingly acknowledge these considerations with some emphasis on education. Observing the rising expenditure on African education and growing enrolments, he translates this immediately into an "increasing mobility of African labour both geographically and up the occupational ladder", p. 199. In contrast, the case can even be made that the apartheid education system has consolidated differentiation within the labour market, including amongst Africans, especially when unemployment and labour migration are taken into account. Again, one can only be astonished at the simplicity with which the apartheid education system is understood and how its effects are realised within the labour market.[52]

This is in part a reflection of the limited way in which the impetus behind institutional change is portrayed in Hofmeyr's account. Almost certainly inadvertently one suspects, Africans, or the opponents of apartheid more generally, are written out of playing a causal role. Thus, apart from the notion that trade unions were ineffective over the period from 1975, the moving force behind reform is associated with, "changes in the attitudes of White management and the government" together with "the increasing recognition by the government of the need to increase the supply of skilled labour", p. 199. The motive for highlighting the limited nature of this account, its exclusion of the resistance to apartheid and its effects, is not to search for an improvement in Hofmeyr's political history but to emphasise how important are a whole series of factors that he ignores in analysing the formation and restructuring of labour markets.

This is an appropriate note on which to conclude. It might be thought that this commentary has been unduly savage and, for those wishing to steer a straight course within the confines of orthodox, neoclassical labour market economics, one that is overburdened with irrelevant factors and abstract considerations. But, as observed at the outset, South African labour market

52 See Chisholm and Fine (1994) for some discussion of the continuing struggle over attempts to sustain racial privilege within education.

analysis is in its infancy. It needs to be even more sharply contested as it takes its first faltering steps. This is so at the levels of methodology, historical understanding and interdisciplinary scope.[53] Otherwise the capacity to understand any of the crucial issues attached to the functioning of labour markets, let alone those of equity, will be severely circumscribed.

Appendix

CLPT as Critical Point of Departure

According to the file from which it was recovered, this appendix was drafted in 2015 but it derived from the hand-written notes for a seminar given at Wits long before. This was probably around 2007, as the draft makes reference to a critique of Lebowitz as forthcoming in 2007, and it appeared as Fine (2008f). This all reflects a reluctance to publish out of respect for the richness of Harold Wolpe's contribution despite my critique of it. The latter can be expressed in a number of ways but one I have not used before is, if there is such a thing as cheap labour power, what does expensive labour power look like and from where does it derive. In short, the underlying analysis (around reproduction through bantustans and articulation of modes of production) is of more importance than its (questionable) expression as cheap(ening) labour power.

Interestingly, similar issues have arisen more recently out of the idea that financialisation (and indebtedness) leads to a reduction in the value of labour power. My response has been that, if this is so, that is what the value of labour power is and, moreover, it is important to see it not so much as its cheapening but as the form in which it is delivered – and differentially across strata and the separate moral and historical elements that make up working class consumption (Fine, 2020 and 2024d). The polished hand-written text now follows.

When I first began to study the South African economy seriously in the mid-1980s, I soon and inevitably came across the Cheap Labour Power Theory, CLPT, for which Harold Wolpe was and remains rightly famous. Its appeal lies in its ability to bring together in a dynamic analysis (i.e. the contradictory tensions) each of the economic and social reproduction of a racially divided working class, the role and periodisation of the state in the specific context of South African apartheid (and, for Wolpe, its distinction from segregation as such), and the bantustan system. Further, it also brought to bear a mix of contemporary

53 For an account of how both industrial relations and labour economics have been impoverished by their lack of dialogue, see Nolan (1993/94).

theory and method, not least drawing upon and promoting the structuralism of Poulantzas and the notion of articulation of modes of production.

As a Marxist value theorist, however, despite these considerable merits, I remained sceptical over the CLPT, not least because of doubts surrounding the idea that labour power could be cheap or, more exactly, what this actually means. For, even if not a value theorist in this vein, if one labour power is cheap, the issue is relative to what; and is some other labour power expensive? Is the implicit comparison with other labour in South Africa, with other countries, with South Africa without the particular form taken by the apartheid reproduction of labour power? The latter is the thrust of the CLPT but what sense does it make to compare the value of labour power as it is with one that is entirely ideal (i.e. requiring the imaginary construction of a less racially oppressive South Africa without the presence of the Bantustan system)? Further, if the value of labour power is cheap (or cheaper) systemically over a long period, surely this is just what the value of labour power is, cheap or expensive, just like the value of bread?

Clearly, what Wolpe has in mind derives from the accompanying notion to the CLPT of the articulation of modes of production. In this context, it reflects the idea that the South African economy is founded upon processes of economic and social reproduction of labour power that draw upon productive activity outside the direct control of capitalist production itself, not least through what was taken to be Bantustan (subsistence) agriculture. Even this is problematic for, in all capitalist societies, labour power is reproduced under non-capitalist relations – in the home through what has come to be termed domestic labour and through 'civil society' and, increasingly with development, state provision including health, education and welfare. Do these make for cheap(er) labour power? Clearly, there has been something different materially, politically and ideologically (and racially) across these within South Africa. Even so, there remains a further serious problem with the CLPT as articulated since, arguably, it both generalises and exaggerates and, hence, homogenises over the reproduction of migrant black labour power, with mining and agriculture taken as ideal types however much they are themselves accurately portrayed. By the mid-1980s, of course, with shanty town urbanisation, much reproduction of labour power was far removed from this ideal of (direct) articulation with Bantustan agriculture without being any the less grounded in racial oppression.[54]

54 Of course, there can be cyclical and seasonal movements between urban and rural environments with support for those from the rural to those located in the urban – although,

The conundrum is, then, that Wolpe's CLPT does seem to capture something of considerable importance about the specificity of South Africa whilst not doing so entirely appropriately. A way forward can be found by interrogating more closely the nature of the value of labour power. This is a concept unique to Marxist political economy. But it has traditionally been defined in two very different ways although often as if they were the same or equivalent. The first is by a quantum of value or labour time, usually as represented by money; but the second is by a quantum or bundle of wage goods. The two might appear to be equivalent, not least as the bundle of goods can be turned into a quantum of value (and corresponding quantity of money) according to the labour time required to produce them. But, for Wolpe, the CLPT is claiming that the material or use value composition of the value of labour power can be sustained, at least in principle and in part in an eroding practice, at a lower value through the contribution made by Bantustan agriculture (as opposed to other non-value contributions). This shows that the two definitions of the value of labour power can be different dependent upon whether value or use value is taken as the defining aspect. Apart from acknowledging different sources of use values in the value of labour power, this difference is also more readily seen once we allow for productivity increase (and the production of relative surplus value) which is itself the systematic consequence of the accumulation of capital. For, in the first case, a given *value* of labour power translates into more goods; whereas, in the second case, it translates into the same amount of goods by definition but a lower value of labour power and, hence, higher profitability.

These are two extremes; the first in which all gains from productivity more or less accrue to labour, and the second in which they all accrue to capital. Which of these is liable to occur in practice? As it were, does the use value or the value aspect of the value of labour power prevail? This indeterminacy has been left unaddressed by appeal to the notion of a standard of living and the phrase, heavily associated with Marx, of its being determined by moral and historical elements – presumably meaning the customary, the cultural and so on. But this is just to give the same problem a different name and what does it mean in practice? In any case, how do moral and historical elements change and, when they do change, how do they affect the value of labour power – is it as a quantity of greater or lesser labour time or as a bundle of goods.

I have an answer to these questions but first I will give an alternative approach that I consider to be wrong as this will allow my own view to be presented more clearly by way of contrast. The view I dispute arises from debate

---

traditionally, urban wages are seen as supporting the rural, not vice-versa. Even so, systemically, the overall balance of support can be in either direction.

with Lebowitz.[55] His argument, first of all, is that Marx and Marxism have been unduly preoccupied with what capital has done to labour rather than the oppositional stance and impact of labour on capital. More specifically, the more united is the working class within and between places of production, the more it will appropriate productivity gains in the form of wages. But capitalism, by its very organisation, divides workers in a way that underpins exploitation, yielding what he calls a *degree of separation*, "dos" for us by way of abbreviation. So, for Lebowitz, the larger is dos the lower is the value of labour power. The degree of separation is also deemed to be decisive in determining the extent to which the productivity increases associated with capital accumulation are appropriated by capitalists (as relative surplus value) or by workers in defence of the *value* of labour power (which would imply higher levels of real consumption of use values).

There is an issue, here, of whether this fairly represents Marx and Marxism in terms of the neglect of class struggle, especially in light of the labour process literature that has, admittedly gone into decline under the twin assault on industrial relations and sociology (by human relations) and political economy (by mainstream economics). For Lebowitz, though, the degree of separation is decisive in determining where the outcome lies between these two extremes of who gains from productivity increase.

My position is different and differently motivated and tends to view Lebowitz's stance as bordering upon a tautology – the more the working class is united in struggle as represented in the dos, the more it has to gain from productivity increase. There is also a dual aspect involved in my approach, corresponding to the two different ways of interpreting the value of labour power – as values or as use values. The first aspect concerns differentiation across and within labour markets. Without going into detail, there are a number different economic and social processes that differentiate the creation and occupation of positions within the production process (and the labour market more generally), and these flow in part from the imperatives of capitalist accumulation itself in terms of skills, hierarchies, and oppositional and organisational conflict in response to reorganisation of, and access to, the work process. Such differentiation, or segmentation as it is usually termed, is variously situated within and across firms, sectors, and occupations. At the very least, this means that the form taken by the value of labour power is not simply the standard enjoyed by all, but one that is determined according to the processes of, and responses to, the restructuring of employment. The value of labour power is

55 My critique is to be found fully laid out in Fine (2008f) with references to Lebowitz.

not even an average from which there are divergences either side, in anything other than a numerical sense. Rather, the value of labour power is the result of a deeply structured and differentiated (re)positioning of the workforce in its economic and social relations as well as in its more narrowly defined rewards in terms of wage differentiation. Indeed, as argued in Fine (1998a), labour market segmentation is not merely a matter of different segments of the workforce but differentially organised functioning within those segments.[56]

To put all of this in Lebowitz's terms, degrees of separation are differentiated both qualitatively and quantitatively and are not homogenised either through some open or underlying process. Significantly, the rather different approach to labour markets taken by my stance was in part motivated by study of the South African labour market, with two separate influences. On the one hand, as point of departure, was whether racial immobility was being eroded in South African labour markets with the demise of apartheid and the anticipated reduction, or not, of racially determined wage differentials. This is, however, a deeply flawed approach if not without empirical interest – for it reduces labour market restructuring to a simple issue of mobility across labour markets as opposed to interrogating deeply entrenched if evolving and differentiated economic and social structures, relations and processes in the formation and functioning of those labour markets. On the other hand, especially in light of work on (female) South African domestic servants, it becomes very clear that these and, say, male mineworkers, are segmented from one another but also belong to very differently organised and reproduced workforces for which a common, or commonly shared, dos would appear to be entirely inappropriate.

In this light, as mutually acknowledged, my differences with Lebowitz reflect substantive methodological issues, not least the relationship between abstraction and causation as well as the location of class struggle in Marxist value theory. These need not be addressed here. But, as indicated, there is a second aspect in the determination of the value of labour power concerning the wage as a bundle of use values, commonly perceived as a material standard of living. Here, I have emphasised three points. First, the way in which that standard is established is different from one commodity to another (and in relation to elements of economic and social reproduction that are not produced by capital directly whether provided by the state or in commodity form outside of capitalist production). More specifically, I have argued that the wage bundle is comprised of a number of separate *systems of provision*, such as the

56 See also Fine (2007c) in debate with Fleetwood (2006) and Fine (1998a).

food, health, housing and transport systems, with these complemented by what I have termed public sector systems of provision.[57]

Second, within each system of provision, norms are established which are neither the same for all nor even an average, but a distinctive mode of provision with corresponding incidence of levels and quality of consumption across different social groups. So, the nature of the moral and historical element is different both within and between different items within the consumption bundle.

Third, then, the way in which the different systems of provision establish the moral and historical element is certainly contingent upon class struggle, and upon the overall value of labour power as it evolves over time. But it is not reducible to these, even if stretched beyond class conflict at the point of production, as a causal role is played by elements along each of the systems of provision as a whole, and through which (in the links between production and consumption) influence is exerted upon the levels and incidence of norms for consumption.[58] Thus, whilst the value of labour power is given at any moment as an abstract and simple determinant, as accumulation proceeds, so the reproduction and transformation of that value of labour power is determined at the more complex levels of differentially segmented and functioning labour markets and the differentiated systems of provision attached to differentiated standards of consumption.

In short, the moral and historical element in the value of labour power as a material standard of living – as opposed to a level of social necessary labour-time – is not determined by class struggle alone, not by production alone, not by conflict between capital and labour alone, and is differentially determined across different elements of consumption. Consequently, it follows that, if the dos is taken as the measure of the extent to which productivity increase is appropriated by the working class, it is an extremely complex and concrete determinant and not one that is logically located at a high level of abstraction such as the value of labour power itself around which the production and circulation of (surplus) value revolves and, from which, the complex determinants of the moral and historical elements can at least initially be abstracted.

In this light, one of the virtues of the CLPT is to have located the value of labour power in the context of the totality of economic and social reproduction.

57 A number of references were given here but see Bayliss and Fine (2021a).

58 A fourth point concerns the attachment of a cultural system to each system of provision through which the meaning of consumption is determined but this is not of direct relevance to what follows – although vital in reflecting and influencing the moral and historical element.

From the understanding of the value of labour power offered here, the CLPT might be usefully reconstructed as a theory of labour market segmentation and a theory of segmented consumption, with the articulation of Bantustan agriculture with economic and social reproduction understood as merely one evolving and differentiated factor amongst others. Of course, this means that the value of labour power in its more complex moral and historical aspects should not be seen as simply coterminous with purchased commodities with a value but also as integrated with other sources of reproduction, whether subsistence agriculture, domestic labour or state provision. These are part and parcel of the ways in which norms are established and what those norms are.

Further, norms of consumption need to be understood in terms not only of different levels of provision to different segments of the population but also by virtue of how such provisioning takes place, not least as the moral and historical element does or does not include public or private provision, subsidised or otherwise and, especially in the current period, open or not to access through credit and of what type and with what consequences (especially important, for example, in housing markets, on the one hand, where capital gains can accrue to wealthier owner-occupiers, as well as over-indebtedness for those on minimal income seeking to sustain norms of consumption). In addition, such norms can evolve continually, as with the rising levels of wages with productivity, be subject to sharp changes that may be consolidated over the course of the rhythm of economic activity, and be subject to change in form and content as, for example, different aspects of economic and social reproduction are commodified (from household or the state) or decommodified as with public provision. These are all part and parcel of 'the moral and historical', alongside other material and cultural determinants.

Such insights suggest that the concerns of the CLPT, and many criticisms of it, can be accommodated by acknowledging that the apartheid value of (black) labour power was differentially underpinned across its various elements as well as being more widely cast than economic and social reproduction through wage labour and Bantustan agriculture.[59] By the same token, the same applies to the post-apartheid value of labour power for which the moral and historical elements in its determination will have been transformed by political transformation and its consequences to an extent and in ways that

59 For the record, an unpublished draft introduction to the section on social and economic infrastructure for the MERG Report observed that its separate components were marked in common by severe racial inequalities, fragmentation of administration, inefficiencies in delivery, lack of mutual integration other than reinforcing deprivation and privilege, centralised control, and differentiated forms of functioning and resistances (Fine, 1996b).

need to be established. As is emphasised by Wolpe himself, from segregation to apartheid and within apartheid itself, economic and social restructuring has been extensive with corresponding implications for reproduction of labour power. Continuing to drive the post-apartheid trajectory has been the Minerals-Energy Complex playing catch up with globalisation of production, financialisation, the corresponding emergence of a black elite, and the neoliberalisation of everyday life. But, as already emphasised, how all of this translates into the value of labour power is contingent on the (re)structuring of labour markets and the (re)structuring of the norms of consumption, the latter themselves attached to (public sector) systems of provision that have been embedded in the newly financialised forms of provision with attendant inequalities, often reproducing and consolidating those inherited from apartheid in the absence of (well-paid) employment and deficient service delivery.

At the expense of self-indulgence, such framing was implicit in the MERG (1993) Report, for which I prepared sections on housing, schooling, electrification and health. Continuing provision in and across these is best understood in terms of differentiated systems of provision and as part and parcel of the reproduction and value of labour power. Each of these sectors posed challenges of their own despite having common roots (and branches) in the apartheid system. And each has been transformed in the transition from apartheid, albeit in ways that have sustained, and even worsened inequalities and converged on neoliberal forms of provision as the current norms. This stands in sharp contrast to universal health care, free at the point of delivery and based on primary and preventative goals as opposed, for example, to a privatised, curative system for the minority, or a public housing building programme for social renting as opposed to financial subsidies to owner-occupation, and so on for schooling and adequate let alone equal access, quite apart from differentiated (forms of) access to clothing, food, social security, transport, energy, etc. In short, the value of labour power has remained not so much cheap as subject to moral and historical elements that continue to reproduce the most severe levels and forms of deprivation and inequality.

CHAPTER 4

Debating the South African Minerals-Energy Complex

Postscript as Personal Preamble

I was delighted that our book on the MEC (Fine and Rustomjee, 1996) was subject to a serious review by Bell and Farrell (1997). At that time, and for some years afterwards, the MEC received very little attention even if subsequently it has become part of the lingua franca. Zav and I drafted a response which was subsequently revised so that page numbers could be put in place, some updating incorporated and an appendix taken out (which is included here).

The changes reflected that a lot was going on at this time. The Asian crisis was looming, there were continuing rumblings of discontent from COSATU, the Post-Washington Consensus was about to be launched and, for me, I was heavily engaged in research around the Developmental State Paradigm, economics imperialism, social capital and more, quite apart from seeking to trace and explain the ANC's embrace of neoliberalism. These and other considerations, if they make their way into the discussion, might seem inappropriate with hindsight but they were hot at the time. I was also heavily engaged in drafting policy papers for NIEP/Cosatu around industrial policy, privatisation, the steel industry and ESOPs (Fine, 1997c and d and 1998c, all reproduced and more in 2025e).

Significantly, response to the MEC framing of South Africa's political economy has always remained muted even after it became commonplace to draw upon it for whatever purpose. Criticism has been even less prominent, see also Chapter 5. The most obvious reason for this is that the empirical evidence of its presence is overwhelming, and the MEC can be deployed instrumentally to explain what does or does not happen, at least selectively. Fair enough but this runs against our own approach which has always been to emphasise the MEC as the South African system of accumulation (in a global context). As such, it has multiple elements (economic and political, and more) and it is shifting over time. In short, it can be seen in terms of the composition of output, core sectors, the role of the state, classes and their fractions, and policies adopted whether succeeding or not. In this light, criticism of the MEC as a framing device is readily adopted through picking selectively upon a few of its features and suggesting they have never been sufficiently weighty or have been eroded.

 | DOI:10.1163/9789004748330_005

Thus, I suspect none would say the MEC is dead because platinum has taken the place of gold. But what of financial(isation) and services more generally? Are we to see the financialisation (and more general restructuring of the MEC through unbundling, globalisation and BEE, quite apart from 'state capture') as indicative of the decline of the MEC or just the new forms that it assumes?[1]

This conundrum indicates that the issue is less whether the MEC exists or not but whether it remains appropriate in capturing how economic and social restructuring and reproduction are occurring within South Africa. But, in our debate with Bell and Farrell, there are also other issues that are raised by the MEC framing but which are not necessarily essential to it – how and in what way did South Africa industrialise, what is import-substituting industrialisation (ISI) and the policies associated with it, were these adopted in South Africa, and were they successful or not. The answers we give are different from those of Bell and Farrell, especially because we look at them through the lens of the MEC.

We were lucky to have Trevor Bell as a reviewer given his prominence as a South African economist, commanding respect across intellectual divides. As emphasised by Vishnu Padayachee (2006) in his obituary notice, Trevor made a rare contribution to the study of South African industrialisation through focus upon (policies to promote) it through bantustan separate development, something generally dismissed by others as token and insignificant. Possibly, an inclination to think otherwise may have encouraged a view of South Africa as having been wedded to (consumer-led) ISI with some degree of success, complemented by the protection offered to consumer goods industries on demand. By contrast, with the MEC on board, industrialisation is all about core mining and energy mega-corporations and the role of the state in relation to them.

1 Introduction[2]

At first sight, the review of our book, (Fine and Rustomjee, 1996) by Bell and Farrell (1997) is most fulsome in its praise. It begins by suggesting, p. 591:

1 Thus, Morrell (1988) can refer to the historical disintegration of the gold/maize alliance – why not the same for the MEC contingent upon the evidence?

2 First published as Fine and Rustomjee (1998). Ben Fine is Professor of Economics and Director of the Centre for Economic Policy for Southern Africa (CEPSA), School of Oriental and African Studies (SOAS), University of London; Zav Rustomjee is Director-General of the South African Department of Trade and Industry (DTI). Each writes in his personal capacity. Note that CEPSA was set up at SOAS in 1992 when I moved there from Birkbeck, with the

> One of the merits of this book is that it gives centre-stage to South Africa's mineral-rich character. It does so in an intriguingly new, unconventional way, in the form of the notion of the Minerals-Energy Complex (MEC).

And it concludes, p. 611:

> Fine and Rustomjee's book raises various other fundamental issues, important both for understanding South African industrialisation in the past and for thinking about its future … Fine and Rustomjee have therefore produced an important book.

What comes in-between, however, is a very different story and features the sort of 'trenchant critique' with which Trevor Bell has been justifiably associated in his previous work, not least in debate with the Industrial Strategy Project (ISP) (Bell, 1995 and 1996; and Kaplan and Lewis, 1996). Specifically, for example, p. 592:

> A major shortcoming of the book is the lack of an adequate statistical picture of the evolution of the economy as a whole, and of the manufacturing industry in particular.

If this were, indeed, fair commentary on our book, the accompanying praise would be undeserved given the book's title and intent. How is this paradox within the review to be explained? It is doubtful, and would be disappointing, to conclude that Trevor had lost some of his sharp analytical edge and had embraced a few skills in flattery in order to render his criticism more effective. We prefer to take the positive commentary at face value so that, despite the critique, Bell and Farrell have accepted our central conclusion – the MEC exists and is central to an understanding both of South Africa's industrial past and its future. Contrary to the use of their own evidence, which is primarily data-based, the reviewers have had the intellectual integrity to recognise that

---

aim of providing teaching, research and policy for South Africa in particular (dovetailing with an ongoing distance learning programme spearheaded by Laurence Harris, starting in Mozambique (where I taught econometrics on occasion) and then extending to South Africa. CEPSA successfully applied for major funding to continue its work in post-apartheid South Africa, granted subject to ANC leadership approval. Frustratingly, post-MERG, this simply proved impossible to get – our training and research was not wanted even at zero cost to the ANC. The irony is that many of those trained at SOAS in the earlier period (funded by the then ODA, later DfID) became stalwarts of the post-apartheid elite. Despite our best intentions, we seem to have provided legs up the greasy pole.

the MEC captures for them much of the material reality of South Africa's political economy.

It is this that is more important for us than any other aspect of their review. It is the first serious academic acknowledgement of the veracity of our approach to South Africa's political economy. Our ideas have primarily been ignored at best, or resisted, misinterpreted, and dismissed at worst. One particularly disturbing interpretation for us is of the MEC as a core set of successful sectors upon which policy for expansion should continue to be focused in the future. In this light, especially given the bewildering pace at which South Africa (and corresponding scholarship and interpretation) appears to be changing, it is worth reviewing – even if at the expense of some self-indulgence – the emergence of the notion of the MEC, for it is not new.

It was first put forward as much as a decade ago, not least in debate with what was to become the economic trends (ET) study of the South African economy (Gelb, ed. 1991), which is notable for its neglect even of the core MEC sectors.[3] At the same time as engaging with the ET approach to the South African economy, study was undertaken of the South African electricity and mining industries and their economic and institutional linkages. This, together with an input-output analysis of intersectoral linkages, was crucial in establishing the notion of the MEC, initially termed the energy-minerals complex (EROSA, 1987a, 1987b and 1988; Fine, 1992a; and Rustomjee, 1990, 1991 and 1994). The change in terminology followed a review of literature on the military-industrial complex which was rejected as an unsatisfactory general model in and of itself, and as a framework for addressing the South African MEC (Fine, 1993b), although it is argued that the South African military-industrial complex has formed part of the MEC (Fine, 1990b).[4]

The MEC concept has proved the continuing basis for difference with the ISP (1995) group (Fine, 1995b). Whatever the substantive theoretical and empirical content these and many other contributions have adopted, they share a common methodological feature, which we have rejected.[5] The contributions have taken one or more abstract concepts, whether racial Fordism from regulation theory or flexible specialisation from neo-Fordism, and applied them as tools to the South African economy. As such, there is a parallel with the

3 Freund (1991) for a minor exception. My research on the MEC was funded over a two-year period by the UK's Economic and Social Research Council (ESRC), from October 1990 to 1992, with a corresponding application for funding being earlier. Zav served as research officer on the project and as my PhD student.

4 For some early history of the MEC, see Fine (1994a).

5 The World Bank and the IMF are, of course, notorious for advising on the basis of preconceived notions and/or models with only token deference to country-specific factors.

standard use of neoclassical economics as a way of interpreting economic performance as succeeding or failing – not necessarily respectively, because of convergence with, or divergence from, the restrictive conditions attached to the ideal notion of perfect competition. Thus, is South African manufacturing competitive, is it Fordism, is it flec-spec? And the list of such explanatory or, more exactly, exploratory tools can be extended more or less indefinitely, and not least to import-substituting industrialisation – an explanation based on whether industrialisation did or did not follow import substitution and, if so, whether successfully or not.

Our methodology is different and we considered it so important that we devoted a chapter of a book on South Africa to a study of South Korea in order to bring out, partly in practice, the substance of our methodology. We wished to avoid the imposition of models on the South African economy. Rather, it was a matter of establishing the nature of the economy from its own historically developed features. We dubbed this the "linkagency" approach since it sought to identify economic and other linkages and the agencies responsible for them. This allowed us not only to identify the MEC, but also to interpret it as a "system of accumulation". In contrast to other work, this approach avoids the interpretation of South Africa as a reflection of either an externally given theory or a stance on capitalism and racism as in the Marxism-liberalism debate.

In short, much of the previous literature on the South African economy has suffered from instrumentalism. There is a tempting parallel, if not parody, with Marxist value theory which orthodox interpretations dismiss since the labour theory of value is not a useful tool or instrument for explaining price and profit. In contrast, Marx was himself concerned with whether value exists or not and, if so (as in commodity-producing societies), what form that value takes. In this respect, Bell and Farrell can be considered akin to Ricardo, since they accept the notion of value (MEC) but find it contradicts itself as an empirical tool (see Pilling, 1980, on such instrumentalism).

Hence, here is a tool for examining the economy – how well does it perform? Despite their empirical criticisms, Bell and Farrell obviously feel that the MEC is quite a good tool and, if we are correct in dubbing the South African economy as the MEC, this should not be surprising. Our methodology is different, however, for we do not see the MEC as a convenient instrument handed to, or invented by, us in order to examine the South African economy. Rather, we see the MEC as the historically shifting form or linkagencies taken by the accumulation of capital in and around South Africa. It is against this interpretation of the MEC that the critique of Bell and Farrell needs to be judged whilst we have also taken the opportunity to review the genesis of our book and some of the work that has followed it.

2 The MEC Core

An appropriate starting point is what the MEC is today. Part II of our book attempts to do this. The first chapter, entitled "The boundaries of the MEC", primarily focuses on the role of the continuing "core" sectors of the MEC. Core in this context can mean two separate but closely related things, and we might be justifiably accused of jumbling up the meanings. First, it can mean those sectors that have always been central to the accumulation of capital in South Africa even if with shifting overall and relative weight. Second, it can be those sectors that are central to accumulation over a particular, shorter period of time.[6]

Now, as instrumentalists, Bell and Farrell wish to define the core as a fixed set of sectors and examine whether its importance has changed over time, in order to question our view that the economy's dependence on the MEC has increased and certainly not decreased. Not of necessity, but symptomatically, Bell and Farrell slip from discussing the MEC core to the MEC itself. For them, using constant prices (whereas we use current prices), the MEC's share of GDP (and not the core's share) peaked in 1964 at 28.9 per cent, ultimately falling to 23.5 per cent in 1993.

For us, however, discussion of the core sectors plays a different role, with the core serving as an empirical or descriptive device and no more. First, it is not a matter of semantics to include some sectors and not others although, admittedly, this is a less fundamental point to them. Rather, we sought to establish the continuing importance of the core sectors of the MEC in both the senses distinguished above. If these core sectors had dwindled to nothing, our book would have been very different. It would have been about how the South African system of accumulation had diversified out of and displaced the MEC. In short, whilst the MEC as a system of accumulation cannot be satisfactorily defined by the weight in the economy of a fixed set of sectors, it is worthwhile to establish the continuing empirical weight of what is to some extent an arbitrarily defined and crudely measured core.

Second, then, our motive for using core sectors for statistical purposes was to serve as an explicit rebuttal of the more or less universal conventional view. If necessarily implicit, this understanding of the South African economy is that it has become less dependent on the MEC as represented by mining or primary production and has, by contrast, industrialised, however successfully and with whatever meaning, on the basis of different sectors. Such a view had been

6 Thus, we were mindful of the significance of the gold and maize alliance at an earlier stage (Morrell, 1988, for its disintegration in the 1920s–to what?).

encouraged by the arbitrary classification of economic sectors, as seen through the prism of the MEC as a system of accumulation. What we would include within the MEC because of its close linkages with mining and energy would be excluded by standard industrial classifications.

Third, in this light, the results of the recalculations of Bell and Farrell do not unduly disturb us. For, that the MEC core sectors continue to occupy 23.5 per cent of the economy is sufficient to establish in these terms alone that they have a continuing weight. But there are other, arguably more important, terms. These are made explicit at the end of the chapter prior to the following chapter's consideration of corporate structure (an aspect of the MEC as a system of accumulation, which is not even mentioned by Bell and Farrell). The argument is that whilst the core sectors continue to carry a heavy, even growing weight, the MEC as a system of accumulation has become characterised by corporate conglomeration across the economy, including finance, so that, "even though strong linkages have evolved within MEC core sectors, the process of accumulation has often encompassed other sectors with varying intensities at different points in time … As a system of accumulation, then, the MEC potentially incorporates all economic sectors, since these have necessarily been associated with each other through ownership and control, through relationships between state and capital or through the imperatives of apartheid" (Fine and Rustomjee, 1996, pp. 91–2).

This quotation is then followed by a discussion of why the identification of the boundaries of the MEC and its core is necessarily arbitrary. The next chapter establishes the corporate linkages for the South African economy which are well known to the point of cliché, although some originality might be claimed for the extent shown to which these are and have been forged through interaction with state corporations.

Fourth, and a relatively minor point in view of the above, we would not accept the rationale behind the recalculations of the MEC's share. The use of constant prices in the case of gold will be of some quantitative significance, not least because its relative price has changed so much. It would be peculiar to downplay the significance of gold to the South African economy because levels of production have stagnated. The weight of economic activity undertaken to produce that gold has increased so much with the decline in mining conditions, both in terms of grade of ore and depth of extraction. In any case, our emphasis would be less on refinement in calculating the MEC core's share and more on the shifting linkagencies to which it is attached.

The discussion of the MEC core brings out some, but not all, of the features of the MEC as a contemporary system of accumulation. There are other features of the South African economy which appear uncontroversial, such as the competitive weakness in consumer goods and the relative absence of capacity in capital and intermediate goods – with stop-go implications for growth through the balance of trade. We were, however, in the context of the history of the MEC – if it exists, how did it get there? – intrigued by two other factors which either seemed to be taken for granted or to be overlooked. First, what had happened to the historical division between Afrikaner and English capital? Second, why had the South African economy experienced successes as well as failures in its industrial development, and what explained these and the balance between them?[7]

3 On Import-Substituting Industrialisation

These issues informed our discussion of industrial development and industrial policy and, in particular, the role played by import-substituting industrialisation (ISI). Once again, we wish to challenge an almost universally standard interpretation – that South African industrialisation was to be perceived in terms of an ISI strategy, underpinned by heavy measures of protection, which was either misguided or not and which had failed or not, although application of these judgements is open to a chronological rhythm. For a typical and recent example, see Jenkins and Siwisa (1997, p. 21):

> The objectives of the industrial/trade strategy adopted have also shifted over time, from an imperative to reduce dependence on Britain and to create productive employment for whites, to the search for a stimulus to economic growth after the 'easy' stages of ISI were completed.

Before engaging with Bell and Farrell directly, two important aspects of our own position need to be clarified. First, we do not take a position on ISI versus export orientation (EO); it is largely a false dichotomy. Indeed, whilst the availability of markets, whether domestic or export, is of considerable importance (as heavily emphasised, along with macroeconomic stability, by Bell, 1995), the role played by trade policy cannot be considered in general and needs to be located in a fuller, usually sector- and country-specific context. In other words, the ISI versus EO controversy provides an inappropriate framework for assessing industrial policy and industrialisation, although it often serves as a metaphor for a different controversy, of state versus market, on which see below.

7 See Kaplan (1987), for example, for the idea of failure in the machine tool industry.

Second, our understanding of ISI as a pattern or path of industrialisation comprises a number of sequenced elements. It begins with protection to promote the production of consumption goods in the domestic market. As domestic capacity expands, it induces knock-on or linkage effects to the production of intermediate and then to capital goods. Consequently, there is liable to be a shifting composition of production, from consumption to intermediate and capital goods, and a shifting composition of imports, as these are sequentially displaced by domestic production in an upstream direction. These processes, however, are not the only ones which affect the composition of production and the trade balance. For example, with growing incomes, the production of consumption goods will continue to expand, possibly even disproportionately, and also serve export markets. With the domestic production of some intermediate and capital goods, others may be required as imports to support domestic capacity.

It follows that the empirical trends in import ratios and shares in manufacturing cannot in, and of, themselves indicate whether ISI has occurred. This is especially so in examining ISI as industrialisation that proceeds through backward linkages. If the share of non-consumption goods rises, it may be as a result of providing domestic inputs to consumption goods, ISI proper, but it is equally compatible with various sectors expanding in parallel with one another. It is a matter of the relations between sectors and not just their relative shares.

Bell and Farrell interrogate our proposition that industrialisation in South Africa has not proceeded through ISI. It is apparent, however, that they take a different view of what constitutes ISI. For us, it is first consumption goods and then diversification to the rest of manufacturing through backward linkages – each word in this definition playing its part. To refute the standard interpretation of South Africa as ISI promoted by protection, it suffices for us to show that the sectoral sequence of industrialisation does not follow the required pattern. We believe that this is shown by our data. It has, what we consider to be, the dramatic effect of demolishing the conventional wisdom by revealing the extent of early industrial production of non-consumption goods.

The understanding of ISI and the associated empirical evidence of Bell and Farrell can now be addressed. Repeating the pattern employed in the discussion of the weight of the MEC (core), they begin by reducing the problem to a few statistical indicators. They then charge us for the way and the (lack of) depth with which we examine these indicators. Finally, they offer more detailed calculations to refute us. In this instance, their understanding of ISI is simply a chronology of the share of sectors in output and trade ratios. At no point do they consider what is, for us, the central point – the pattern and sequencing of linkages between sectors of the economy. How this can have been overlooked is puzzling to us, since it is a theme that recurs again and again throughout the book – in the discussion of South Korean industrialisation and, for South Africa, both for past and future prospects.

In short, our view of the MEC is as one which failed to promote the forward linkages from its core sectors. This is opposed both to the view of those who see South African industrialisation in terms of ISI (and the creation of backward linkages) and to that of Bell and Farrell who perceive it in terms of shifting import and value-added shares. We devote a chapter of the book to establishing that the history of industrial policy in South Africa is not, as traditionally perceived, one of protection to promote ISI (although protection does support domestic production of consumption and other goods) but the creation and support of the MEC core industries, with limited impact on forward diversification.

Indeed, quite apart from failing to integrate forward from the MEC core, the South African economy failed to integrate backward from protected consumption industries – another nail in the ISI coffin, as interpreted by us. One purpose throughout much of the book is to examine the creation of backward and forward linkages in manufacturing, and the corresponding role played by policy, itself reflecting the balance of economic and political interests. For this reason, whatever our other criticisms, we consider the ISP interest in filières and the Monitor Group's approach to clusters to be a strength. In this light, our dual emphasis on forward and backward linkages is acknowledged in a strangely inconsistent way for the interwar period, for Bell and Farrell both accuse us of "more or less exclusive focus on developments in MEC sectors", p. 604, and then point out that "much attention is given to food products", p. 604. We do, however, emphasise that the outcomes are mixed across sub-sectors but that protection is the only systematic and general element of industrial policy. This is not, however, ISI, and did not induce it.

4 The MEC as a System of Accumulation

The topic of policy brings politics to the fore. Once again, the interpretation of Bell and Farrell is a considerably stripped-down version of our own approach to the MEC as a system of accumulation. For them, it appears as if policy is a balance between economic efficiency and political interests, as in their discussion of steel and Sasol, for example. In the case of Sasol, reference is made in the review to Bell's (1993) hypothesis that it was not initially a response to sanctions but an appropriate commercial response to prevailing economic conditions. If so, it is not apparent how this undermines the notion of the MEC as a system of accumulation. They seem to interpret the politics of the MEC as the predominance of its associated interests over those of efficiency where the two criteria conflict. Our approach is considerably more nuanced than they allow. It explicitly rejects crude identification of the apartheid state with exclusive promotion of Afrikaner interests for the simple reason that such was impossible given the power held by English capital. Policies were not, and so cannot be, legitimately read off as simply reflecting economic or political interests. As we are at pains to show, policies necessarily represented compromises (and conflicts) that were differentiated from sector to sector and from issue to issue, with greater or lesser success from a narrowly interpreted perspective based on economic efficiency.

Consequently, our emphasis on state enterprises, and on Iscor and Eskom in particular, is justified since these have been wrongly interpreted as having been state-owned, national and hence Afrikaner capitals. To address the creation and development of these corporations is to unravel the complex interaction between economic and political power and interests. It could give rise to 'positive' outcomes, around the MEC core, despite the necessary collaboration with English capital. But, by the same token, exactly the same configuration of general economic and political interests appears to have precluded greater interventionist industrial policy, as in steel-using industries, for example.

This, of course, is our main point and it is stunningly overlooked by Bell and Farrell. It is also argued for in the case of steel in the post-war period in Fine and Rustomjee (1995) in commentary on Cross (1994). Bell and Farrell's reference is to South Korea and its establishment of a steel industry as a strategy for industrialisation (against the advice and support, it should be added, of the World Bank). If they did it (some decades later it should be observed how much more has been achieved in so short a time), why is it so special compared with South Africa? The answer is South Korea's flying-geese strategy, fully discussed in our earlier chapter, through which a sequence of steel-using (not least shipbuilding) and other industries were established.[8] This is notably absent in South Africa's industrial policy, even though it did manage to establish a steel industry through state intervention. This is so despite the affinities between the South Korean and South African conglomerate structures – the chaebol and mining houses, respectively – with each diversifying ownership across sectors. Whilst we do not wish to make a fetish of industrialisation through economic linkages – other factors alone or in combination are equally,

8 For a discussion of the continuing weaknesses in the South African steel industry, see Fine (1998c).

if not more, important – it is a key contrast between the two economies both in policy and outcome.

Moving from the interwar period, what we do identify, in general, is a shifting pattern of compromise over the post-war period. Roughly, the 1950s signalled the building-up of Afrikaner financial capital, the 1960s its expansion into mining and the erosion of divisions between large-scale Afrikaner and English capital, and the 1970s a concerted policy on the part of the state to promote MEC core sectors. This only proved possible after the settling of accounts within Afrikaner interest groups (as discussed by O'Meara, 1996). It is also imperative to recognise that, whatever the differences between English and Afrikaner capital, there was a common reliance in practice on use of the apartheid labour system. This, however, has itself been heterogeneous (see Fine, 1998a). Consequently, at no point has coherent industrial policy been adopted to promote industrial linkages, a deficiency that persisted into the 1980s and 1990s as policies of monetarist liberalisation, and then the crisis of apartheid, precluded such an industrial strategy.

Throughout, the lack of such vertical integration and development is what we mean when pointing to South Africa's low level of diversification which, unfortunately, Bell and Farrell interpret in the much narrower sense of a wider spread alone in the composition of output. This is the only explanation for what we consider to be the unfair accusation of having misled our readers over the extent of the growing diversity of production. We do not dispute growing diversity of output, but satisfactory integration across sectors in such diversification. Bell and Farrell also suggest that, as relations between MEC and non-MEC sectors are independent, there is no reason to endow one rather than the other with causal priority. This is, however, to overlook the economic and political power and interests attached to the sectors concerned, as is evident in the total lack of reference by Bell and Farrell to evolving corporate structure and ownership, where the commanding position of the MEC has been indisputable.

5 Future Prospects

The answer to the question of how the MEC got to be where it is, is to be found in the brief outline above. Greater detail can be found in our book, other contributions listed in the references here and, hopefully, subsequent research. The final chapter of our book, the publication of which from delivery of manuscript unfortunately took two years, suggests some implications for future research. The momentum of our own collaborative academic work was considerably reduced by the shift to policy analysis around the 1994 election, with involvement in the ANC's Department of Economic Policy (DEP), the Macroeconomic Research Group (MERG, 1993), ISP – for which Rustomjee (1993) contributed a sector study – and with Rustomjee's ultimate appointment to the DTI.[9]

But what about the future and what are the policy implications? As argued in Fine (1997c), there is currently disarray within the World Bank, and between it and the International Monetary Fund, as the Senior Vice-President and Chief Economist of the World Bank, Joe Stiglitz (1998), in particular has sought to reject the neoliberal Washington Consensus and replace it with a Post-Washington Consensus that is more state-friendly.[10]

This creates both opportunities and responsibilities for South Africa. It is in a position both to deploy more interventionist policies than have previously been encouraged by the Washington Consensus, and for these to offer experiences and precedents for other developing countries less favourably placed. Otherwise, the agenda of the Post-Washington Consensus, of the market-conforming state, will command the development policy agenda just as the Washington Consensus did previously. It will at best offer a pale and weak version of Keynesianism/welfarism and modernisation. South Africa's potential to meet needs in industry, as well as elsewhere, must be forced both intellectually and programmatically beyond such limited perspectives.

But where does this leave the role of the MEC? As shown in Fine (1997b and c), the MEC continues to incorporate considerable economic and political power, with strategic emphasis being placed on the globalisation of its own operations. This has considerable implications for the formation and impact of macroeconomic policy, as well as for industrial policy, where the development of economies of scale and scope in manufacturing continues to be constrained by limited domestic commitment on the part of conglomerate capital. Bell's (1997) commitment to protection for preserving markets and for macroeconomic stability is notable not only for the absence of consideration of economies of scope (as opposed to scale), but also for the limited account offered of the political forces currently underpinning excessive trade liberalisation and macroeconomic austerity. This is so despite the careful empirical exercise suggesting that low-wage black employment is most at risk from trade liberalisation (Bell and Cattaneo, 1997). As Fine (1997c) argues, the erosion of protection

9 Note the unresolved tensions around industrial policy in the MERG (1993) Report between our position and that of the ISP. See also Fine (1994b) in debate with Nattrass (1995) and Fine (1997b and c).

10 See Hildyard (1998) and Fine (1999a) for critical accounts of the Post-Washington Consensus.

is a significant index of the loss of economic and political weight behind the sectors concerned, and macroeconomic austerity is designed to allow for the removal of exchange controls and the free movement of South African conglomerate capital out of the country.[11]

Unless such issues are satisfactorily addressed, the objective of black advancement will be primarily confined to a minority for the narrow purpose of attaining social and political stability. Whether directly through the corridors of power or indirectly through the perceived need to establish an elusive 'business confidence', the MEC remains at the heart of policymaking and exerts a profound influence on social and economic reconstruction.

More specifically, we are increasingly being told that, as far as economic policy goes, there are no alternatives and that policy is neither to the left nor to the right, but simply good or bad. It is a matter of speculation how long such confidence in existing policies will persist until similar confidence is placed in the altered policies that will inevitably follow. To entrench conservative interests, there is a need to promote sections of black business to serve as a buffer against more extensive assaults on the structure of ownership and modus operandi of corporate capital. Similarly, the delivery of social programmes is a matter of satisfying an equally elusive people's confidence. In the realm of debate, policymaking and politics, these goals and issues can only be satisfactorily addressed by acknowledging the central presence of the MEC.

Appendix

Postscript

As mentioned in the Preamble, an earlier draft made fuller reference to the Post-Washington Consensus as providing an opportunity for South Africa itself to take a lead in promoting progressive policies as well as supporting them more generally in scholarship, policy, ideology and policy in practice upon the back of the disarray in which the Washington Consensus found itself in the mid-1990s. It is after all the height of irony that South Africa should have so fully and willingly embraced policies associated with the Washington Consensus (and so much of the policy advice of the IMF and World Bank) just at the time when it was, at least in the world of scholarship and ideology, being abandoned for the Post-Washington Consensus. What follows is the text that was deleted from an original draft, presumably for reasons of length and/or to focus more

11 See Fine (1996a) for an example of how economies of scale can justify protection.

narrowly, if briefly, on South African policy debates. That the Post-Washington Consensus should have disappointed in policy practice, and more generally across scholarship, ideology and world vision, was subsequently addressed in Fine et al. (eds) (2001) and Bayliss et al. (eds) (2011). Maybe things would have been different had South Africa stood up for the PWC and beyond.

Opportunity for Opportunism Missed

Despite our firm response to the review of Bell and Farrell in other respects, the area of policy is the one in which we are most disappointed with their contribution. For it is behind times both in the literature that it considers and in the way that it considers it. In particular, their closing section places the debate over industrial policy on the terrain of market versus the state, with an agnostic position in view of the World Bank's (1993) Report on East Asia. This is unsatisfactory for a number of reasons.

First, the vast majority of World Bank contributions in this and other areas are not of a scholarly and balanced standard. It is strange that the critical standards displayed in the rest of their Review should be abandoned in this context.[12] Second, then, it is not a matter of differing opinions of equal weight. The World Bank literature has been subject to devastating criticism in the past as is demonstrated in our Chapters 2 and 3, and this ritual slaughter has continued unchecked since our book appeared.[13] Third, in any case, the dichotomy of state versus market is a false one. Rather, it is a question of how underlying economic and political interests are represented both through the state and through the market, the perspective adopted throughout our book and which renders otiose the reminder from Bell and Farrell that policy is endogenous, particularly in the light of our critical discussion of the developmental state by what we term the economic and political schools.[14] Fourth, even if in a limited way and in an attempt to retrieve the policy and intellectual agenda, these points have already begun to be accepted within the World Bank itself, not least in the latest World Development Report (World Bank, 1997, The State in a Changing World) and most notably in Stiglitz's (1998) latest contribution appealing for the creation of a Post-Washington Consensus.

12 See Wade (1996), in particular, for an account of the lack of independence of the World Bank's East Asia study.

13 See Amsden (ed.) (1994), Fine and Stoneman (1996), the special issue of *Journal of International Development*, vol 9, no 6, 1997, devoted to the World Bank's assessment of privatisation, and Bayliss and Fine (eds) (1998). For an even longer view, see Fine (2025b).

14 See also Fine and Stoneman (1996).

CHAPTER 5

Engaging the MEC: Or a Lot of My Views on a Lot of Things

Postscript as Personal Preamble

This Chapter derives from a paper prepared for a workshop arranged by Vishnu Padayachee at the University of KwaZulu-Natal, June, 2008 (although the actual location, as was commonplace for such events was in a beautiful country-side retreat). Assessing the MEC was the theme, and I was designated to present the opening to put the case positively against which other participants could respond. As will be apparent, I took the opportunity to lay out in detail a wide-ranging account not only of the MEC itself but also of its history and methodological and theoretical foundations. As a relatively small workshop with invited participants only, all under some obligation to circulate papers in advance so that best use could be made of the time available, I expected that my paper (prepared well in advance) would have been read in advance. Judging from the list of invitees, I was anticipating heated discussion and a tsunami of criticism.

As a result, I made my presentation brief and to the point, wishing to leave as much time as possible for criticism and response. But I was shocked to see Vishnu's face of surprise as I finished my brief opening (especially relative to the length of my paper) as he clearly expected me to go on for much longer. I suspect the same was true of the other participants as commentary was limited and strained, offering little criticism for me to answer. After the event, I recall being bitterly disappointed, in part for having let Vishnu down, but also as what I had hoped to have been an opportunity for debate and, by winning, to promote the MEC framing across South African political economy.

My presentation was ultimately published in *Transformation*, for which a special issue had been planned to come out of the workshop. The published paper was drastically shortened and I have five or more versions of it as such on record. This Chapter restores the longer as well as including some of the material added to the later, shorter version (in part as an Appendix to this Chapter). Significantly, the only other paper apparently derived from the workshop came from Bill Freund (2010) for I do not recall the availability of others with the possible exception of Roberts and Rustomjee (2010), each endorsing the MEC framing in particular interpretations of South African industrialisation

 | DOI:10.1163/9789004748330_006

as a developmental state around core MEC sectors (Freund, 2013 and 2018, leading in his hands to pessimism about future post-apartheid prospects, Fine, 2025e, Ch. 2).

In retrospect, this is all a bit sad, and a sorry commentary on the state of South Africa's political economy quite apart from the political economy of South Africa. Much of the content of my long piece had long been available, not least as it drew heavily upon a contribution to a Perth conference at the turn of the millennium (Fine, 1999b). The major elements were all in place covering not only the nature and gestation of the MEC and the 'MEC' but also some of its key aspects – the failure to diversify from core MEC sectors, the stop-go of growth as the sucking in of imports with growth brought about balance of payments problems, the enduring problem of (illegal) capital flight, the unnecessarily high exchange and interest rates to cover balance of payments not least to support the value and impact of capital flight, and the prospect developmentally of at most a renewal of core MEC expansion.[1] In this light, there is huge potential to criticise the MEC approach from unsympathetic quarters. At a general level, as the MEC changes, so it can be designated as no longer existing, or never having existed. And for particular elements, the core, the conglomerates, the state, the composition of output, etc., change in one or other of these alone can be taken as evidence of the absence of the MEC. None of this is to suggest the MEC approach is sacrosanct, only that it can be partial in coming to a judgement over its veracity. In the event, criticism was and remains muted.

Nonetheless, the MEC Workshop was indicative that change was in the air after a decade and a half of neoliberal policymaking with the prospect of renewing the political economy of South Africa in the wake of dissatisfaction with the post-apartheid experience. Clearly, Vishnu felt debate around competing approaches could be broached through taking the MEC as focus. But I had myself been heavily absent(ed) from the South African policymaking and research scene for a decade or so, if actively continuing training and teaching in alternatives, in response to demands placed upon me. Yet, I found upon renewal of engagement that little had moved on. Whatever we said at the time of the transition remains valid. And all the talent that had been progressive in the struggle against apartheid found itself in the enviable position of

1 Note that financialisation warrants what is a relatively early presence in my work in this contribution. Understanding the importance and impact of stop-go and of a high exchange rate were also prompted by knowledge of Britain's economic history not least, respectively, from the relatively poor growth performance during the golden age after the second world war growth and the return to gold in the 1920s.

opportunities for enrichment and status through private and/or public opportunities, with corresponding habituation to neoliberal and pro-government modes of thought. South African political economy was in the doldrums. In this light, as in part anticipated in the Perth piece, there was much to worry about as far as progressive research was concerned in the post-apartheid period (and see final paragraph of this Chapter, its Appendix, and Chapters 1 and 11).

This was, then, a context in which patience was running out with ANC neoliberalism – something that had been tolerated as essential in light of the powers and wishes of global capital. That this had required a historic compromise was argued most forcibly at the Perth conference by Eddie Webster and his co-author (Webster and Adler, 1999) for which, in the immediate aftermath of being exposed to it, I offered a riposte reproduced here as an Appendix. In the event, the discontent within South Africa beyond the world of scholarship expressed itself in the rise of Zuma and 'state capture' in place of Thabo Mbeki's continued Presidency. It is not getting what you want that is the problem, it is wanting it when you get it.

1 Introduction[2]

"The Ego Reminiscence Ratio (ERR) (the proportion of a person' speech devoted to their past – 'when I was …' and 'I remember when …' etc.) is supposedly higher among men than women, rises with age, on retirement leaps to a new high level, is higher in the evening than the morning, and rises sharply with the consumption of alcohol" (Chambers, 2005, p. 67).

In a contribution reflecting upon ten or, more exactly, twenty years of the 'MEC', I have found it more or less irresistible not to dwell upon my own intellectual history and its role in making the MEC. This may have meant that I have descended much too far into a sad exercise in self-indulgent nostalgia around my own contributions and flawed aspirations, and even been reduced

2 Initial draft for discussion and only to be cited as such. Thanks to Vishnu Padayachee for comments on a first draft. This is the last of three papers written more or less simultaneously over the past couple of months. Inevitably, there is some overlap but it is relatively limited other than as indicated. Fine (2008a and b) focus more on the current character of the MEC and the putative character of South Africa as a developmental state with the latter also addressed in Fine (2007b). Together these papers represent a renewal of work on South Africa after a ten-year break and, in so short a time after so long an absence, inevitably fail to do full justice to material developments as well as the available literature. Apologies both to the reader and to those whose contributions have been overlooked and even misrepresented.

to levelling recriminations against others involved.[3] But, hopefully, the account that follows is not entirely wasted in that its self-centredness does seek to offer something over and above a set of what are rapidly becoming forgotten intellectual traditions and the rationale for them. First is to emphasise the richness of the analytical content and energy that went into study of the MEC. Second is to promote the notion itself in scholarly, rhetorical and policy circles for still capturing better than any other term the continuing dynamic of the South African economy. And third is to inspire wider application of the MEC to the past, present and future although this needs to be done through a judicious combination of appropriate theory, its limitations, and its sensitivities to South African realities.

In this light, the following section gives an account of the way in which the 'MEC' came into being as a result of my engagement both with the South African economy and the ANC as the latter took its first steps in drafting economic proposals with the prospect that they might be implemented. To begin with, I appear to go off on tangents, taking a step or two back from South Africa itself to highlight the broader intellectual, political and ideological influences at the time that informed the notion of MEC, ranging over Marxist value theory, the British economy, Thatcherism and more. As a result, the MEC is shown to have been a careful and thorough mix of theoretical and empirical elements, and not a terminological and dogmatic fix for empirical and polemical purposes. This is not the place to replicate a specification of the MEC but it is worth emphasising how much it has been misunderstood even by those who support it, let alone those who do not. For, whilst the MEC is centred on a core set of sectors, it is much more than this in the economic, political and ideological connections that it does or does not forge more generally. As such, it is an instance of what might now be termed a system of accumulation, applied to South Africa in particular, seeking to examine how specific, concretely defined, economic interests give rise to corresponding patterns of accumulation of capital and the consequences that flow from this as such a system evolves.

For this reason, and partly through exploration of the relevance of the developmental state literature for understanding the South African economy, considerable effort was spent in exploring the South Korean economy for comparative purposes. The results of this found their way into the beginning of Fine and Rustomjee (1996), and might now appear anomalous. A more general

3 The following does offer heavy critique of others that hopefully will cause neither offence, disappointment nor surprise. Those mentioned have been good friends and without whom much of what I have accomplished would have been impossible. The option is surely open for them to respond in terms of their own continuing contributions and trajectories.

framework around linkages and agencies was also constructed to underpin the notion of system of accumulation (Fine, 1992c),[4] and has been taken up by others such as Lee (2002) for the South Korean car industry and Saraswati (2007) for Indian IT, with other doctoral students working on topics such as South Korean and Japanese steel, and Nigerian oil. The point is to examine the rhythm of relations between state and private capital, patterns of outcomes including developmental success and failure, and the incidence of policy with corresponding causes and effects.

If section 2 provides the background to the launch of the MEC approach, section 3 offers an account of the generally negative, or lack of, reception encountered by the MEC once the post-apartheid government was in place. In a sense, the MEC suffered a fate parallel to that of the MERG (1993) project, if in the realm of ideas as opposed to policy, and much less acutely. The same forces that brought it into being were to disown it before there was any chance of secure and sound foundations across scholarship, rhetoric and policy.

This is despite, as argued in section 4, the continuing relevance of the MEC for understanding the South African economy. Here, considerable emphasis is placed upon the extent to which the post-apartheid economy has, at least until recently, been dominated by the globalisation and financialisation overhang attached to its domestic conglomerates. Directly and indirectly, policy has been dictated by, if not confined to, the imperative of allowing for the conglomerates' orderly and beneficial export of capital. On the other hand, it seems as if policy is now working itself once more towards a state-led expansion of the MEC core, reminiscent of the 1970s, through renewal of public investment in state corporations, especially around energy and transport but with as much private participation as can be engendered (domestic conglomerate, FDI and, of course, parasitic BEE). This is a matter of enormous importance for contemporary debate, both in teasing out what is happening as well as in offering and strategising for alternatives.

In addition, section 5 suggests directions in which the MEC might be deployed in examining both the past and broader socioeconomic aspects of the South African formation. Apart from history and policy, it ranges over topics such as labour markets (at some length), social and economic infrastructure, and technology, although these are only offered as suggestive avenues for further research.

---

4 Note that this working paper was one of eleven that had been delayed in issue waiting upon my move from Birkbeck to SOAS in April, 1992. Six of these concerned work on the MEC, all but this one subsequently published in one form or another, the other five concerning detailed empirical research on UK household acquisition of consumer durables!

The concluding remarks express concern over the fate of radical scholarship and thinking around South Africa, with concepts such as race, class and capital no longer deployed as once they were. Possibly greater attention to the MEC might offer some remedy by emphasising the economic without degenerating into economic reductionism, and by drawing on theory without neglecting specificity.

In short, in looking back upon a decade since the publication of Fine and Rustomjee (1996), I begin in Section 2 with reflection on how the idea of the MEC came into being. This is followed by an account in Section 3 of the continuing evolution of the MEC after the democratic transition, emphasising the roles of both financialisation and export of conglomerate capital. Section 4 suggests how the MEC could provide a much broader fulcrum on which to understand South Africa's economic and social history (and prospects). And the concluding remarks reflect upon the challenges facing scholarship in the years ahead.

2 The History of the 'MEC'[5]

I was first approached to contribute towards ANC economic policymaking in 1984. At that time, I was an academic at Birkbeck College, University of London, but I had also taken a half-time post on secondment as joint research editor to the Industry and Employment (I&E) Branch of the Greater London Council which was about to be abolished by Mrs Thatcher.[6] Its various activities were to be devolved to higher or lower levels of government, with the exception of five functions, including economics, for which it was considered there would be no need for a dedicated, London-wide authority.[7] Secure in the knowledge that its policies would never be implemented, and drawing upon its workforce

---

5 This section offers an expanded and revised account first given in an unpublished paper for a conference in Perth, Australia in 1999. Later versions of that paper excluded this account (Fine, 1999b) but added a critique of Webster and Adler (1999) (see Appendix to this Chapter) who presented at the Perth Conference. It also draws upon an unpublished paper (Fine, 1998b), originally presented to the TIPS Conference in Johannesburg, September, 1998, although that paper focused much more on an early critique of the newly-emerging Post-Washington Consensus, and its implications for scholarship and policy in theory and practice.

6 My co-editor was Teresa Hayter.

7 The others were general strategic planning, policing, ethnic minorities, and women. Greater London government was subsequently reinstated in 2000, by the Blair government, with transport as its major function and with Ken Livingstone returning in triumph and continuing as Mayor until his defeat by Boris Johnson in May, 2008. The current mayor, Sadiq Khan, lives on the same street as me!

of almost two hundred, including many economists,[8] I&E created a wealth of policy documents including the *London Industrial Strategy* (LIS), and the *London Labour Plan* (LLP) (GLC, 1985 and 1986), to both of which I was a contributing editor.[9] The first of these was heavily influenced, at least for a number of sectors, by the newly emerging flexible-specialisation, flec-spec, approach associated with Piore and Sabel (1984) which subsequently proved influential in South Africa through the Industrial Strategy Project (ISP, 1995), see below. The Director-General of I&E was the inspirational Robin Murray, who fell for and propagated the flec-spec approach in a big way, having previously been based at the Institute of Development Studies (IDS), University of Sussex.

I was totally sceptical about the flec-spec approach, and this entailed considerable if generally cordial conflict with Robin Murray over the policy documents. My opposition was based on both theoretical and empirical reasoning, and was well-informed by knowledge of the literature as I had jointly taught with one of flec-spec's leading proponents, Jonathan Zeitlin, on a course on the economic history of the UK over the past century.[10] I was also mindful of the desire, if not the need, for the London Industrial Strategy both to make a grand statement (as political and ideological opposition to Thatcherism) and yet to be attached to some sort of rationale for the limited policies that the GLC was capable of implementing given its resources, powers and circumstances. For the UK, given the major role played by multinationals in Britain's deindustrialisation, and the decline of inner-city manufacturing, the GLC was powerless to intervene in the major changes going on at that time in the absence of a supportive and determined central government that was most notably absent. Far from the veracity of flec-spec dictating GLC policy, the inability to intervene other than at the level of small-scale firms rendered it an attractive policy framework to lend ideological support to those limited GLC interventions that were within the bounds of possibility. In practice, such industrial interventions were little short of disastrous with, paradoxically, much loss-making

8 Affectionately dubbed GLCSE since many of these were drawn from the CSE, the UK Conference of Socialist Economists.

9 The *London Financial Strategy* was redlined as far as my participation was concerned. Ken Livingstone has been notably favourable to the City as a global financial centre and, as such, as an asset to the London economy.

10 Sabel and Zeitlin (1985), for example, for the astonishing notion that mass production was, in a sense, a big historical accident, against which the beloved and idealised flec-spec is the delayed triumph of an alternative industrial logic.

compensated for by capital gains on industrial property purchased but never used for industrial workshops.[11]

The early eighties also marked the end of a period of concern about the long-term performance of the British economy, its having given way to debate around the putative productivity miracle of Thatcher's second term of office. Fine and Harris (1985) both critically assessed the earlier literature and also offered an explanation of its own, drawing upon a series of contributions on the performance of the British economy. We centred on the lack of coherent long-term industrial planning in the UK, pointing to the interaction between economic and political factors. British finance had been short-term and international in its orientation, unlike its West German and Japanese counterparts. Both in its lending and in its direct and indirect influence over policy – financiers in high places and the rule of the money markets, respectively – British banks had had no interest as such in providing long-term finance for, and as a lever upon, the restructuring of British industry. This had itself been dominated by multinational corporations with global strategies, deploying the British workforce on the three low basis, low investment, low productivity and low wages. The latter reflected, contrary to popular wisdom, the weakness of the British trade union movement, despite its reputation for militancy, and especially in pushing successfully for industrial policy. In short, neither individually nor collectively through the state, were the three great powers in the UK able or willing to adopt appropriate industrial strategy. Policy remained piecemeal, uncoordinated, without long-term objectives and, given these characteristics, subject to shifts and turns. In this respect, Thatcher's economic policies, even privatisation, were to be understood as highly interventionist, even if under the guise of *laissez-faire* ideology, and to reflect considerable continuity, rather than a break, with the practices of the past.[12] In a word, research on the British economy had been informed by a focus on industrial restructuring as the basis for explaining and promoting economic performance and that the

11 The true story of social criteria sacrificed to commercial imperatives and the wasted investments in, to put it kindly, undeserving firms has never been told. Loyalty to the GLC, especially under the threat of abolition, and simple lack of facts made available, has muted criticism. For the price of a drink or three, I am happy to redress the balance, and Vella Pillay, as a board member of the GLC's Greater London Enterprise Board, would have been able to tell even more. For an 'official' account, see MacIntosh and Wainwright (eds) (1987). For critique of flec-spec in the South African context, see Fine (1995b) but also Fine (1998a, Ch. 4) for a more general critical assessment.

12 See Fine (1997d and e) for consideration of South African privatisation and, most recently, for Sub-Saharan Africa but of relevance for South Africa, Bayliss and Fine (eds) (2008).

organisation and promotion of economic and political interests was decisive in governing outcomes.

At the same time as all of this, I was also serving as an economic advisor to the British National Union of Mineworkers (NUM). One of the outcomes of the year-long 1984/85 strike against pit closures, a concession to stop the pit deputies from joining the strike which would have closed all mines for legal reasons, was for the workforce to have the right to go to an independent tribunal in case of proposed pit closure. Economic evidence submitted to the tribunals focused on the 'social' costs of closure, comprising redundancy payments, unemployment benefit, lost output, lost direct and indirect taxes, and the knock-on effects to other industries, the local community and balance of payments through lost expenditure and sales.[13] On a wider scale, especially with the privatisation programme of the Thatcher government, it became apparent that coordinated expansion across state (nationalised industries) and private capital was being wasted from the past and jeopardised for the future, given linkages between coal, electricity, steel, water and car manufacture for example. For polemical purposes, I described this as if a kamikaze pilot were making his way through the input-output table of the British economy.

Other than the above, and my position within the British Communist Party as firmly opposed to its Eurocommunism sect that not only promoted new social movements but also increasingly saw class and trade unions as their

13 Tackling these issues was brilliantly pioneered by the late Andrew Glyn (1984). In the event, victory at the Tribunal proved Pyrrhic. The Coal Board still insisted on closure even against Tribunal recommendation, interpreting the wording of the agreement by the letter rather than the spirit, in the sense of only having to take Tribunal conclusions into account and not to be bound by them. The employer also threatened punitive redundancy terms in case the workforce undertook the option of Tribunal reference. See Fine (1990a) for a full account for the issues covered in this paragraph. Note, though, that this experience came in handy given the opportunity in the Labour Market Commission, see below, to question Chris Stals, then Governor of the Reserve Bank and just prior to the announcement of GEAR. When asked by me the reason for high levels of unemployment in South Africa, he responded that the Bank's model indicated that real wages were too high. This led me to ask at what level of real wages would the Bank's model give rise to full employment, to which there was no answer, twtwna. Asked if there was a case for housing finance to be subsidised to generate employment and provide cheap homes, he responded that this was a microeconomic question but that he would have to advise government of the negative macroeconomic implications. Asked for his response to the idea of a subsidy to keep gold mines open, he replied this was a microeconomic question but that he would have to advise government of the negative macroeconomic implications. I pointed out that gold contributed 40% of foreign exchange and this was surely a macroeconomic question, twtwna. Stals continued in post until 1999.

antithesis, I had no qualification to advise on South Africa.[14] But, no doubt reflecting the ANC's first tentative steps towards constructing post-apartheid policy, I was asked to join a small group led by Laurence Harris, Economic Research on South Africa (EROSA), set up as the counterpart to the earlier RESA, Research on Education for South Africa. The latter had been organised by Harold Wolpe, and I involved myself in RESA as an outsider as much as I could. Inevitably, this placed me in contact with Harold's wider and earlier work concerning the reproduction of labour power and articulation of modes of production as well as the political formulations around colonialism of a special type and so on.

Because of longstanding work on the coal industry (Fine, 1990a, for example), my first task for the ANC, through the EROSA group, was to assess the prospects for mining. As a lefty with no particular previous experience of South Africa, my knowledge was predominantly gleaned from the anti-apartheid movement, with its emphasis in the economic sphere focusing on trade boycotts and the role of direct foreign investment by multinationals into South Africa. However, my entry into research was dominated by two publications, each of crucial and complementary significance. One was the Report of the Commission of Inquiry into the Electricity Industry (de Villiers, 1983), and the other was Duncan Innes' (1984) account of Anglo-American. From the two publications, I gained an understanding, respectively, of the significance of the state and of domestic corporate capital in the economy, and, by means of a short and obvious analytical step, the interaction between the two. After more detailed research on mining and energy and on corporate structure, I early on formulated the notion that South Africa had been dominated by what I ultimately termed the Minerals-Energy Complex (MEC).[15] In brief, the MEC is to be understood in terms of the concrete form of accumulation of capital taken in South Africa, centred on a core set of sectors, but reaching beyond them

14 As further background, the Alternative Economic Strategy (AES) had been put forward by the Communist Party of Great Britain and the left of the Labour Party in the context of decline of industrial trade unions but rise of white collar unionism. See London CSE Group (1979) for which I was a co-author as well as Fine et al. (n.d.).

15 My first EROSA (1987a and b and 1988) papers covered electricity, coal and gold. Until the DEP (Department of Economic Planning, later Policy) was established within South Africa, EROSA appears to have played a major research role in formulating economic policy although, like MERG after it, the primary goal was creation of indigenous research capacity. Note that the notion of mixed economy for South Africa, now forgotten, emanated from EROSA through Laurence Harris. It seems to have been designed to defend the role of the state in the economy whilst appeasing *laissez-faire* critics. In retrospect, it appears to have had the opposite effect, smoothing the way for GEAR through the adoption and marginalisation of the RDP.

in terms of corporate control and influence. By the same token, the relations between private capital and the state are imperative to the nature and evolution of the MEC. It should be apparent how earlier work on the UK informed, but did not dictate, that for South Africa.

From these origins, and in light of the term itself, it would be natural to perceive the MEC as primarily a descriptive category contingent upon an empirical assessment of the South African economy. This interpretation has probably been all too common, leading to the idea (itself empirically correct or not) that the MEC has never existed or has ceased to exist in light of the economy's changing composition of output. And, there was, indeed, a very strong commitment in proposing the notion of the MEC to grounding analysis in empirical realities. But there is a sense in which this is also extremely misleading. For there were two more important, analytically prior and complex elements underpinning the conceptual construction of the MEC. First of these was to have drawn upon, often by way of departure, a wide range of theoretical debates that were prominent at the time and in which I was an active participant. These included Marxist value theory, the theory and practice of developmental states, the periodisation of capitalism (and the role of internationalisation, monopolisation and the state), and the apparent parallels with the idea of Military-Industrial Complex.[16] In some respects, the adoption of the MEC occurred despite the inclination to avoid both the economic reductionism and empiricism that it would appear to imply. And, as a result, it was underpinned with a careful and more general methodology involving what was termed a linkage-agency, linkagency, approach.[17]

Just as the MEC did not emerge in an intellectual vacuum, so it was heavily influenced by the imperatives of policy making or, at least, proposing. At this time, as mentioned, I had been heavily embroiled in the Alternative Economic Strategy being put forward by the left of the Labour Party and the Communist Party of Great Britain, as an advisor to the British National Union of Mineworkers in its formally arguing against pit closures before an Independent Tribunal, and as a research editor for the Industry and Employment Branch of the Greater London Council that was about to be abolished by Mrs. Thatcher.[18]

Through these three elements of theory, empirical realities and policy concerns, the MEC was and continues to be understood as an evolving system of accumulation specific to South Africa, incorporating corresponding structures, relations, processes and agencies as well as a particular, evolving composition

16 See Fine and Harris (1979 and 1985), Fine (1992 and 1993b) and EROSA (1992).

17 See Fine (1992c and 1993a).

18 See London CSE Group (1979), Fine (1990a) and GLC (1985 and 1986).

of output. In a sense, it was possibly fortunate that the MEC had in its own way attained some sort of maturity by the time it was discovered as such in the mid-1980s, casting a bright light not only on its own past but also on what has now become its future. It had already benefited from the massive public sector led investment programme around mining and energy in the 1970s, major political conflicts around large-scale capital had been resolved as Afrikaners had been incorporated and, as conglomerates, the mining houses had both developed major financial interests and were deploying them to extend ownership and control beyond the core MEC sectors.

Having formed the notion of the MEC, it served as a focal point for academic and policy work over the next decade. Such efforts were primarily geared towards serving the ANC although, as part of a wider exercise in training and research. A two-year research project from the UK's Economic and Social Research Council was successfully applied for, beginning in 1990 and ultimately giving rise to Fine and Rustomjee (1996), with my co-author playing at least an equal part in filling out the analysis of the MEC, see also Rustomjee (1994). In policy work, I was heavily involved in MERG (1993), taking responsibility for the contributions on housing, schooling, electrification and health, quite apart from the inconsistent compromise with ISP, see below, in the chapter on industrial policy. MERG, as is often overlooked, had primarily been set up to develop research capacity not to deliver it. I remember very clearly being informed in early 1993 by Vella Pillay, then heading MERG, of the request from the highest level to prepare an alternative policy framework to that on offer from the World Bank and outgoing government. I responded with gentle resistance on the grounds that this would undermine the longer-run goal of creating indigenous capacity, with resort to outside expertise whenever something important or urgent was required.[19] But I deferred to the priorities of the moment (and the movement). However, by this time, both the substance of economic policy and the way it was produced (from on high at one extreme as with GEAR as opposed to organised root and branch discussion in the earlier period leading to the RDP) had changed dramatically. Within six months of its having been commissioned and even before it was published, the MERG

19 It is worth noting that apart from holding an MSc in Economics through part-time study from Birkbeck (where I had taught), Vella had long held a senior post in the London office of the National Bank of China with major responsibility for currency holdings and dealings, and he continued after retirement to be economic advisor to the Bank until 2002. Whilst MERG was often dismissed as wildly unrealistic, it should be acknowledged that its head probably had more experience and training in the necessary pragmatism than those who were so readily dismissive.

Report was disowned by the leadership of the ANC. My work became oppositional and oriented primarily around the trade union movement (Fine, 1994b, 1995a, 1997c and d, 1998b and c, and 2000c). However, I was asked, to my surprise, by the then Labour Minister, Tito Mbweni, to serve as a foreign expert to the Presidential Labour Market Commission (LMC, 1996).[20] But otherwise, this heralded a ten-year period of limited study of the South African economy, more by way of a collapse of demand than conscious and deliberate exercise of personal choice.[21]

The preceding gives some account of how the MEC emerged as an organising framework for understanding the South African economy – in light of attention to everything from input-output tables to Thatcherism. But there were also wider intellectual influences at work that are readily forgotten. Especially important were debates within Marxism, straddling Marxist political economy and value theory in particular, and the response to the influence of French Marxism, both Althusserianism and regulation theory. Whilst taking a firm stance on value theory, albeit expressed in an Althusserian vernacular for which I do not feel primarily responsible, Fine and Harris (1979) were more concerned both to define the current period of capitalism and to draw upon previous work on the British economy (Fine and Harris, 1985). This involved emphasis on a dual periodisation of capitalism: by laissez-faire, monopoly and state monopoly capitalism and, correspondingly, by the internationalisation taken by the forms of capital as commodity, money and production. At the same time, the neoliberal Washington Consensus was at its height of influence, together with concerted opposition in the form of the developmental state paradigm and adjustment with a human face.

This all created a heady mix of analytical elements with which to address the South African economic formation. In addition, especially in light of the relative decline of the US and UK economies, defence economics had emerged to prominence primarily arguing both for crowding out effects (as opposed to tempering stagnationist tendencies, a position that had always been untenable

20 My colleagues at SOAS, John Sender and John Weeks, collaborated with Guy Standing to produce the ILO (1996) background report for the Commission.

21 There were minor exceptions in writing, primarily reflecting an overhang from the past as opposed to new activity (Fine, 1997a, b and e, and 1999b; and Fine and Padayachee, 2000 and 2001) after which a gap until 2007. I also did not push some of these papers for publication but I can offer electronic copies of those interested for all unpublished papers cited here other than those of EROSA which would have to be found in hard copy and dusted off from an attic somewhere.

despite its influence),[22] and more widespread undermining of economic performance through technology policy, etc. Inevitably, this brought the notion of military-industrial complex (MIC) to my attention, long associated with President Eisenhower and then JK Galbraith (1967). But this notion seemed limited in addressing the US economy as a whole (as did the monopoly capital thesis for neglecting internationalisation) and discouraged, if anything, the adoption of the notion of MEC for South Africa for fear of unduly rigid structuralism, functionalism and misunderstanding by association.[23] But, in the event, reason and realism prevailed with the notion of the MEC understood as the form taken by the accumulation of capital as it evolved in South Africa, incorporating specific relations, sectors, structures and dynamics.

3 The Reception of the MEC

I am not in a position to pass serious judgement on the reception of the MEC in scholarly, policy and more popular discourse. I have not studied how and how much the idea has been deployed and am otherwise subject to bias irrespective of my own paternal/maternal rights. I am liable to take note of the use by others where it might otherwise escape notice but I have also, over a ten-year period, been aloof from the South African scene. Being of a modest disposition, despite the evidence of this paper to the contrary, I have not sought to push the MEC on others and certainly not to investigate and applaud or contest its use or rejection. The exception that proves the rule is the debate between Bell and Farrell (1997 and 1998) and Fine and Rustomjee (1998).

For the first time, for the purposes of this paper, I made a Google search for 'minerals-energy complex' and came up with 15,000 or so entries. I suspect this reduces to half if Amazon and the like and Patrick Bond are excluded. I also suspect that you need to score at least a million or so to be considered to have made any sort of impact.[24] But, possibly reflecting my prejudices, and despite the Google references across an impressive array of applications and users, generally extremely positive and/or taking it for granted, the MEC does

22 For an account of its unusual origins in the work of Paul Sweezy, see Fine (1988, 1990a and 2009i).

23 Nonetheless, I did furnish on demand a policy paper from EROSA on the South African military-industrial complex, inspired by the policy work on conversion (from military to civilian production) at the GLC and SAMIC's attachment to the MEC (EROSA, 1992). See also Fine (1993b).

24 By way of comparison, social capital, on which I have worked and published extensively, googles 11 million entries and, when Fine is added, this reduces to half a million.

not seem to be prominent. Most significant is the failure even to acknowledge it by those who would, presumably, reject it.

Whatever the merits, then, of the MEC in these terms, it has not prevailed other than amongst a minority of both committed and occasional adherents. Why is this so or, more constructively, tracing where the MEC is or is not used, and how and for what purposes, is a potential source of investigation within the sociology of knowledge. From the earlier account, it is apparent that the MEC became associated very rapidly with dissident scholarship, rhetoric and policy stance. What follows is a harsh, even offensive, judgement but economic analysis and policy around the time of the transition became either the prerogative of mainstream, narrow-minded orthodoxy or of non-economists. The depth of understanding incorporated in the MEC may not have been appreciated in any sense of the term. Nonetheless, its close correspondence with the empirical realities of the South African economy did, and continues to, allow for it to be embraced at different levels of understanding. So the antipathy to the MEC runs deeper and must be sought elsewhere.

My first visit to South Africa was in 1987 at the request of the ANC to review the work of the Economic Trends, ET, group. ET was run by Stephen Gelb and was strongly supported from NUMSA through participation of Alec Erwin. The organising framework for ET was the idea of racial Fordism, inspired by Gelb. This was a point of difference with, from my perspective, the framework of regulation theory crudely and inappropriately imposed upon the South African economy (Gelb, ed. 1991). My impression of those engaging in the sectoral studies within ET was that it allowed them to do their research, and they were prepared to go along with the framework as long as it did not get in the way. Very few positively used it, and it was probably inapplicable at any level of detail (and, reflecting an element of underconsumptionism, unable to address the fate of non-consumption sectors – why should gold and capital and intermediate capital goods be restricted by race).

It was, however, indicative of personal and intellectual opportunism that grew out of all proportions as the Industrial Strategy Project emerged out of ET. Intellectually, ISP also took its inspiration from French Regulation theory, especially in its flec-spec, post-fordism version, and it was spearheaded by Raphie Kaplinksy (a disciple in this respect of Robin Murray at IDS) and gathered together a number of those who had previously studied at Sussex. Of course, from an MEC-perspective, irrespective of the merits of flec-spec in the wider world (its now having declined to nothingness other than in the perpetually evolving global commodity/value chain approach), the ISP had practically nothing to say about the major sectors of the South African economy and, with minor exceptions, ISP was inevitably self-limiting to those sectors that might be interpreted within its analytical orbit. To me, this seemed like the GLC rationale turned upside down. For it, you could only work with small-scale industry, so flec-spec was adopted. For ISP, flec-spec was adopted, so you could only work with small-scale industry.

Inevitably, ISP and MEC were entirely incompatible but ISP prevailed in discursive circles merely by weight of numbers, resources and connections (with NUMSA and Alec Erwin in particular). In retrospect, it has had little or no impact upon policy and, at most, survives on the margins most notably in the group around Mike Morris, whereas others including Kaplinsky have moved on, possibly as if they had never subscribed to the approach.[25] At most ISP served the role of creating a smokescreen around debating and formulating industrial policy. In this respect, it conformed to two holy cows in the economic historiography of South Africa that the MEC approach had been determined to slaughter, not least in securing foundations for future policy and the challenges that it posed. First is the belief that South Africa's industrialisation had been based on a (failed) import-substituting industrialisation around consumer goods. On the contrary, this was to focus attention on the wrong goods and the wrong policies. For South Africa's industrialisation had been the consequence of development, if within limits, around the core MEC sectors. Accordingly, it remains the gap between this core and the consumer goods industries that needs to be filled by active intervention.

Second, then, South Africa's industrial policy had primarily been seen in terms of protection of consumer goods. But equally if not more important has been the support given to the MEC through the formation and promotion of state corporations such as ESKOM, ISCOR and SASOL, and the coordinated expansion of private and state capital around the MEC and MEC-related sectors. In this light, industrial policy for the post-apartheid economy looks very different from the intra-sectoral fiddling attached to the ISP and its failure to get to grips with the core structures, processes and dynamics of the MEC, let alone the entrenched economic and political interests to which they are attached, alongside the addition of an evolving Black Economic Empowerment (BEE), partially realigned from SME promotion to corporate incorporation.

25 Note that Dave Lewis has become more rounded in his stance on the MEC, possibly reflecting his co-directing the Labour Commission but especially in coming up against the conglomerates as head of the Competition Board. See Lewis et al. (2004).

4 Post-apartheid Economy

Elsewhere I have argued that the post-apartheid economy has continued to be dominated by the MEC but with new features coming to the fore (Fine, 2008a). From an early stage, it was emphasised that the South African conglomerates had been frustrated in their attempts to globalise their operations by exchange controls from 1985 and by the stigma attached to apartheid (Fine, 1997c), with Rustomjee (1991) having studied illegal capital flight before working with me on the MEC. But globalisation has also increasingly meant financialisation of corporate governance. The two together have exercised a profound effect on the South African economy and, equally, on macroeconomic policy as the imperative of corporate shifting of capital overseas on favourable terms has underpinned the adoption of policies more or less indistinguishable from IMF orthodoxy. Incredibly, the South African economy now has a financial sector that is presumed to account for one fifth of its GDP. But how is it possible that so much by way of financial services should be required to move the real economy (and South Africa has a trade deficit in financial services and so cannot use the UK excuse of earning foreign exchange by providing services abroad)? The answer is that it cannot. Rather than finance servicing the real economy, it is the other way around. One quarter of the real economy is taken to support financial services which are then added on to the level of real output to make up GDP, see below.[26] Whilst there is much evidence to support this view, it does require further theoretical and empirical investigation of some sophistication.[27] Analytically, there is the need to close the gap between how macroeconomic policy is conceived, presented and implemented and how it responds

26 In a study of Ghana (Boateng and Fine, 2000), it was found that the World Bank claimed both that productivity had been increased in agriculture by shedding labour in response to its commercialising policies and that the displaced labour had found employment in the informal sector. But there did not seem to have been any increase in real output across other sectors. The conundrum was resolved by noting that there had been a massive increase in stressed street selling, more people selling the same amount of goods but putatively increasing the level of commercial services. This is an ideal example of the overexpansion of the commercial sector, indicative of the role of the financial sector in some respects, and also of relevance to the functioning of labour markets, see below.

27 Ndikumana and Boyce (2008) examine the extensive capital flight and external debt characteristic of Sub-Saharan African economies, referring to the "revolving door" effect whereby aid inflows sustain private capital outflows. For South Africa, the revolving door has drawn partly upon exporting the domestically generated surplus and also partly upon inward short-term capital movements that places the external account in a state of immanent crisis as discussed.

to and promotes the process of capital export and speculation alongside the continuing functioning of other aspects of the economy.

This offers a very different starting point than the orthodoxy, not least the idea that the stability of the economy, however targeted, is being traded off – and possibly too strongly – against growth or other economic objectives such as expansion of expenditure on health, education and welfare. Such is the view of Stephen Gelb, with his account organised around the notion of a generally unachievable trilemma of exchange rate stability, independent monetary policy, and inflation targeting (Gelb, 2005, for example). But this trilemma approach is based on a false analytical framework from within orthodox macroeconomics – one that separates the short from the long run, is organised around equilibrium, and which treats monetary policy independently of its insertion within a financial system (as opposed to a limited set of markets for assets). This means that the decisive issue governing macroeconomic performance and policy for South Africa even within this narrow perspective, the pressure for capital control liberalisation for domestic conglomerate globalisation and financialisation, is more or less overlooked. The dilemma faced by policy was how to allow capital export as far as possible without bringing down the value of the Rand and, thereby, undermining the worth of capital export itself. This was complicated by the inflow of volatile short-term finance to fund the long-term outflow, something always placing the economy on the edge of financial crisis, thereby justifying neoliberal macroeconomic management. Meanwhile, levels of investment within the domestic economy have remained limited, not primarily because of the lack of attraction to inward investment but because of the external orientation of domestic conglomerates and their failure to invest in the domestic economy at required levels.[28]

Yet, no one in the orthodoxy seems to be able to explain this lack of investment without descending into appeal to ad hoc factors that are blown out of proportion. Thus, in a major report from the World Bank, Clarke et al. (2007, p. 14) conclude that the "investment climate is mostly favourable – power is cheap and relatively reliable, the burden of regulation is not excessive, corruption is low, the ports function relatively well, access to finance does not seem to be a major problem for most enterprises, and most people trust the court system". So, in order to explain why private investment has been so modest in South Africa, other reasons have to be put forward such as exchange rate instability, cost of skilled labour, labour regulation, and cost of crime, and even that their study is too early and insufficient time has passed for the favourable

28 For some work on these issues, see Bond (2003), Andrews (2005) and Mohamed and Finnoff (2004).

factors to have worked through. Significantly, these factors are only hypothesised after the others have failed (and should have been incorporated into the original analysis rather than used to excuse its failings). Capital flight by financialised domestic corporations is, though, notable for its absence! Gelb (2006, p. 4) himself even argues that it is the shadowy presence of alliance opposition to GEAR, despite its absence in formulation, that led to its failure in implementation, discouraging in-flow of capital as GEAR was not perceived to be credible enough.[29] No doubt, this also all weighed heavily on Trevor Manuel's mind as he reduced capital controls on domestic conglomerates and granted permission for them to list overseas.[30]

There is, of course, some evidence to support this interpretation of financialisation-globalisation overhang, although not as much as there should be because such matters have scarcely been investigated on these or other terms. But, indicative of the high level of pressure for disinvestment and how it has increased, Mohamed and Finnoff (2004, p. 2) estimate that *illegal* capital flight from South Africa rose as a percentage of GDP from 5.4% between 1980 to 1993 to 9.2% from 1994 to 2000. From the South African Reserve Bank, Wesso (2001) reckons from 1991 to 2000 that there was an overall net, foreign direct investment, FDI, capital outflow at R386m per quarter. This is not broken down into inflows and outflows and the impact of capital controls is set aside on the grounds that there is no reliable index for capital mobility so that there is no way to account for the impact of capital controls, p. 64. This is a bizarre neglect of responsibility – not to investigate the importance of something because it is difficult to index, especially in light of his own asserted judgement that volatility in net direct investment had been "mainly due to South African firms receiving exchange control approval to invest offshore", p. 68 (see also p. 75).

Chabane et al. (2006) report on a different aspect of disinvestment by domestic conglomerates, providing evidence in support of the position adopted here. For, "Rather than London listings enabling conglomerates to raise capital to fund investments in South Africa, there has been a much more striking pattern of outward acquisition and investments ... total stock of outward FDI has grown from $8.7 billion in 1995 to $28.8 billion in 2004", p. 559. Permission for listings, as pronounced by Trevor Manuel in his 2000 budget speech, has been dependent upon: foreign expansion being integral to the company, that it should be an international concern with high share of revenue outside of

29 Note the contrast with Webster and Adler (1999) where labour is perceived to have conformed to a beneficial if constrained compromise with capital as opposed to frightening it off.

30 The following dozen or so paragraphs draw more or less directly from Fine (2008d).

South Africa, that there should be monetary and balance of payments benefits, and an advantage (to whom?) in raising capital. It is not even clear whether all or some of these criteria need apply and, implementation in practice is discretionary, and secret in application and response by the Minister. There is reference to advantage and benefit to the company and to the balance of payments, although the connection between these and the broader contribution to the economy, and the disadvantaged within it, are diffuse to say the least!

Significantly, Chabane et al. (2006) also report a peak of unbundling deals by domestic conglomerates in 1999, accounting for R80b, p. 555. This also coincided with a spate of mergers and acquisitions between South African and off-shore companies. It is surely not accidental that this followed the raising in the previous year of investment abroad limits to R50m per company outside SADC and R250m per company within SADC. Further raising of the limits and easing of controls have followed in subsequent years. But it does not take a corporate genius to work out that you get more out of the country if you break up a conglomerate into separate companies and benefit from multiple allowances![31]

More generally, the EIU (2007, p. 54) reports for South African financial services that, "The sector is one of the largest and most deregulated within the emerging markets, with sophisticated banking, bond and insurance markets accounting for around 20% of GDP and 1.3 million jobs in total". But does it do its job. It would appear not. For, putting it unduly extremely, apart from taking one quarter of what is produced by the rest of the economy, financial services are, from a variety of perspectives, entirely unproductive. They produce nothing at all other than acts of exchange between willing parties and, increasingly, acts of exchange that only involve, at most, paper products. Yet, in an economy and society in desperate need of transformation, they have grown at almost twice the rate of GDP over the last decade or so but offer no services directly at all to 40% of the population.

In a sense, then, the highly financialised South African economy absorbs a quarter of what is produced and, to add insult to injury, leaves less produced as a consequence, as well as dictating much of macroeconomic policy. To sustain the Rand, for example, reserves were depleted from $4.3b at the end 1995 to

31 Note that Gelb (2005) in a footnote discusses such restrictions in terms of allowances "per project" as opposed to per company but I have no evidence of this. If he were right, companies would have an incentive to unbundle projects into multiple components in order to increase overall allowances available. The bigger point, though, is either lax discretion (specification, enforcement and monitoring of criteria) within whatever are the limits involved, or SARB is essentially making industrial and other policy both undemocratically and with limited powers (to ease capital controls or not upon application).

$2.2b by the end of 1996. Much the same occurred again in 1998, with the use of $1.2b to protect the Rand. This all sheds light on the traditional defence given for South African macroeconomic policy. Trevor Manuel offered the following rationale before the inquiry into the collapse of Rand in December 2001, instigated by accusations that the collapse had been engineered by speculators to make money, and cited in Steyn (2004, p. 126), emphasis added:

> Some commentators have called for a "big bang" approach to exchange control relaxation. At the same time, however, most of the same commentators have recognised the complexities and pitfalls inherent in capital account liberalisation. Mindful of these complexities, government's stated commitment has always been clear and unequivocal – we are committed to a gradual process of exchange control liberalisation that takes into account critical *sequencing* considerations. A sustainable development path requires that certain *conditions* be in place before proceeding to full capital account convertibility.

This is extremely revealing for depending upon appeal to sequencing and preconditions before capital controls can be lifted. This is now accepted as appropriate, even by neoliberal commentators after what has been the extent of financial instability created across the world economy by what is now perceived to have been too rapid a lifting of exchange and especially capital controls without preconditions in place. But, within Central Bank policy and the academic literature, these issues are primarily concerned with regulation, control and transparency of *short-term* capital movements. This is not what has been the South African problem but the long-term overhang of disinvestment attached to domestic conglomerates. Indeed, South Africa would pride itself on its degree of conformity to international financial standards, especially those necessary for allowing regulation of short-term capital movements.

In short, the problem is not one of preconditions and sequencing other than in handling the overhang of disinvestment by South African domestic conglomerates. As Steyn comments, "The debate about a 'big bang' rears its head every now and then. But Manuel prudently chose a gradualist approach, and reforms were timed to coincide with periods when the economy appeared able to withstand the change". But what was the change that was necessary to withstand could not be clearer:

> There can be no doubt that the easing of exchange controls contributed to the rand's slide during the period that Manuel has been finance minister. After years of isolation, the pent-up demand for foreign investment

> by institutional investors and companies was huge. The extent of this demand is illustrated by the fact that, from the introduction of the asset-swap mechanism in 1995 till its abolition in early 2002, institutional investors invested R100 billion abroad.

If, as is to be believed overall from the book in which Steyn contributes, Trevor Manuel is to be judged as a success in his macroeconomic policy, that success resides in managing the outflow of capital by the domestic conglomerates and, it should be added, presenting it as something else in terms of macroeconomic objectives.

Ten years ago, I did raise these issues sharply in terms of the role to be played by the South African financial system (Fine, 1997c).[32] At that time, with the emergence of the Post-Washington Consensus, with Stiglitz to the fore, the idea of different types of financial system had been accepted by (non-neoliberal) orthodoxy, especially with two ideal types – Anglo-Saxon and Japanese-German. Whilst the first putatively involved short-term financing through markets without commitment, the second was based on long-term investment with non-market coordination between banks and industry and presumed to overcome informational asymmetries and short-termism. Irrespective of the empirical veracity of such ideal types in practice, I argued that this overlooked the external power relations and dynamic governing both industrial and financial policy. South Africa, in particular, offered a striking example of both Anglo-Saxon-type banking and conglomerate ownership across banking and industry, with no apparent inner problems of coordination since both sides were owned by the same conglomerates. Consequently, the main issue for South Africa was, and remains, how to transform the financial system into one that provides finance for investment for both economic and social restructuring and development. If anything, I underestimated the importance of financialisation as such, seeing it as merely a means for globalising conglomerate's real activities rather than, increasingly, as a defining aspect of the current stage of capitalism (Fine, 2007a).

Yet, over the past few years, there has also been a shift in the (macroeconomic) policy rhetoric away from GEAR, with explicit commitment towards more state intervention, especially in public investment. Worthy of more investigation is my suspicion that this represents a judgement that handling the overhang of globalisation and financialisation has been accomplished, and there is now to be a renewal of the state-led strategy characteristic of the 1970s,

32 Also the unpublished Fine (1997a) but see Aybar and Lapavitsas (2001).

marked by the expansion of core and directly related MEC sectors.[33] At a more general level, this may also reflect a second phase in the neoliberal project that has financialisation as its defining moment (Fine, 2008c and e and 2009h). An earlier phase, as a sort of shock therapy, simply released market forces as far as possible, with finance to the fore. Now, it requires the state not only to temper the worst excesses that have resulted (keeping the lights on) but also to intervene more extensively to support continuing financialisation as such (financial rescues at enormous cost) and, in the case of South Africa as more generally, its dependence upon the surplus produced elsewhere in the economy from which it cannot escape.

This is not to say that the MEC as a collaboration between state and private capital remained inactive during the GEAR period. Indeed, the state-owned Industrial Development Corporation (IDC) was the major domestic manufacturing investor in the period, often creating jobs at a capital cost of between R5m and R8m in capital per worker, hardly conducive to employment creation (Roberts, 2004, for a wide-ranging discussion). But that this expansion of the economy, even around MEC sectors, should take second place relative to conglomerate globalisation and financialisation is strikingly illustrated by the electricity crisis, again subject to further research and as much as confidentiality, or secrecy, will allow. Ten years ago, as I was withdrawing from work on South Africa, electricity supply was so much in excess supply that power stations under construction were being mothballed. There was the prospect of export of power not only throughout Africa but also into Europe. Reports of capacity shortage and outages upon renewal of work on South Africa were initially received on my part with disbelief. But there's no denying when the lights go out or, of greater pertinence, when the mines stop working. Does this represent erosion of the MEC's interests and/or failure to meet them?

How did this come about? I am not convinced a full explanation is yet available and would involve close interrogation of individuals involved in decision making (not least through an open public enquiry). Within Africa and elsewhere in the developing world, in electricity and for other social and economic infrastructure, privatisation has not delivered, after an initial burst of enthusiasm, the necessary levels of investment. And nor has what has been

33 This overhang of frustrated globalisation and financialisation is very different from that associated with Bob Brenner's (1998) explanation for the world slowdown, although there is evidence that South Africa's incumbent position in the domestic economy discourages foreign direct investment. For critique of Brenner, see Fine et al. (1999 and 2005) but note that explanation of the world slowdown in terms of financialisation implies an over-accumulation of financial assets but an under-accumulation of real capital – in contrast to much of the Marxist rhetoric of the day.

delivered been entirely satisfactory in outcome (Bayliss and Fine, eds, 2008). Unfortunately, the emergence of South Africa's need for new capacity coincided with the late realisation and acceptance that privatisation was not going to deliver, nor even be delivered. For the last four or five years, the World Bank has accepted this and has fallen back upon a strategy of promoting state-led private participation. If the private sector won't do it by itself, the state must make conditions and resources more conducive for its participation. Significantly, the recent report on ESKOM from the World Bank (Kessides et al. 2007) basically concludes that it had performed well but that it still makes sense to promote public-private initiatives where possible, something that has become a matter of dogma where previously the Bank sought to depend upon privatisation alone.

Even so, over the past fifteen years, there have been any number of plans for restructuring electricity supply. I recall in the early 1990s being invited to a one-to-one breakfast with Alan Morgan, then Chief Executive at ESKOM, at the Savoy Hotel, London. I am not sure whether either of us knew what the other was doing there, although he presumably had more of an idea than I did. I formed the impression, though, that, as a fishing exercise on his part in terms of ANC intentions, he had less of an agenda of his own to pursue than a desire to see settled the institutional framework within which to run the business.[34] It should be recalled that this was a time when any number of schemes were being proposed for the new democratic constitution, including a Swiss canton for the Afrikaners, and the same applied to the economy with scenario syndromes, including any number of schemes for the whether and the how of privatising electricity, itself complex across arrangements for generation, distribution and marketing quite apart from the issue of electricity supply to those previously unconnected.[35]

Such uncertainty has remained to the present day, in part contingent upon hope and uncertainty about how and how much the private sector would participate. This goes a long way towards explaining the failure to make the necessary investment in increasing capacity. For the decline in the reserve margin has slowly but steadily evolved over the past decade and recognisably revealed itself in acute form. And yet there has been no capacity added to generation

---

34 There were fears, for example, of some sort of management buy-out as a means to privatise, wildly unrealistic in terms of the investment levels required.

35 Note that in my contribution to MERG on electrification, considerable emphasis was placed on the positive contribution that could be made by ESKOM because of its institutional capacity to deliver but that this should be also harnessed for diversification into electricity use by the newly connected.

between 2002 and 2006.[36] To some extent, this represents a failure of coordination across government departments with this, and corresponding powers, residing predominantly within the Ministry of Finance and the Presidency, at the expense of other Ministries. Otherwise, surely, those of Mineral and Energy Affairs, Trade and Industry and Public Enterprises would have collectively prevailed in expanding provision?

But of crucial importance, and generally overlooked, is the role played by the domestic conglomerates that have had much to lose themselves in the wake of the power cuts. Why did they not press for expansion of capacity on a timelier basis? Historically, of course, the conglomerates have benefited from, even taken for granted, state provision of by far the cheapest electricity in the world (together with profitable contracts for providing coal to power stations). Over the past decade, and for much longer,[37] their individual if not necessarily their collective interests have been served by globalisation and financialisation of their assets, and certainly not tying them up in ESKOM, privatised or otherwise. And the scale of investment required is staggering, over R300 billion over the first five-year period alone or of the order of 17% of GDP.[38] In crude, crowding-out terms, it was a matter of government committing this investment itself or allowing the conglomerates the equivalent to export as capital overseas. Both sides seem to have made the same choice at their mutual expense in terms of electricity supply. Significantly, this need not have been the case by reference to different relations between the state and capital. With 'negotiation' over the new minerals bill, Black Economic Empowerment essentially appropriated 25% of the nation's mineral resources at the expense of the conglomerates and worth R55 billion (Hamman et al. 2008).[39] So, in this arena at least, the state was prepared to act to redistribute wealth but without regard to its creation through deploying such revenue for providing electricity generating capacity.

36 All figures here taken from UBS (2008).

37 I have previously argued that privatisation under the apartheid government would have to have been coerced on South Africa's conglomerates because of their unwillingness to commit resources to the domestic economy, Fine (1997d).

38 As reported in Business Day, 15 May 2008, in wake of a speech from Alec Erwin, "The government and the state-owned enterprises plan to invest about R568bn over the next three years. But the public enterprises department estimates the cost of doubling electricity capacity over the next 16 years, including nuclear power, at about R1,3 trillion. Local sourcing of supplies for this would limit the programme's negative effect on the balance of payments and reduce its vulnerability to global market conditions".

39 The initial demand was for BEE to appropriate 50% of mineral rights, but this was dropped not so much at protest from conglomerates as from the collapse in the value of their mining company shares and fear of biting the feeding hand.

But there are much broader implications even than this. For, as far as industrial policy is concerned, it points to the absence of coherence and determination in policy in South Africa in a rather different way, the definition or understanding of industrial policy itself let alone how and whether it has been implemented. There has been an extraordinary narrowing of understanding of what is meant by industrial policy and the capacity to implement it. Striking is the claim of Morris et al. (2006, p. 206) that, "The industrial policy designed by the Industrial Strategy Project ... *and adopted by the new democratic South African regime* was founded on a view that 'competitive advantage must also be derived from intra and inter firm cooperation'", emphasis added. It is a moot point whether ISP offered very much by way of policy, whether it was adopted, and whether it engaged at all with the major policies being adopted and influencing the progress of industry. Appropriately, Dave Kaplan (2007, p. 91), a leading member of ISP and for a time Chief Economist at the Department of Trade and Industry, concludes that, "First, industrial policy should not, in the current context be too ambitious. Second, given limited governmental capacities, a more prominent role should be accorded to the business sector". As indicated, he bases these conclusions on the limited institutional capacity to deliver policy. This raises questions over why, if this is the case, industrial policy has not been more extensive (and failed) since there can be no presumption that limited capacity to deliver policy entails limitation of policy to that capacity, why existing capacity has been distributed as it has (to macroeconomic management and to the financial sector for capital export, and, of course, to BEE), and why it has not been distributed elsewhere, and what is being done to raise institutional capacity (Fine, 2008a).

In this light, consider trade policy, for example. In the past, this was very much a matter of protection on demand to small-scale Afrikaner capital to secure survival. With minor exceptions, this has been cast aside in the post-apartheid period, with tariff reduction exceeding WTO membership requirements, MEC core sectors the main beneficiaries, and black labour-intensive employment the main casualty (Fine, 1997c). This paper also forcibly argued within the confines of orthodoxy itself that industrial as trade policy is fundamentally flawed in relying upon notions of effective rates of protection – as, outside a two-good world, such a notion cannot be properly defined theoretically, cannot be properly measured empirically even if it could be defined, and even if it could be defined and measured, effective rate of protection reduction is not necessarily beneficial.[40] The broader conclusion is that trade cannot be considered legitimately in isolation from other elements of industrial policy. As you have

40 See also Deraniyagala and Fine (2001 and 2006).

to have a trade policy (even if neoliberal), it follows that you have to take a stance, however wittingly, on other areas of policy with which it interacts.

By contrast, for Kaplan, a virtue is made out of a narrow definition of industrial policy, and a narrow definition is made into a necessity. For, in addition, Kaplan praises the Western Cape microeconomic development strategy as a model that might be followed by central government. But it is worth noting what view is taken by those themselves who have responsibility for implementing that model in light of the power crisis, citing McDonald (2008, Ch. 1):

> A survey of business attitudes in Cape Town undertaken in late 2006 by the Western Cape Investment and Trade Promotion Agency (Wesgro) underscored these corporate concerns. Some 71 per cent of firms interviewed cited "electricity reliability" as the second largest "constraint" on business growth in the city (after crime), noting that unreliable electricity supply had a "serious debilitating impact on their business".

From this can be drawn four implications. First, it is necessary to slaughter the two holy cows in the economic historiography of South Africa – that (flawed) industrialisation took place through protection of consumer goods, and that industrial policy was essentially a matter of tariff protection. Second, then, the notion of industrial policy should be much more widely stretched to incorporate whatever is necessary to guarantee industrial success including, as indicated here, the question of national and local power supply. Of course, this is not a matter of throwing in everything that you can think of but of incorporating those issues that are of significance to success for specific interventions. Third, as already suggested and more specifically, this is neither a matter of leaving power supply to the private sector nor of the absence of the institutional capacity of government to deliver. Rather, government has failed to intervene out of deference to the private sector. Fourth, and possibly most important, this all suggests that it is not possible to have an effective industrial policy unless it is extensive. For no or little policy even with limited capacity, relying on the 'market', can arguably be worse than an imperfectly implemented policy with ambition. Even if the 'market' (i.e. conglomerates) know best and have the best capacity, they do not necessarily do best – just as we would not, presumably, leave defence policy to the arms manufacturers on the grounds that they know best what are weapon capabilities and how to use them.[41] Those with superior resources may have unacceptable motives

41 I do recall that, as discussant at the TIPS conference, Kaplan's fiercest objection to Fine (1998b) was to my closing comment, especially as emphasised by him that conglomerates might be coerced if not cooperating, see Concluding Remarks to the Appendix

and pursue them dysfunctionally for the rest of the population and even for themselves – although South Africa's conglomerates are probably not ruing their failure to take on Eskom's electricity supply on their own account.[42]

Diversity of outcomes – for electricity supply, on the one hand, as opposed to BEE enrichment, on the other, through mineral leases – arises out of the tensions in the structures and dynamics of the MEC and its location within the South African economy today no less than in the past, as with the formation of state corporations in the 1930s but with limited integration across the rest of industry. It is necessary to see the present as the history of the post-apartheid economy in the making as the MEC unfolds even if it does not unravel.

5 From History of "MEC" to History of MEC

It was always my ambition as an academic that the MEC approach should be extended to incorporate other areas of study than the immediate and recent functioning of the South African economy and the policy implications that flowed from this. Inevitably, in rooting the MEC in its past and gaining a hold over its character and dynamic, the history of the MEC was engaged, both within Fine and Rustomjee (1996) and also on other occasions, most notably in Fine (1992a and 1994a) and Fine and Rustomjee (1992 and 1995). But, as with the slaughter of the holy cows of industrialisation and industrial policy, there is considerable re-investigation and re-interpretation of the past that might be engaged. This should go back to the emergence of mining, and draw readily on existing scholarship that has much more easily and fully identified the intersection of race, class and economic and political interests.

This might also go some way towards redressing the balance in existing MEC work in its undue pre-occupation with what capital (and the state) did as opposed to the actions of labour, trade unions and other organisations of resistance and change. Work had begun on South African labour markets, not least in view of attachment to the Labour Market Commission. But most

---

to this Chapter. In contrast, his own inclination is that, "a more prominent role should be accorded to the business sector", presumably without coercion and with the results already experienced post-apartheid and before. The point is not so much our disagreements over the need for voluntarism or coercion but that, at the least, this should be acknowledged and debated rather than passed over by default in the context of the realities of what the conglomerates have been doing.

42 The current tortuous passage to electricity renewables, and self-generation in light of black-outs, is another story.

of this remained unpublished.[43] My own approach grew out of a critique of segmented labour market theory. The latter has an interesting history. It arose out of the idea of dual labour markets, itself associated with a dual industrial structure of highly paid, careered, monopolised, capital-intensive stable employment as opposed to flexible low-paid, unstable jobs in a competitive sector.[44] Inevitably dual led to multiple labour markets in deference to empirical realities, and explanation for these structures was offered in terms of broad socioeconomic determinants both from the nature of jobs supplied (industrial or employer characteristics) and who got to fill them (employee characteristics).

Until the mid-1980s, the idea of segmented labour markets was entirely rejected by mainstream economics in deference to theoretical and empirical models based on human capital (although these always left an unexplained residual by major socioeconomic characteristics such as gender and race). Significantly, with the emergence of the market imperfections approach to economics, segmented labour market theory was appropriated by the mainstream, and is interpreted in terms of endogenously created labour market structures in which initial differences in worker characteristics could be exaggerated into much larger differences in outcomes. Despite this, mainstream empirical work on labour markets has continued to take human capital as its starting point as a means to measure levels of market imperfections in the rewards accruing to workers. In this vein, in an early contribution in the post-apartheid period, Hofmeyr (1994) argued that labour market outcomes had already become less discriminatory and more integrated (i.e. not segmented) because wage differentials had declined once correcting for "non-racial" attributes such as levels of education or regional location.[45]

This is interesting empirically but absurd analytically (Fine, 1998a, p. 110),[46] since it takes major labour market determinants such as location and education as if they are not part and parcel of systemic racialisation and segmentation of labour markets. We know, for example, that the major source of differences in pay between men and women is due to occupational segregation. When men and women do the same job, they tend much more to be paid the same. So, if we correct for occupation in looking at pay differentials, they will be drastically

43 But see Fine (1998a).

44 As I pointed out, the flec-spec school adopted a similar dualism but reversed the benefits of the two types of industry. Piore is the connection between the two.

45 See also Hofmeyr (1993).

46 I drafted an extensive critique of Hofmeyr but it never got to be published, ultimately Fine (1994d) which also incorporated criticism of the World Bank's approach to South African labour markets and especially Fallon (1992).

reduced. And much the same applies to so many factors in which men are more favourably placed than women, and it is this that has to be explained in and of itself and in relation to the functioning of labour markets.

My own approach has been different from both mainstream and radical versions of segmented labour market theory, and is much more careful in understanding the nature of labour market segmentation and of segments themselves.[47] For each of the other approaches, if slightly differently, suggests that socioeconomic factors are thrown together and generate labour market structures with corresponding outcomes in terms of workforce, wages and conditions. By contrast, although such factors are both present and of huge importance, they are complemented by and channelled through the *internal* workings and generation of labour market structures. These might be sectorally specific ("vertically" determined as, for example, in migrant labour to the mines), "horizontally" determined (fluidity across sectors as for those with generic skills or professions), or some combination of the two. In short, it is a matter of recognising not only that labour markets are segmented from one another, with correspondingly different outcomes, but that they also are internally structured and function differently from one another. In other words, labour market segments are only formed concretely out of the organisation, structures and practices attached to (access to) work itself and cannot be entirely read off from broader determinants. I suspect the simplest and most obvious way of recognising this is by reference to the South African mining labour force as opposed to its domestic servants for example.

To a welcome extent, the differentiation of the South African labour markets (not market) is being recognised (as is inevitably so for case studies of particular labour markets where specific internally generated conditions are acknowledged). It is essential, for example, to reject the idea of a simple dichotomy between formal and informal employment, since each category is itself highly differentiated in wages, conditions and mode of functioning.

47 My interest was first prompted by the wish to explain increased female labour market participation in advanced countries and its relationship to standards of living (Fine, 1992b). This has also inspired a very different understanding of how real wages are determined in terms of norms of consumption that do not derive entirely from labour markets themselves as a result of wage levels paid (this itself representing an attempt to get to grips with the meaning of the value of labour power both in value terms and in its 'moral and historical elements'). See Fine (1987 and 1998a) but also Fine (2007c and 2008b). It is significant that my understanding of labour markets should have been informed by attention both to female labour market participation and to its intersection with consumption on which I was also heavily engaged (Fine and Leopold, 1993; and Fine, 2002, for example). See also Appendix to Chapter 3.

Further, the intensive effort on identifying the poor in South Africa, in which (un)employment is a key element, has also revealed corresponding differentiation of working conditions and categories of labour. But to explain these, identification of the internal workings of particular labour markets is imperative.

Consider, for example, the study of Heintz and Posel (2008). By simple scrutiny of the empirical evidence, they do acknowledge differentiation within the informal sectors, not sector. But they do so in order to emphasise the lack of *mobility* across the informal sectors, and take this (alongside overall levels of demand) as the determinant of low levels of informal activity and higher levels of unemployment relative to other countries. The problem here is that (im)mobility between sectors is being asked to do too much analytical and causal work.[48] It has to stand for race, gender, sector and all of the other internal and external factors that shape labour markets (and the extent of mobility itself). In effect, we are implicitly being asked to suppose what would be the effect of abolishing all occupational segregation within and between (informal) labour markets. This might offer a nice measure of labour market discrimination by access to jobs or otherwise but it does not allow us to understand how labour markets are structured and interact with one another.[49]

A more promising approach is to be found, in principle, in industrial sociology and, especially, labour process theory and an explanation for labour market segmentation built upon, but not reduced to, the division of labour within enterprises and the corresponding hierarchies that are formed out of technical change and command of production and/or work. Unfortunately, the pioneer of this approach in South Africa, Eddie Webster, has increasingly moved away from examining (the organisation of) work as such (itself a general trend across the literature with decline in labour process theory, and the associated industrial relations and sociology being redefined as human resource management) and has sought to impose a relatively crude external typology of work types on South African labour markets (Webster and von Holdt, eds, 2005, for example), although this may be motivated by a wish to impose a calculus of

48 To be fair, they do acknowledge, "Barriers to mobility may exist not only between formal and informal labour markets, but also into, and *within*, informal activities themselves", p. 30, emphasis added. Even so, it is not apparent that presence of "barriers" or not is the way to understand the social relations, structures and processes that are attached to labour markets.

49 In my own approach, I have deployed the concept of labour's "access" to work to indicate a much broader notion than degree of mobility between employments. This allows account to be taken of the conditions governing employment within a segment as well as those differentiating between segments.

economic interests upon heterogeneous sections of the workforce in terms of their wage and employment prospects under different types of policy.[50]

What is the significance of the MEC for all of this? First and foremost, the MEC is a major employer of labour and, consequently, is both a source of labour market segmentation and labour market segments, not least as its own more general dynamic both draws upon and contributes to economic and social reproduction. In this respect, there is a correspondence with the potential for the location of the MEC in the historiography of South Africa, since its formation and transformation of (racist) labour markets have been so peculiar. Second, as already indicated, even if not serving itself or in its related sectors as the direct employer of labour, the MEC has a more or less indirect influence upon segmentation elsewhere in the economy, not only influencing levels of employment and unemployment but also the more general conditions in which they operate (and much the same is true of state employment in setting standards in relation to which the private sectors function). Third, then, even where the MEC would appear to have no direct impact upon employment as in some if not across all of the informal sectors, it does, nonetheless, have a profound influence both by virtue of its presence in the economy as a general force and by vacating but constraining the space for alternatives. The most obvious example of this sort of thing, pervasive across the world if with peculiar characteristics within South Africa as elsewhere, is the retail system and its dependence upon both formal and informal types of retailing (Valodia et al. 2007).

I am acutely conscious that the preceding account for labour markets has implicitly drawn upon a tripartite structure of MEC core, MEC related, and MEC detached. The boundaries between these in practice are inevitably fuzzy, not least in the wake of financialisation and conglomeration as there are multiple criteria involved ranging over ownership and productive and other linkages. In addition, the nature of the connections in socioeconomic terms are heterogeneous. As a result, the classification is admittedly rough and ready and at most serves as the basis for further investigation both within and between the categories themselves in order to specify their exact nature.

Three examples are illustrative. For MERG, for example, Zavareh Rustomjee identified what we dubbed a manufacturing-agricultural complex, MAC. This is highly differentiated across products and producers but the relations between manufacturing and agriculture have, not surprisingly, often been found to be mediated by the conglomerates. Similarly, for MERG, if in a different way, the

50 The contrast is most sharp, for example, with Webster (1985). I am intrigued in anticipation of the paper to be presented to the workshop, Bezuidenhout and Webster (2008), not least in light of developments since Fine (1998a) was drafted. I have not followed this up.

role of MEC-finance had profound implications for provision of social and economic infrastructure, most obviously for electrification, insidiously so for the privatisation of health provision through insurance companies, and in the priority given to finance as opposed to simply building in provision of housing. Further, as argued in an early paper, the national system of innovation, or technological performance of the South African economy, has been profoundly influenced by the MEC (Fine, 1993a). Essentially, these examples demonstrate the need to recognise both the capitalistic nature of the South African economy, its specific features and their more general direct and indirect influence on economic and social life even where capital itself is not directly involved.

6 Concluding Remarks

It should be apparent how earlier concerns confronted in work on political economy in general, in policy for the GLC and the British miners, and on the British economy, have had an influence on my understanding of the South African economy and on how economic and social policy needs to be understood and formulated. On the other hand, unlike the contributions of many others, neither an analytical scheme nor comparative experience has been imposed on South Africa in an as if way, from racial Fordism through flexible specialisation in the academic arena and from the unmistakeably neoliberal GEAR to the rhetoric of developmental state in government practice and rhetoric, respectively.[51] Rather, analysis has proceeded from the economic and social realities of South Africa itself, as captured by the notion of the MEC both as an appropriation of those realities and an investigative tool. This involves an understanding pitched at different levels of analysis, ranging from consideration of individual sectors, for example, to the shifting configurations and dynamics of economic and political power. Whilst I believe that the case for continuing to understand the South African economy in terms of the MEC remains incontrovertible, I am sufficiently sensitive to the realities of the South African situation to recognise that this view remains little known let alone accepted. However, I can still press, whether through an understanding based on the MEC or not, that the major issues of political and economic

51 Elsewhere, I have given a more general account of the shifts in scholarship, rhetoric and policy in practice (and their degrees of realism) in the putative shift from Washington to Post-Washington Consensus (Fine, 2001; Fine et al. eds, 2001; and Jomo and Fine, eds, 2006). In an age of neoliberalism as financialisation, we are now entering a phase in which the state is being required to temper the effects of what has gone before and, or in order, to allow the process to continue (Fine, 2008c and e).

power be addressed in understanding what is going on and formulating policy responses. Currently, the South African conglomerates may not make policy but they do heavily influence its scope and impact. Any chances for success depend upon their commitment, voluntary, coerced and/or transformed, to social and economic restructuring at home.

Such advice to putative policymakers has its counterpart in academic endeavour. The democratic transition in South Africa seems to have been associated with an equally remarkable shift in the orientation of scholarship, especially where political economy is concerned. Whilst the apartheid era was marked by oppositional scholarship of the highest quality and originality, not least in debating the relationship between capitalism and racism in the South African context, the associated methodologies and critical stances involved seem subsequently to have been lost. No doubt, there are a number of reasons for this: a loyalty to the ANC; the loss of academics to government posts; the shift in the broader intellectual environment; the imperatives of policymaking as opposed to oppositional polemics; the enhanced capacity for South Africa to be included as another case study for continuing or new orthodoxies; and so on. In other words, just as there have been powerful economic, political and ideological factors underlying the dynamic of South African industrial policy, and economic policy more generally, so there have been heavy influences behind what might be termed the neutralisation of the traditional radical perspectives attached to academic research on the South African economy. If I have managed to restore some of these, not least in terms of the heavily negative influence exerted by the World Bank from without and by government from within, I consider that I can congratulate myself on a job half done. To finish off, it is also necessary to persuade others of the need to renew the commitment to an analysis of South African capitalism that is based on both continuities as well as shifts in the structures and dynamics of economic and political power in which the MEC continues to play a decisive role.

Appendix[52]

Historic Compromise or Own Goal?[53]

The first version of this Chapter was drafted before having a chance to consult Webster and Adler (1999), a version of which was presented at the Perth

52 As elsewhere, this Appendix is marked by concerns and references that may no longer be as topical as they were deemed to be at the time of drafting.

53 Title added for this Volume.

conference. It seems appropriate to offer a commentary in light of considerable differences with my own general approach as well as interpretation of contemporary developments in South Africa. One third of their paper is devoted to a general discussion of "bargained liberalisation" as a desirable form of class compromise. This is discussed first. It is followed by a critique of their assessment that a stalemate has prevailed in South Africa over the past decade, but with improving prospects for a more favourable outcome.

At one level, it is more or less impossible to depart from their general conclusions. It is better to reach a positive-sum outcome through (class) compromise than a negative-sum outcome through conflict. By this means, only two marginalised extremes, in principle and practice, offer themselves as alternatives on the right or left depending, respectively, on whether you favour outright victory for capital or labour. Once posed, thus, in the stark, static terms of the simplest game theory, without reference to time or place, it becomes a matter of filling in the dynamic and the detail of case studies from the past or from contemporary capitalism. But it is crucial to recognise that the interpretative framework has already been set in place – the only alternatives are success through class compromise or failure through the extremism of right or left, of capital or labour.

Although the problem is initially posed in class terms, the analytical content of the general framework proceeds otherwise, at least by one step removed. Thus is posed an "estrangement between the economy and society", p. 348, a "balance between the market and society", p. 349, the "terms on which a country engages with the global economy", p. 348, and there is an air of analytical opposition between market (equals globalisation and liberalisation) versus the state (a filter for domestic interests and compromise). These structural oppositions are complemented by processes, which are equally aloof from social and historical specificity and straddle class divisions, although the language of, and application to, capitalism are immanent. Thus, there is the putative double transition from apartheid, comprising democratisation and economic restructuring, even if alongside increasing liberalisation, globalisation and increasing flexibility.

Now, with the notable absence of good governance and community development, these are precisely the terms under which both Washington and Post-Washington Consensus have comprehended development over the last twenty years. Each of these concepts has been subject to extensive critical unpacking, whether for their self-serving construction in general or their departure from class analysis in particular. In this light, W&A provide an exemplary illustration of the shifting nature of scholarship on South Africa, from focus on notions of race and class rooted in the realities of apartheid to the bland generalities of modernisation and its progeny.

Nonetheless, out of the vision that these concepts allow, W&A do descend one step closer to home by applying them to post-war developments, both in the developed North and the developing South. For the North and its post-war boom, there is reliance upon one model fits all with minor modifications. A compromise must have been struck between capital and labour for if one, capital, is too powerful, economic and social reproduction is dysfunctional and, if it is the other, then profitability and accumulation are stymied.

There are very serious problems with this account. First, it is not well-grounded theoretically, relying exclusively on distributional arguments, albeit ones that are extended to welfare and other elements of economic and social reproduction. Essentially, no account is taken of the productivity increases that accompany accumulation and which can allow rises in profits and wages. The issue is why does this dynamic process break down – the answer cannot be found in the limited terms covered by W&A.

Second, if there is one outstanding aspect of Brenner's (1998) account of the contemporary malaise of world capitalism, it is to demonstrate that distributional arguments around the power of labour are inconsistent with the evidence. Rather, as critics of Brenner have argued, rather than Brenner himself, it is necessary to examine the restructuring of capital in both its national and international dimensions, and in markets, finance and production and not just or primarily in distributional (and demand) terms.[54]

Third, W&A do make some concessions to diversity of experience for the North by reference to Esping-Andersen's theory of welfare regimes and also by reference to the work of Richard Freeman. As I have shown in detail elsewhere in drawing upon a wide-ranging survey of the literature, and despite its popularity,[55] Esping-Andersen's approach is marked by considerable theoretical and empirical weaknesses. Theoretically, Esping-Andersen draws upon a correspondence between underlying structures and welfare outcomes in terms of archetypal regimes, a more sophisticated version of, but departure from, the class-based approach that preceded it as welfare is perceived as functional and legitimising for capital but also a drain upon it (Gough, 1979, for example). Empirically, the three welfare regimes he identifies have increasingly been shown to be unable to accommodate diversity within and across countries in

54 Brenner confines himself to competition between three nations, Japan, Germany and the United States, and ultimately deploys an explanation based on the depressing effect of large-scale incumbents upon investment. For wide-ranging criticism, see *Historical Materialism*, vol 4, no 1, 1999, and vol 5, no 1, 1999. Later, see Fine et al. (2005).

55 See Fine (2000b) drawing upon Fine (1999c and 2000a). Later, more mature and more easily accessible work on welfare can in part be found in Fine (2024c).

welfare programmes. Further, Esping-Andersen has himself moved towards understanding welfare provision in more orthodox terms, such as "risk management", rather than as a form of integrating economic and social reproduction under capitalism. Significantly, W&A refer positively to Richard Freeman, a mainstream labour economist who has deployed corresponding models of welfare systems.[56] In short, W&A have trailed a literature that has shifted away from the political economy of the welfare state towards the management of welfare subject to constraints (global or otherwise).

Fourth, as with the welfare state, the idea of globalisation has come to the fore. While it is inevitably qualified in the literature by local discretion, yielding the notion of glocalisation or the like, the economic analysis is flawed for the international as for the domestic economy from which it has been simply transposed. Globalisation is perceived as a competitive constraint on all economies as the mobility of capital drives each down to lower standards of wages and welfare. But there is one simple conundrum – if wages, etc. are being driven down, who is benefiting, especially as productivity is also increasing driving down prices and raising incomes? There is a fallacy of composition here. It could be resolved by appeal to the notion of globally deficient effective demand. This would then require a very careful analysis of gainers and losers, and how these cut across the various sectors and interests of the economy and welfare. Such finesse is notably absent from the grand overview of W&A and, it should be added, of their application of it to South Africa.

Fifth, there is a presumption that, whatever the exaggerated claims for globalisation, it takes its most severe form in finance, p. 350. This is, however, to misunderstand the nature of finance itself (which is structured both nationally and internationally), and of financial systems and their international differences. The significance of national control and regulation, and how industry, finance and government are integrated remains and even increases with internationalisation of finance.[57]

Finally, W&A present their account as running against an analytical and ideological tide in which "the idea of class compromise – indeed, of the very notion of societal bargaining – has fallen into some disfavor", p. 351. This is to

56 The same is true of Rodrik to whom W&A refer favourably. But the leading and most progressive economist in this vein is Tony Atkinson. He is able to put forward the virtues of bargained compromises, at least as strong as any proposed by W&A, in opposition to the transatlantic consensus (inequality is inevitable), without need to refer to class (individuals are his analytical starting point), and with ultimate reliance upon the economic and social analysis that flows from market imperfections (Atkinson, 1999).

57 For a case study in case of the stock exchange in Germany, see Lütz (1998). More generally, see Fine (1997c and 2000a).

mistake the intellectual and political climate at the end of the millennium. It has already turned against neoliberalism, more in principle than in practice, but is seeking an accommodation with it. The question is with what will neoliberalism be replaced. It is certainly not an antipathy to compromise, as most noticeable in the emergence of Third Way, for which the notion of class is the victim. Only in this sense do W&A swim against the current. Otherwise, both terminologically and analytically, they conform entirely to an emerging orthodoxy which fundamentally accepts the propositions of neoliberalism as half-truths that need to be tempered by recognition of market and non-market imperfections and humane values.

W&A's treatment of the "Southern compromise" is no less ambitious in its generalisations. Essentially nothing is added analytically to the "parallel", p. 353, account offered for the North other than a more complex underlying class structure and an additional hurdle of democratisation to negotiate.[58] Significantly, the only illustration offered in any detail draws upon Heller's work for Kerala.[59] Only reference is made to Heller (1995), no doubt prompted by its extremely supportive title, and bald conclusions of the sort that, p. 666:[60]

> Its very success in transforming Kerala's social structure created a structural dilemma, the existence of a redistributive-welfarist state in a dependent capitalist economy, in which the politics of class struggle became counterproductive.

There is, however, an alternative interpretation of Heller's work. He emphasises how working class conflict won victories for labour and welfare, although compromise was ultimately reluctantly embraced. Heller argues that redistributive-welfare strategies prevailed for thirty years before the transition became necessary. Even subsequently, gains have been sustained by "an interventionist state and the politically hegemonic position of the working class", p. 645 and from his abstract. The supposed transition, however, was arguably not due to the pressures of globalisation, with Kerala little integrated into the world economy, but because of the newly-emerged political imperatives of an unsympathetic and unsupportive central government.

58 Note how this corresponds to the view of the Post-Washington Consensus that the developing countries have a different composition of output and a greater depth and breadth of market and institutional imperfections than their developed counterparts.

59 Lambert (2000) provides a detailed critique of W&A by reference to the Australian model.

60 See also p. 647, "Kerala would thus appear to substantiate the oft asserted thesis that, in the long run, high levels of labour militancy produce negative-sum economic outcomes."

A number of other features stand out from Heller's contribution irrespective of how it is interpreted. First, Kerala's achievements were made in the absence of large-scale and powerful capital.[61] Second, the negotiated compromise is not a consequence of incorporating capital to engage in positive sum self-interest but to compensate for its failure to do so, p. 652/3:

> Data from the manufacturing sector in four South Indian states found that Kerala has by far the highest labour productivity … no evidence that Kerala's industrial workers earn higher wages or have lower productivity than the national average. Moreover strike data for the 1980s shows Kerala well behind India's four main industrial states. Nonetheless, capitalists operate with bounded and ideologically coloured information … it follows that Indian capital would shy away from Kerala. In 1988, private investment from outside the state accounted for less than five per cent of investment in ongoing major industrial projects.

Third, as is recognised in all the literature on Kerala, its economic and social development has been founded on a radical land reform. Fourth, a general neglect in the literature on Kerala, and as Törnquist (1999, p. 119) reports, remittances from the Gulf as well as from elsewhere in India make up between 10 and 30% of Kerala's income, both sustaining the economy and undermining its ethos as young migrant workers have funded parents' unproductive expenditures.

Fourth, as emphasised by Heller and others, Kerala has benefited from an extraordinarily rich 'civil society', reaching down through each layer of social organisation. Indeed, although absent in the work cited by W&A, Heller (1996 and 1999) has been increasingly drawn not only to strengthen his redistributive class compromise interpretation of Kerala but also to attach it to an understanding based on social capital. This is in order to explain the importance of civil society in both phases, those of redistribution and compromise. Yet, as I have argued elsewhere, in great depth and detail, social capital is a leading concept in promoting the Post-Washington Consensus and the extension of its economic to social analysis, Fine (2001)[62] – although Heller is extremely unusual in connecting social capital to trade unions and the state.

61 "The state in Kerala still lacks an appropriate partner in the form of a sizeable indigenous bourgeoisie and is working with what is even by Indian standards a rather underdeveloped industrial base", p. 665.

62 And, most recently, for social capital (and India), see Fine (2025c).

In addition, fifth, the notion of social capital is notable for its total disregard of economic analysis other than in insisting that the social is important to the economic. Accordingly, it is hardly surprising that Heller is incapable of explaining why investment and growth has not blossomed in response to the class compromise adopted in Kerala. For, however rich the factors deployed, they are all read through the redistributive/welfarist framework. In short, the division between positive-sum compromise and negative-sum conflict is at best an extremely blunt and self-serving instrument in disentangling the dynamic of economic and social development.

In this light, the transition from Kerala to South Africa in W&A's account displays a triple displacement. First, how well does Heller account for Kerala – his political economy is weak? Second, how well do W&A account for Heller – it is to do his contributions a disservice to reduce them to simple game-theoretic terms however much he may himself do this from time to time? Third, how well does Kerala translate to South Africa – hardly at all in view of the five points just listed, and surely the wealthier but far more unequal South African economy has several decades of redistribution to enjoy before it needs compromise?

Nevertheless, against this broad background, W&A locate recent developments across South Africa's double transition, suggesting that failure to deliver more progress on the economic and social fronts derives from a stalemate between capital and labour that dates at least from the late 1980s. Further, W&A are in part optimistic about the prospects for a bargained liberalization in view of achievements across the six pre-conditions they identify, p. 375. Of these, three are perceived to be satisfied: government and labour are facing increasing stalemate in view of labour resistance; institutions exist to forge bargain; and "surprisingly", the international context is more conducive in wake of the Post-Washington Consensus with explicit reference to Joe Stiglitz. As the three other conditions are not yet considered to have been met, suffice it not to discuss them other than to note that W&A are unduly optimistic over them: the parties have to recognise that compromise is better than stalemate, opposition within parties be contained, and innovative strategies be adopted.

Otherwise, for the international context, those that had high hopes have already had them rudely shattered with the (forced) resignations of Stiglitz and Kanbur.[63] These were in part deemed to be a consequence of interference of US Treasury Secretary, Larry Summers, previously notorious as Stiglitz's

63 Stiglitz was Chief Economist at the World Bank, and Ravi Kanbur was lead author for the Bank's annual World Development Report (on poverty). For later discussion of the limitations of the Post-Washington Consensus, see Fine et al. (eds) (2001), Bayliss et al. (eds) (2011) and Fine (2025b).

predecessor for having advised that developing it would make sound economic sense for developing countries to serve as dumping grounds for developed's toxic waste. In particular, he is reputed to have redrafted sections of Kanbur's report dealing critically with the impact of globalisation.

Whilst the institutions that have been put in place since 1994 are consistent with bargained liberalisation, they also conform to repressive tolerance, incorporation or whatever. Institutions and legislation as such tell us very little. What seems indisputable is the period has witnessed considerable weakening of labour market conditions, capacity and influence, not least in loss of leading personnel to government and the private sector, job losses and the weakening politics of the Tripartite Alliance. Nor is there any evidence of increasing recognition of stalemate by big business. Its economic policies have essentially been adopted.

Rather than address the foregoing in detail, it is appropriate to offer an alternative interpretation of events, even within the W&A framework. On the one hand, the stalemate that they seek is surely to be found in the 1980s – a period of zero net investment, mounting national and international opposition to apartheid, international debt freeze in 1985 following mismanagement of the economy with financial liberalisation in the 1980s just as the gold price began to fall from its peak (and similarly for energy prices), an end of the public sector led investment of the 1970s that even the World Bank confessed had crowded in private investment, and so on. In this light, the early 1990s was the most favourable time at which to bargain a settlement and, indeed, one was reached almost entirely favourable to capital to put it crudely. Subsequent developments have reflected that settlement and built upon it rather than witnessing progress towards reconciling political with economic restructuring. This is all reflected in the early intervention by large-scale capital in the 1980s to reach a rapprochement with the ANC and the decline of the Mass Democratic Movement (MDM) around and through the form taken by the negotiation of the constitutional settlement.

It would take too long and is unnecessary to go over the evidence presented by W&A to support this alternative view. Readers can form their own judgements. There are, however, significant errors and omissions that I feel particularly well-placed to correct. Whilst often only of minor detail in the bigger picture, they are symbolic of an alternative reading of recent developments.

First, MERG is described as having been established by progressive academic economists. This is not quite right. It arose out of the mission recommendations of the Canadian development agency, IDRC. The aim was to strengthen policy research capacity amongst black economists not, in and of itself, to develop policy alternatives. MERG was, however, asked in early 1993 – from the highest levels – to prepare an alternative framework in light of dissatisfaction with the increasingly aggressive policy initiatives and activities of both big business and the World Bank and IMF. I remember being against meeting this request for, not for the first time, it would have meant sacrificing creation of long-term capacity for short-term gain in policy proposals.

Nonetheless, the work went ahead but W&A are wrong to claim that the ANC's Department of Economic Policy, of which I was a member, initiated MERG or this particular task. Indeed, it opposed and impeded the latter, whether for reasons of institutional, political or personal rivalry. Trevor Manuel was head of DEP and Tito Mboweni his deputy. At discussion of the penultimate draft, Manuel unsuccessfully insisted that the independence of the Reserve Bank not be discussed let alone opposed. He has become Minister of Finance and Mboweni ultimately became Minister of Labour before succeeding to Governor of the Reserve Bank. It is true that the MERG document was dropped[64] – again from the highest levels – a sharp shift in the leadership over the middle years of 1993, culminating in the constitutional guarantee of Reserve Bank independence and the secretive negotiation of an unneeded $850 million loan from the IMF. Nor is it the case that the RDP and MERG (Report) personnel overlapped. The RDP was the first economic policy document in which I, for one, did *not* participate. In addition, the RDP was notable for beginning to abandon the widespread, participatory discussion of such documents through the MDM.[65]

Second, much is made by W&A of the labour legislation, the job summit and the Labour Market Commission. Having served as an advisor to the latter, I take a different view, more along the lines of its being rhetoric. The job summit was a late in the day proposal from the Commission aware that it had been convened for over a year without having any concrete proposals to put forward for job-creating policies with any substance. Similarly the mining summit is confessed by W&A on being about how to make orderly closure and job losses (and to my knowledge, no proper and full social cost-benefit has been made of such closures).[66] Meanwhile, formal job losses continue despite considerable labour market flexibility as documented by the companion research report to

64 MERG itself did not "disappear" as reported but was transformed into the National Institute for Economic Policy, NIEP.

65 More detail and retrospective on these issues is to be found throughout the three Volumes on South Africa.

66 Along the lines of those conducted and won by the British NUM before an independent tribunal only to be ignored (Fine, 1990a).

that of the Labour Market Commission, ILO (1996), and W&A's opinion to the contrary, p. 349.[67]

Third, W&A put forward three arguments for the shift in ANC economic policy at the decisive moment in 1993 – the collapse of the Soviet Union ("the most important factor"), pressure from international actors, and lack of progressive economists. No doubt, all of these played a part but none is decisive. The collapse of the Soviet Union was too far away in time and place. Pressure from international actors had been resisted (why otherwise sign an unnecessary deal in secret?) as had the arguments of right-wing economists.[68] It is inescapable that the shift was made out of choice, not least to smooth the way for the constitutional settlement, and not because of these factors, consistent with though they are.

In this light, what is notably absent from W&A's account for South Africa is the role of capital. This is true of lack of attention to its structures (domestic, international, sectors), its interests (industrial and trade policy quite apart from macro and labour markets) as well as its activities (globalisation, especially net outflow of investment). Indeed, the narrative from 1994 onwards centres almost exclusively on the relations between the state and labour, possibly an unintended acknowledgement that capital has been pretty well satisfied. No explanation, for example, is offered for the WTO offer on tariff reduction that exceeded what was required (essentially because large-scale capital has little interest in promotion of production for the domestic market of the commodities involved). Most important, as recognised in the MERG document, macro and other policies are severely constrained and even counterproductive unless substantial use is made of domestic financial resources for reconstruction and development, with commitment to building the institutional

67 Guy Standing organised the research and was co-author with my colleagues John Sender and John Weeks. Paradoxically, Standing's work is referenced by W&A in earlier discussion of labour market flexibility as underpinning the need for compromise across North and South. Yet South Africa has presumably managed to escape its influence.

68 It only takes one economist to convince a politician and one a day for almost a year is not enough if the politician is unwilling. Twenty years ago, 364 academic UK economists signed a letter to the Times arguing that Mrs Thatcher's policies had no theoretical or empirical foundation. It probably had the reverse of the intended effect, if any. Further, whatever the capacity and weight of progressive economists, *they* were influenced by the loyalty commanded and demanded by the ANC, quite apart from their movement into entrepreneurship, consultancy culture and government posts. For some, this evolution has not been so dissimilar from those economists attached, for example to the World Bank and the like, that had been opposed in the past but who gained considerable influence and government posts before moving to or straddling the private sector – revolving doors for some but not the many.

capacity to deliver rather than relying upon the benevolence of the market, supplemented by subsidy.

Omission of such considerations is indicative of a more deeply rooted problem. The limited treatment of capital not only renders it too homogeneous and too simply partitioned into global and domestic – the vast majority of South African capital is both. It also sets aside an inescapable facet of the double transition that is totally overlooked by W&A in their framework of bargained liberalisation between given, if diverse, parties in the context of the South. This is the process of creating and restructuring classes themselves. The class structure does not remain static, and Pilger's crude if symptomatic polemics aside, p. 347, a black bourgeoisie, big and small, is in the process of formation whilst longstanding, large-scale conglomerate capital is busily internationalising in diverse ways. If any bargained liberalisation is going on, these are the parties doing it, with labour and other interests increasingly sidelined.[69]

---

69 A significant omission in W&A's account is any mention of land reform and agriculture – especially in the context of the South and recent developments in Zimbabwe. How many white farms have been taken over in South Africa, even with compensation? Is it too cynical to suggest the lack of prominence of such issues reflects a lack of interest on the part of aspiring capitalists?

CHAPTER 6

Political Economy for the Rainbow Nation: Dividing the Spectrum?

Postscript as Personal Preamble[1]

I was both surprised and delighted to receive an invitation from the South African Sociological Association to deliver a plenary lecture to its Annual Conference in 2009. I was honoured to be acknowledged by a discipline other than my own but, more important, considered this might represent a (re)turn to political economy within South African sociology and social science more generally. As far as I knew, the only label that would have been attached to me at that time was the MEC – MERG had yet to become the victimised *cause célèbre* of the neoliberal turn in ANC policy upon anticipation of assuming government.

However, the Conference theme(s), "Making Sense of Borders: Identity, Citizenship and Power in South Africa", did not seem to lend itself to a straight account of the MEC, other than through an account of the exercise of (economic) power. But, as chance would have it, I had in one way or another been working directly or indirectly on these themes in work unrelated to South Africa, often in major research projects and over long periods. I had no reason to believe that an audience of South African sociologists would be aware of any of this. As a result, I felt I had an opportunity not only to introduce the political economy of the MEC to an audience of sociologists but also the results of my other endeavours. I might, thereby, not only promote this other work but gain credibility for it and for the MEC as value added.

More specifically, I had launched a scathing critique of the (mainstream) 'economics of identity' as part and parcel of my more general programme of research on economics imperialism (Fine, 2024a–c, and 2025a and b). This had dovetailed with my longstanding work on consumption, and its material culture (Fine, 2002 and Bayliss and Fine, 2021a most recently), themselves providing broader framings with potential applicability to borders, citizenship and power. The Conference focused my attention on how the notion of

1 "The pure spectral colors form a continuous spectrum, and how it is divided into distinct colors is a matter of culture, taste, and language", http://en.wikipedia.org/wiki/Color.

 | DOI:10.1163/9789004748330_007

being South African (the putative Rainbow Nation) was being reconstructed as part and parcel of the post-apartheid condition. For me at least, the following issues loomed large: the redefinition of Black Economic Empowerment (being reduced to ownership of private capital, particularly large-scale in practice); the increasing citizenshiplessness nature of South African capitalists with capital flight and corporate unbundling and incorporation into global value chains to the fore; and solidarity across the southern African region in wake of its history of support in the struggle against apartheid and the longstanding role of migrant labour to the mines and more.

Sorry to report that all my dreams were shattered. Neither at the Conference nor subsequently were there any hints of taking these initiatives forward, at least with me. Why is for someone else to discover whether personal or indicative of the evolving nature of South African sociology.

1 Introduction[2]

JULIET
O Romeo, Romeo, wherefore art thou Romeo?
Deny thy father and refuse thy name;
Or if thou wilt not, be but sworn my love
And I'll no longer be a Capulet.
ROMEO
[Aside] Shall I hear more, or shall I speak at this?
JULIET
'Tis but thy name that is my enemy:
Thou art thyself, though not a Montague.
What's Montague? It is nor hand nor foot,
Nor arm nor face, nor any other part
Belonging to a man. O be some other name!
What's in a name? That which we call a rose
By any other word would smell as sweet;
So Romeo would, were he not Romeo call'd,
Retain that dear perfection which he owes
Without that title. Romeo, doff thy name,
and for thy name, which is no part of thee,
Take all myself.

Romeo and Juliet, Act 2, Scene 2, 33–49

2 Prepared from Fine (2009h).

I must apologise for hauling you back to schooldays by such a long and familiar quotation from Shakespeare. My excuse for doing so is because of the dazzling light that breaks from *Romeo and Juliet* upon our conference themes of citizenship, borders and identity. Juliet is clearly struggling with how to reconcile the material with the discursive world, both wishing them to be cast asunder whilst recognising that they cannot be – whereas Romeo, at least, for the moment, is content to confine himself to introspective deconstruction. But I leave you to impose your own interpretations and, no doubt, the outcomes would be as diverse as the academic literature on our conference topics. I cannot hope to match the rich potential of such an exercise. Instead, in truly moving from the sublime to the ridiculous, I offer a mundane vignette or two from my own experience in serving upon the South African Presidential Labour Market Commission that sat between 1995 and 1996 (LMC, 1996). As an international advisor, I was present at most discussions and at questioning of witnesses, and was even allowed to interrogate them myself.[3]

The issue of migrant workers from the southern African region came up as a topic for discussion amongst the Commissioners, not least for its impact on employment and unemployment. To my astonishment, an ideology of the meaning of nationhood rapidly came to the fore, with jobs for South Africans as a first call not only upon the nation-state but as a way of consolidating it as such. In an instant, before my eyes, anti-apartheid solidarity and the history of (migrant) labour evaporated as Commissioners warmed to their topic. In a jaw-dropping moment, the discussion turned to the efficacy of different technologies for policing porous national borders, reluctantly accepting that they might prove to be both ineffective and/or unacceptable. I should observe that these were not township or urban dwellers engaged in xenophobic violence but carefully chosen representatives from the new, and not so new, elite across public and private life.[4]

At this time, we examined Bobby Godsell as a representative of the Chamber of Mines.[5] Intriguingly, he took a genuinely 'liberal' view of labour markets in the region, arguing for free mobility across national borders, at least to the mines. This was a period, although not so long ago, when labour

3 I suspect this should not have been allowed as I was not a member of the Commission itself but its proceedings were conducted informally with costs as well as benefits as will be seen. See Fine (2008b) for an account of my questioning of Chris Stals, then Governor of the Reserve Bank.

4 It would be an interesting exercise to trace forward, and trace back, the subsequent trajectories of the Commissioners – a sort of *Bridge of San Luis Rey* for the new, and old, South Africa. What brought us there together and, fatal accidents apart, where were we going?

5 See previous footnote in light of his appointment as Chair of Eskom in July, 2008.

on the mines was more extensive in numbers and geographical origin than now, with wages and working conditions less attractive both in absolute and relative terms. When I raised the issue of strategies for, and management of, international recruitment and remittances, I was assured that administration for these within the region had been reformed and now served the interests of the employees themselves. I then requested that the Minutes of the Chamber of Mines deciding on these matters be deposited with the Commission. At this point, my jaw dropped to its lowest point as, in refusing, Godsell's liberal persona transmogrified into a mind-blowing rant about no longer living in the Marxist past and obsessions with conflicts long since settled.[6]

Unfortunately, the Commissioners did not decide to insist upon receiving the evidence that I had requested upon their behalf (possibly reflecting a lack of experience of their powers) and even seemed apologetic for the offence that *I, myself,* had caused. But the lessons I wish to draw concern the extraordinary speed and extent to which citizenship, borders and identity can be redrawn, exhibiting equally remarkable degrees of continuity and change across both material and ideological elements. Of course, this should not come as a surprise to those versed in the theoretical and/or empirical investigation of these topics.

I suspect I was somewhat more innocent in this respect at the time. But I am immodest enough to suspect that the reason I am here is not to reflect upon my naiveté on these topics but because of my work on the South African economy which will be known to many of you, and to which I return below. But I am also equally modest enough to suspect that many of you will be unaware of my work on identity (if hardly citizenship and borders, lest the latter be concerned with landed property as opposed to national frontiers although the two are not entirely orthogonal). On identity, my work falls into two parts. The more recent, Fine (2009d), offers a critique of the treatment of identity within mainstream economics, not least by Akerlof and Kranton (2000),[7] in which identity is treated as a matter of choice within an individual utility function albeit with attached externalities and social outcomes/equilibria in terms of size of groups with different identities and mutual dispositions to one another. In other words, identity is simply market imperfections handled by other means, an ideal example of what I have termed "economics imperialism" in its more rounded version. Significantly, Akerlof, a Nobel Prize Winner for

6 At least, he might be said to have done his homework on the person interrogating him.

7 This initiated a stream of contributions, addressed in my own critique as well as some of the other criticisms from within heterodox economics.

Economics, is perceived as incorporating sociological insights into economics, and his work on identity does range over references as diverse as Homi Babha and Michael Burawoy. But the treatment of their work would, I suspect, be unrecognisable to them given the method, concepts and theory deployed.

I mention this critique of identity, an example of the much more wide-ranging and contemporary assault on the social sciences by 'economics imperialism' in order to highlight the rational choice milieu in which I am situated but which, I suspect and hope, most of you as (critical) sociologists do not need to engage let alone escape (Fine and Milonakis, 2009). My more substantive contribution on identity derives from the study of consumption and the consumer with which there is no reason why a South African audience should be familiar. Coincidentally, this work was already well-established at the same time that I was serving on the Labour Market Commission (Fine and Leopold, 1993, through Fine et al. 1996; and Fine, 1998d and 2002). I am extremely hesitant, quite apart from a fear of teaching grannies how to suck eggs, in extrapolating from its general results for the consumer to the more general and distinct subject matter of citizenship, borders and, my focus here, identity. But nothing ventured, nothing gained.

I begin in the next section by summarising my conclusions for the nature of (consumer) identity (or culture) as being characterised by the 8 Cs, as Constructed, Construed, Contextual, Contradictory, Chaotic, Closed, Collective and Contested. This is followed by an account of neoliberalism suggesting that it is legitimate and imperative as a category of analysis if necessarily to be understood as being based upon the current era's dependence upon financialisation, itself having gone through two phases, each of which inconsistently draws upon shifting and diverse combinations of scholarship, rhetoric, policy in practice, and representations of reality. Section 4 provides some account of the notion of South Africa as having been dominated by a system of accumulation organised around the Minerals-Energy Complex (MEC). It suggests that the post-apartheid economy, not for the first time, has seen a shift in the mode of operation of the MEC, not least with significant impetus towards providing for orderly financialisation and globalisation of conglomerate assets, that is export of capital.[8] The final section tentatively extrapolates from the contradictions of consumer politics to suggest that, whilst finance is an increasingly identifiable target for mobilising for progressive alternatives, the prospects for success in this regard require both going beyond the travails of finance itself

8 Note that this section has been deleted as it reproduces what is already present in Chapter 5.

and forging unity, not homogeneity, across fragmented struggles and the identities to which they are attached.

2 Identifying Identity

My approach views the material and cultural as inextricably intertwined and systemically based on structures, relations, processes and agencies that are reproduced or transformed in attachment to one another. In case of (commodity) consumption, this gives rise to particular systems of provision – the food system, the housing system and so on – which are self-defining and attached to corresponding cultural systems with which (consumer) identities are formed, acted upon and transformed. These cultural systems are themselves subject to what I term the 8 Cs.[9]

First identity is Constructed by which is meant not merely in thought or disposition as much as out of the material practices engaged and, thereby, offering themselves as potential elements to be incorporated, or not. What it is to be South African looks very different before and after apartheid, for Labour Market Commissioners dealing with unemployment as opposed to representatives of the Chamber of Mines dealing with employment.

Second, identity is Construed since its construction is not reducible to the material practices nor do these determine more than the context that is worked upon in thought and dissemination, constraining and/or inducing how identity is conceived. Accordingly, identity is not simply constructed and received but reflected and acted upon and transformed. In this respect, identity is remarkably fluid especially in response to changed circumstances or in one context as opposed to another. Solidarity with the region as an aspect of liberation gives way to nation-building, whilst it is more or less impossible to find anybody these days who supported apartheid, Mrs. Thatcher, Mao, or financial deregulation.

Third, identity is Contextual, not simply in the limited sense of the way in which varieties of different universal elements are or are not present but that meanings themselves are both variable and created not chosen by circumstance. This is similar to, if not reducible to, the invention of the nation, tradition, and identity itself both in conformity to, and in violation with, past and present practices and beliefs.

9 Initially, I began with just 5, but have subsequently extended to 10 after which I closed the season on additions. The extra two are Commodified and Conforming (Fine, 2013b; and Bayliss and Fine, 2021a, for a retrospective).

Fourth, identity is Contradictory not simply in the sense of the multiplicity of competing claims made upon it (see next C) but also in the material practices that underpin them. National identities, in particular, require *universal* principles applied in practice on a restrictive basis, no more so than in rights to cross borders, and access to employment and other rights. More generally, we know only too well that, even where they exist, formal freedom and equality before the market, the state and civil society are underpinned by contradictory practices that inform the construction and construal of identities across race, class, gender and so on.

Fifth, hardly surprisingly then, identity is Chaotic because of the inevitability of the multiplicity of identities attached to the multiplicity of practices in which we engage at both individual and social levels. We switch between identities, and beliefs and actions across them, even as they are formed and transformed. Indeed, it is precisely the capacity and inclination to subjugate multiple to single identities that is conducive to exclusion and intolerance.

Sixth, identity is also Closed in the sense not only of who does or does not belong but in how it is defined, by whom, and out of which practices. This is, of course, the rationale underpinning the demand for grassroots activism (as well as elite rule at the other extreme). But this is itself no guarantee of an approved inclusion as opposed to a shifting if select constituency.

Seventh, identity is Contested (Conflictual) not only in who is or is not included but, even given this, in (re)defining content and meaning in correspondence with material practices. Identity is both discovered and created in the domain of conflict as much as that of unexamined everyday life, revealing and creating powers, governances, solidarities and hidden meanings.

Last, identity is Collective, not a Romeo or a Juliet, an (individual) arm or leg, but Montagues and Capulets, forged out of common bonds and conflicts, enduring or otherwise. Yet, whilst the understanding of identity depends upon the use of simple categories such capital and labour (and other partitions, dual or otherwise), the relationship between categories, such as class, gender and race, and identity cannot be rigidly determined, not least because of the other Cs.

3 Is Neoliberalism Dead (Was It Ever Alive) – Long Live Neoliberalism?

I am acutely aware that the force of my proposed 8 Cs is liable to be pushing against an open door as far as sociologists are concerned (as opposed to the economics of identity that I have in part taken as my point of departure), especially in emphasising the diversity and complexity of identity. The great difficulty, though, is in how to negotiate the passages between the general issues and determinants and the more concrete and specific, or the contextually home-grown as it were. This is most apposite for a discussion of the crisis of neoliberalism which is both material and ideological. At the time of writing, the ideology of free markets has given way to successful demands for extensive state intervention, even if especially to sustain the financial system that is on the verge of, or even beyond, collapse and is, in any case, prompting a major recession whose depth, breadth and duration remain uncertain. Does such overt renewal of state intervention signal the end of neoliberalism or is it neoliberalism reinventing itself in a new form?

Significantly, questions over the nature of neoliberalism, even whether it is a legitimate category of analysis, had already been raised prior to the current crisis. As Castree (2006, p. 6) concludes, "I suspect 'neoliberalism' will remain a necessary illusion for those on the … left: something we know does not exist as such, but the idea of whose existence allows our 'local' research finding to connect to a much bigger and apparently important conversation". One major reason for the scepticism over neoliberalism concerns its diversity and complexity across time, place and issue, with a corresponding lack of distinctiveness as far as the neoliberal component is concerned in the local application – Bush is surely neoliberal but he nationalises banks and insurance companies! This problem has been explicitly addressed by Ferguson (2007) in the context of social policy, for he appropriately charts the extent to which the rationale for a Basic Income Grant (BIG) in South Africa has often been provided by progressives in deploying arguments that are borrowed from the neoliberal portfolio. He reasonably asks, p. 83/4:

> When activists, trade unionists, and others opt to seek concrete economic improvements for the poor by adapting to the reality of neoliberalism and speaking its language, are they simply falling into a trap by allowing issues of power and policy to be framed within a grotesque liberal vision of society that reduces all human activity to the pursuit of capital by (more and less impoverished) 'entrepreneurs'? Or are they using the space that democratization has opened up to create new and potentially promising forms of political struggle – not acquiescing in an overarching (and anti-poor) neoliberal design for society, but rather taking up and creatively redeploying neoliberal concepts and discursive moves in the service of a fundamentally different political end?

He concludes that, "We will also need a fresh analytic approach that is not trapped within the tired 'neoliberalism versus welfare state' frame that has until now obscured many of the key issues from view", p. 84.[10]

There are two separate issues involved here although they are closely related. One is whether neoliberalism is too heterogeneous to allow let alone warrant an acceptable characterisation. No one can doubt the diversity to which it is attached and, yet, it also seems to capture the grander, possibly illusory, character of the past thirty years or more, not least by comparison with the putative Keynesian era that preceded it. Are we in danger of throwing out the neoliberal baby (even as it has grown-up) with its mucky and murky bathwater? Second, though, is the strategic purchase to be made of neoliberalism. Should it be contested as a descriptor of our reality or rejected, not least in the attempts to replace it with something else?

These conundrums can be addressed, even resolved, by appeal to three aspects of neoliberalism that do render it a reality and one that must be strategically contested.[11] First, and brought sharply into relief by the current crisis and the responses to it, neoliberalism, and its counterpart in globalisation, are heavily underpinned by an extraordinary expansion and promotion of financial activity. This goes far beyond the proliferation of the financial markets themselves, and corresponding speculative activity, for it is the extension of those markets (not their inner parasitism in the form of derivatives, for example) to an ever-expanding range of activities associated with both economic *and* social reproduction that has marked the neoliberal era. Such developments are well-captured by the notion of 'financialisation', signifying not only the greater weight of finance in economies but its greater scope of application (Fine, 2007a and 2009a and e). Dos Santos (2009) and Lapavitsas (2009) have emphasised the extent to which banking had made its profits out of the financial services attached to the reproduction of the workforce (as opposed to dominance of industry).[12] To put it pithily, the expansion of markets in general (for which read private capital) under neoliberalism (as with all aspects of privatisation and commodification) has underpinned the expansion of finance

10 Nor is Ferguson alone in questioning the liberal use of neoliberalism in addressing social policy. For Molyneux (2008, p. 775), "The term neoliberal is widely used as shorthand to describe the policy environment of the last three decades. Yet the experience of the Latin American region suggests that it is too broad a descriptor for what is in fact a sequenced, fragmented and politically indeterminate process."

11 See Fine (2009a and e) on the issues that follow.

12 They now term this financial expropriation of wage revenue but see Fine (2008f) for a different view.

in particular. Further, financialisation, as the key distinguishing feature of the neoliberal era, is what justifies the term both in itself and in its effects by marking the contrast with, and even the reversal of, the previous Keynesian period.

This is not simply a matter of macroeconomic policy but the heavy subordination of economic and social policy more generally to the dictates of the promotion of markets in general and especially of finance. What the critical literature reveals from a variety of perspectives is that financialisation:[13]

1. Reduces overall levels of accumulation of real capital as financial instruments and activities expand at its expense.
2. Prioritises shareholder value, or financial worth, over other economic and social values.
3. Pushes policies towards conservatism and commercialisation in all respects
4. Extends influence more broadly, both directly and indirectly, over economic *and* social policy.

Thus, first and foremost, neoliberalism is underpinned by financialisation as the key defining characteristic of the world economy over the past thirty years, this both explaining and, to some degree, concealing its significance as such through appeal to a state-market dualism that does not fit the neoliberal age comfortably as the concept's critics correctly observe.

Second, though, it is necessary to untangle neoliberalism into two broad phases. The first is appropriately understood as the 'shock' phase although of much wider, if less dramatic, applicability than to the transition economies of eastern Europe alone, although they are indicative. This is the classic phase of neoliberalism in which the role of markets is pushed with limited regard to the consequences. It is aptly summed up in the phrase 'Just do it', and ranges over user charges through to privatisation. The second phase, dating from the early 1990s, has two aspects. On the one hand is the need to respond to the dysfunctions and conflicts that have resulted from the first phase. On the other hand, as most dramatically revealed by the current financial crisis, is the imperative of sustaining and not just ameliorating the processes of financialisation. Symbolic of this is the level of state funding that is being made available to sustain the financial system in circumstances of extreme crisis when, in better times, such funding could not be made available for health, education and welfare. I can do no better to indicate both the scale and the priorities involved than by quoting Hall (2008, p. 6):[14]

---

13 For my own account, see Fine (2007a).

14 See also Naudé (2009) on the G-20 Summit, "Many have already remarked on the fact that huge amounts of money have been found at short notice to bail out banks, but that

- the total value of the renationalisations of banks and insurance companies in the USA, UK and the rest of Europe is approximately equivalent to reversing about half of all the privatisations in the entire world over the last 30 years
- the USA renationalisation of the insurance company AIG is by itself equivalent to reversing all the privatisations that have taken place in the former communist states of central and eastern Europe since the collapse of communism.
- the UK government liability for the debts of Northern Rock alone is greater than the combined total value of all the private finance provided through PFI and PPP schemes in the UK and the rest of the EU over the last 17 years.
- Another way of seeing the scale of the rescue is to note that the total cost of constructing sewers and water systems throughout the world's cities, to provide household connections for water and sewerage for over ¾ of the urban population in developing countries, would require only about €280 billion – about 5% of the guarantees already given to the banks.

In short, we see that in the later, if now critical, phase of neoliberalism, preserving finance takes absolute precedence over all other aspects of state economic intervention, including those associated with privatisation (out of which, of course, finance has, at least in the past, done extremely well).

Third, then, is to acknowledge that neoliberalism needs to be disaggregated into separate components around scholarship, ideology, policy in practice and putative representation of reality. These are not necessarily consistent with one another, and do shift over time, place and topic, and in relation to one another. In general, there are tensions between the different components that remain unresolved. Broadly, though, in the context of development for example, the shift between the two phases of neoliberalism can be identified with the shift between the Washington Consensus and the Post-Washington Consensus. For the latter, in particular, justifies piecemeal intervention to enhance the imperfect workings of markets and institutions – although policies in practice might even be adjudged to have strengthened on those associated with the Washington Consensus (Van Waeyenberge, 2007).

money to bail out the world's bottom billion can never be mobilized. Contrast for instance the $50 billion agreed on for developing countries at the summit with the estimated $8.4 trillion for bailing out banks. As Oxfam recently remarked, the latter amount is sufficient to end extreme poverty worldwide for 50 years."

4 From Neoliberalism to the MEC[15]

In short, if 'neoliberalism' is to be sustained by reference to financialisation, its two broad phases, and the shifting inconsistencies across rhetoric, scholarship, policy and representation of reality, what forms does this take in case of South Africa? I have always been wary of telling South Africans about their own economy as my harshest criticism of other economists is for those – from the World Bank through to the latest Harvard group advising, or legitimising, Treasury – who impose preconceived and generally flawed ideas on the South African economy rather than starting from its economic realities.[16] There is a need for dialogue between identifying such realities, and the judicious choice and development of appropriate theory to explain them, quite apart from the role this all plays in policy formulation and implementation. As it were, the 8 Cs need to be applied to the South African economy as well as its citizens' identities and borders!

5 Neoliberalism Changes Gear?

In brief, the twenty or more years from the debt freeze of 1985 have marked the passage to liberalisation of capital controls and have allowed for the globalisation and financialisation of South African conglomerates. This all sheds some light on the shifts in policy from RDP to GEAR to AsgiSA, and from neoliberalism to a putative developmental state. No doubt the latter reflected at least in part a futile response to the profound dissatisfaction with the previous Mbeki leadership within government, and the results of its associated policies. There is general agreement, official denials to the contrary, that macroeconomic (and other) policy, especially with GEAR, has been neoliberal. As Hart (2002, p. 17) puts it, there is a need for "in-depth historical and ethnographic studies grounded in particular places, but closely attentive to wider connections", of which one would appear to be for South Africa, "that political liberation and emancipatory promises coincided with the ascendance of market triumphalism on a global scale, defining the terrain on which the newly elected democratic state came to embrace neoliberalism". But there might be nagging doubts about this in light of the extent of support to social expenditure, the limited

15 Much of the account here draws more or less directly from Fine (2008d) which in turn has been incorporated into Fine (2008b and 2009f).

16 Most recently, see Fine (2009b and c) in debate with Hausmann and Andrews (2009).

extent of privatisation that has been achieved, and the recent shift towards a more interventionist and even developmental state stance.

These reservations, however, reflect a misunderstanding about neoliberalism in practice in respect of the three features previously outlined, rendering South Africa in the position of exemplary illustration of neoliberalism in many respects, especially if departing reductionist accounts in the absence of contestation. As Hart (2008, p. 680) puts it, "The key challenge, both analytical and political, is to produce concrete concepts that are adequate to the conditions with which it they [sic] are seeking to come to grips". Hendricks (2008), for example, offers an outstanding account of how the South African state has ensured privileged pensions (of apartheid civil servants and new black elite) at the expense of increase in the national debt and more potentially progressive use of government expenditure. As he suggests, the fully funded pension scheme involved runs against (neoliberal) trends elsewhere (more dependent on pay-as-you-go), especially in the developing world. The same is true of the extent to which South African government indebtedness has been internal as opposed to external, with the state pension funds accounting for an increase from R31 billion to R136b in respective total indebtedness of R66b and R297b between 1989 to 1996. In this light, the apparent breach with neoliberalism in South Africa in view of provision and level of universal pensions takes on an entirely different character, the crumbs spun off from advantage elsewhere as opposed even to the alleviation of social tensions. Similarly, in 2004, South Africa had the capacity to deliver R3,637 per capita expenditure to 40% of the white population in municipalities but only R146 for the poorest 20% of the black population (a gap of 25 times) (Makgetla, 2007, pp. 150/1). Institutional capacity in providing health services in the private sector, serving a fixed number of people, and so declining to 16% of the population, has risen from 4.5 times to 7.1 times the level of expenditure in the public sector between 1997/98 and 2002/3, taking 59% of health expenditure overall (Schneider et al. 2007, p. 296).[17]

Recall also that South Africa embarked upon GEAR in the second phase of neoliberalism and merely adopted ameliorative policies appropriate to local conditions whilst promoting financialisation. That there should be inconsistencies across this adoption of policies, ideology, representation of reality (BEE, two economies, etc.) and (limited) scholarship is par for the (neoliberal)

17 As documented in Fine (2008d) in the context of institutional capacity to deliver policies (lack of which is used as an excuse for failing even to try). With plenty of examples to highlight, there would appear to be plenty of capacity to deliver the policies that have priority, and little effort to build capacity for alternatives.

course. The results have been tragic but have descended into farce with the claim of developmental state status, with South Africa far removed from any such resemblance (other than around serving conglomerate and related interests). That casual declarations of politicians should be taken so seriously and so quickly by the intellectual community is astonishing even if the wish for something different, and potentially more progressive, in political framework and orientation is understandable, in part as a weapon seized from, and to be used against, those who introduced it.

For, broadly, the politics of the current period are heavily marked by the transition from apartheid in which the ideological *and* organisational unity around its abolition has been dissipated. Struggle against the consequences of South Africa's neoliberalism have been both extensive and fragmented and, correspondingly, weakened and undermined. What are the challenges ahead and how might they be met?

Much insight can be derived by drawing upon the following quote from Sir Josiah Stamp, reputedly the second richest man in the UK in the 1930s, a manager for Nobel industries, head of the British chemical company, ICI, a member of the board of the Bank of England, and even head of the British Inland Revenue Service:[18]

> Banking was conceived in iniquity and was born in sin. The bankers own the earth. Take it away from them, but leave them the power to create money, and with the flick of the pen they will create enough deposits to buy it back again. However, take it away from them, and all the great fortunes like mine will disappear and they ought to disappear, for this would be a happier and better world to live in. But, if you wish to remain the slaves of bankers and pay the cost of your own slavery, let them continue to create money.

This is a most wonderful exposé of the power and ethos of money, how it can and must be overcome, and the contradictions between ideology, scholarship, practice and representation in the expression of the identity of a particular individual.

But it is also limited in a number of ways. First, it focuses exclusively on distributional issues – who gets what rather than how much there is to get – and without specifying the mechanisms by which this is done other than through the flick of a pen. Indeed, as suggested here, financialisation not only draws

---

18 See http://en.wikipedia.org/wiki/Josiah_Stamp,_1st_Baron_Stamp.

upon ever greater rewards, it does so by reducing those that are available to others. Second, Stamp only structures power and privilege by reference to the bankers versus the rest of us. This is by no means either central, given finance's dependence upon industry, nor sufficiently refined in terms of differentiation within classes of slaves and enslaved, as well as by race and gender and so on. Third, as observed, how and whether the flick of the pen or some other mechanism reproduces inequalities, that go beyond fortunes at one extreme and slavery at the other, is itself highly differentiated from the restructuring of the economy and labour markets through to the separate elements of economic and social provision across housing, health, education and so on. Such differentiation in practice both by process and constituency (employed/unemployed and so on) is itself a source of fragmentation to be acknowledged and overcome in order to sustain progressive advance, both to secure and make secure alternative policies and outcomes.

In this light, with some renewed trepidation in view of the dangers of false extrapolation, I return once more to earlier work on the consumer and consumer politics. Elsewhere, Fine (2005), I have argued that the latter is self-limiting for the following reasons. First, as we are all consumers, consumer politics is caught in the contradiction of presenting particular interests as if they were general, and this cannot be sustained the more effective the politics becomes and particular interests are promoted or defended. Of course, this is not unique to consumer politics as the same is true of citizenship, human rights, and, within borders, nationality, and so on. Thus, the most basic consumer politics of campaigning against higher prices tends to identify manufacturers, retailers, even government as purveyor of taxes and subsidies, as the other. But to be defined as opposition is equally to fragment the universal category of the consumer and to open up the 8 Cs previously enumerated in creating the identity of consumer politics.[19]

Second, consumer politics is not only about price and quality but also concerns the ethics of consumption itself, ranging from sustainability of the environment to the working conditions and wages of sweatshops and child labour. This implies, once again, not only that the consumer's politics are differentiated and subject to the 8 Cs but, even if not recognised as such, the consumer is also prised away from the market and attached to social issues more generally.

---

19 As chance would have it, my uncle was instrumental in setting up the Consumer Association in the UK, an organisation whose most well-known product is the magazine *Which*, that has primarily become a means of advising middle-class purchasers on tested products. At its origins, though, it was perceived to be a communist conspiracy simply by virtue of challenging the price and quality of manufacturers' products!

The consumer becomes a citizen and, correspondingly, the politics becomes broader and different, not least attaching itself to a discourse of rights and needs as opposed to equality (and inequality) before the market alone.

Third, as consumer politics evolves, it inevitably traces its concerns not only across the broader terrain of citizenship but also backwards to the origins of products in the systems of production, distribution and exchange. This can lead to, or even be inspired by, antipathy to private provision, with demand for public provision instead as with health, education, and so on. It can depart the narrow focus on the product and its terms of availability to address, as mentioned, conditions of work and for the environment. The result is to reinforce the tensions across the consumer/citizen and universal/particular interests and divides and to transform consumer politics into something else that further reinforces those tensions and divides. For, in case of *public* consumption (notably absent from postmodernist, discursive accounts), the issue becomes one of the welfare state (and, not surprisingly, commercialisation of public services is concerned to present citizens as consumers and not vice-versa). Otherwise, it is a matter of, for example, trade unionism and the environmental movement. Consumer politics is limited because it becomes different and something else the more it succeeds.

And, as with struggles over water and electricity, it may never have been consumer politics in the first place. But, in light of Stamp, the general conclusion that I draw from this, for South Africa as elsewhere, is that policy and provision have to be insulated, at least as a first step, as far as possible from the flick of the pen of financialisation as opposed to being embroiled and integrated within it. Currently, the antipathy to neoliberalism and finance as its vanguard is at a higher point than for a long time in view of the iniquity and sin, let alone downright dysfunction, with which it is associated. But this is no guarantee of progressive alternatives, not least as finance will seek or automatically turn on its destructive powers if not appropriately served. Outcomes will depend upon the strength and unity of popular movements. And, I suspect, the failure to deliver more progressive policies in South Africa in the past by the post-apartheid government has reflected a wish not to provide the basis for more progressive and potentially oppositional movements. Be mindful that every act of state provision potentially creates a constituency for continuing, enhanced and widened provision.

Here, though, there is a striking difference with consumer politics. For, as argued, it begins with an ideology of universal common interests in principle that is illusory and cast asunder as it is pursued in practice, as conflicts emerge over what are the issues, and how they should be defined and struggled over. By contrast, the politics of provision more generally (for jobs, justice, basic needs and an alternative society) begins with fragmented struggles in practice and the task of forging them into a common purpose, a dialectical task of definition, leadership, organisation and popular participation. Identity, citizenship and the negotiation of their multiplicity of borders need to follow, rather than be imposed upon, such processes.

CHAPTER 7

Amnesty International?: The Nature, Scale and Impact of Capital Flight from South Africa

Postscript as Personal Preamble

Co-authored with Sam Ashman and Susan Newman, undertaken alongside other ventures with them (and others) at the same time, I was and remain both pleased with, and proud of, this contribution. It attempted to put (illegal) capital flight from South Africa on the map. It certainly succeeded as far as my own work on South Africa is concerned, and I began to sound like a cracked record even to myself as I emphasized again and again – what is the point of debating economic policy and how to improve economic performance if as much as 20% of the surplus you generate is leaving the country rather than providing for much needed public and private investment. It is hardly rocket science after all but the roar of the engines seemed to fall on deaf ears, and still does.[1]

Not that we were the first to put capital flight on the map as it was highlighted within the apartheid period. But what made our contribution particularly appropriate is that it was prompted by the South African Reserve Bank's offer of an amnesty to those who had breached its regulations. As argued, even if not in such harsh words, this was a particularly foolish initiative. It exposed SARB to ridicule. First, it had studiously ignored illegal capital flight. Second, having brought this to everybody's attention by offering an amnesty, it intended to make it entirely legal in the future. Third, there was little incentive from miscreants to comply with a confession.

In short, this dagger at the heart of the economy's miserable performance (and antithesis to the anticipated massive inflow of foreign direct investment that had inspired GEAR) was to be condoned as it had been throughout the post-apartheid period. My suspicion is that it was some half-baked idea to raise a bit of revenue without the consequences and symbolism having been thought through. Interestingly, we took up the issue in the press, with an article appearing in *Business Day* if I remember correctly. This solicited a phone

1 For an update, see Fine (2024e).

 | DOI:10.1163/9789004748330_008

call declaring an interest from the Chief Economist at the inland revenue service, SARS, as illegal capital flight is not simply a matter of lost resources to the economy but of lost tax revenue to the state. We never heard any more and suspect the well-meaning official was told to leave it alone. In the great scheme of things, this is indicative not only of the 'state capture' to come but also of its deep roots in the pre-Zuma period.

The abstract for the original article that follows offers a neat summary. I particularly like the reference to the post-apartheid dividend that has now long since passed out of optimistic expressions for the future. And, whilst the calculations are rough and ready and open to considerable dispute, this is not the point. Rather, where is the investigation, policy and action by Government of the sine qua non of developmental progress?

The South African Reserve Bank (SARB) announced in July 2010 its intention to introduce a new amnesty for illegal capital flight. For a flat rate fee of 10% of the value of the assets, corporations and individuals disclosing their illegal expatriation of capital prior to February 2010 would receive no further penalties and be allowed to keep their assets offshore under the "Voluntary Disclosure Programme" (VDP). SARB sees this as a first step towards the complete legalisation of outflows.

Such capital flight is not new but it has worsened significantly since the defeat of apartheid. As a percentage of GDP, it increased from an average of 5.4 % per year between 1980 and 1993 to 9.2 % between 1994 and 2000, and averaged 12% between 2001 and 2007, finally peaking at a staggering 23% in 2007. The vast majority of (illegal) capital flight arises out of transfer pricing by conglomerates, especially in and around mining, and forms part and parcel of a more general adjustment of such conglomerates to the imperatives of financialisation and globalisation in the wake of an apartheid backlog. In this sense, capital flight has been the most important form taken by the post-apartheid dividend, and has dictated and conformed with other less than satisfactory economic and social developments attached to the post-apartheid era, including elite Black Economic Empowerment. The impact has been to intensify falling domestic investment in productive activities, declining capital stock across almost all productive sectors, macroeconomic austerity and vulnerability, and deindustrialisation of the economy, further entrenching unemployment, poverty and extreme inequality in the provision of basic services. Rather than focusing on the motives of individuals, our approach emphasises that capital flight is a consequence of broader shifts in the global economy and the historical trajectory of South African economic development.

1 Introduction[2]

How can South Africa attempt to pursue a new economic development trajectory which breaks from constraints of the old? That question was posed by some during economic policy debate towards the end of 2010 as the Cabinet announced a New Growth Path for the country that would "place employment at the centre of government economic policy" and put the economy on a "production-led trajectory" rather than the consumption-led growth of recent years. Measures proposed included the creation of five million jobs over the next ten years with the aim of cutting the official unemployment rate from 25% to 15% by 2020. Growth in six key economic sectors is to be promoted (infrastructure, agriculture, mining, the green economy, manufacturing and tourism).[3] The Cabinet also proposed to integrate macroeconomic and microeconomic level interventions to create more 'inclusive' growth. The specific details of the New Grow Path documents were not known at time of writing as they were to be presented to business and labour forums before being made public, and a series of policy announcements are expected over the first half of 2011. But Finance Minister Pravin Gordhan elaborated on the New Growth Path to a degree in his Medium Term Budget Policy Statement in October 2010 which announced, in addition to the above, a *cut* in the budget deficit and a major *relaxation* of South Africa's exchange controls.[4] International headquarter companies based in South Africa will be allowed to "raise and deploy capital offshore without exchange control approval" from January 2011. This will allow for assets to be taken out of the country without paying the current 10% exit levy. Exchange controls on domestic companies are to be reformed to remove barriers to international expansion. Exchange controls and limits on offshore investments for individuals are also to be lifted, as are restrictions on the 'blocked assets' of emigrants. Gordhan would not estimate the amount of the outflows that might result. But the intended direction of policy with regard to capital flows is crystal clear. The South African Reserve Bank (SARB) had already issued a media statement in July 2010 stating its intention to

---

2 Reproduced from Ashman et al. (2011). Thanks to editors and referees for extremely helpful suggestions and comments.

3 For details of the Cabinet's announcement see, "Cabinet Statement on the New Growth Path", October 26th, 2010, http://www.info.gov.za/speech/DynamicAction?pageid=461&sid=14034&tid=23221.

4 Pravin Gordhan, "Medium Term Budget Policy Statement", October 27th, 2010, http://www.treasury.gov.za/documents/mtbps/2010/mtbps/speech.pdf Gordhan also acknowledged when interviewed that the thrust of the New Growth Path is not all that new. See B. Boyle, "Government Mind Shift to Create Jobs", *Business Times*, October 31st, 2010, p. 3.

implement an "Exchange Control Voluntary Disclosure Programme" (VDP), effectively an amnesty for illegal capital flight, as part of the gradual liberalisation of exchange controls.

SARB formally, if far from extensively, invited comments from South African individuals and entities on the proposed scheme to be submitted by the 2nd of August, just three months before the scheme was due to be implemented in November 2010. There may have been some tension between informing those who might benefit from the scheme, i.e. those who had illegally exported capital and might wish to wipe the slate clean, and highlighting the process of illegal capital flight much more generally to those liable to take a much more critical stance on the issue. Such is the motivation of this article, and it is based on comments submitted to SARB by the Corporate Strategy and Industrial Development (CSID) research programme at the University of the Witwatersrand. CSID's submission to SARB focuses upon the extent of capital flight from South Africa and the developmental implications of capital flight in terms of domestic investment foregone. This Chapter can, however, take the opportunity to locate the formal submission in a more rounded and academic account than is possible or, more exactly, appropriate in a document submitted to government apparently intent upon a particular course of action that can be deemed to be questionable in terms of its equity, motivation, impact and analytical underpinnings. Nor, as will become apparent, is this some trifling matter as very large quantities of resources have been involved, and the extent of illegal capital flight reflects both the interests that have been served by economic policy and a particular prism through which to view South Africa's post-apartheid political economy. As reported below, at its peak, capital flight from South Africa was more than double the sorely inadequate levels of domestic investment, a telling indictment of priorities and their impact on corresponding outcomes in a society dominated by extreme levels of unemployment and poverty.

Specifically, the VDP amounts to a flat charge of 10% of the market value of the assets for individuals and companies who disclose their illegal expatriation of capital prior to February 28th, 2010. The VDP and Amendment of the Exchange Control Regulations were also signalled by SARB as part of a gradual liberalisation of exchange controls and so amount to the "regularization" of formerly illegal capital outflows prior to implementation of the proposed legalisation. This process will allow large amounts of capital to remain offshore to the disadvantage of the population as a whole through the negative impact capital flight has had, and continues to have, on the balance of payments either directly in terms of earnings taken out of the country or indirectly in terms of the knock-on effects of lower availability of levels of domestic resources contingent, of course, on how these would have been used if retained within the country. Further, the VDP and Amendment of the Exchange Control Regulations will, as part of an ongoing process of the liberalisation of capital controls, be liable to increase the ongoing expatriation of wealth from South Africa and further contribute to low levels of domestic investment, so perpetuating unemployment, inequality and poor domestic development even if SARB's neoliberal dogma suggests otherwise.

In addition, the VDP and Amendment to the Exchange Control Regulations have been proposed with apparently very little investigation or quantification of capital flight from South Africa by SARB itself. Yet capital flight has plagued South Africa for five decades. Apartheid governments repeatedly turned a blind eye to capital taken out of the country illegally by large conglomerates (Fine and Rustomjee, 1996, pp. 11, 174, 247). One exception to this lack of investigation by SARB is Brian Kahn's 1991 estimate that total capital flight between 1970 and 1985 amounted to US$15.38 billion at 1985 prices. Mohamed and Finnoff (2005) estimated that capital flight as a percentage of GDP increased from an average of 5.4% a year between 1980 and 1993 to 9.2% of GDP per year between 1994 to 2000. More recent calculations by Newman (2009) using the same method found that capital flight between 2001 and 2007 was on average 12% of GDP per year. This figure increased year on year from 2001 and peaked at 23% of GDP in 2007. In particular, trade mis-invoicing remains a significant channel for capital flight by companies.

Capital flight on such a scale has profound implications for South Africa's economic performance. The issue requires further research and far greater public debate, not least because SARB's plans will inevitably conflict with other policy measures designed to achieve the New Growth Path proposed by the government. Indeed, regularising capital flight for it to become legal could have the effect of scuppering any attempts to adopt more progressive and interventionist economic policies.

We also argue that SARB's use of the term "regularization" disguises the extent to which individuals and companies have not only broken the law with regard to exchange controls but have also evaded taxation in so doing. The proposed new measures come as other countries have adopted measures to reign in capital moved abroad for purposes of tax avoidance and evasion. Critically, however, the expatriation of wealth from South Africa has serious implications in terms of foregone domestic investment. It was recently estimated by Fofack and Ndikumana (2010) that if only a quarter of the stock of its capital flight was repatriated to, and invested in, sub-Saharan Africa, the sub-continent would go from trailing to leading other developing regions in terms of domestic investment. The continued expatriation of resources from South Africa is of particular concern given falling domestic investment in productive activities, declining capital stock across almost all productive sectors, deindustrialisation that has further entrenched the high levels of structural unemployment in the country, and strains on levels of public sector investment.

It is in this context that the proposed VDP and ongoing process of the liberalisation of exchange controls should be seen. Most methods of measuring capital flight include both legal and illegal capital flows. Whilst liberalisation is likely to reduce illegal capital outflows motivated by the circumvention of current exchange controls, it will not necessarily do anything to reduce the extent to which wealth continues to be expatriated, only make it legal instead of illegal. Yet this wealth, if properly utilised domestically, holds the potential for enhancing social and economic progress. To achieve developmental outcomes, an alternative VDP could require the repatriation of a certain proportion of the wealth (illegally) taken offshore. We argue that this should be part of an alternative process of "regularization" that leads to the gradual control of capital flows in a manner that is conducive to domestic investment, the reduction of unemployment and a more equitable economic development path.

To date, much of the capital flight literature has focused on individual motives for the expatriation of capital. Capital flight has been seen as a consequence of political or economic instability (Kindleberger, 1937). More recently, capital flight has been explained as a portfolio choice based on the balance of risks and returns in an increasingly financially integrated global economy (Collier et al. 2001). Capital flight is often defined as illegal capital flows either associated with criminal activities, tax avoidance or a desire for the hidden accumulation of wealth (Kar and Cartwright-Smith, 2008). Rather than focusing on the motives of individuals, our approach emphasises that increases in capital flight or outflows from South Africa need to be located in the context of broader shifts in the global economy and the historical trajectory of South African economic development that has resulted in an industrial structure that is highly skewed towards mining and related industries. We also suggest that further liberalisation of exchange controls is peculiarly inappropriate in South Africa as, under the impact of the global economic crisis, even the major neoliberal international financial institutions, such as the IMF, are confessing themselves to have been wrong or too dogmatic in the past, cautiously recognising the legitimate role to be played by capital controls in regulating flows of capital and guarding against instability due to hot flows of money.

This then begs the question of why South Africa should have turned such a blind eye to (illegal) capital flight in the past and now seek to "regularize" it in the future. The answer is to be found in the extent to which the interests of conglomerate capital have managed to exert continuing influence over economic policy in the post-apartheid period, not least as such domestic conglomerates have both adjusted to the imperatives of globalisation that were constrained under apartheid whilst fully embracing over the past twenty years the processes of financialisation that have so obviously accelerated with such disastrous consequences for the world economy (Ashman et al. 2010b).

In this light, we begin by contextualising capital flight both as an aspect of globalisation and neoliberalism in general and in relation to the particular forms these have taken in or, more exactly, out of South Africa. For, as argued, the Minerals-Energy Complex (MEC) that has dominated the South African economy from the end of the nineteenth century has adjusted in the post-apartheid period by embracing the processes of financialisation in which the export of domestic capital has played a leading role (Fine and Rustomjee, 1996). Whilst illegal capital flight was also characteristic of the apartheid era, and is equally prevalent for much of Africa, its sheer volume in the post-apartheid economy, as calculated and presented, is particularly noteworthy. As suggested, the retention, or retrieval of such capital is a potentially rich resource for meeting developmental goals. This renders imperative, as argued in our conclusion, that consideration of the VDP needs to go far beyond a casual granting of an amnesty to those who confess and pay a penalty (and why should they bother given the goal of allowing such transgressions to be legal in the future). Rather, capital flight needs to be fully investigated alongside reconsideration of how and for whom financial policy has been implemented, and policed, and how and for whom it should be designed in the future. Whatever the merits of 'truth and reconciliation' as far as illegal capital flight is concerned, it must surely render acceptable in the future what we forgive (for 10%) from the past.

2 Capital Flight and the Political Economy of South Africa

The South African Government is committed to the wholesale liberalisation of capital flows into as well as out of South Africa. This stance is in line with policy recommendations that have emanated from numerous international panels and commissions charged with providing policy advice to the Government, most notably the recent Harvard Panel (2006–2008), the World Bank Commission on Growth and Development (2008) and the OECD (2010).[5] The rationale for liberalising capital flows comes from the perceived need to narrow the gap between domestic savings and investment through attracting

5 See the debate between Fine (2009b and c) and co-author, Ricardo Hausmann, the leader of the Harvard Panel (Hausmann and Andrews, 2009).

capital inflows. In addition, an increase in foreign assets is presented as reducing South Africa's external vulnerability "through income inflows and by supporting two-way demand for the Rand."[6] What is notable from these analyses is the absence of any discussion of capital outflows, either in terms of extent or in terms of implications for domestic investment.

Mainstream economic explanations of capital flight downplay its significance in terms of the outflow of resources that might otherwise be deployed domestically to achieve better social outcomes. Capital flight is explained as a rational market phenomenon in which economic agents exercise portfolio choices based upon the balance of risk and reward. In this way, capital flight is no more than an outcome of the market mechanism acting towards the efficient allocation of resources, in part in light of more or less conducive policy environments.

We take a different view that breaks both methodologically and theoretically from the idea that capital flight is a rational response, and more or less efficient reflection, of market and institutional imperfections. Rather, we situate capital flight within the context of broader systemic developments at the global level and the specific form that they take for South Africa, with its own peculiar history and trajectory. In particular, drawing on earlier work, we characterise the system of capital accumulation in South Africa as a Minerals-Energy Complex (MEC), where accumulation has been *and remains* dominated by, and dependent upon, a cluster of industries, heavily promoted by the state, around mining and energy – raw and semi-processed mineral products, gold, diamond, platinum and steel, coal, iron and aluminium. This is not simply a matter of the weight played by the mining and energy sectors but also their determining role throughout the rest of the economy (Fine and Rustomjee, 1996). The MEC has defined the course of capitalist development in South Africa since its minerals revolution of the 1870s, in such a way that extraction came to be based on the extreme exploitation of black labour, achieved through a system of migrant labour. The discovery of precious metals and minerals produced a rapid inflow of British capital that quickly established control over the mining industry. The dominance of mining, and its need for large-scale capital investment (due to deep and dispersed gold deposits), rapidly produced concentration in mine ownership in the hands of six finance houses or producer groups which consolidated their stranglehold over production, distribution and marketing through the Chamber of Mines.

6 Pravin Gordhan, "Medium Term Budget Policy Statement", October 27th, 2010, p. 18, http://www.treasury.gov.za/documents/mtbps/2010/mtbps/speech.pdf.

The process was facilitated by an uneasy compromise between Afrikaner political power and foreign, 'English', economic control and ownership of mining capital. State corporations, especially for steel and electricity, served the MEC, as did labour control. But policies for diversification of industry out of the core MEC base remained weak. In the 1960s, however, the emergence of an Afrikaner mining house was negotiated (anticipating later black economic empowerment), and dysfunction between large-scale capital and the politics of state intervention was eroded. There was potential for a developmental state sort of strategy. But the 1970s witnessed the collapse of the post-war boom, raising prices of both gold and energy, and thereby consolidating state-conglomerate strategy around MEC core sectors associated with mining, energy and associated heavy industry.

This was followed in the 1980s by the gathering crisis of apartheid itself. Yet the effect of sanctions was paradoxical. Exchange restrictions mostly confined financiers to the domestic economy – with the exception of the illegal capital flight that took place – forcing them to invest in established MEC sectors and acquire the foreign subsidiaries made available by disinvestment. The quantity and range of the conglomerates' holdings thereby multiplied across the board and, while the mining industry remained a staple outlet for 'trapped' domestic finance, the domestic financial sector also became particularly prominent alongside illegal capital outflows. Paradoxically, the incorporation of finance under mining house control, together with conglomeration as domestically confined finance was used to acquire assets more generally across the economy, gave the impression of the decline of the MEC itself although this is better understood as a shift in the form and scope of its influence beyond simply being confined to mining and related sectors alone.

In addition to the historical specificities of the South African economy, patterns of capital outflows from South Africa need to be situated in relation to broader shifts in the global economy and how these shifts have played out in the South African context. Flight from fears of post-apartheid control in the 1980s no longer prevail in the post-apartheid period. But the neoliberal era of capitalism has been associated with the increasing 'financialisation' of the global economy from which South African conglomerates had been partially excluded in the apartheid period. Financialisation, as a term, describes and is associated loosely with the proliferation of financial markets, institutions and actors that have emerged since the collapse of Bretton Woods. Under this broad term is included the increasing importance of institutional investors; the expanding range of financial activities in the economy; the expansion and proliferation of a range of financial services and instruments and a whole range of financial institutions and markets including the now infamous sub-prime mortgages. One consequence of these changes has been the extraordinary growth in the value of financial assets, which, in the USA, grew from four times GDP in 1980 to ten times in 2007 (Crotty, 2009). If, as in the Efficient Markets Hypothesis (McKinnon, 1973; and Shaw, 1973), unregulated financial markets operate efficiently, mobilising and allocating funds for investment, the ratio between financial assets and GDP would surely be falling. Financialisation has also witnessed huge rewards to those involved in finance, and widening inequalities against previous trends, together with the penetration of finance into ever more areas of economic and social reproduction.

But financialisation is much more than simply the proliferation of financial markets and assets. Critically, non-financial companies have diversified into, and gained an increasing share of, profits from their financial activities, a development accompanied by the increasing financing of investment from retained earnings or borrowing on open markets. The neoliberal period has witnessed the expansion of speculative assets at the expense of real investment and has been characterised by the weakening of labour and the strengthening of capital.

In sum, then, the effects of financialisation can be summarised as: reducing overall levels and efficacy of real investment as financial instruments and activities expand at the former's expense even if excessive investment does take place in particular sectors at particular times; prioritising shareholder value, or financial worth, over other economic and social values; pushing policies towards fiscal conservatism and commercialisation in all respects; extending influence, both directly and indirectly, over economic and social policy; and placing more aspects of economic and social life at the risk of volatility from financial instability (Ashman et al. 2010b).

As discussed above, economic sanctions in the 1980s served to consolidate the domestic power of the mining conglomerates. The opening up of the South African economy with the demise of apartheid freed previously 'trapped' capital to seek rewards from opportunities opened by financialisation. Since 1994, major South African corporations have primarily pursued a strategy of corporate globalisation in the form of the increasing internationalisation and financialisation of their operations. This has entailed the export of domestic resources and control, and the relisting of major corporation on the London stock exchange such as Anglo American, de Beers, Old Mutual, South African Breweries, Liberty, Sasol, and Billiton. The reason for such relisting is to make it possible for large amounts of capital in the form of dividends and other payments to be moved out of South Africa legally, unbound by the exchange control restrictions that have been in place for South African residents until now.

This capital flight was in part a consequence of capital's fear of its loss of political (and, hence, economic) control brought about by the end of apartheid (Mohamed, 2010). But it was also because the end of apartheid coincided with important changes in the global economy. South African corporations thus took the opportunity to internationalise their operations and to participate in the mergers and acquisition frenzy of the 1990s which also saw increasing concentration within many domestic sectors despite conglomerate unbundling (Chabane et al. 2006). Corporations have concentrated their operations on core sectors and sold off diversified interests in South Africa but with an increase in levels of corporate concentration within sectors in the South African economy even if overall conglomeration across sectors has declined. Raising 'stakeholder value' has driven the process at the expense of other goals such as employment creation and industrial development. Rather than channel investment into productive activities and the accumulation of capital stock, investment has increasingly been channelled into the acquisition of financial assets under the control of, and/or with close links to, the conglomerates with origins in mining.

The financialisation of South African conglomerates and the creation of a new black elite through Black Economic Empowerment, with reduced incentives to engage in and promote policies for economic and social investments, have had a major impact on politics and governance and, correspondingly, policy in South Africa since 1994. The non-negotiable, neoliberal Growth, Employment and Redistribution programme (GEAR), adopted in 1996, emphasised fiscal austerity, deficit reduction and pegging taxation and expenditure as fixed proportions of GDP. Through GEAR, the government's stated macroeconomic priorities became the management of inflation, the deregulation of financial markets, tariff reduction and trade liberalisation as well as limiting government expenditure. The irony is that while the rationale offered for these policies was to attract foreign direct investment, their effect in practice was to increase the outflow of domestic capital – even while the hoped-for long-term inward investment failed to materialise. These policy goals mirror the neoliberal economic policies adopted in much of the global North and the policies of structural adjustment imposed on the South.

By understanding capital flight within the broader context of financialisation and corporate restructuring on a global scale and within South Africa, systemic implications over and above the domestic investment foregone are apparent. Neoliberalism – of which financialisation is a crucial part – has affected the 'uneven and combined development' of capitalism on a world scale, generally limiting the potential for successful economic performance where finance, and its associated policies, exercise an upper hand. For, financialisation and corporate restructuring have consolidated the power of international conglomerates, subordinated macroeconomic and other policy to financial interests, resulting in the reproduction and deepening of North-South inequalities and underdevelopment in the South.

Yet, whilst financialisation is associated with slowdown in general over the period since the end of the post-war boom, there have been pockets of development for those who have sheltered themselves from the more dysfunctional forms of finance, used the state to promote (private) real accumulation, controlled wage increases relative to productivity increase, and found both domestic and international markets to serve. China is the most glaring example now, but the East Asian 'developmental states' preceded it. With some sectoral exceptions around its core and traditional areas of mining and energy, South Africa provides an example of the precise opposite of this form of capitalist development. Whilst the post-apartheid state has intervened extensively, it has been to conform to both the interests of a financialising and globalising domestic (increasingly internationalised) capital, with historical roots in the mining houses of the past, and at the expense of broader developmental goals and strategies. Whilst it is important not to paint too homogeneous a picture across different sectors of the economy and corresponding interests, as well as the formation and incidence of different economic and social policies, such is the core thrust of post-apartheid developments, together with the creation and incorporation of a black elite through enrichment in part via these very processes.

South Africa remains an extreme case within the configurations of uneven and combined development; an advanced industrial economy and first world lifestyles exist with abject poverty and unequal social relationships and resource distribution of all kinds.[7] The picture of slow growth, declining investment, rising unemployment, rural degradation, and income and wealth inequality that characterised the economy towards the end of the 1990s remains little changed over a decade later (Freund and Padayachee, 1998). The terms of the post-apartheid settlement, the establishment of liberal democracy and political rights alongside economic inequality and with property ownership intact, have been combined with intensive globalisation, financialisation and corporate restructuring of the economy.

7 South Africa is now, 'officially', the most unequal society in the world. The poorest 20% of South Africans receive 1.6% of total income while the richest 20% benefit from 70% according to the South African Government's Development Indicators, 2009.

3 Capital Flight and Economic Development

The following empirical discussion of the nature and extent of what we call capital flight from South Africa – as opposed to the more neutral term of outflows – can be set in the context of the impact that capital flight has upon the pattern of economic development. Ndikumana and Boyce (2008) estimate that capital flight (defined as the voluntary exit of private residents' capital for either a 'safe haven' or for investment in a foreign currency) for a sample of forty sub-Saharan African countries amounts to 420 billion in real US dollars over the thirty years from 1970 to 2004. They further estimate that, including interest earnings on past capital flight, the total is $607 billion. Just 25% of the stock of capital flight from the forty countries surveyed by Ndikumana and Boyce amounts to more than twice the total volume of debt relief these countries received. Widespread capital flight from Africa co-exists with dramatic increases in the volume of capital flows at the global level, of which sub-Saharan Africa's share of inflows remains small and of which South Africa takes the lion's share. Sub-Saharan Africa's share represents 10% of global net private capital flows to developing countries, with South Africa receiving over 50% of gross market-based capital flows to the region (World Bank, 2006).

Africa as a whole has the highest proportion of assets held abroad of any region (Collier et al. 2001) and, as a substantial proportion of these assets are held abroad as liquid assets, especially bank deposits, this has been interpreted as a net savings gain for the recipient countries. If only a quarter of the assets estimated to be held abroad were repatriated and used to finance domestic investment in the source countries, sub-Saharan Africa's ratio of domestic investment to GDP would rise from 18.5% to 29.6%, and the liquid nature of many of the assets held abroad means that the transaction costs associated with the repatriation of these assets would be relatively low (Fofack and Ndikumana, 2010). Moreover, this would allow the sub-continent to move close to the minimum threshold of investment generally considered necessary to achieve the rates of growth required for the successful achievement of the Millennium Development Goals (UNECA, 1999). Much economic literature suggests that deepening financial intermediation to increase savings and raise tax revenue can increase domestic resources and so accelerate growth but this literature neglects the important contribution that repatriating capital flight can make to agendas for resource mobilisation and economic growth (but see UNCTAD, 2009).

Capital flight is, therefore, a significant drain on available funds for investment and, in the context of discussion of the active promotion of equitable economic development policies, there is a need for measures not only to reduce capital flight but also for the introduction of capital repatriation schemes to boost domestic investment and growth. Repatriated capital would raise domestic saving, widen the taxable base, raise government revenue which could be used for increased public investment, and so contribute to capital formation, a key to long-term growth.

One of the most discussed cases is that of Chile where capital repatriation was brought about using programmes of debt-equity swaps. Nigeria also successfully recovered half a billion dollars of capital from Swiss banks in 2005 (World Bank, 2007) – though marginal compared to the US$240 billion stock of capital flight from the country. The UN has been discussing ways of both preventing illegal capital flight and introducing means to repatriate illegally transferred funds since the passing of UN General Assembly Resolution 55/188 in December 2000. A recent study by Beja (2010) on the relationship between cross-border capital flows, financial depth and governance in ten Asian countries found that well-managed cross-border financial flows are associated with desirable outcomes such as economic expansion along with rising individual incomes and welfare. By contrast, unmanaged flows produced perverse outcomes such as interruptions and/or deterioration in economic performance. The empirical findings from Beja support the proposition that government should apply capital flow and trade management techniques, together with better governance in administering the domestic economy to reduce unreported flows. Developed or improved capacity enables a country not only to internalise funds more effectively but also convert them more fruitfully into outcomes that lead to progress and development, p. 22. South Africa could learn much from a serious study of international experiences of dealing with capital flight and of devising measures to bring about capital repatriation. Measures to curb capital flight and to repatriate wealth taken abroad should be considered an integral part of a developmental agenda. This is not to suggest that repatriation of capital flight is sufficient in and of itself to promote development but it is a significant source both of resources and of commitment to alternative policies that might use such resources developmentally.

4 Calculations for Capital Flight from South Africa

Capital flight has been variously defined in the literature. In its broadest sense it can be defined as all outflows that would yield a higher rate of social return if invested in the domestic economy. A variant of the broad concept is a narrower approach to capital flight as 'hot money'. These are resident outflows that accrue in the short term. Narrow definitions of capital flight distinguish it from other capital flows on the basis of: volume (whether or not the capital flow is normal or abnormal given the historical experience of an economy);

motive (reflecting individual uncertainty of the investment environment and wider portfolio decisions); legality (with only illegal outflows, usually through trade mis-invoicing, defined as capital flight) (Schneider, 2003; and Epstein, 2005). We take a broad definition here, as we are concerned with the issue of the expatriation of wealth and its implications for domestic investment and potential impact on economic development.

Capital flight is typically measured as various unreported components of capital outflows in the Balance of Payments (BOP). Here we employ the World Bank residual method taking account of current account adjustment through trade mis-invoicing.

Capital flight is thus measured as the sum of the change in the stock of external debt (DDEBT) and net foreign investment (NFI), minus the current account deficit (CA) and the change in net stock of foreign reserves (DRES) and mis-invoicing (MISINVt).

$$ADJKFt = DDEBTt + NFIt - (CAt + DRESt) + MISINVt \tag{1}$$

The measure of capital flight shown in equation 1 allows us readily to decompose capital flight in order to study, not only changes in the extent of capital flight but also its character in terms of its different channels that are likely to reflect changes in the policy environment as well as wider developments in the global economy and economic restructuring in South Africa. Figure 7.1 charts our measure of capital flight as a percentage of GDP for the period 1986–2009.

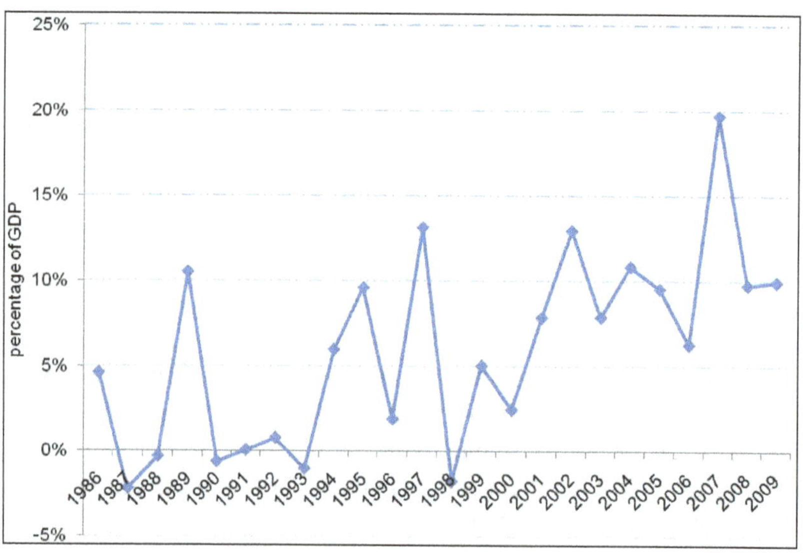

FIGURE 7.1 Capital flight as a percentage of GDP 1986–2009

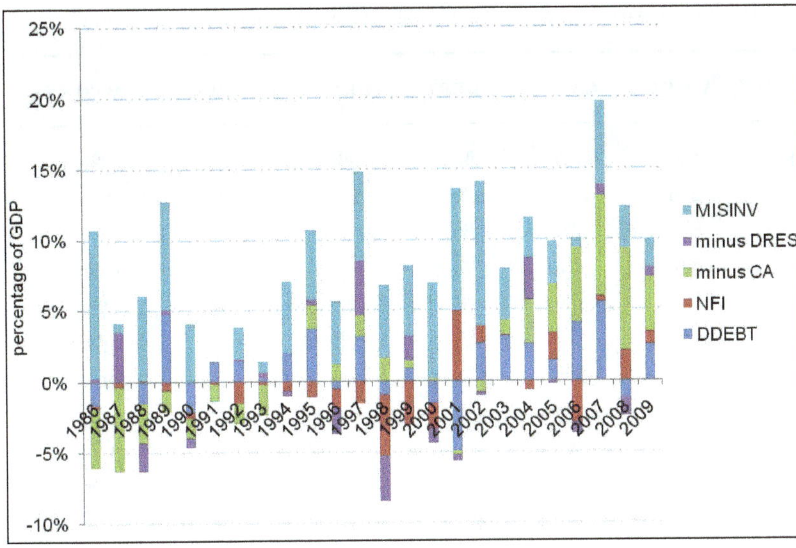

FIGURE 7.2 Breakdown of capital flight into components of unrecorded capital flows as a percentage of GDP

Figure 7.2 shows adjusted capital flight broken down by its various elements. This is shown in Table 7.1. In addition to the increasing volume of capital flight over the period, the composition of capital flight has also changed.

TABLE 7.1 Breakdown of components of capital flight as percentages of GDP

	ADJKF	CA	DDEBT	DRES	NFI	MISINV
1986	5%	4%	-2%	0%	0%	10%
1987	-2%	6%	0%	-3%	0%	1%
1988	0%	3%	-2%	2%	0%	6%
1989	11%	2%	5%	0%	-1%	8%
1990	-1%	1%	-2%	1%	0%	4%
1991	0%	1%	1%	0%	0%	0%
1992	1%	2%	1%	0%	-2%	2%
1993	-1%	2%	0%	0%	0%	1%
1994	6%	0%	2%	0%	-1%	5%
1995	10%	-2%	4%	0%	-1%	5%
1996	2%	-1%	-1%	2%	-1%	4%
1997	13%	-1%	3%	-4%	-2%	6%
1998	-2%	-2%	-1%	3%	-4%	5%

TABLE 7.1 Breakdown of components of capital flight as percentages of GDP (*cont.*)

	ADJKF	CA	DDEBT	DRES	NFI	MISINV
1999	5%	-1%	1%	-2%	-3%	5%
2000	2%	0%	-2%	1%	-2%	7%
2001	8%	0%	-5%	0%	5%	9%
2002	13%	1%	3%	0%	1%	10%
2003	8%	-1%	3%	0%	0%	4%
2004	11%	-3%	3%	-3%	-1%	3%
2005	10%	-3%	1%	0%	2%	3%
2006	6%	-5%	4%	1%	-3%	1%
2007	20%	-7%	6%	-1%	0%	6%
2008	10%	-7%	-1%	1%	2%	3%
2009	10%	-4%	3%	-1%	1%	2%

SOURCE: SEE APPENDIX 1, TABLE 7.3

In their study, Mohamed and Finnoff (2005) calculated Adjusted Capital Flight for the period 1980–2000. They found that between 1980 and 1985, capital flight followed the trend in debt conforming to the notion that capital flight was induced by economic uncertainty. Between 1986 and 1993, however, capital flight was lower than during the period of the debt crisis as South Africa was forced to run a trade surplus. This period also saw in increase in the illegal share of capital flight through increased trade mis-invoicing. Capital flight as a share of GDP has been increasing since the end of apartheid. Capital flight has shown a positive trend throughout the period shown (1986–2009), peaking at around 20% of GDP in 2007.

Illegal capital flight through systematic trade mis-invoicing is likely to be motivated by a desire for tax evasion rather than its being a response to political and economic instability. A closer look at the sectoral patterns of capital flight through systematic trade mis-invoicing shows that the vast majority of capital outflows through trade mis-invoicing occur in the ores and metals sectors (see Table 7.2). This pattern of capital flight reflects the continued dominance of the mineral and energy sectors in the economy. Recognising the scale of capital flight that takes place through trade mis-invoicing is important. Not only does this flow of capital need to be perceived as damaging to economic development, but changes in exchange controls will also not curb the capital flight that takes place through trade mis-invoicing. Other policy responses are necessary.

TABLE 7.2 Trade mis-invoicing by sectors 1995–2006 (USD millions)

	All food items (SITC 0 + 1 + 22 + 4)	Agricultural raw materials (SITC 2 less 22, 27 and 28)	Ores, metals, precious stones and non-monetary gold (SITC 27 + 28 + 68 + 667 + 971)	Fuels (SITC 3)	Manufactured goods (SITC 5 to 8 less 667 and 68)	Chemical products (SITC 5)	Machinery and transport equipment (SITC 7)	Other manufactured goods (SITC 6 + 8 less 667 and 68)	Iron and steel (SITC 67)
1995	1.59	1.06	7.83	2.25	−24.21	−3.92	−18.70	−1.60	2.18
1996	2.05	0.93	10.81	2.52	−21.76	−3.73	−16.39	−1.64	2.21
1997	2.05	0.90	7.94	2.47	−23.23	−3.73	−17.49	−2.01	1.38
1998	2.55	0.98	7.81	2.27	−22.40	−3.37	−18.15	−0.88	2.01
1999	2.80	0.90	12.69	2.33	−15.02	−3.41	−11.66	0.05	2.49
2000	2.11	1.02	12.18	2.42	−14.43	−3.28	−12.03	0.89	3.27
2001	2.79	0.98	9.49	3.02	−13.47	−3.17	−10.47	0.17	2.36
2002	2.71	1.11	10.22	3.08	−12.86	−3.11	−10.06	0.31	2.44
2003	3.50	1.36	14.39	3.63	−17.17	−3.80	−14.26	0.90	3.39
2004	3.95	1.51	18.88	5.06	−22.16	−4.38	−20.11	2.33	6.10
2005	4.06	1.55	23.72	5.65	−27.30	−4.85	−23.23	0.78	5.90
2006	3.27	1.34	31.68	4.50	−32.77	−6.14	−25.82	−0.81	6.16

Positive value represents an outflow of capital: (Calculations by CSID based on UNCTAD Comtrade database 2009).

SOURCE: SEE APPENDIX 1, TABLE 7.3

5 Capital Controls, Wealth Repatriation and the Prevailing Policy Framework

The extent to which capital flight is seen as damaging to economic development depends upon the prevailing economic development policy framework. As noted above, there is now at least growing rhetorical support within government, following the pressure and political changes associated with Zuma assuming office, around the need for a New Growth Path to bring about structural change in the economy in order to address high levels of inequality and poverty, persistent unemployment and large unsustainable imbalances in the economy which exist as a result of the legacy of apartheid. The New Growth Path is presented as one that is employment-led. That is, rather than a residual effect of growth policies, the creation of decent work opportunities through the restructuring of the economy are said to be placed at the centre of economic and industrial policies. These shifts in posture have been accompanied by the establishment of new institutions, notably the Economic Development Department and the National Planning Commission, supposedly to work collectively with the Treasury and the Department of Trade and Industry in the formulation and implementation of economic and industrial policy – though much debate continues about the extent to which these bodies share a collective vision. As argued above, important differences remain within the government over the direction of economic policy and government commitment to the liberalisation of exchange controls and restrained fiscal policy will conflict with the goal of employment creation.

If job creation is to be placed centre stage, there is an important role to be played by capital controls that are designed to minimise the types of capital flight that are detrimental to more equitable social outcomes. A strong goal of policy should be to restrict the types of capital outflows that hinder development and to redirect these resources in order to maximise social returns. Further research needs to identify the specific types of capital outflows that undermine economic development, and which need to be targeted using capital controls and other trade measures. Where capital flight is motivated by tax evasion, the enforcement of restrictions on capital flight either through improved cross border trade controls to reduce mis-invoicing or better enforcement of capital controls could potentially improve social outcomes. 'Odious debt' is another example of capital flight that is damaging to the domestic economy (Jayachandran and Kremer, 2006)· This involves external borrowing by governments that is turned into private asset accumulation abroad by domestic residents, with corrupt dictatorial regimes to the fore. But the process is simply more widespread and more complex in case of illegal capital flight given that government borrowing may be required to fund such private capital outflows for whom and by whatever complex channels. It is also important to note that the proper management of cross-border flows will only be translated into positive developmental outcomes in co-ordination with appropriate industrial and other policies.

And so capital controls on outflows, as opposed to further liberalisation, need to be part of the policy framework. As is well documented, financial liberalisation to reduce financial repression became a standard recommendation of international finance institutions and a donor conditionality whilst capital controls became anathema. Finance ministries across the developing world absorbed the idea that liberalisation is necessary to improve the functioning of the financial sector and to attract international capital to the extent that alternative ideas and paths were not even discussed, despite widespread evidence that deregulation has tended to create financial fragility, a greater propensity to crisis, has had negative deflationary and developmental effects and has not attracted higher levels of long term FDI (Ghosh, 2005). An increasing connection between financial liberalisation, crisis, and capital flight has also been observed, with the Mexican, Russian and East Asian financial crises of the 1990s as obvious examples before the current global crisis.

One effect of the current crisis has been to bring about an extraordinary about-turn in the thinking of the International Monetary Fund in relation to capital controls. In February 2010, an IMF policy note argued that, "capital controls are a legitimate part of the toolkit to manage capital inflows in certain circumstances" (Ostry et al. 2010). It recognises that capital controls can be used to prevent inflows of hot money from boosting the value of the home currency and so undermining the competitiveness of exports and that capital controls can reduce vulnerability to sudden changes in financial market 'sentiment' which can have ill effects on domestic growth and employment. Dani Rodrik (2010) wrote of this document, "In the world of economics and finance, revolutions occur rarely and are often detected only in hindsight. But what happened on February 19 can safely be called the end of an era in global finance."

At the same time, the IMF also acknowledged that, "we thought of monetary policy as having one target, inflation, and one instrument, the policy rate" (Blanchard et al. 2010). The IMF even provides evidence that developing economies with capital controls were affected less badly by the sub-prime crisis and its effects than those which did not. But whilst remarkable, the IMF's 'mea culpa' is also severely limited. It provides no explanation for how they got it wrong for so long, and its changed thinking has not affected its policy advice and conditionalities in practice. The limited nature of the self-critique can be seen in the brief attention paid to capital outflows where it is argued that liberalising outflows may offset net inflows but, "on the other hand, greater assurance that capital can be repatriated may make the country an even more attractive destination for foreign investors" (Ostry et al. 2010, p. 10).

In the case of South Africa, capital flight has been associated with a commitment to liberalise exchange controls, with an overvalued exchange rate to raise the value of exported assets denominated in rands, and a high interest rate to attract volatile short-term capital to balance long-term outflows. Such policies, and others under the rhetoric of prudent macroeconomic management, have both damaged the performance of the economy and placed it on the cusp of instability, not least because exchange controls are eased the better the economy performs and there is always the risk of flight of hot money. Further, whilst the domestic financial services sector, now commanding one-fifth of GDP, has been the fastest growing over the post-apartheid period, it has signally failed to meet the basic needs of the vast majority of the population – both literally and directly as 40 % of the population receive no financial services at all, and indirectly in the failure to mobilise resources for development. Thus, rather than channel investment into productive activities and the accumulation of capital stock, investment has increasingly gone into the acquisition of financial assets. In South Africa, then, financialisation has produced a particular combination of short-term inflows (accompanied by rising consumer debt largely spent on luxury items) and a massive long-term outflow of capital. Significantly, capital flight through systematic trade mis-invoicing has been concentrated in mining sectors.

6 Conclusions

The analysis presented in this Chapter has argued that capital flight from South Africa needs to be understood not in terms of the motivations of individuals but in the context of the country's evolving political economy and its interaction with broader shifts in the global economy. South Africa has long been dominated by minerals extraction and what has been dubbed its Minerals-Energy Complex. Sanctions against apartheid confined finance to the domestic economy and to the dominant mining sectors, financing conglomerates as they bought up the holdings made available by disinvestment. The end of apartheid combined fear about loss of economic and political control, on the one hand, and the opportunity to participate in the global trend towards both internationalisation and financialisation, on the other. The end of apartheid thus coincided with important changes in the global economy, and neoliberal macroeconomic policy has facilitated the 'escape' of this previously 'trapped' capital. So, whilst capital flight from South Africa is not new, it has worsened since the defeat of apartheid. If we are correct in our calculations, and despite its importance official estimates simply do not exist, capital flight peaked at as much as 23% of GDP in 2007. Capital flight should thus be treated as a major economic issue, and a major determinant of economic performance – albeit a negative one – with the majority of illegal capital flight taking place as a consequence of transfer pricing by corporations, specifically in and around mining. Moreover, capital flight is not only an issue of concern for South Africa but for Africa as a whole, which has the highest proportion of assets held abroad of any region in the world, thus introducing the need for capital repatriation schemes as integral to a progressive development agenda.

Yet despite its scale, much of the policy making world in South Africa seems happy to continue turn a blind eye to (illegal) capital flight, preferring instead to legalise further outflows of capital. We have argued that the South African Reserve Bank's 'Voluntary Disclosure Programme' effectively amounts to an amnesty for capital flight and, given that the proposed 'amnesty' is part of an ongoing process moving towards the complete removal of exchange controls, the emigration of wealth is likely to increase in the future rather than to fall – in contrast to theories of capital flow that predict movement from wealthy to poor countries. SARB's proposal for an amnesty for capital flight at 10% as a move towards total freedom of legal capital export can be seen as comparable to a policy to grant an illegal firearm ownership amnesty as a move towards allowing legal ownership without a licence at all. South African conglomerates took the 'post-apartheid dividend' abroad, much of it illegally, and now they look set to be granted a voluntary amnesty for doing so again at very little cost to themselves, with no incentive to declare, and with the promise of total freedom in the future.

For its part, SARB, as part of a public debate, needs to open discussion of the extent to which it has considered certain key questions surrounding capital flight in order to ensure full transparency and accountability regarding the policy. These questions should include: Why is SARB offering a capital flight amnesty now, at this time? What estimate does SARB make of how much revenue will be generated by its proposal and what proportion of illegal flows this represents? Has SARB estimated the amount of money that has left the country illegally/undeclared and, if so, what conclusions has it reached about South Africa's situation that can be made public? Why, if this activity has been illegal in the past and there is now the promise of it being legal (and given complete freedom) in the future, does SARB consider that there is any incentive for anyone to declare their activities or resources? And, finally, what measures are currently in place to investigate illegal capital flight to which the amnesty applies, how many prosecutions or other actions have been undertaken in the past with what effect, and what measures are proposed to discover and deal with those who do not take advantage of the 'amnesty'?

More generally, our findings and analysis further underline the necessity for capital controls on outflows, as is now belatedly recognised even by the International Monetary Fund. This shift in thinking has not been reflected in the policy debate in South Africa to date, and there would seem to be a contradiction at the heart of government economic policy – pursuing a New Growth Path and job creation at the same as cutting the budget deficit, maintaining high interest rates, and relaxing exchange controls. If this is not recognised by both SARB and government more broadly, the effects of the loss of capital (and foreign exchange) will continue to be felt through an ongoing crisis in the level of investment with all the obvious implications this has for record high levels of unemployment, entrenched inequality, and the ongoing failure to confront the legacy of the apartheid past.

Appendix 1

TABLE 7.3 List of data and sources

Acronym	Description	Source
DDEBT	Annual change in total foreign debt	SARB quarterly bulletin
NFI	Net foreign investments	IMF BOP
FDI	Foreign direct investments	IMF BOP
PORT	Net portfolio equities	IMF BOP
CA	Current account	IMF BOP
DRES	Annual change in international reserves	IMF BOP
X	Total exports of country	IMF DOTS
M	Total imports of country	IMF DOTS
PX	Value of trading partner's exports to country	IMF DOTS
PM	Value of trading partner's imports to country	IMF DOTS
CIF	Cif/fob factor	IMF DOTS

Appendix 2

Technical Details

Capital flight is typically measured as various unreported components of capital outflows in the Balance of Payments (BOP). Here we employ the World Bank residual method taking account of current account adjustment through trade mis-invoicing. Capital flight is thus measured as the sum of the change in the stock of external debt (DDEBT) and net foreign investment (NFI), minus the current account deficit (CA) and the change in net stock of foreign reserves (DRES)

$$KF_t = DDEBT_t + NFI_t - (CA_t + DRES_t) \quad \text{(i)}$$

The World Bank measure captures all legal financial outflows that are not accounted for in the balance of payments. Given that systematic trade mis-invoicing – namely export under-invoicing and import over-invoicing – is an important channel for illegal capital repatriation, we follow Boyce and Ndikumana (2001) in measuring adjusted capital flight $ADJKF_t$ as the World Bank measure for mis-invoicing ($MISINV_t$).

$$ADJKF_t = DDEBT_t + NFI_t - (CA_t + DRES_t) + MISINV_t \quad \text{(ii)}$$

Trade mis-invoicing is measured as the sum of under-invoicing of exports ($MISX_t$) and over-invoicing of imports ($MISM_t$).

$$MISINV_t = MISX_t + MISM_t \quad \text{(iiia)}$$

Export under-invoicing and import over-invoicing are, respectively, measured as the trade discrepancy for exports (DX_t) and imports (DM_t) divided by the shares of the major trading partners in South Africa's total exports (X_MT_t) and imports (M_MT_t) as shown in equations 3b and 3c. This adjustment is made because the export (DX_t) and import (DM_t) discrepancies are obtained as this between South Africa and its major trade partners using data from the IMF's Direction of Trade Statistics (DOTS) given in equations iiid and iiie.

$$MISX_t = DX_t / X\_MT_t \quad \text{(iiib)}$$
$$MISM_t = DM_t / M\_MT_t \quad \text{(iiic)}$$
$$DX_t = PX_t - CIF_t .X_t \quad \text{(iiid)}$$
$$DM_t = M_t - CIF_t.PM_t \quad \text{(iiie)}$$

PX_t is the value of trading partner's imports from South Africa as reported by the trade partners and PM_t is the value of the same trading partner's exports to the country reported by trade partners; and X_t and M_t are South Africa's recorded exports to and imports from trade partners, respectively, as reported by South Africa. CIF_t is the adjustment made to account for the cost of freight and insurance computed as the ratio of cif to fob values.

CHAPTER 8

Neoliberalism, Varieties of Capitalism, and the Shifting Contours of South Africa's Financial System

Postscript as Personal Preamble

This Chapter was initially written for a special issue of *Transformation*, with the theme of the Varieties of Capitalism (VoC) approach to South Africa. As will be apparent, I was not and never had been favourably inclined towards the approach, initiated by Hall and Soskice (eds) (2001).[1] In a nutshell, there is only one capitalism although it is best understood, as is increasingly popular and in part in response to VoC, as being variegated and contradictory across time, place and level of analysis (from the global to the sectoral, across the totalities of economic and social reproduction). The VoC approach shares with the Welfare Regimes Approach (WRA), the Developmental State Paradigm (DSP) and the Social Compacting Paradigm (SCP) deep historical origins in the post-war boom and its conditions and possibilities. Paradoxically, each of these emerges just as, or even after, the so-called Keynesian/welfare period is coming to a close, to be displaced by what is now a longer-lasting period of

1 Full disclosure. I first came across David Soskice in 1969 when I was starting out as a graduate student in economics at Oxford, having taken a first degree in mathematics (and recruited as such by Jim Mirrlees – background in maths more important than in economics for postgraduate study). I was employed to teach maths to a small class of fellow postgraduate students (yes, even in those days, they had students do what was considered the mundane teaching – also, not a single female on the course nor the staff teaching it from my experience, although Sue Himmelweit registered for a PhD and Heather Joshi attached to development and Oxford Institute for Economics and Statistics). But to be paid I had to get each tutor to sign off on each of their students. Soskice did not do this despite repeated requests from me. I have no idea why, was I a bad teacher, did he not approve of his students having to learn maths, should students be self-financing and contribute to teaching without being paid, or whatever? I needed the money – I recall my grant for living expenses at that time as a postgraduate was £670 per annum (Oxbridge got £20 extra per year if my memory serves me well). For comparison, my starting salary at Birkbeck three years later was around £1750, with stagflation around the corner. Needless to say, this unfortunate oversight on Soskice's part is in no way reflected in keenness of my critical take on the VoC approach.

 DOI:10.1163/9789004748330_009

neoliberalism, As a result, in the case of VoC, neoliberalism appears as one of the choices across the varieties of capitalism not its current stage. Significantly, if corrected in later work, finance (and financialisation) does not appear in the founding definition of the varieties and their institutional configurations.

As a result, our critique of VoC in a South African context runs over some of its financial history and, unsurprisingly, takes the MEC approach as critical point of departure. Financialisation and neoliberalism also figure prominently as does a critique of mainstream financial economics. But my advice to others, especially research students engaged in empirical studies and literature reviews, whether incorporating VoC or otherwise, is not simply to dismiss. Rather why not adopt a dual approach? What has the VoC approach, for example, got to say about South Africa (the strengths and weaknesses of its insights and, especially for the latter, its omissions and misfits). What is it trying to explain how, why and with what? And what parts of reality does it capture however well. And, in light of all of this, what has South Africa got to say about the VoC approach, highlighting strengths and weaknesses as before?

I must be getting lazy as, once again, I reproduce an abstract to give the idea of what the Chapter contains. It focuses on the role played by both national and global finance in comparative economic performance. It critically examines financial economics, arguing that both the Efficient Markets Hypothesis and the New Financial Economics, with its emphasis on market imperfections, information asymmetries and financial systems, fail fully to explain theoretically the specific role played by finance in the economy and the emergence of specific financial systems. It cannot provide, therefore, an adequate account of variety in capitalism. Neither, however, can the Varieties of Capitalism literature which rejects excessively homogenising visions of institutional convergence but which foregrounds institutional variety without providing an adequate theory of institutions or a deeper theory of capital and capitalism. The argument is demonstrated through an examination of the changing nature of South Africa's financial system from the apartheid to the post-apartheid periods and its insertion in both national and global economies. Financialisation, it is argued, incorporates a global dynamic into the economic and social formation of class interests and national economies which is seen clearly in the South African case. The argument therefore provides a critique of both mainstream financial economics and the Varieties of Capitalism literature and sheds light on the relationship between finance and the real economy and the nature of contemporary capitalism.

1 Introduction[2]

What best explains variety within capitalism and what role is played by the financial system within this explanation, and in comparative economic performance? Further, what is the role of finance in the economy and how do we account for different financial systems and their significance? 'Financial systems' are an important dimension of the New Financial Economics that has developed as a critique of the Efficient Markets Hypothesis. But, arguably, this approach, with its emphasis on market imperfections and information asymmetries, fails fully to explain theoretically both the specific role played by finance in the economy and the emergence of specific financial systems. It cannot provide, therefore, an appropriate account of variety in capitalism. Neither, however, can the Varieties of Capitalism (VoC) literature do so, even if rejecting excessively homogenising visions of institutional convergence. For it foregrounds institutional variety without providing an adequate theory of institutions nor a deeper theory of capital and capital*ism*. Indeed, this approach acknowledges the importance of finance, and yet finance is not one of the five defining components of Hall and Soskice's (2001) initial binary and static typology of Western capitalism into liberal and co-ordinated market economies. From a deeper perspective, capital accumulation has contradictory dynamics and conflicts, as well as institutional compromises, and so analysis must address the changing formation and balance of class interests and conflicts, and do so recognising the importance of global forces and dynamics, as opposed to the methodological nationalism of the Varieties of Capitalism approach (Peck and Theodore, 2007; and Streeck, 2010).

In this Chapter we propose an alternative view both to New Financial Economics and to the VoC approach. We argue that it is necessary to look at the relationship between specific configurations of productive and money capital, and different state policies towards banking and finance, and how they change over time. Money capital has a clear and essential role in Marx's analysis of the total circuit of industrial capital but the articulation between the different forms of capital is historically constructed and contingent (Marx, 1978; and Orhangazi, 2011). We argue that global factors should be viewed as causally mediated at the national level, and that global factors themselves need to be understood within a broader periodisation of capitalist development.

2 First appearing as Ashman and Fine (2013a).

Neoliberalism and, with it, financialisation may have produced more or less unified policy recommendations but these have produced diverse outcomes in different contexts. Finance alone does not, and cannot, account for national diversity but needs to be integrated into an understanding of specific (national) systems of accumulation. But with the financialisation of the global economy, finance has become an increasingly important determinant, exacerbating combined and uneven development both within South Africa and across the global economy and incorporating a global dynamic in the economic and social restructuring of national economies contingent upon the formation, representation and evolution of class interests.

This argument is illustrated through a discussion of South Africa's financial system, but it is worth noting that there is little application of the VoC approach to South Africa, in line with the general neglect of developing economies within this approach (one exception being Nattrass and Seekings, 2010). The South African financial sector is by African standards large and well developed as a consequence of the historical role played by British imperial capital and then Afrikaner finance capital which produced a unique conglomerate structure whereby a small group of conglomerates, or "axes of capital" (Fine and Rustomjee, 1996), came to own and control both the major corporations and finance houses. These strengths were compounded by sanctions against the apartheid regime which saw considerable withdrawal of international capital and the 'trapping' of large amounts of domestic capital – though accompanied by illegal capital flight. Liberalisation since the early 1980s, in line with World Bank policy recommendations (for the World Bank on the role of foreign banks, see dos Santos, 2011) but pursued from within by domestic class actors (Carmody, 2002) has, particularly with the adoption of GEAR from 1996 onwards, allowed for considerable liberalisation of the financial sector in a process similar to the repeal of the USA's Glass-Steagall Act. The consequences, in conjunction with the financialisation and internationalisation of capital, have been dramatic. The classic period of the Minerals-Energy Complex, MEC, see below, has been followed by the emergence of a 'Financialised MEC'.

The Chapter is structured as follows. In section two we make some general observations about the VoC approach. In section three we look at Financial Economics and the shift from the Efficient Market Hypothesis to the Inefficient Market Hypothesis. In section four we look at financialisation as a dynamic and contradictory process of change across many levels. In sections five and six the merits of our alternative are demonstrated by reference to the shifting contours of the South African financial system and its insertion within both national and global economies. In section seven we draw some conclusions.

2 Varieties of Capitalism

It is important to recognise that the VoC approach has its origins in the post-war boom even if it only emerged and shot to prominence in the early noughties, something which itself warrants explanation. That these origins might be overlooked is a consequence of the very different material and intellectual environment that accompanied the post-war boom as opposed to the first decade of the new millennium. For, during the post-war boom, much attention was focused on the differing growth performances of (already developed) national economies, with Germany and Japan to the fore, and the USA and, especially, the UK as laggards. Significantly, the prospect of global recession did not enter the picture until the eruption of the stagflation of the 1970s. Moreover, as is already apparent, the post-war boom induced a focus upon comparative economic performance at the *national* level, as if the global were secure, and could be addressed in terms of differences in national policies and modes of policymaking and corresponding institutions. Reference to the global was far off although some attention could be paid to the role of multinational corporations as potentially eroding, even challenging the capacity for, independent national policymaking.

Intellectually, the post-war boom was marked by a tripartite (not just macro and micro) division of economics into (Keynesian) macroeconomics, microeconomics with the conditions for Pareto-efficient partial or general equilibrium as point of departure for benevolent state intervention, and a diverse range of applied fields covering the public sector, industrial and other policy, and institutional design and performance around industrial relations, corporate structure, etc. Not surprisingly, differences in comparative performance could, in part, be associated with differences in national financial systems, with contrasts drawn between Japan and Germany as bank-based, and the USA and the UK as market-based, see below. For the latter, in particular, there had been a longstanding debate over whether the 'City' had been responsible for the UK's relative (industrial) decline.[3]

The collapse of the post-war boom shattered this somewhat complacent configuration of material and intellectual reference points. Remarkably, especially in retrospect, it was not so much the demise of Keynesianism that is surprising as the extreme form of monetarism that was soon to replace it, with a corresponding redrawing of the content and emphases of mainstream

3 See Ingham (1988) for a relatively late contribution to the debate and also Fine and Harris (1985).

economics as a whole (that also, paradoxically given the crisis of capitalism, witnessed the marginalisation of the heterodox alternatives and radical political economy that had prospered to some degree in the 1960s). The New Classical Economics (NCE) not only turned the tables of hegemony within the discipline by subordinating macroeconomics to microeconomics, it also did so under the umbrella of the most extreme assumptions and conclusions – reliance upon representative agents, rational expectations, perfectly working markets, the existence of unique, stable, efficient equilibrium, and the ineffectiveness of state intervention other than to distort micro-markets. Both business cycles and short-term fluctuations were taken to be the consequence of random shocks. And, with the increasing prominence within the discipline of microeconomics and homo economicus, applied economics with its strong inductive content became displaced by deductive methods and mathematical modelling.

The 1970s also witnessed the growing hegemony of neoliberalism, its counterpart in globalisation and, even more recognisable now in the wake of the global crisis of the noughties, the meteoric rise of finance at both national and global levels. More immediately, though, in the 1980s, the reaction against the NCE took the role of market imperfections as its critical point of departure. Rather than challenge the microeconomic apparatus upon which the NCE had been constructed (and even restore the macro and inductive, as opposed to the micro modes of reason, attached to the Keynesian period), the new market imperfection, especially asymmetric information, economics accepted optimising individuals as deductive starting point, but located them as subject to imperfect information, transaction costs, etc., and not necessarily efficient equilibrium.[4] In short, the price of restoring the propositions that markets might work imperfectly and that there might be a corresponding role for the state to correct them was to accept the shift consolidated if not pioneered by the NCE of subordinating macroeconomics and applied economics to microeconomics.

This also had a number of further consequences. The first, as with 'economics imperialism', was to extend even further the scope of application of economics and to make it more palatable, as it were, to its victims. For, unlike earlier extensions of microeconomics to the non-economic in which the latter was treated as if in the presence of perfectly working markets, market

4 Note that market imperfections economics derives from two main sources. One, focused on here, is asymmetric information, most closely associated with Stiglitz. The second is increasing returns to scale (or externalities) pioneered by Krugman but with little or no application to finance as opposed to geography and trade (Fine, 2010d).

imperfection economics treated the non-economic as if it were the, possibly path-dependent, response to market imperfections. As a result, a whole new set of fields was established or renewed, from the new institutional economics through the New Financial Economics, see below, to the newer development economics (not least with Stiglitz's launch of the Post-Washington Consensus). Second, the policy consequences of the new micro-foundations were to suggest that there is scope for state intervention to improve economic performance, subject to correcting market and institutional imperfections on a piecemeal basis, presuming it can be demonstrated that outcomes will be superior to leaving things to the market (given scope for rent-seeking, corruption, and the generally but not universally favourable role played by the market through competition). Third, and often overlooked, the new approach otherwise lacked any systemic vision precisely because of its micro-foundations – in contrast to Keynesianism (get aggregate demand right) and monetarism (leave things to the market). It was, in effect, incapable of explaining comparative economic performance other than as a sack of more or less indefinite differences in market and institutional imperfections.

And it is precisely this vacuum within the market imperfection economics that, consciously or not, the VoC approach opportunistically found itself capable of filling.[5] It did so through an eclectic and selective amalgam of the older, inductive traditions from the Keynesian period and the newly established market imperfection microeconomics. This explains VoC's chronology in terms of the prior need for availability of microfoundations but the latter's deficiencies for addressing comparative performance for which analytical inputs derived from elsewhere. It also explains its primary preoccupation with "economies at relatively high levels of development because we know them best and think the framework applies well to many problems there" (Hall and Soskice, 2001, p. 2).[6]

5 The market imperfection economics based on increasing returns, etc., does purport to explain systemic uneven development on the basis of where corresponding advantages (first) accrue or not, as in the new economic geography (Fine, 2010d).

6 They immediately continue, "However, the basic approach should also have relevance for understanding developing economies as well". Such promise would, or should, inevitably lead to confrontation with the developmental state paradigm as the two share so much in common in view of the state-market dichotomy, methodological nationalism, focus on imperfect markets and coordinating institutions, etc. Arguably, however, the developmental state approach is both richer and less ambitious in scope. For discussion of the developmental state approach in relation to South Africa see Ashman, Fine and Newman (2010a) and for discussion more broadly see Fine et al. (eds) (2013).

From this perspective, it would be possible, but mistaken, to read VoC for its exclusive reliance upon microfoundations and market imperfection economics as it seeks "to connect the new microeconomics to important issues in macroeconomics" (Hall and Soskice, 2001, p. 5). And it does, after all, focus on the firm (but a small step from the optimising entrepreneur), draws upon game theory as technique (fundamentally individualistic in matching strategies to outcomes) and, within a single page of the founding introduction, it is possible to find referenced all of the corresponding conceptual jargon – transaction costs, principal-agent, adverse selection, shirking, hierarchy, incomplete contracts, capabilities, and coordination, whilst posing this as "relational" (Hall and Soskice, 2001, p. 6). But such microfoundations are complemented by their marriage with an ad hoc mix of more or less arbitrary elements drawn from political science, sociology and the social theory in general attached to what is deemed to be comparative political economy.

Consequently, "five spheres" are taken as the building blocs of capitalism's national varieties – industrial relations, vocational training and education, corporate governance, inter-firm relations, and intra firm-employee relations. Finance is notably absent from this list and, yet, it immediately serves as a reference point for differences in national economies. Thus, p. 16:[7]

> British firms must sustain their profitability because the structure of financial markets in a liberal market economy links the firm's access to capital and ability to takeover to its current profitability; and they can sustain the loss of market share because fluid labor markets allow them to lay off workers readily.

This mixed presence of finance is indicative of, and conducive to, further tensions within the approach. One is around the ideal types of liberal and coordinated market economies (LMEs and CMEs) given that so many different (five or more?) spheres can be variously configured in relation to one another.

---

7 See also pp. 22–24, and p. 19 where it is suggested that there is an inverse relationship between stock market capitalization and employment protection. And again, p. 29, "Liberal market economies usually lack the close-knit corporate networks capable of providing investors with inside information about the progress of companies that allows them to supply finance less dependent on quarterly balance sheets and publicly available information. The relevant contrast is with CMEs, where firms need not be as attentive to share price or current profitability in order to ensure access to finance or deter hostile takeovers." This is all substituting the hypothesis of inefficient for efficient markets as sole explanatory device, or IEMH, see below.

In addition, the role of the global is in part taken as external shock that might disturb national economies from their equilibrium (although the approach is also deemed to be dynamic, necessarily in a limited sense). But, especially in the domain of finance, the global is seen as potentially determining even though the whole thrust of the approach is to emphasise the role of national institutions as a source of diversity of outcomes in response to globalisation. Indeed, it is suggested that, "Financial deregulation could be the string that unravels coordinated market economies", p. 64.

The incidence of finance within the VoC approach, then, is peculiar. Acknowledged as possibly dynamic and globally determining, it fails to appear within the "five spheres" of institutionalised national economies whilst figuring most prominently as such in comparisons of national economies as case studies. In part, these ad hoc formulations might be explained as a matter of intellectual and material chronology. For, of course, the VoC approach did not have the benefit of hindsight of the global crisis of the late noughties which might have catapulted finance more securely into its five, or more, spheres.

But the VoC approach did have the benefit of the New Financial Economics which, based on market imperfection economics, had not only been established in the 1980s but, as will be seen in the next section, had already been found to be somewhat inadequate to the past, continuing and increasing complexities and roles of both national and global finance. For, as the string of finance unravels into the noughties, its role in comparative economic performance could hardly be reduced to the relations between banks and industry in funding investment, as had been simplistically presumed by the New Financial Economics. As a consequence, the VoC approach could hardly credibly call upon market imperfection financial economics, not least because, whilst finance had long since moved beyond the industry/bank relationship, the New Financial Economics had remained stuck and unchanging. Significantly, for example, two or more decades later, Stiglitz continues repeatedly to refer back to his classic joint article with Weiss to explain the potential dysfunction of financial systems (Stiglitz and Weiss 1981), as if finance itself, let alone theory, had failed to move on, see Stiglitz Report, for example.[8]

---

8 UN (2009, p. 47/8) which, commenting on neoliberal orthodoxy, suggests, "But this standard view ignored key advances in economics in the last quarter century – and especially results relating to the inefficiency of markets when it is recognized that information is always imperfect and asymmetric. Such informational asymmetries are also an inherent characteristic of financial markets. Theoretical arguments have been bolstered by a wealth of historical experience and econometric evidence suggesting: (a) that markets are generally not self-correcting; (b) that financial markets in particular are usually characterized by 'market

So, in the next section, it is shown why the New Financial Economics was inadequate for purpose, both in terms of its own object of enquiry – the role of finance in the economy – and for the VoC approach. Perhaps this explains why finance occupies such an ambiguous position within the approach and, as will be suggested in Section four by reference to 'financialisation', attempts to fix it remain inadequate. For unlike the VoC approach, financialisation appropriately locates finance as an evolving (and contradictory) process rather than as an institutional compromise, or evolving equilibrium.

3 From EMH to IEMH

Following the collapse of the post-war boom, financial economics in the early 1970s within the mainstream increasingly became dominated by the efficient market hypothesis, EMH. As Larry Summers has so eloquently put it as co-author (Summers and Summers, 1989, p. 166, emphasis added):

> The ultimate social functions are spreading risks, guiding investment of scarce capital, and processing and dissemination the information possessed by diverse traders ... *prices always reflect fundamental values* ... The logic of efficient markets is compelling.

For the early proponents of the EMH, the composition of financial assets in underpinning real investment was essentially irrelevant (the Modigliani-Miller hypothesis) but, in more refined form, the EMH reflected the following five sequential propositions: all available information is incorporated into the pricing of assets; surplus profits can only be temporary within financial markets; asset prices adjust rapidly as more information becomes available; asset prices reflect the value of corresponding real assets; and the real economy is served efficiently by efficient financial markets in terms of the volume and composition of investment. Policy-wise, finance should be deregulated to allow for financial deepening and the creation and use of a fuller range of financial assets in line with saver and investor needs.

These propositions are open to dispute on their own terms (Guerrien and Gun, 2011). However, within these terms, the EMH gave rise to what might be dubbed, as its alter ego, the Inefficient Market Hypothesis (IEMH). Drawing upon the broader notion of market imperfections as a consequence of

failures'; and (c) that failures in financial markets have systemic consequences for the economy." Where's the power and vested interests?

informational asymmetries, the New Financial Economics began to emphasise not only how financial markets might be inefficient but also give rise to institutions (and regulation) in response to those inefficiencies.[9]

As a result, the approach examines financial systems, recognising a structural separation between those that lend and those that borrow money, and the potential for non-market relations between them. This separation can itself be explained by the productivity of specialisation – in various aspects of finance as opposed to productive entrepreneurship – but the distinguishing analytical content of this approach in the most recent literature is in the informational asymmetries and uncertainties that surround financing. First, if I am to lend money, how am I to know who is a good and who is a bad risk? Second, how am I to be sure that the loan is being used for the purpose for which it has been made? Third, how am I to guarantee that the borrower, who is in a better position to know, is accurately reporting firm performance and prospects. Nor are all the problems on the side of the lender. For, fourth, a borrower needs to know that a lender will tide a firm over an unforeseeable and unfortunate time of difficulty rather than, for example, forcing bankruptcy and collecting on any arrangement for default collateral. Fifth, what is to happen in the event of an unpredicted or unpredictable outcome, one not covered explicitly by contract? Who is to bear the unforeseen losses or gains and how?

Despite its apparent novelty, the financial systems approach lay within the mainstream, even if vanguard, of orthodox neoclassical economics. It yielded as such, at least in principle, a range of remarkable results, not least the eclipse of the financial liberalisation approach which is merely a special case of a financial system in the absence of contractual costs and of informational asymmetries and uncertainties. The alternative of the EMH is deemed fatally deficient in two telling respects. First, it is incapable *theoretically* of addressing the specific role played by finance since it treats it as one market amongst many. For Stiglitz (1985, p. 134), in commenting on the traditional, financial liberalisation approach:[10]

9 Much as the market for 'lemons', or second-hand cars of dubious quality, might induce reputable dealers to organise a collective warranty system (Akerlof, 1970).

10 Note that Stiglitz sees the polar opposite of the toilet paper view of banks as the Populist one of the late nineteenth century that considers, "that banks were running the country". He concludes that, "economic theory ... is more consistent with what I shall loosely refer to as the Populist view ... Shareholders do not control the firm, and managers do not necessarily act in their interests", p. 134. Quite apart from its implications for the role of banks, consider the significance of the conclusion if the firm is understood as the economy, shareholders as the general populace, and managers as the government!

> Banks are like suppliers of pencils or toilet paper; each supplies a necessary ingredient in the production process of the firm, and there is no more reason to ascribe control to banks than to suppliers of other inputs.

Second, not surprisingly, the financial liberalisation approach has a limited ability to explain the emergence of different financial systems, how they function empirically, and how they might be improved other than by deregulation. Indeed, it even denies these are of significance.

More constructively, by contrast, the IEMH is able to show, first, that a deregulated financial system, leading to financial deepening, can be inefficient since the degree of certainty and efficacy of contracting can be enhanced by imposing financial regulations. Second, it points to the importance within the financial and industrial system of the methods of monitoring investment prior to, during and after the application of funds; further, traditional monitoring devices such as stockholder meetings, threat of takeover, and dependence on external finance have weaknesses as well as strengths. Stockholders find it difficult to organise collectively, and meetings can be stage-managed by better-informed management. Apart from the costs that can be imposed by an incumbent management, those contemplating takeovers need to distinguish between poor performance and poor circumstances in evaluating a firm – and doing so may incur investigative costs from which others benefit in following a share-purchase lead (free-riding). And reliance upon external finance as a disciplining device is limited to the extent that managers can deploy retained profits (Stiglitz, 1985).

Third, deregulated financial systems can lead to short-termism at the expense of long-term commitment on the part of finance to the goals of growth and productivity increase. For Stiglitz (1985, p. 147):

> Keynes, in the *General Theory*, expressed a concern that investors in the stock market were merely concerned with short-term gains, not the long-term returns. Today, increasingly, similar allegations are brought against the managers of many of America's largest enterprises: the heads of these enterprises are financial experts, not production experts. Their job is to allocate capital. And their perspective is not unlike that of the Keynesian investor: they wish to find under-priced assets, just before those assets are discovered by others, so that they can reap a short-term capital gain. Their behavior is not surprising: what incentive do they have to be concerned about the long-term prospects of the firm or the productivity of the economy?

Fourth, unregulated financial systems can lead to inefficiently high rates of interest, discouraging productive investment and, paradoxically, reduce the rate of return to lenders as only ever more risky borrowers are prepared to borrow. This can also lead to a knock-on effect in which there is an increased demand by savers for existing financial assets, thereby artificially inflating their prices.

Fifth, a resolution of all of these problems is in part deemed to be possible through the closer collaboration between contracting parties, rather than reliance upon the anonymity of deregulated market forces, so that reputation can be built into and support long-term financial arrangements. Consequently, how banks relate institutionally to industry is of crucial importance.

On the basis of these propositions, the financial systems approach has generally been inclined towards favouring what has been termed bank-based financial systems – those most notably, if not exclusively, associated with Japan and Germany.[11] For these countries' banks, often with a 'main bank' in the lead, are presumed to have an intimate interaction with the firms to which they lend, monitoring performance intensively, providing long-term finance and, most important, securing long-term plans for restructuring in times of 'distress', reflecting a systemic reputational effect, or implicit contract, on both sides. The bank is prepared to take a huge risk with a poorly performing company which, in turn, during better times, does not take advantage of the possibility of turning to other banks or sources of finance and imposing competition for its banking business. The systemic outcome can be one of lower interest rates and higher levels of long-term industrial investment. This is in contrast with the so-called market based system which is supposed to be typical of the USA and, especially, of the UK, for which a greater proportion of funds is obtained through internally generated finance (retained earnings) and anonymous external funds, more likely on a short-term basis even if competitively determined.

Given the strengths of these results, and the apparently sounder correspondence to empirical evidence in the functioning and structure of financial markets than is allowed for by the financial liberalisation school, it would be natural to expect the drawing of immediate policy conclusions – to move towards, and to expect movement towards, a bank-based financial system. Such a conclusion is, however, both premature and insufficiently nuanced for the following reasons. First, however the theory is investigated empirically,

11 Classic references within the financial systems approach are, respectively, Corbett (1987) and Cable (1985).

it is entirely based on deductive principles around market imperfections without prior reference to the modern nature of finance itself. Indeed, banking is construed in terms of a set of archetypical assets (short- and long-term, for example, or overdrafts as opposed to equity) and regulations concerning the extent of liberalisation of the financial system and the degree of state intervention through monetary policy. Correspondingly, the market- as opposed to the bank-based system is readily and correspondingly associated with the predominance of different types of assets and regulations. In practice, however, the distinction between the two forms of banking is nowhere near so sharp, nor does it readily translate unambiguously into different types of assets and regulations.

Second, by the same token, the theory is based upon a variety of functions, undertaken in sequence over the lifetime of investment projects. Purely in the relations between finance and industry, this involves screening proposals, constructing contracts with terms and conditions, monitoring outcomes, and dealing with them when they fall outside contractual stipulations. Once again, such functions do not necessarily correspond consistently with one another along the single dimension of a continuum between market- and bank-based financial systems. A short-term loan, for example, in the form of an overdraft, may be readily rolled over by a bank with a longstanding industrial customer. This has been typical of Japanese but not of UK banks, for example, rendering it difficult to distinguish the two banking systems empirically if purely examining the stock and form of bank credits to industrial enterprises.

Third, the character of a financial system is not purely dependent upon the terms of its structural separation from industry and how they interact with one another. Nor are the intrinsic structures and functions of these two components invariant since there are different types and dynamics of industry as well as of finance. Moreover, each and their interaction are dependent upon broader socioeconomic factors, something acknowledged by the VoC approach in its insistence upon the importance of how different institutions interact with one another. Indeed, the VoC approach suggests how, relative to the CME, the LME can be conducive to more adventurous initiatives in pursuit of technological change in view of ease of availability of short-run finance and detachment from coordinated institutions subject to inertia. Thus, "the institutional frameworks of liberal market economies provide companies with better capacities for radical innovation, while those of coordinated market economies provide superior capacities for incremental innovation" (Hall and Soskice, 2001, p. 41).

There are, then, limitations on the use of IEMH for the VoC approach, especially as the former has failed to move on even in the wake of the global financial crisis. There are two obstacles in its way. First, and paradoxically, despite the alleged superiority of the bank-based over the market-based system, drawing on departure from EMH, asymmetric information between contracting parties, and the supposedly superior performance historically of bank-based systems, financial and national developments have gone in precisely the opposite direction. The financial string has, indeed, unravelled! Second, the IEMH has no way of explaining this. Again, we can illustrate this by reference to Stiglitz who increasingly draws upon the vested interests and ideology of finance to explain what has occurred, and why his own common sense and more sophisticated theory has not prevailed. But this ought better to serve as a (partial) starting point rather than as a conclusion. And, of course, it is totally incompatible with an approach based on asymmetrically informed, if optimising, individuals.

4 From IEMH to Financialisation

It is, then, a virtue of the VoC approach that it locates finance not only in terms of intrinsic microfoundations but also in relation to its extrinsic interaction with other institutional forms and effects. But this does not mean that the VoC approach gets these right in content as well as emphasis. In some respects, this is difficult to assess in principle since the approach is so open across the institutional forms it can incorporate, its reliance upon both these and microfoundations, and its greater or lesser appeal to equilibria and dynamics, path dependence and inertia, globalisation and national specificity, and cooperation and coordination but also culture, power and (class) conflict. As a consequence, it is conceivable that any critical analysis could be reconstrued as lying within the VoC approach.

This may or may not be so of the use of the term 'financialisation' to characterise the nature of contemporary capitalism over the past thirty years of neoliberalism and which, coincidentally, emerged at much the same time as the VoC approach in the early noughties, (Goldstein, 2009; but see also Arrighi, 1994). In brief, financialisation has involved: the phenomenal expansion of financial assets relative to real activity (by three times over the last thirty years); the proliferation of types of assets, from derivatives through to futures markets with a corresponding explosion of acronyms; the absolute and relative expansion of speculative as opposed to or at the expense of real investment; a shift in the balance of productive to financial imperatives within the private sector whether financial or not; increasing inequality in income arising out of weight of financial rewards; consumer-led booms based on credit; the penetration of finance into ever more areas of economic and social life such as pensions, education, health, and provision of economic and social infrastructure; the emergence of a neoliberal culture of reliance upon markets and private capital and corresponding anti-statism despite the extent to which the rewards to private finance have in part derived from state finance itself. Financialisation is also associated with the continued role of the US dollar as world money despite, at least in the global crisis of the noughties, its deficits in trade, capital account, the fiscus, and consumer spending, and minimal rates of interest.

And, however financialisation is defined, its consequences have been perceived to be: reductions in overall levels and efficacy of real investment as financial instruments and activities expand at its expense even if excessive investment does take place in particular sectors at particular times (as with the dotcom bubble of a decade ago); prioritising shareholder value, or financial worth, over other economic and social values; pushing of policies towards conservatism and commercialisation in all respects; extending influence of finance more broadly, both directly and indirectly, over economic *and* social policy; placing more aspects of economic and social life at the risk of volatility from financial instability and, conversely, places the economy and social life at risk of crisis from triggers within particular markets (as with the food and energy crises that preceded the financial crisis). Whilst, then, financialisation is a single word, it is attached to a wide variety of different forms and effects of finance with the USA and the UK to the fore. And, even if exposed in acute form by the crisis, its expansion over the last few decades has been at the expense of the real economy despite otherwise extraordinarily favourable 'fundamentals' for capitalism in terms of availability of new technologies, expansion and weakening of global and national labour forces, and the triumph of neoliberalism in political and policy arenas.

Now, as is apparent, the notion of financialisation has been used in many different ways and some, no doubt, are more compatible with the VoC approach than others. Where financialisation sits least comfortably within the VoC approach is where it is perceived as incorporating a global dynamic in the economic and social restructuring of national economies contingent upon the formation, representation and evolution of class interests. This is precisely of significance for the passage from apartheid to post-apartheid economy.

5 From Apartheid to Post-apartheid Economy and Financial System

The economic and political history of any country both shapes, and is shaped by, the financial system. The elements which make up a financial system are not only complex, as discussed above, they are historically and socioeconomically specific and they change over time. South Africa has a well-developed and sophisticated financial sector, particularly in comparative African terms, as a consequence of the particular pattern of its imperial past. Whilst rejecting South African exceptionalism as such, it can be argued that the peculiar form of the concentration of power in the financial and corporate sector makes it historically unique and not a clear example either of an LME or a CME, a distinction which is highly problematic to begin with (Aybar and Lapavitsas, 2001).

A number of dimensions of the South African financial system are of particular importance historically both prior to and during the apartheid era. First, as has been emphasised by conventional descriptive histories (Amphlett, 1914; and Jones, 1994, 1996 and 2009), is the domination of the banking sector by London-based imperial banks. But, and rather less analysed, is the relative lack of importance of these banks in providing funds for accumulation. The Standard Bank of British South Africa, established in 1862, and Barclays Bank Dominion Colonial and Overseas (BBDCO), formed through a merger in 1926, both had headquarters in Britain, expanded into colonial markets in South Africa, survived various economic crises, and absorbed over time numerous small banks which had largely served agricultural needs. They expanded gradually outwards from their original based in the Cape Colony, particularly following the discovery of gold in the Transvaal. By 1910 the two main imperial banks held over 90% of the total capital of banks in South Africa (Verhoef, 2009a). The imperial banks benefited greatly from the minerals revolution both as service providers to the mining sector, first in Kimberley and then in Johannesburg, but these banks were far from being central to the funding of industry. Deep-level mining needed considerable capital. The rapid concentration in the mining sector gave rise to an oligopolistic industrial structure. By the early 1930s mining was controlled by six mining houses which controlled all the major mining groups, with minerals giant Anglo-American to the fore (and which had interests in both Standard and Barclays). This pattern is hardly surprising, but each of the mining houses established their own finance houses to raise capital from overseas, and it was precisely this control over the financial sector which helped establish the dominance of the mining conglomerates. Productive and financial capitals were intertwined (Innes, 1984).

Second, this pattern was to inspire Afrikaner capital which until the Second World War was heavily represented in agricultural production but had little representation in mining or secondary industry, such as it was (Giliomee, 2003; and O'Meara 1983). The phenomenon of 'poor whites' would increasingly exercise the minds of the Afrikaans-speaking elite. The 'scorched earth' policy of the British during the war of 1899–1902 had devastated agriculture and increased the urbanisation of poor and unskilled whites. Santam (the South African

Trust and Insurance Company) was formed in 1918 to establish a South African insurance company based on Afrikaans speakers, and Santam established Sanlam (the South African National Life Assurance Company) as its life assurance subsidiary in 1918 with an overlapping board of directors. These had three strategic goals: to contribute to the growth of the South African economy; to encourage Afrikaners to develop a propensity to save; and to strengthen Afrikaner (and all South African policy holders') participation in the South African economy in contrast with foreign-owned insurance companies which expatriated profits (Verhoef, 2009b, pp. 124–5). Sanlam was to be central to the development of Afrikaner nationalism and Afrikaner capital and within twenty years it was the fourth biggest insurance company in South Africa. Similarly, what would become Volkskas Bank was established by the Afrikaner Broederbond in 1934 as a people's savings bank, but it was some time before it was able to compete with the imperial banks and Nedbank, the third commercial bank (originally Dutch) considerably smaller than Standard and Barclays (Verhoef, 1992a and b).

At the Economic People's Congress in Bloemfontein in 1939, organised by a broad spectrum of Afrikaner institutions to address the poor white question, Tienie Louw of Sanlam proposed the establishment of an investment company to provide capital for Afrikaner business, modelled on the finance houses of the mining conglomerates. He did so on the grounds that, "If we want to be successful, we need to use the capitalist system in a similar fashion as displayed by the gold mining industry" (Verhoef, 2009b, p. 128). The FVB (Federale Volksbeleggings or Federal People's Investments) was established with Sanlam having a controlling shareholding and overlapping members of the board of directors. Through FVB, Sanlam was critical in channelling Afrikaner savings and agricultural surplus into the development of an 'Afrikaner' industrial base (O'Meara, 1983).

The heavy promotion of Afrikaner finance capital in the 1940s and 1950s, with the aid of the state, allowed Afrikaner capital to break into areas once the domain of English-speaking capital. Minerals and energy then became the vehicles through which Afrikaner capital integrated into the industrial core of the economy. The state, particularly under the National Party from 1948 onwards, promoted the development of Afrikaner capital, through a shifting mixture of compromise and conflict with English capital but critically through the creation of state-owned sectors in electricity, Eskom, and steel, Iscor, but also chemicals and fuels which complemented mining conglomerate needs and provided a growing link between the state and the private sector (Clark, 1994; and Fine and Rustomjee, 1996). The Industrial Development Corporation, established in 1940, had by 1956 invested £40.7 million in Sasol (the state-owned coal-to-oil conversion facility), 77 percent of its investments in industry (Fine and Rustomjee, 1996, p. 159). The state formed The National Finance Corporation in 1949 and, in doing so, did much to create a local long-term capital market. The NFC invested its deposits in Treasury Bills and in mining house debentures and was particularly important in financing the huge development of the Orange Free State Goldfields in the immediate post-war period (Fine and Rustomjee, 1996, pp. 154–155; and O'Meara, 1983, pp. 148–9). Indeed, the NFC channelled funds from Anglo American's diamond operations to its mining interests in the Orange Free State and so represented a shift from private sources of finance to institutional ones and in addition helped erode differences between English and Afrikaner capital.

FVB secured Afrikaner capital's entry into the almost wholly English-owned mining industry initially through guaranteeing Volkskas bank loans but then through Bonuskor (created by Sanlam in 1946). Bonuskor took the bonuses of policy holders and invested them in shares in listed companies on the Johannesburg Stock Exchange. Bonuskor and FVB established their own mine holding company Federale Mynbou Beperk or FM (Federal Mining Limited) in 1953. FM broke into coal (in part in co-operation with Anglo-Vaal), gold and asbestos and became increasingly interested in diamonds, eventually co-operating with Anglo-American, through Genmin, though AAC wanted to ensure FM's operation in diamonds came under the de Beers Central Selling Organisation.[12] FM eventually controlled Genmin and, in 1974, Genmin took over the Union Corporation Company, a British owned gold mining company, creating Afrikaner control of the second largest gold mining house, renamed Gencor in 1975 (Jones, 1995; and O'Meara, 1983).

FVB also developed into an industrial holding company and by the late 1980s had assets of R259 million (Verhoef 2009b, p. 133). By the 1970s FVB managed nearly thirty industrial enterprises, Federal Industries, Federal Chemical Investments, Federal Telectra, Fedfood, Fedservices. O'Meara (1996, p. 139, Table 3) estimates that in 1954/5, Afrikaner ownership of mining was 1% which increased to 10% by 1963/4 and 18% by 1975. Over the same period for manufacturing and construction the share rose from 6% to 10% to 15%, while in finance it rose from 10% to 21% to 25%. The capital market remained small

12 A confidential letter (cited in Verhoef, 2009b, p. 141) from Anglo's Harry Oppenheimer to the chairman of the FM board stated that should FM "or any other company over which it exercised effective control (including General Mining) make any new diamond discoveries or were invited to hand any new diamond venture, such discovery or venture would be offered in the first place to a new company to be formed for that purpose, and the capital of the new company would be owned 51 per cent by de Beers and 49 per cent by Federale Mynbou."

relative to European standards, and foreign capital and internal financing by mining houses remained important. Nevertheless, personal and corporate savings increased by 1,654 % between 1948 and 1958 (from £13m to £215m); the surplus of public authorities increased by 125% (from £28m to £63m); and in 1958 share capital and deposits of permanent building societies were £512 million (Innes, 1984, p. 148).

Anglo formed its own merchant bank in 1955, Union Acceptances Limited, supported by Barclays Bank and was, by 1968, the largest merchant bank in the country (with assets worth R142m) and also the seventh largest bank (Innes, 1984, p. 206). Other merchant banks followed UAL: the Central Finance and Acceptance Corp backed by SANLAM; the Accepting Bank for Industry funded by the IDC; and the Philip Hill Acceptance Co. a subsidiary of a London firm. By the 1960s, the growth and development of Afrikaner finance capital had begun to erode the dominance of the British imperial banks, Standard and Barclays. The National Finance Corporation, private merchant banks, Volkskas, Trustbank – established by Sanlam and FVB in 1955 (Verhoef, 1992a) – plus building societies and life insurers emerged. In particular, Volkskas benefited greatly when the National Party after 1948 transferred to it the accounts of state corporations and government municipalities.

The very rapid growth of merchant banking from the late 1950s onwards, under conglomerate control, reinforced the close connection between finance and industry. A major series of mergers, including financial ones, increased concentration in the economy. Most important of the financial mergers were those led by Anglo's Union Acceptance Limited which joined with Syfrets Trust Co. owned by insurance firm the South African Mutual Life Association Society (later to become Old Mutual) and which was backer of Anglo's Rand Mines which merged with manufacturing conglomerate Tomas Barlow to form Barlow Rand in 1971. The combined group then merged with the originally Dutch-owned Nedbank Group (then the third largest commercial bank) to form in 1974 Nedsual (Nedbank and Syfrets-UAL Holdings). Three groups, Standard, Barclays and Nedsual thus dominated banking, with Volksas in fourth place, and both Anglo and Old Mutual had expanded significantly into finance, especially given Anglo retained a minority stake in both Barclays and Standard. Anglo then took over the Schlesinger financial group so gaining controlling stakes in Eagle Life Assurance and Western Bank (seventh largest) and Sorec Ltd (second largest property company) (Innes, 1984). All the major finance groups had significant industrial and property holdings with the exception of Standard/Liberty Life which remained purely financial.

The concentrated control of the financial sector has contributed to concentration and centralisation of Nedsual capital and also shaped industrialisation around the MEC core.[13] Hence, understanding of finance needs to be integrated into a broader understanding of the dynamics of accumulation in a particular place and time. South Africa's system of accumulation, the MEC, produced, and was produced by, a powerful and concentrated financial system with uniquely close ties/overlapping ownership structures with productive capital and strong state support. These origins (of which an international dimension is constitutive) shaped the financial sector until deregulation, internationalisation and financialisation provoked further, if changing, patterns of integration and accumulation. Perhaps paradoxically, conglomerate control of the financial sector did not prevent but led to increasing speculative investment and to high levels of illegal capital flight.

In the climate of growing isolation and international sanctions (following the Sharpeville massacre), the Franszen Commission of the early 1970s led to eight amendments to the Bank Act. It regarded the banking sector as economically strategic and was concerned that foreign-controlled banks held 73% of total commercial bank deposits, recommending that foreign control be reduced to below 50%, and new entries by foreign banks were effectively prohibited (Itzikowitz, 1992; Singleton and Verhoef, 2010; and Innes 1984). Anglo increased its share in Barclays, thus allowing the bank to deflect criticism whilst, "At the same time the strong links which Anglo had with Nedsual and Standard laid the basis for an extremely powerful alliance to be formed between Anglo, Barclays, Standard, Nedsual (with its attendant Dutch connections) and the Old Mutual" (Innes 1984, p. 217). In the wake of the debt crisis of 1985, when international banks led by Chase Manhattan refused to release $10 billion to South Africa, and in the economic and political climate of the time, foreign banks withdrew from South Africa. Barclays Bank sold its stake in 1986 and Barclays National was renamed as the more patriotic sounding First National Bank and later absorbed into the FirstRand Group. Standard Chartered sold its share in the Standard Bank of South Africa, again to South African interests. This upheaval meant that for a short period, the banking sector was almost entirely domestically owned (Singleton and Verhoef, 2010).

But it is not simply a matter of intra-financial relations. Accumulation within South Africa had witnessed a passage from an uneasy compromise between Afrikaner and English capital to their integration, with a corresponding subordination of small-scale to large-scale Afrikaner capital. Equally, just as English capital spread its ownership and control over most sectors, including finance,

13 One objection to the MEC analysis is that its focus on mining and energy fails to grasp the importance of the insurance industry in the history of South African capitalism. As should be clear from the analysis presented here, this is to miss the point.

so the major mechanism through which Afrikaner capital grew, concentrated and integrated was by means of finance (with extensive support from the state). But, as will be seen in the next section, from its role of catalyst in forming and resolving intra-class capitalist conflicts, finance has increasingly taken on significance on its own account.

6 The 1980s Onwards: Deregulation, Internationalisation and Renewed Concentration

Growing demand to isolate the apartheid regime led to an increase in sanctions and the withdrawal of foreign capital in the 1970s and 1980s. From the 1970s onwards, sanctions and relative isolation tended to increase domestic concentration. It was the de Kock Commission, appointed in 1977 and reporting in 1985, which facilitated a massive transformation of the South African financial system with its advocacy of the liberalisation of the financial sector, in line with international trends. As seen above, financialisation as a structural change has affected many developed economies since the 1980s and is associated with the liberalisation of interest rates, exchange rates, credit ceilings, the privatisation of state-owned banks, and removal of barriers to entry. Financialisation is also associated with large financial and capital markets, increases in financial transactions, in real interest rates and higher returns to the financial sector and a larger share of income accruing to the sector and holders of financial assets.

De Kock's framework was the financial liberalisation approach and, as such, demonstrated scant attention to the functioning of the financial system as a whole, and argued for monetary policy to be conducted by the 'market mechanism' as far as possible: for specialised bank categories to be abolished in order to "stimulate competition"; liquid asset requirements were superseded by cash reserve requirements; new capital requirements were imposed, as prescribed by the Basel accord; foreign banks were allowed to establish branches and buy shares in South African banks; and the latter were permitted to establish offshore interests. Legislation in 1990, amended again in 1994, removed all distinctions between deposit-taking institutions and led to the transformation of almost all of South Africa's building societies into banks which, in turn, became targets for takeover by the larger banking groups. In 1995 there was the abolition of the dual exchange rate system and the end of capital controls on non-residents. Today South Africa's capital market is large relative to GDP and significantly more liberalised than other BRIC countries (for example, Abiad et al. 2008; and Schindler, 2009). Financial services' (which includes finance, insurance and real estate) contribution to GDP has risen from 11% 1980 to 15%

in 1990 and 21% in 2010. It is the single largest sector of the South African economy in terms of contribution to GDP and its growth has outstripped all other sectors.

The restructuring of the financial sector and the emergence of a small number of specifically financial conglomerates has resulted, with the sector, and the financial system as a whole, being dominated by the 'Big Four' commercial banks. But the restructuring of the financial sector has occurred alongside general corporate restructuring which has seen the 'unbundling' and overseas relisting of many major conglomerates alongside new participation by overseas capital in the financial system. The Big Four are (Bankscope, 2012):

Standard Bank: in which the Industrial and Commercial bank of China now has a 20% stake, and which is the biggest bank in Africa (by assets) and which controls the Liberty Holdings group which includes Liberty Life Insurance (the third biggest insurance company in South Africa today) and Stanlib (the largest unit trust company and second largest investment manager);

ABSA: the Amalgamated Banks of South Africa, formed in 1991 through the merger of 'Afrikaner' groupings previously under Sanlam – particularly Volkskas and Trust Bank. In 2005 Barclays returned to South Africa and bought a controlling stake in Absa whilst Sanlam undertook extensive unbundling and delisted;

The First National Bank: now part of First Rand Limited financial services conglomerate which is dominated by Rand Merchant Bank and Remgro and which includes Wesbank, Momentum Insurance and Asset Management;

The Nedbank Group: controlled by Old Mutual, previously South African Mutual. Old Mutual demutualised, relisted on several stock exchanges in 1999, established London headquarters and has extensive global holdings. Vitali et al. (2011) found that 147 corporations control 40% of the monetary value of all transnational corporations. Of the top 50 firms in the centre piece of their 'bow tie' of control, 45 are financial firms and Old Mutual is placed 30th of the world's most powerful corporations (see also Du Boff, 2011, for suggestive if not convincing critical comments on the methodology of Vitali et al.).

The assets and market share of South African banks are given in Table 8.1. The banking sector is not only extremely concentrated, it has become more so. The number of fully registered banks in South Africa increased from 35 in 1994 to 44 in 2000. But 2001–2003 saw a major clearing out of the sector (Figures 8.1 and 8.2) as (smaller) banks were acquired by larger banks (e.g. Imperial Bank, Mercantile Lisbon and McCarthy Bank), others dissolved (e.g. Regal Treasury and SAAMBOU, the seventh largest bank in terms of assets at the time) while others (African Merchant Bank, Brait Merchant Bank, Cadiz Investment Bank and Corpcapital Bank) did not apply for renewal of their

TABLE 8.1 South African Banks: assets and market shares in 2010

Bank name	Bank assets (Rbn)	Market share
The Standard Bank of SA	781 947 804	25.5%
ABSA	663 076 327	21.6%
FirstRand Bank		18.8%
Nedbank	546 961 735	17.8%
Investec Bank	201 501 528	6.6%
Imperial Bank	578 078 265	1.9%
Citibank N.A.	51 068 333	1.7%
Deutsche Bank	34 910 860	1.1%
African Bank	28 103 931	0.9%
JP Morgan Chase	25 758 392	0.8%
Caylon Corporate and Investment Bank	15 918 044	0.5%
Standard Chartered Bank	13 274 633	0.4%
The Hong Kong and Shanghai Banking Corporation	12 871 226	0.4%
Capitec Bank	10 793 359	0.4%
Societe Generale	8 584 122	0.3%
China Construction Bank	6 524 014	0.2%
Mercantile Bank	5 959 348	0.2%
Bank of China	4 760 807	0.2%
The Royal Bank of Scotland	1 879 659	0.1%
Teba Bank	3 520 766	0.1%
Albaraka	2 638 585	0.1%
HBZ Bank	2 065 276	0.1%
Grinrod Bank	2 105 980	0.1%
State Bank of India	2 099 982	0.1%
Bidvest Bank	2 340 742	0.1%
Sasfin	1 550 210	0.1%
The SA Bank of Athens	1 221 759	0.0%
Habib Overseas Bank	734 270	0.0%
GBS Mutual Bank	788 009	0.0%
Bank of Taiwan	738 066	0.0%
Bank of Baroda	455 251	0.0%
VBS Mutual Bank	259 292	0.0%
Total assets	3 069 936 863	100%

SOURCE: BASA (2010)

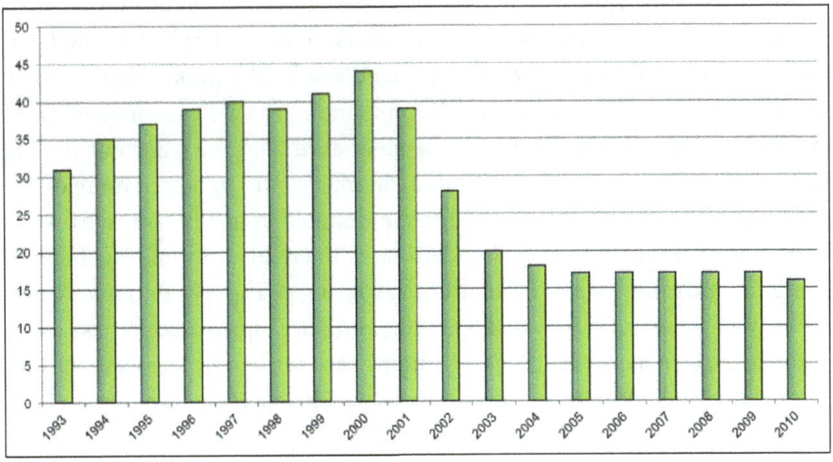

FIGURE 8.1 Number of registered South African banks
SOURCE: BASA (2010)

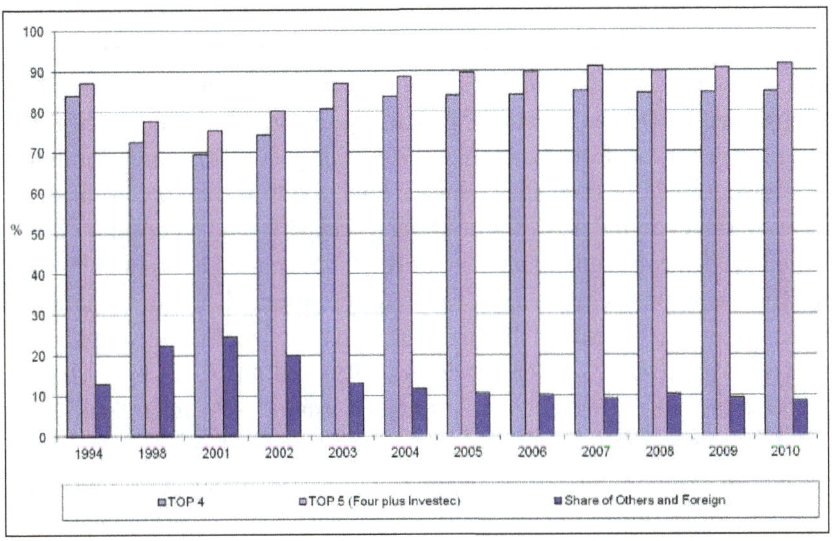

FIGURE 8.2 Market share of assets for selected years: South African banks
SOURCE: BASA (2010)

licences at the end of 2002. In addition, BOE, the sixth largest bank, was absorbed by Nedbank (Hawkins, 2003).

The National Treasury and the South African Reserve Bank commissioned a Task Group to examine competition in South African banking (Falkena et al. 2004). The Report of the Task Group found that the concentration levels of the South African banking industry are high, but not out of line with other emerging markets. However, it argued that in market segments, rather than at firm level, concentration is even more marked. For example, the 'Big Four' banks accounted for 93% of total deposits made by the public in June 2003, but they accounted for 95.4% of credit card lending, 92.3% of mortgage loans, and 89.5% of instalment finance (Falkena et al. 2004, p. 34). Each of the Big Four has a scale monopoly (25% or more market share) in one or more of the retail market segments, "FNB has a scale monopoly in instalment sales, ABSA in mortgages and credit cards, Standard Bank in credit cards and Nedbank in overdrafts and other loans" (Falkena et al. 2004, p. 34). The concentrated nature of the financial sector is show in Figures 8.3 and 8.4. Concern about these levels of concentration led to the Banking Enquiry established by the Competition Commission in 2006, the specific focus of which was retail banking and the level and structure of charges made by retail banks (Competition Commission, 2008; see also Falkena et al. 2004; and Hawkins, 2003).

The leading institutions of the financial system, then, are the few highly concentrated commercial banks whose profitability considerably outstrips their European counterparts (Figure 4) and which are part of larger financial conglomerate groupings. These institutions have extensive branch networks and hold short-term assets and liabilities and, it would seem, largely oversee their own regulation. Deregulation of the financial sector has not increased funds for industry nor the diversification of the economy. Indeed, finance for industry has continued to stagnate (Ashman, Fine and Newman, 2010a). Instead, however, since around 2004 South Africa has experienced a consumer boom fuelled by high commodity and asset prices and increased household borrowing. High asset prices inflated the capacity of households to borrow and this consumption growth, though limited to around the top 20% of the population, saw total household debt nearly double from R0.7 trillion in 2006 to R1.3 trillion in 2011 (SARB, 2011). Household debt stands at around 65% of GDP, and loans and advances to the household sector exceed loans to the corporate sector (SARB, 2011). The commodity boom and rising asset prices attracted short-term capital inflows, contributing to a strong Rand which further strengthened the consumption boom and led to a surge in import demand. Imports have grown, as has the financial services sector as seen above, while the share of agriculture, industry and manufacturing has fallen. Net flows of portfolio investment were ten times higher than FDI flows in 2010 (SARB, 2011).

These flows keep the value of the Rand strong, make cost of labour and inputs higher, and make long-term FDI less attractive. Large portfolio inflows and outflows also increase the volatility of the exchange rate, which tends also to discourage FDI. Portfolio investments keep equity prices higher, which further exacerbates elite consumption. High returns to equities 'crowds out' more

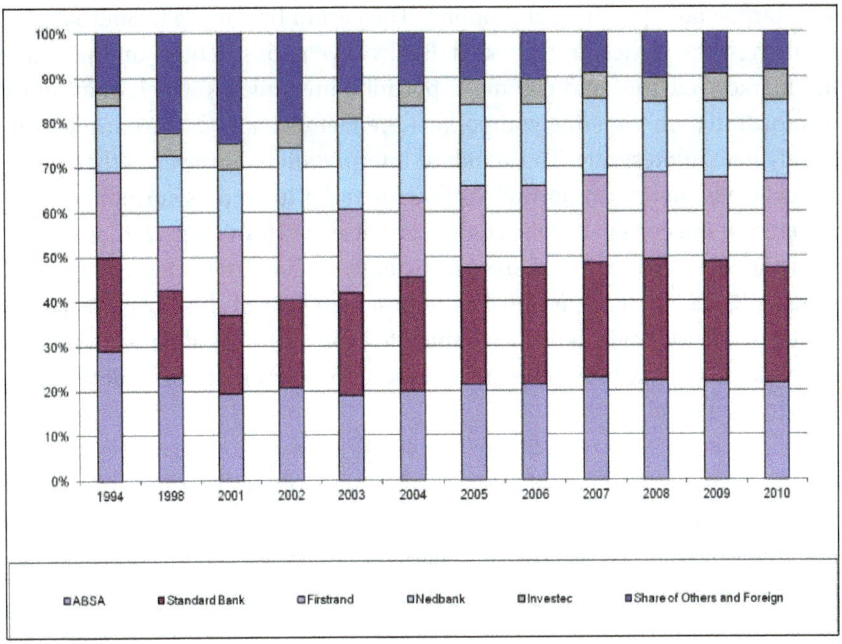

FIGURE 8.3 Market share of assets of South African banks
SOURCE: BASA (2010)

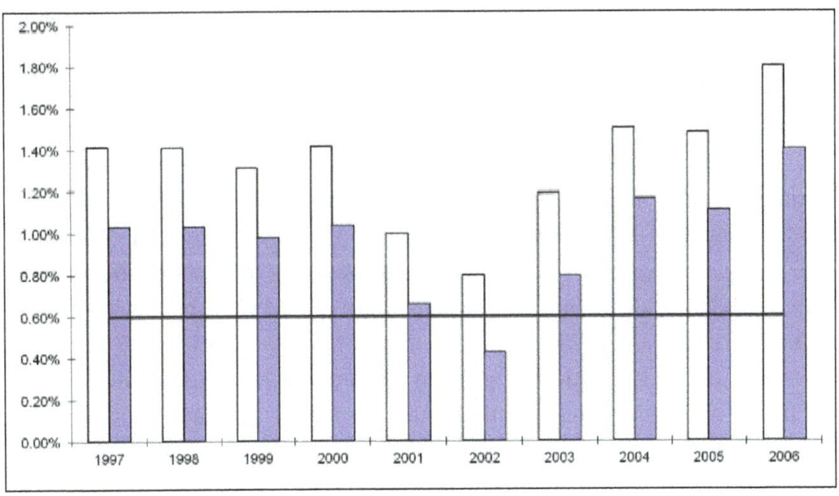

FIGURE 8.4 Return on assets – South African banks
SOURCE: BASA (2010)

long-term lending to the real economy. The cost of borrowing in South Africa is amongst the highest in the world. Banks have no restrictions on their capital market activities and can make portfolio investments which offer quick returns. Inflation targeting compounds the factors above by favouring a relatively high interest rate. The standard interpretation, however, is that South Africa needs short-term portfolio inflows in order to fund its current account deficit. But the current account deficit is worsened by the repatriation of dividend income. South Africa has consistently suffered negative net income transfers. In 2009, income transfers represented 56% of the current account deficit, while the trade deficit accounted for only 21% (World Bank, 2011). The portfolio inflows are thus necessary to fund the outflow of profits that the portfolio inflows earn!

Lack of attention to the financial system's capacity to finance investment continues to be a striking theme of the literature on the South African financial system (for example, Van Wyk et al. 2012). Oligopolistic competition in the financial sector means that the banks are overextended in some assets at the expense of others. Oligopolistic competition in financial markets results in inefficiency, and the failure to produce a full range of financial markets. This is the opposite of the theory motivating liberalisation. Liberalisation in practice, as demonstrated by South Africa, leads to greater concentration amongst financial institutions, higher costs of finance, and the proliferation of asset markets not necessarily broadening the net provision of the scope of financial services. The stagnation in levels of investment is not because of the nature of the financial system as narrowly conceived in the mainstream literature. For it remains heavily influenced by the role played by corporate conglomerates. They continue to dominate the industrial core of the economy, which remains in minerals and energy, whilst pursing internationalisation and financialisation strategies of their own. Their oligopolistic domination can discourage new investors because of the difficulties of breaking in to concentrated markets and because of the difficulty of negotiating joint ventures. This is true of domestic capital also. Oligopolistic concentration and divisions between sectors can produce stagnation in levels of investment as a consequence of market power whilst the conglomerates' international vision leads to the growing importance of foreign capital markets, and also widespread, illegal and staggering levels of capital flight (Ashman, Fine and Newman, 2011).

How, then, has the South African financial system evolved, and what are the forces driving this evolution? During the last decade or so, the South African economy has experienced consumption-led growth, with household consumption outpacing output and income growth. This 'growth path', facilitated by the financial system, has only served to exacerbate high levels of unemployment and inequality and to hold back development. Macroeconomic policy since 1994 has focused on low inflation, a strong currency, a liberalized trade regime and an increasingly open capital market. All of these have benefited financial interests, and the broader corporate interests so intertwined with the financial sector in South Africa both historically and today. Interests within the financial system may block or promote particular types of both financial and non-financial policies. Finance tends to oppose interventionist industrial policy because it may be threatened by the way that finance is to be raised and deployed by such a policy. Similarly expansionary macroeconomic policy may well be opposed, in so far as it gives precedence to (public) welfare over conventional macroeconomic policy targets which are conducive to the profitability of the financial sector (inflation targeting and protection of financial assets).

So, as Zysman (1983, p. 80) argued in a different context some time ago, "the structure of the national financial system affects the capacity of the national policy executive to intervene in the industrial economy" and "since the financial system is a constraint on action and an influence on the power relations in the economy, it is an element shaping the arena for industrial and economic politics." Our discussion of South Africa surely illustrates these two points. The South African financial system cannot be expected to reform itself nor to promote investment in industry/broader employment generation unless it is made to do so. Pressure to do this will not come from corporate South Africa whose conglomerates retain a powerful influence over the financial sector and which are pursuing internationalisation abroad whilst remaining highly concentrated and profitable at home.

7 Conclusions

The discussion of the evolution of South Africa's financial system, under the impetus of global and national factors and forces, has demonstrated the more general theoretical arguments made in this chapter. We have argued that the Financial Systems approach, which has emerged within the discipline of economics, is only marginally superior to the financial liberalisation approach for drawing lessons from comparative experience. It has yielded some surprising results about the potential and necessity for government regulation and intervention, but it has done so on the narrowest of theoretical foundations, and its analysis is incapable of addressing the complexity, variety and the key causal elements of financial systems in practice. The Varieties of Capitalism approach, which has emerged from a broader range of disciplinary locations, is also unsatisfactory given its methodological nationalism and failure to provide a deeper understanding of capital and capitalism, its conflicts as well as its institutional compromises. In the hands of Hall and Soskice in particular, the approach employs a firm-centric view of institutional variation in order to "theorize macro-level diversity from a starting point in microeconomics", whilst its reliance on parsimonious taxonomies instead of causal analysis narrows "the spectrum of economic variation to a single, privileged continuum of difference internal to the advanced capitalism of the Northern Hemisphere." (Peck and Theodore, 2007, pp. 745 and 750, respectively) In the hands of others, the VoC approach is reduced to common sense (Bruff, 2011) or vacuous appeals to the necessity for history (Hodgson, 1996).

As we have seen, some important questions are at stake. First, is the financial system to be viewed narrowly as financial institutions and activities alone or is it to be conceived more broadly as the system by which industry/the economy in general is financed? For that understanding it requires consideration of the interaction between financial and other institutions and how they mutually undertake financial functions. Systemic connections exist between industry and finance, but they take different forms and have different outcomes. And second, if – as we have argued – specific historical trajectories and class relationships and the patterns of the emergence and interaction of different forms of capital and the state, shape capitalist development in particular place and time, how do we theorise causal processes of change through time?

Addressing these questions has important implications for the comparative political economy of capitalism, and its financial systems, more generally. In our alternative approach to both Financial Systems and Varieties of Capitalism, financialisation has been identified as a causal factor in the evolution of national financial systems/systems of accumulation. But various factors at various different levels causally mediate the processes of financialisation in dynamic ways and so financialisation should not be seen simplistically as a force for convergence. Instead, financialisation needs to be incorporated into conceptions of the variegated and combined and uneven nature of capitalism and the uneven and interdependent development of national and regional capitalisms. Capitalism's general tendencies play out in specific ways in time and space. Much the same can be said about neoliberalism, of which financialisation is a critical part. Whilst clearly international in nature and containing commonalities in its restructuring programmes, its outcomes vary economically and institutionally, and it cannot be seen as a source of simplistic economic or institutional convergence. That this broad viewpoint is vital historically and analytically should be clear from our discussion of the South

African system of accumulation and the non-developmental (broadly understood) role played by finance within it. One consequence of the MEC and now the 'Financialised MEC' is that South Africa has a large, powerful and sophisticated financial system which is undertaking its own internationalisation strategy into other parts of Africa whilst 37% of the population do not even have a bank account (Finscope, 2011) and at the same time as there remain crisis levels of unemployment and crisis levels of productive investment combined with critical levels of capital flight, both legal and illegal. Yet, remarkably, all these dimensions remain overlooked in the still largely complacent literature on the South African financial system.

CHAPTER 9

The Meaning of Marikana

Postscript as Personal Preamble

Even for those, such as myself, for whom the post-apartheid transition nestled securely and comfortably somewhere between massive disappointment and equally massive disaster, the Marikana massacre came as a huge shock as it did more generally. In retrospect, two features stand out, over and above how Marikana is indicative of what and how much had gone wrong. The first is just how greater the shock and reaction would have been across the world if Marikana had taken place under apartheid. And, second, by the same token, how much more and for how much longer it would have been marked as symbolic of what post-apartheid South Africa had become. For some reason, the passage from apartheid seems to have anaesthetised crimes against the people as well as condoning those complicit in those crimes and similar even if on a lesser and less direct scale. The comparisons with the Sharpeville massacre and the Soweto uprising are telling.

1 Some Underlying Determinants[1]

The mining core of South Africa's economy saw, in 2012, the most explosive and significant strike wave since the defeat of apartheid which challenged the terms of settlement in the industry and the low wage regime on which it rests. At Marikana, it involved the killing of 34 Lonmin strikers by police on 16th August. These events, and the response to them by the Tripartite Alliance of the ANC, COSATU and the SACP, starkly reveal the economic and social issues in South Africa today, highlighting how many features of the apartheid system have not been so much preserved as reproduced and even intensified.

Further, the strike wave threw the labour movement into acute crisis as many members of the National Union of Mineworkers led the strike wave by rejecting the union's politically powerful but industrially conservative leadership.

1 This article first appeared in shorter form in Think Africa Press, http://thinkafricapress.com/south-africa/state-mining-industry-run-mangaung-marikana. It also appeared in various other shorter versions, not least Ashman and Fine (2013b). The Chapter draws upon Ashman and Fine (2013c).

 | DOI:10.1163/9789004748330_010

Many workers had joined the Association of Mining and Construction Workers' Union (AMCU), the rival union formed in 1999. Further, most notably at Lonmin and elsewhere, workers sought to negotiate with employers directly, and not through any of their union representatives. 'Fear' of industrial unrest in the mining sector and worries about weakening economic growth continued to dominate the business headlines over early 2013.

Once more, then, the industry is in the grip of a crisis, which the media all too often suggests is terminal despite the ongoing scale of South Africa's mineral wealth. Against this backdrop, we suggest that there are four systemic factors underpinning events at Marikana and South Africa's political economy more generally. Mining starkly exhibits these central features – monopolistic industry structures, tight corporate control, vertical integration, and the co-option of emerging black capitalist interests. It also reveals the continuing emphasis of the post-apartheid economy on exporting minerals over local beneficiation, the diversification of the economy, and greater employment generation. Critically these events have drawn attention to the ongoing scale of South Africa's mineral wealth and the industry's continuing dependence on cheap, black, and often migrant labour. In April 2010, a Citigroup Report identified South Africa as the world's richest country in terms of its mineral reserves, valued at $2,500 billion. Platinum group metals constituted $2,300 billion, the bulk of this value, all located in the Bushveld Ignateous Complex (BIC) geological formation spreading across Gauteng, the North West and Limpopo Provinces. This area also contains the world's largest chromium and vanadium reserves and produces ferrochrome, nickel and other minerals.

Platinum is one of a family of six chemically-similar elements that make up the platinum group metals (PGMs). South Africa is estimated to hold 87% of the world's PGM reserves and accounted for 76% of world platinum production in 2009. Since the early 1990s, platinum has been the fastest growing sub-sector within the mining industry and, consequently, the BIC area has been the fastest-growing South African region, exceeding 15% in some years. Meanwhile, significant restructuring of firms around platinum means the sector is dominated by Anglo American Platinum (80% owned by Anglo American) and Impala Platinum, which also dominated the sector during apartheid, together with the third largest producer, Lonmin. These firms have successfully converted their old-order mining rights and have retained control over a large part of BIC platinum production by entering into joint-venture partnerships with domestic black capital.

The latter were BEE beneficiaries of the process by which the state effectively nationalised privately held mineral rights through the enactment of the Minerals and Petroleum Resources Development Act (Capps, 2012a and b).

The MPRDA required incumbents to convert their rights under the new Act. At the same time, much akin to the way in which the National Party leveraged economic space for Afrikaner capitalists in the decades following 1948, the post-apartheid state has also been subject to pressure by emerging black capital to do the same. It has done so through favourable MPRDA mineral rights allocation, as well as through the support of state institutions like the IDC, to finance the growth of black capital. A larger proportion of merger and acquisition activity in South Africa has, however, been financed by the country's financial sector. Existing communities, which owned BIC mineral rights under Bantustan legislation, have also acquired ownership stakes in the old and new mines. The Bafokeng, for example, own a significant share of Impala Platinum and have listed their assets, Royal Bafokeng Holdings, on the Johannesburg Stock Exchange. The joint ventures with emerging black capital tend to shoulder a disproportionate share of the risks, often being the first to reduce output so not to depress commodity prices further. The scale and pace of growth has also increased the sector's systemic dependence on bringing in labour from other areas of South Africa.

Against this backdrop, as suggested, there are four systemic factors underpinning events at Marikana.

The first is the nature of South Africa's extractive economy, highlighted by the notion of the Minerals-Energy Complex (*MEC*). The MEC refers to the core set of heavy industries, powerful vested interests and institutions which evolved around minerals extraction and processing and their interaction as a distinctive system of accumulation whose dynamics and linkages have long determined South Africa's pattern of industrialisation (Fine and Rustomjee, 1996). Critical actors in the MEC were the six mining houses that grew out of the minerals revolution in the late nineteenth century, established the migrant labour system, fused with Afrikaner finance capital in the 1960s, and diversified ownership out of the minerals and energy core so that by the 1970s and 1980s they dominated the whole economy. The concentration of both industrial and money capital in the MEC core rested both on state support provided for key sectors, particularly through the establishment and development of energy parastatals, and beneficial tariff and pricing policies, combined with the extreme exploitation and political oppression of the black majority.

The political settlement of 1994 protected white capital, despite more radical demands from parts of the liberation movement. Since 1996 the ANC has reduced capital and exchange controls and allowed conglomerates to move their primary listings abroad, which they have combined with intensive unbundling at home. This has involved selling some of their (often less productive) assets to the aspirant black bourgeoisie which was regarded by many as an essential buffer against more extensive attacks through wealth redistribution and other and more far-reaching progressive policies.

These developments have both reproduced and transformed the MEC's determining influence across the economy. The foreign listings and unbundling of the big productive capitals have meant a (domestic) focus on their productive, mining core *and* an emphasis on the internationalisation (and financialisation) of their operations. Simultaneously, this unbundling has led to the emergence of distinctively financial corporate groupings with an increasing amount of domestic power as the financialisation of the economy has intensified.

The post-apartheid economy then could be said to have been dominated by the 'three Fs'- capital *flight*, *finance*, and *foreign* ownership albeit served with a side-order of BEE. Illegal capital flight has, for example, denuded the economy of the vital resources needed for investment and development, at times haemorrhaging abroad as much of the economy's resources as have been retained at home for real investment. This itself, on the other hand, has meant the economy's three Fs are complemented by four lows – low investment, low productivity, low employment and low wages.[2]

In platinum, capital's restructuring created the Anglo American Platinum Corporation (Amplats), formed as Anglo broke up its old JCI holdings into JCI Ltd (gold, ferrochrome, base metals); Johnnic (industrial holdings); and Anglo Platinum which amalgamated with Anglo's Rustenberg Platinum Holdings. Amplats is listed in London and controls 40% of global output. In 2001 Amplats was the first South African company to make $1 billion profit.

Impala unbundled from Gencor and also listed in London, with Lonhro renamed Lonmin in 1999, divesting itself of non-core assets. Anglo-Swiss multinational Xstrata has a 25% stake in Lonmin. Xstrata is also one of South Africa's biggest coal producers, and an important supplier to Eskom. Commodity giants Glencore and Xstrata were negotiating a merger throughout 2012.

The platinum industry starkly exhibits the central features of South Africa's political economy – monopolistic industry structures, tight corporate control, vertical integration, and the co-option of emerging black capitalist interests. The evolution of platinum extraction also reflects the continuing emphasis of post-apartheid economy on exporting minerals over local beneficiation, the diversification of the economy, and greater employment generation. Black

2 Later, I added a fifth, low economic and social infrastructure (Fine, 2025e, Ch. 13).

capitalist interests, it appears, fully supported the aggressive response of the firms and the state in attempting to break the strike at Lonmin. Evidence to the Farlam Commission of Inquiry has revealed how Lonmin senior management had written to government ministers requesting that, "The State should bring its might to bear on this crucial sector of the economy using resources at its disposal to resolutely bring the situation under control." Emails from Cyril Ramaphosa – former general secretary of the NUM, now Lonmin executive – reveal he used his position in the ANC to lobby the government for action in support of Lonmin, calling the strikers "dastardly criminal" and demanding "concomitant action" be taken.

The second issue that Marikana reveals is that much remains of the century-old migrant labour system, despite nearly two decades of reform of the apartheid labour market system. The mining industry remains wedded to its apartheid past in its dependence on cheap black labour. Lonmin workers were striking for a pay rise from around R4,000 to R12,500 per month. Pay scales are complex, particularly as labour brokers (formally banned under apartheid) now hire approximately one-third of the workforce across mining as mine employment has been increasingly casualised, particularly through the sub-contracting of 'non-core' surface jobs.

The migrant labour system, as established by the mining houses at the end of the nineteenth century, entailed both racialised workplace organisation and a regional system of labour recruitment that drew in labour from across Southern Africa (Jeeves, 1985). One damning feature of this system were the compounds where mineworkers were housed and which functioned as a key means of labour control. Workers' annual work cycle only allowed for breaks at Christmas and Easter. The migrant labour system also meant the devastation of the 'labour-sending' areas which were forced to rely on mineworkers' remittances. The Eastern Cape supplied labour to the gold mines of the Witwatersrand from the 1890s onwards, and the area remains today both one of the poorest regions of the country and a labour-sending area – particularly the villages of the former Transkei 'homeland' around Lusikisiki, Bizana and Flagstaff, origin of a number of the miners shot at Marikana. Measures to shorten the length of time between mineworkers' home visits, such as building airstrips (common near to Game Reserves) have not been taken.

However, the mining houses developed a strategy of stabilising the migrant workforce through a combination of repeat, long-term contracts and more localised recruitment. Mine managers began to question the worth to them of the compound system, in part at least because hostels were becoming bases of union organisation in the 1980s. Anglo American, for example, argued that hostels were becoming unmanageable, that they were exploited by the National Union of Mineworkers (NUM) to "foment unrest", and that a policy of home ownership would have the greatest impact on "worker and social stability" (Bezuidenhout and Buhlungu, 2010, p. 250). Major change, then, has been the decline in the number of migrants from outside South Africa. For example, of the 52,000 total workforce at AngloPlats in 2012, 45,000 were from South Africa, 3,677 were from Mozambique, 1,600 were from Lesotho and 280 from Swaziland. This change has been combined with an increasing number of workers drawn from the areas more local to the mines, particularly high in platinum where many workers originate from across the North West Province and Limpopo. So more short distance migration has grown along with peri-urban settlement, and further devastation of rural labour-sending areas as employment opportunities have declined even further.

But whilst the compounds have been abandoned by mining companies, it has not resulted in affordable decent housing for mineworkers, whether state or company provided. Family accommodation schemes have been introduced for those who live near to the mines, but this often takes the form of a subsidy for a bond to purchase a house, which has only been taken up by a minority of better off workers. Despite pressure to deliver alternatives, privatisation of housing provision has really amounted to a living out allowance whereby workers are given a cash allowance to 'live out'. Many workers simply use this allowance to supplement their pay by living in the zinc shacks of the 'shack lands' which have sprung up around the mines. The appalling living conditions indicate that the social and labour plans of the MPRDA have been ineffective, reflecting the failure of the government to enforce its own policies.

Former NUMSA official and industry consultant Gavin Hartford (2012, p. 1) argues that 'the specific migratory and housing conditions of migrants have led to a double economic burden; that the collective bargaining processes and institutions failed dismally to hear the signs of discontent and address the causes; that the company leadership in HR and the line management functions is complicit in this failure; and that the solutions require a radical re-think of the future of migrant labour, of collective bargaining, of the manager/employee interface at shaft and mine level."

The third issue that Marikana exposes is the lack of adequate and coordinated planning of the development of such a large and important part of South Africa. Local municipalities are responsible for dealing with local development. But haphazard and unplanned development of the built environment has been rampant. This is at a time when the largest municipality in the BIC appears to have collapsed completely. Last year the Auditor-General failed to complete its audit of Rustenberg. Auditors were unable to express an opinion on the municipality's accounts. In the previous five years, Rustenberg received five successive qualified audits. Yet this has been one of the fastest growing parts of South Africa, and Rustenberg appears now not to be served by anybody amidst a myriad of uncertainties, including over land tenure.

The fourth issue upon which Marikana has shone the spotlight is the informal financial sector and growing levels of unsecured debt. The growth of micro-lending has been phenomenal recently despite legislation such as the Usury Act aimed at protecting the poor. According to the National Credit Regulator, South Africa's debt sits at R1.3 trillion, of which almost 10% is unsecured credit. Some 62% of unsecured credit agreements come from those earning less than R10,000 a month, and 22% are from those earning less than R15,000 a month. Moneyweb estimates that, for South Africans earning between R3,500 and R10,000 a month, as much as 40% of their income goes toward covering loan repayments. Of 19.6 million credit active consumers in 2012, 9.2 million of them are 'impaired', i.e. three or more payments in arrears, or with an adverse listing or judgement or administrative order against their name. This often takes the form of garnishee orders when employers are ordered by the courts to deduct debt repayments directly from workers' salaries. Many mineworkers were striking for higher wages in part either because garnishee orders were leaving them with little on which to live or because they were indebted to the unsecured lenders operating either outside the mines or in the cash loan shops that have grown up. There are at least thirteen 'micro-lenders' in Marikana alone.

This growth of borrowing for consumption is a consequence of an amendment to the Usury Act passed in 1992 which removed price controls on small loans (those under R6,000 and with a duration of less than 36 months), in theory to open up the market for small borrowers previously excluded from the lending of the big banks. It did this by removing the legislation restricting the interest rate. Small lenders then in theory would be able to cater to small borrowers' needs, whereas having a ceiling on the interest rate, it was argued, was making it hard for micro lenders to cover their costs. The National Credit Act of 2007 then capped the interest rate for unsecured loans at 31% in order to try to control this kind of lending, but this regulation was arguably too little, and somewhat too late.

It is too early to say what will be the lasting effects of this crisis. Amplats announced 14,000 job losses in January 2013, the biggest in that company's history, blaming falling world market prices as demand from the European car market (which use catalytic converters in car engines) has fallen. But as the four shafts to be closed are to be kept under 'care and maintenance' this tends to suggest that the company is taking the opportunity to increase profitability by limiting global supply, pushing prices back up, and at the same time trying to break the new militancy amongst workers. Also both the company's and industry expert reports (for example, that provided by European platinum manufacturer Johnson Matthey) argue that, whilst labour unrest in South Africa has affected supply, demand for platinum remains essentially stable given the likelihood of recovery in car production in Japan (following the natural disasters of 2011) and growth in the markets in China and India. Nevertheless, the job losses threaten once more to turn a crisis of profitability into a social crisis for labour.

Is the tough stance of the government in the face of the strikes indicative of the future as debate continues over the minerals sector? Of course, one possibility is that the ANC government will largely leave things as they are, with the industry resting upon the same low pay and state support as in the past. Another course, flaunted during the BRICS summit in Durban in March 2013, is for there to be a greater degree of co-operation over price and marketing between the big producers within South Africa and between South Africa and Russia – the largest global producer of palladium – in order to stabilise prices, the so-called 'OPEC option'. But to our mind this omits the question of industrial diversification. Platinum in particular could be the basis of an industrial diversification strategy focused on keeping downstream secondary industries within the domestic economy by concentrating on catalytic converters (and hence creating socially useful 'green jobs' helping to reduce greenhouse emissions), fuel cell technology and electricity generation. But all of this is resoundingly absent from public discussion, including from the National Development Plan.

Much of the current discourse centres around the Farlam Commission of Inquiry established by the ANC. From our perspective, while it is important for clarity to be obtained on the events around the day of the Marikana massacre, the focus should be broadened to examine the four root causes outlined above. Nevertheless, Marikana is the epitome of today's MEC, reflecting both the economic and social failings of post-apartheid development for the majority across so many dimensions. It reveals the continuing power and determining role of the MEC and white monopoly capital, the virtually unconditional support given to it by the ANC and its newly enriched black elite, the persistence – albeit in changing form – of migrant labour, the appalling pay, working and living conditions of mineworkers and the confused and opportunistic complicity of sections of the labour movement to all of the above.

2 The Present Crisis

But what of the new crisis in the mining sector? The collapse of global commodity prices – including coal, platinum, iron ore, nickel and gold – has produced a new crisis in the mining industry. Employers are proposing thousands more job losses. Anglo in particular has said it anticipates shedding 53,000 jobs over the next few years. Both Anglo and Lonmin have blamed the crisis on depressed commodity prices, erratic power supply, and rising labour costs.

Key 'stakeholders' met recently at a mining 'Phakisa', ostensibly to develop a shared vision of how to transform the industry and bring about improved levels of investment in line with the goals of the National Development Plan. Its aim also was to 'fast track' solutions to critical development issues, in particular how mining can contribute to beneficiation and broader industrialisation.

However, in reality, the agenda seems to have been dominated by the mining industry's plans for further drastic job losses combined with extensive new mechanisation of the sector. In a sane world, the mechanisation of many mining jobs would be good thing. But as we do not live in a sane world, the job losses threaten once more to turn a crisis of profitability into a deepening of the social crisis of labour. The government seems to hope that job losses can be compensated for by increased employment in the sectors which provide inputs into mining, particularly capital equipment.

But if the MEC, South Africa's system of accumulation, is to be changed, it means diversifying out of the core sectors and using minerals for much more systematic industrial diversification, aimed at developing downstream secondary industries within the domestic economy as well. Allowing mining capital to call the shots is not a recipe for success.

CHAPTER 10

Across Developmental State and Social Compacting: The Peculiar Case of South Africa

Postscript as Personal Preamble

At the time of the transition from apartheid, the vast majority of those who had fought so hard for it expected at the least to benefit from sort of policy mix that would bring development in the form of growth and welfare provision that had characterised the post-war boom in the west (and east Asia). Some, no doubt had other and higher priorities, for a class of black capitalists, for socialism of some sort despite the fall of the Soviet Union, and for a renewal and transformation of South Africa's role in the region and the continent.

These hopes and aspirations were primarily dashed in an instant by the policies adopted by the first ANC-led government. But, given time, hope springs eternal if often in diluted forms especially as neoliberalism takes hold. So, twenty years later, with Mbeki dismissed and Zuma in his place, National Development Plans, New Growth Paths, Developmental States and Welfarism were once more, if cautiously, being mooted.[1] And, emboldened by the shift in ANC leadership that had been engineered by progressive forces, trade unions felt they had the muscle to bring about radical change.

This is the context in which my cynicism could run riot. In particular, it focuses upon what I have called the Developmental State Paradigm and the Social Compacting Paradigm. Like the Varieties of Capitalism Approach and the Welfare Regimes Approach, from my perspective these framings were heavily rooted in the conditions of the post-war boom (however accurately and appropriately) that had spawned them and so, accordingly, were insensitive to contemporary neoliberal conditions that had already lasted longer than the post-war boom itself. In a sense, pinning hopes on these perspectives involved a double displacement – that the conditions underpinning them no longer existed on a global scale and, within South Africa itself, economic and political factors were not conducive even to begin to satisfy what was necessary to be either a development state and for partnership across state, industry and trade unions to forge economic and social policy.

1 For previous commentary on these, see Chapter 8 and Fine (2025e, Chs 11 and 12).

 | DOI:10.1163/9789004748330_011

Instead, the nature of neoliberalism is brought to the fore,[2] its dependence upon financialisation, and the consequences for the restructuring of the Minerals-Energy (and Finance) Complex. There are also hints of declining political conditions and the prospects for corruption to take hold. Sadly, we are well into the unravelling of the Tripartite Alliance as alliance and of its individual elements.

1 Introduction[3]

This Chapter is concerned with the shifting fortunes of the Developmental State Paradigm (DSP) and the Social Compacting Paradigm (SCP) and, with some reference to South Africa, how they do or do not have continuing presence and relevance. For each, there is a dual trajectory in terms of an evolving intellectual content, on the one hand, and an evolving set of global and national circumstances on the other. I show that both paradigms have increasingly diverged from the material realities that they are intended to confront. This is primarily because of the neglect of financialisation as the key characteristic of the past thirty years, which itself underpins neoliberalism. Whilst, in the post-war boom, both developmentalism and neo-corporatism offered some purchase on material realities and the prospects for policymaking, this has been eroded or, more exactly, transformed by financialisation. Unless the latter is satisfactorily addressed, neither (state-led) development nor (social) compacting can be expected to succeed, or be progressive, in any meaningful sense.

Nonetheless, neither paradigm has been killed off even though both have been hard hit by neoliberalism if in different ways and with different timings. The SCP, in the form of neo-corporatism, prospered by claiming to explain the post-war boom in general and for differential success within it for developed countries (the more corporatism, the better the performance). Ultimately, though, the SCP became much less ambitious, seeking to carve out a niche for itself in the slower growth and more unstable conditions of the neoliberal period, thereby diluting, shifting and even broadening what could be (defensively) targeted or (positively) achieved by compacting.

---

2 And its two phases crunched together in South Africa, and a third phase added in later work (Fine, 2024d).

3 Reproduced from Fine (2016a) drafted whilst benefitting from being a research professor visiting the Institute of Economic and Social Research at Rhodes University.

The DSP has suffered a similar if later fate, tied more to the fortunes of the East Asian NICs (Newly Industrialised Countries) than the developed economies. It was at its height during the East Asian miracle, in its opposition to the dogma of the Washington Consensus, but was already in decline prior to the East Asian crisis of 1997/98. Like the SCP, it too has diluted, shifted and broadened, with the notion of the developmental state increasingly being deployed to refer to any positive intervention by the state just as social compacting serves as a rhetorical device to support any cooperative compromise between potentially conflicting interests. As a result, I suggest that both the DSP and the SCP have become 'buzz' concepts, more or less freely applied across a wide range of diverse contexts, without necessary reference to longstanding traditions and experiences and to broader and deeper causal factors and goals.

This is all of particular relevance to South Africa. It is shown to have been hard hit by financialisation in the post-apartheid period, and the favourable conditions most associated with the DSP and the SCP have been substantially eroded with the internationalisation and financialisation of conglomerate capital and the incorporation of a new black elite. Despite, or even because of, this, recent policy documents have been drawn to a greater or lesser extent to both the DSP and the SCP. For the DSP, there is the projection of future aspirations with negligible attention to the realities that would be necessary to underpin them either by reference to the classic features of erstwhile East Asian NICs as developmental states or the conditions characterising the dynamics of an evolving class structure of contemporary South Africa. For the SCP, there is an abiding interest in, and paper commitment to, the role of social dialogue, particularly in light of the Tripartite Alliance of the African National Congress (ANC), South African Communist Party (SACP) and the Congress of South African Trade Unions (COSATU), but, once more, scant attention has been paid to the shifting conditions in which the Alliance collaborates, or not, which has witnessed the emergence of a new elite and the increasing reduction of compacting to moderating the demands for more progressive, effective and equitable policies (leading to questions over whether the Alliance serves or potentially breaks with such an outcome).

The Chapter proceeds in Section 2 by interpreting the DSP as a middle-range theory, charting its shifting content as such by highlighting what it does, and does not, incorporate within its explanatory framework and scope of analysis. This leads to a discussion in Section 3 of the nature of financialisation and its relationship to neoliberalism, and the problems this poses for the DSP. This is followed in Section 4 by an account of the SCP also as middle-range theory. Its trajectory, as well as that of the DSP, is ultimately broadly set in the context of financialisation as underpinning neoliberalism, with the latter having gone through two phases (shock therapy and its aftermath), each broadly attached to particular mixes of scholarship, ideology and policy in practice. This allows in Section 5 for an account of how the post-apartheid economy has been subject to financialisation, internationalisation, and the formation of a new black elite in which the conditions for, and policies associated with, both the DSP and the SCP have been eroded rather than strengthened. Paradoxically, this has meant these paradigms have proven more attractive for underpinning policy documents especially where they primarily serve ideological functions far removed from serious scholarship and policy in practice, as is illustrated by reference to the National Development Plan. The concluding remarks question under what conditions the paradigms (in and of themselves and in relation to material conditions) might be usefully deployed in policy making.

2 The Developmental State Paradigm

Although not acknowledging itself as such, what I will term the Developmental State Paradigm (DSP) might be classified as an almost ideal example of what Robert K. Merton defined as middle-range theory.[4] The latter offers an integration of the theoretical and the empirical, situating itself somewhere between grand theory and case study, and it is marked by its workability in explaining social outcomes by reference to underlying causal factors without being either unduly deterministic or insensitive to diversity and specificity. In the case of the DSP, its middle-range approach was prompted by the successes of the East Asian NICs as its subject, but its object was different if related. The DSP became prominent by the 1980s as the spearhead of opposition to the Washington Consensus in both theoretical and empirical terms. For, theoretically in the inductive traditions of modernisation theory associated with the old or classical development economics, the DSP sought, successfully, to show that the East Asian miracles had been the consequence of extensive state intervention, especially industrial policies and their accompaniments. In other words, developmental success depended upon rejection of the Washington Consensus, and the analyses and prescriptions associated with it.[5]

4 Neatly, in terms of what follows, his son, Robert C., was awarded the Nobel Prize in Economics in 1997, together with Myron S. Scholes, for discovering "a new method to determine the value of derivatives", the Black–Scholes(-Merton) formula, http://www.nobelprize.org/nobel_prizes/economics/laureates/1997/.

5 Although eliminating reference to the DSP as such, Ha-Joon Chang (1994, 2002, 2007 and 2010) has been at the forefront of this sort of continuing assault on the Washington

I suspect that the term middle-range is taken as pejorative, not least because it is suggestive of lack of depth, something that will be shown to be characteristic of the DSP in a number of respects. But, equally important, is the extent to which middle-range theory lacks breadth, almost inevitably so given its design to address specific empirical case studies. In addition, even so, the middle-range is potentially extremely extensive, rather than fixed and focused, depending upon the exact balance and scope of application of the incorporated theoretical and empirical content. As will be seen, the DSP has shifted emphasis from preoccupation with questions of national, if especially industrial, development to those of piecemeal development, with corresponding shifts in analytical content and focus.

But, for the moment, consider the target for the DSP as it shot to prominence in opposition to the Washington Consensus. First and foremost, it was concerned with the circumstances and the policies that make for latecomer, catch-up industrialisation. Each of these terms is important in defining, that is narrowing, the scope of the DSP, and in projecting its significance back in history (from Alexander Hamilton and US protectionism, through Friedrich List and German industrialisation, to Latin American ISI and beyond to East Asian miracles) and to future prospects. But latecomer, catch-up industrialisation is only one broad stage in the process of industrialisation, leaving aside other stages in industrialisation as well as other, and integral, aspects of development itself. Thus, for example, the DSP has generally overlooked the earliest stages of industrialisation,[6] that is the transition from agrarian society, as well as the later stages which involve moving *beyond* and not just *to* the technological frontier (which is inevitably a moving target as the first-comers do not accommodate by standing still).[7] By the same token, until lately for reasons that will become apparent, the DSP has tended to have very little to say about economic activity other than industry (what about agriculture) other than through the lens of industrialisation and/or industrial policy. This has implied a sore neglect of health, education and welfare for example (and demographics,

---

Consensus, with a corresponding convergence towards more mainstream market imperfections and institutional economics (Fine and Van Waeyenberge, 2013).

6 See Frangie (2011) for a rare juxtaposition of the developmental state with primitive accumulation and the process of state formation itself.

7 See Al-Jazaeri (2008) but also, put neatly, by Kim (2012, p. 158), "A study of the Korean state's activism since the early 2000s sheds new light on two outstanding issues in the literature on East Asian developmentalism ... First, how do erstwhile developmental states catalyse economic activity in an open, yet more regulated, economic environment? Second, since the nation-building phase of industrialization has largely been achieved, how do former developmental states support companies beyond catching up?"

again apart from some deference to labour force requirements especially in terms of skills).

Such wider considerations place the DSP as middle-range theory under critical scrutiny in two opposing fashions. On the one hand, it begs the question of the approach's empirical scope of application across stages of development and in terms of the notion of development itself. Confining these narrowly was to some extent extremely convenient for advocates of the DSP in their conflict with the Washington Consensus over the virtues of state intervention as exemplified by the East Asian NICs, not least as less rounded achievements in social policy (and democratisation) could be sub-contracted and confined to that other critical tradition (of the Washington Consensus) that emerged at the same time – adjustment with a human face – with few points of contact between them. And, especially for the economic school of the DSP (see below), case studies chosen for prominence could be the star performers even if at most establishing intervention as a necessary but not sufficient condition for successful industrialisation (as has been endlessly observed by critics of the DSP and opponents of picking let alone creating winners – on a rough count, state intervention fails as much as it succeeds).

On the other hand, there is the issue of what middle ground is occupied by the DSP as theory. Are its principles confined, by accident or design, to a limited phase of industrialisation, should they apply more widely, and, if so, does this indicate their strengths or weaknesses? Of course, such questions cannot be answered without interrogating DSP theory itself, something which is not necessarily made explicit as an amalgam of the theoretical and empirical. Broadly, though, I have identified what I have termed two schools within the DSP literature, the economic and the political (although the latter is heavily influenced by the sociology of development).[8] The economic school places emphasis on the role of state interventionism (industrial policy) in correcting systemic market failures associated with economies of scale and scope, coordination of complementary investments, targeting finance for investment, and so on (and, especially, in the phrases of Amsden and Wade, respectively, "getting the prices wrong" and "governing the market"). In a word, the developmental state for the economic school is exemplified by POSCO, the South Korean, initially state-owned steel corporation, built against World Bank advice on grounds of comparative advantage and spearhead and emblematic of the country's subsequent industrialisation.

8 For my previous work on the DSP in general, see Fine (2004 and 2006) and Fine et al. (eds) (2013), and Fine and Rustomjee (1996) for relevance for South Africa at an early stage.

To a large degree, the economic school has relatively little to say about whether appropriate developmental policies will or can be adopted on these terms, being more focused on insisting that such policies are pre-conditions for success. As a result, the economic is complemented by the political school. Its focus is upon whether the state is characterised by political or other conditions that allow it to be developmental (as opposed to being captured by non-developmental interests for example) without questioning what this means in practice. It has no need to refer to POSCO, and its symbolic mantra is, or ultimately became, one or (two) words – (embedded) autonomy.

Of course, market imperfections and embedded autonomy are ideal examples of middle-range concepts. Their adequacy for purpose in their chosen application within the DSP is not, for the moment, my immediate concern. Rather, it is to observe that as theoretical principles they are universal bordering on the ahistorical and asocial, and not confined to either latecomer, catch up or, indeed, any form of industrialisation. Thus, for example, the transition from agrarian to industrial society is surely as much a matter of market imperfections as for later stages. And, how did feudal or slave societies ever get out of their predicament whilst being bound by something considerably less, or more, than and certainly different from (latecomer) embedded autonomy?

Such reflections over a broader historical sweep suggest that the DSP, whether by accident or design, depends for its appeal on confining itself, as it has in practice to a greater or lesser extent, to latecomer, catch-up industrialisation. For, otherwise, the middle range involved stretches the credibility of allowing the grander questions to be ignored – such as what are the nature and causes of the (nation-)state and of development itself. Here I place emphasis upon three critical weaknesses of the DSP upon which it is dependent if only so much more apparently so once locating the approach more broadly in historical scope.

First is how the DSP is structured by taking the state-market dichotomy (possibly complemented by civil society) as foundational. This is understandable given the goal of countering the Washington Consensus on its own terms of market versus state, if coming down on the opposite side of the divide in the debate. But, on longer and alternative views of development, and even of the performance of advanced capitalist economies, the market/state dichotomy appears much less appealing once addressing the form and content of economic and social transformations that are far from reducible to, nor run along the lines of, the state/market divide. This is especially so of class interests, and of economic interests more generally, as these both evolve and are represented through both the state and the market. In any case, the state is itself a major player in as well as upon the market.

Second, then, it is not the case that class interests are absent in the DSP. But they tend to be confined to consideration of capitalists alone, involving a double reduction in not only focusing solely on capital but also on its relationships to the state as more or less exclusively constituted out of the latter's embedded autonomy in administering industrial policy on capital's behalf and in its collective interest (however defined, formed and pursued). Most obviously, this means conceiving the state in terms of the ministries, institutions, networks and personnel for making policy, at the expense of broader considerations of the politics of (inter- and intra-) class conflicts. And, on the longer view, there is a failure to address how class structure is transformed by development, with the emergence of new (fractions of) classes and shifts in the balance and forms of power between them.

Third, the DSP is thoroughly grounded in methodological nationalism and, in particular, the idea that each and every nation-state can develop subject to adoption of appropriate policies.[9] Again, this is not to suggest that the global is overlooked by the DSP as much is made of how to relate to international capital in trade, finance and access to technology. What is done in terms of the DSP, though, is to overlook the systemic functioning of the world economy in which each nation-state is an integral, rather than independent, part. As Gray (2011, p. 318) puts it in the context of South Korea:[10]

> Most analyses have adopted either an approach that analyses state transformation in terms of changes in the underlying domestic social relations of production, or have viewed neoliberal state transformation as stemming from international factors, namely the pervasive nature of neoliberal ideology and/or the coercive manoeuvrings of the US along with the international financial institutions. The argument ...[here] is not simply

9 See Pradella (2014) for methodological nationalism as the longstanding basis for the DSP.

10 See also Gray's (2011b, p. 595) study for Taiwan, "moving beyond attempts to understand transformation through national comparative ideal type models", or as Song (2011, p. 297), drawing on world systems theory and the state derivationist approach, puts it for South Korea in light of the putative demise of its developmental state, "Once the Korean developmental state is analysed in the light of the new framework, its transformation cannot be understood either as a transition from an interventionist to a non-interventionist state, or from the national to the global. The Korean state remains a capitalist state, be it understood to be the old developmental state or not, and it is no less integral to global capital accumulation. The transformation of the Korean developmental state must be seen as the rise of a new modality of social domination within the capitalist mode of production, rather than the reversal of the domination of 'the state' over 'capital' (or 'the economy'), of the 'national' (internal) over 'the global' (external) or vice versa, which are the presuppositions of practically the entire existent literature on the subject."

> that both 'levels of analysis' are important in the explanation of the state transformation, but that these 'levels' in fact need to be understood as inter-related and mutually constitutive.

Such an argument is particularly important in conjunction with those that came before concerning the weaknesses of the DSP, not least as classes of international and domestic capital mutually evolve both across and through both state and market.[11]

In making these points, reference has already been made to the evolution, or demise, of developmental states themselves, not least those of the East Asian NICs, although those that came earlier in Latin America, primarily through import-substitution industrialisation (ISI), are also perceived to have suffered a similar fate. There has also been a corresponding evolution of the literature making up the DSP itself. This has been made up of a number of strands, both broadening and shifting its content. First has been to respond to the supposed demise or death of the developmental state with reference to a number of separate elements or influences. Most obvious was the impact of the East Asian crisis of 1997/98, especially as it came on top of a revisionist literature that had suggested the region's miracle had been a myth, as popularised by Krugman (1994). Also important for the decline of the DSP was the move from Washington to Post-Washington Consensus (PWC), allowing in principle for limited and piecemeal concessions on state interventionism in response to identifiable market and/or institutional imperfections (without ever acknowledging that this shift had in part been provoked by the critical contributions of the DSP which never warrants a mention in the PWC universe, see below).

11 Thus, as Gray (2011b, p. 587) observes for the birth of the East Asian NICs in general, "As with Japan and South Korea, the US had deliberately sought to nurture economic growth and self-sufficiency in Taiwan as part of the wider geopolitical aims in East Asia". And, equally, combinations of such factors, with the irresistible attraction of the Chinese mainland to Taiwanese investment and declining US hegemony in the region, arise with the putative demise of the Taiwanese developmental state, p. 590, "In Taiwan, development thus brought forth new social forces that arose to contest the authoritarian developmental political system. The social movements that emerged were of four distinct types. The first protested against the state's inaction in the face of new issues, such as consumer protection, pollution, rising housing costs, and conservation. The second focused on state policies regarding ethnic groups and minorities' language rights, land control, and cultural identity and preservation, as well as the care more generally of disadvantaged groups. The third challenged the state's corporatist control over key social groups, such as workers, farmers, students, women, teachers and intellectuals. The fourth emerged to challenge the rules surrounding political sensitive issues, such as the ban on private contacts between Taiwan and mainland China, and human rights."

But, equally, prior both to the crisis and to the emergence of the more state-friendly Post-Washington Consensus, doubts were already being expressed about the continuing viability of the East Asian NICs on the grounds that the embedded autonomy required for their success would be undermined by that success. For latecomer, catch-up industrialisation brings with it a class of industrialists who are increasingly deemed not to be inclined to be subject to state control. More generally, successful industrialisation also creates other demands and from other classes that derive from the associated strains of economic and social development, whether it be for higher wages and welfare (from organised labour and social movements in Latin America) or democratisation.

Significantly, the understanding of the developmental state as its own gravedigger, to coin a phrase, offered an unwitting acknowledgement and bringing back in of some of those factors that had been omitted in establishing the DSP. This is clearly the case in terms of incorporating the role of evolving classes and class interests as underpinning the relationship between state and market. And, especially in the context of the East Asian NICs, it involved due deference to the impact of systemic global factors, not least as domestic capitals sought to gain access to international financial markets and, thereby, free themselves from state controls against this in terms of sources and application of funds. Second, though, this is indicative of the strand in the DSP literature that sees it draw upon a necessarily cumulative set of case studies both by country and by stage and nature of industrialisation (or development more broadly). For the economic school, given its self-selection bias towards success, this is much more muted than for the political school, which is more able to accommodate both success and failure in terms of meeting, or not, the conditions for an increasingly qualified notion of autonomy with, of course, the addition of the moniker, embedded, to form the "oxymoron", embedded autonomy, being the first step in the process.[12] As a result, we are subsequently offered different ideal types to suit different types of developmental states, from the networked for Eire[13] through to the neoliberal for Singapore and, for Botswana,

12 See Mkandawire (2012, p. 18) for observing that, "Peter Evans coined ... the oxymoron-like expression, 'embedded autonomy'".

13 For an account, see Breznitz (2012) who takes a constructivist ideational approach, p. 106, interrogating how an ideology across neoliberalism and developmentalism reconciled these in practice, p. 107, "This ideology, which was transformed into a 'taken-for-granted shared mental model' starting in 1958, led Irish policymakers to devise and implement economic policies on the basis of two opposing ideas: neoliberal free-market principles and a strong developmentalist ideal. Facing severe economic crisis and emigration, the government made job creation the national objective. The organizations designated to achieve it were granted immense power and influence. The strong focus on job creation

the development-oriented gate-keeping state (Hillbom, 2012).[14] Further, not only is there an accumulation of ideal types of developmental states, these are complemented by an ever-expanding range of explanatory factors across social, cultural, political and institutional variables.

Third is a strand in the literature that questions whether the developmental state is dead after all, especially as the East Asian crisis becomes less a distant memory and is seen more as an obstacle that is overcome through the renewal of state-supported growth.[15] As already indicated, this in part reflects the heterogeneity attached to continuing state intervention in the neoliberal era as opposed to, or in conjunction with, the presumed loss or lesser autonomy of the state relative to an increasingly powerful class of capitalists. It dovetails with another distinct but closely related literature that claims that industrial policy is alive and well, not least in the USA where neoliberal ideology dare not allow it to be known by this "toxic" name (Wade, 2012, p. 224). But elsewhere than the USA:

> A majority of middle-income countries – in Latin America, sub-Saharan Africa, Middle East and North Africa, and South Asia – have fallen behind the West in relative average income since the 1980s. Many are now seeing their manufacturing sectors stagnate or shrink in the face of East Asian competition. Some are pressing the World Bank to give more assistance in industrial policy ... This may turn out to be an early phase in the emergence of a new set of global policy norms in favour of a more 'developmental' state, qualifying the near-consensus around the norms of a 'regulatory' state.

led IDA to develop an orientation favoring MNCs. Application of these policies lured a stream of MNCs to Ireland. At the same time, investing in local industry, which necessitates a long timeframe and did not have an immediate benchmarked job creation impact, was viewed as economically protectionist and market distorting activity to be avoided."

14 See Tsukamoto (2012) for Japan's neoliberalised developmental state, and Liow (2011, p. 241) for whom, "Once a developmental state, Singapore has undergone much structural changes to its economy in the past decade. The economy has gradually been deregulated, liberalised and privatised to conform more to the neoliberal model. However, existing interests embedded within the developmental state prevents a transition to a full-fledged neoliberal regulatory one. Instead what emerges is a type of hybrid state, in the form of the neoliberal-developmental state." Note that, as with Breznitz from previous footnote, the neoliberal developmental state, equally middle-range oxymoronic as embedded autonomy, is engaged only at the expense of departing from, or at least refining, the DSP's account of economic interests, state-market dichotomy, and the role of international capital.

15 For Petropoulos (2011), this can involve the substitution of expanding and furnishing domestic demand through state intervention across the East Asian NICs and especially in China.

This is unduly optimistic since, as Wade (2012, p. 225) himself acknowledges, support for more extensive industrial policy even of a limited kind has minimal support within the World Bank. Indeed, even its major proponent, Justin Lin (the Bank's Chief Economist until June 2012), suggests that, "less than 10% of World Bank economists are sympathetic to his arguments" and, as argued by Fine and Van Waeyenberge (2013), Lin is more realistically interpreted as seeking to constrain rather than to promote state intervention as far as industrial policy (and more) is concerned.

As a fourth strand, the notion that the developmental state is alive and well, or has been resuscitated in East Asia or elsewhere, is, however, far from confined to a more realistic and empirically grounded account of industrial policy. Indeed, as argued in Fine (2013a) following Cornwall and Eade (2010), the developmental state is best understood currently as a failed buzzword (and fuzzword) within development discourse. It is a buzzword in the sense that, in combining together the other strands in the DSP literature and deploying them, and more, across many issues within development, the concept has lost its original roots in explaining systemic industrialisation and ranges freely across more or less any topic however narrow or broad and however distant from industrial policy. In this respect, it is like other buzzwords such as participation, citizenship, empowerment, sustainability, transparency, accountability, corruption and governance. In effect, wherever there is any example of success in state intervention, this can be interpreted as indicative of the presence of a developmental state whether by sector or across economic and social functioning more generally. The attachment to development and the state, to economic and social transformation in general, and to industrialisation in particular, is suspended. And the concept of the developmental state is wide-ranging but reduced to an ethos of favouring some degree of state intervention, generally increasing and more than allowed for by neoliberal orthodoxy. The latter is the key to the developmental state being a *failed* buzzword since success, or wide-scale use of the fuzz and buzz, depends upon adoption, certainly acknowledgement, by the World Bank, so dominant is it in development discourse both in setting the analytical agenda and skewing content within it. As far as the World Bank is concerned, the developmental state might just as well never have existed, whether in the literature or the real world itself.[16]

---

16 Thus, for example, in his proposal for a new development economics, there is no reference by Lin (2012), even by way of critical departure, to the DSP (apart from a title in references) despite his putative shift towards embracing industrial policy.

In short, the DSP has both been marginalised in its core mission of promoting state intervention in the form of industrial policy as a means to development, and it has been spread across a much wider and diffuse range of applications. To what extent, however, does this reflect the reduced opportunities to prosper for what might be deemed to be developmental states? Certainly, this has also been a strong current within the literature both against and subsequently within the DSP. Initially, the idea of non-replicability of national conditions (get yourself invaded by Japan and/or become an aid beneficiary of the USA in the Cold War) was strong, especially as a second line of defence amongst those begrudgingly accepting the evidence of industrial policy as a source of East Asian success. But it has subsequently given way to doubts within the DSP camp itself over whether global conditions remain conducive to developmental states along the lines experienced by those of the past. Thus, for Evans (2008), drawing incoherently and superficially upon new growth theory, new institutional economics and the capability approach, the developmental state of the 21st century will be oriented around the knowledge economy as opposed to manufacturing, with broader participation and rewards than those confined to an industrialising elite coordinated by a state bureaucracy.[17]

3 The DSP in the Age of Financialisation

Evans' (2008) approach raises his middle-range theory (and its preferred, contested and, to considerable degree, misinterpreted elements in growth, institutions and capabilities) to grand theory and overlooks what has been a considerably more important factor in determining what has to be negotiated in twentieth century (state) developmentalism. This is the extraordinary growth of finance over the past thirty years, something which Evans falsely and distortedly takes at most as indicative of the need to be service- and not manufacturing-oriented in the twenty-first century.[18] On the contrary, the role of finance has increasingly been to limit the prospects for development. Such is best understood by reference to the notion of financialisation. Across a new

17 See also his contribution in Williams (ed.) (2014), a collection that might be interpreted, largely inadvertently, to illustrate the propositions offered here, both in general and for South Africa in particular. Interestingly, in contrast to Evans, those such as Lin (2012) who disregard the DSP altogether continue to regard industrialisation and industrial policy as central to development (and Lin even suggests light targeting of industries a decade ahead in the process of development, as revealed by those who are to be emulated).

18 To be fair, Evans does not seem to have the benefit of the global crisis by which to assess the role of finance and its implications for development.

but rapidly expanding, predominantly heterodox, literature, the notion of financialisation has pointed to a number of different features of contemporary capitalism, mainly drawing upon the USA and UK as its leading sites.

In brief, financialisation has involved:[19] the phenomenal expansion of financial assets relative to real activity (by three times over the last thirty years); the proliferation of types of assets, from derivatives through to futures markets with a corresponding explosion of acronyms; the absolute and relative expansion of speculative as opposed to, or at the expense of, real investment; a shift in the balance of productive to financial imperatives within the private sector whether financial or not; increasing inequality in income arising out of weight of financial rewards; consumer-led booms based on credit; the penetration of finance into ever more areas of economic and social life such as pensions, education, health, and provision of economic and social infrastructure; the emergence of a neoliberal culture of reliance upon markets and private capital and corresponding anti-statism despite the extent to which the rewards to private finance have in part derived from state finance itself. Financialisation is also associated with the continued role of the US dollar as world money despite, at least in the current crisis, the United States' deficits in trade, capital account, the fiscus, and consumer spending, and minimal rates of interest.[20]

However financialisation is characterised, its consequences have been: reductions in overall levels and efficacy of real investment as financial instruments and activities expand at its expense even if excessive investment does take place in particular sectors at particular times (as with the dotcom bubble of a decade ago); prioritising shareholder value, or financial worth, over other economic and social values; pushing of policies towards conservatism and commercialisation in all respects; extending influence of finance more broadly, both directly and indirectly, over economic *and* social policy; and placing more aspects of economic and social life at the risk of volatility from financial instability and, conversely, placing the economy and social life at risk of crises from triggers within particular markets (as with the food and energy crises that preceded the financial crisis). Whilst, then, financialisation is a single word, it is attached to a wide variety of different forms and effects of finance with the USA and the UK. And, even if exposed in acute form by the current

---

19 The next two paragraphs taken from Fine (2011a).

20 I observe here, in passing and for future reference, that the policies adopted by the USA and some other developed countries have been exactly the opposite of those advised, or should that be imposed, on developing countries experiencing similar crises in the past. As Ha-Joon Chang has been at the forefront of arguing in the context of historical paths to development, those that have traversed it insist, "Do not do as we *did*, do as we say" to which should be added the nostrum, "Do not do as we *do*, do as we say".

crisis, its expansion over the last few decades has been at the expense of the real economy despite otherwise extraordinarily favourable 'fundamentals' for capitalist economies in terms of availabilities of new technologies, expansion in supplies of labour, weakening of labour and progressive movements more generally, slow increases in economic and social wages under the influence of neoliberal policy, and the end of the Cold War.

In these terms, if implicitly and incompletely in retrospect, the role of financialisation in the Asian crisis and, at least temporarily, the presumed demise of the East Asian developmental states, is apparent. To a large extent, those who regret the demise perceive it in terms either of the liberalisation (and internationalisation) of domestic finance or the undermining of coordinated industrial policy. But both of these were operative and were mutually reinforcing. As Rethel (2010, p. 499) suggests:

> As the East Asian economies became increasingly integrated with the world economy, it was more difficult to afford the insulation necessary to maintain the developmental state system of old. Similarly, capital markets increasingly competed with banks as main sources of funding. Major pillars of the old developmental state system were gone.

Further (Rethel, p. 510):

> While in the developmental state model of old, the consumption needs of households had been subordinated to the financing needs of economic transformation, since the crisis, private consumption is increasingly seen as an important driver of domestic growth.

This is all perceived as having drawn the NICs towards the Anglo-American forms of financial architecture and governance, something that was accelerated by the East Asian crisis and the responses to it (but eventually giving rise to neoliberal developmental states?).

But it is not simply that financialisation has eroded or transformed existing developmental states; it has also constrained or, more exactly, transformed and conditioned how they can be achieved even if by way of exception, as opposed to universally (as suggested by the optimism attached to methodological nationalism in the face of neoliberal globalisation pessimism). This is because financialisation is associated with the strengthening and/or emergence of national financial elites, and the increasing integration of such elites with international finance. The result has been to reduce levels and efficacy of investment, and not only to subordinate policy to short-run financial gains but also to change the nature of the way in which policy is made with the shift towards the interests of finance and forms of governance that reflect this. In terms of the DSP vernacular, financialisation involves an embedded (or should that be disembedded?) autonomy in which the interests of finance come to the fore and for which developmental gains are accidental or incidental rather than integral.[21]

Such observations are drawn much too generally, of course, and should be seen more as setting the conditions under which developmental states do or do not emerge (and not that no development does or can take place at all). In the case of China, and in much development elsewhere of a more systematic or systemic kind, a necessary condition is the extent of insulation from financialisation, particularly the extent to which finance for investment continues to be subject to state direction. For Ireland, the forms taken by its financialisation and development have been sharply revealed by the current crisis. The South African experience is explored below after considering "social compacting".

4 From Developmental State to Social Compacting

Significantly, there is very little overlap between the DSP and the Social Compacting Paradigm (SCP)[22] literatures even though each is concerned with the forms of governance and corresponding institutions and policies that make for superior economic functioning.[23] Indeed, it is far from clear that there is an SCP in the same way that there is a DSP, with no equivalents, for example, to

21 Significantly, Leftwich (2010), a leading member of the DSP's political school, bemoans the lack of attention to agency, and despite his focus being on the role of elites in creating developmental aspirations, or not, there is not a single reference to finance! The single exception that proves the rule is to be found on p. 102, "It is in this context that the role of agency becomes critical, at least in the world of *real politics*, that is in shaping institutional responses to political, economic and social challenges – such as the financial crisis of 2008–2009, political instability and violence in the context of failed or unconsolidated states, or the threat of nationwide HIV/AIDS epidemics that currently ravage many countries in the south." Thus, finance, or its crisis, is merely something to which elites need to be able to respond developmentally (as opposed to being seen as both causal and, in large measure, beneficiaries). This is of significance for social compacting, see below.

22 There is a neat coincidence of acronym with the Structure-Conduct-Performance tradition within industrial economics, for which corporate power and behaviour lead to outcomes as opposed to classes, political processes and policies.

23 A major exception to prove the rule is Mkandawire (2012), possibly a consequence of his addressing the SCP in the context of South Africa at a time when the DSP is also to the fore.

Johnson, Amsden, Wade and so on (and corresponding classic associated contributions), although country case studies are more readily identifiable (especially in Scandinavia).[24] Yet, each paradigm is deeply rooted in methodological nationalism, is state interventionist in ethos, and is firmly opposed to neoliberalism. But, whilst the SCP can, like the DSP, be thought of as middle-range, there are a number of major differences between them. First, whilst also concerned with industrial performance and whilst there is a longer and more wide-ranging history to the SCP, especially if it is associated with corporatism as a constituent part, see below and also Molina and Rhodes (2002) on which I draw extensively, the SCP derives primarily, if not initially, from an interest in the comparative performance of *advanced* capitalist economies, rather than on latecomer, catch-up economies. A typical question within the SCP is: why are some *developed* countries more successful than others in terms of growth and stability, especially over the post-war boom and its slide into neoliberalism?

Second, the SCP has focused upon what interests are represented and/or how they are represented, especially through the state (as opposed to how the state imposes or coordinates developmental goals for the DSP). Thus, for the SCP from the 1980s onwards, "two conceptions of neo-corporatism ... became 'official' with ... [the] distinction [made] between 'neo-corporatism 1' (a structure of interest representation) and 'neocorporatism 2' (a system of policy making)" (Molina and Rhodes, 2002, p. 308). Indeed, there emerged affinities with the divisions between economic and political schools of the DSP (Molina and Rhodes, 2002, pp. 309–310):

> In the 1980s and 1990s, the study of corporatism followed two main paths. The first was the study of corporatism as a political phenomenon ... as a system of representation and a process of policy making. The second, which was related but assumed a distinct place in the literature, focused

24 Thus, for Reinert (2012, pp. 7/8), "The same best years of growth were found in the Nordic countries, which were long seen as a very successful Third Way between capitalism and communism. The Swedish case is interesting because the formula for industrial success after WW II can be personified in three individuals, Schumpeterian economist Erik Dahmén (1916–2005), who for decades worked for *Stockholms Enskilda Bank*, the bank's owner Marcus Wallenberg (1899–1982), and social democratic politician Gunnar Sträng (1906–1992). Sträng held ministerial posts in the Swedish government from 1947 until 1976, the last 21 years as Minister of Finance. Industrialist Wallenberg and his advisor Dahmén had lunch every Wednesday, and capitalist Wallenberg and social democrat Sträng met, often in secrecy, to solve the big issues. This type of arrangement developed the Fordist wage regime – that the fruits of industrial productivity were shared between capital and labor – and the accompanying ratchet wheel effect of welfare capitalism: wages could only go up, not down."

> on the systemic effects of corporatist institutions. This literature became methodologically separate from the first. Whereas the first path of study explored the varieties of corporatism across different countries (and sectors), the second concentrated on the links between systemic features and socioeconomic outcomes.

But these characterisations are somewhat misleading in practice, since the interests and processes addressed focus especially if not exclusively, on those concerning capital and labour (as opposed to capital-state relations as for the core of the DSP). It is these that primarily underpin the role of the state analytically (as opposed to a state-market dichotomy) as well as the state, in turn, mediating between these classes.

Third, whilst both SCP and DSP share a market-imperfection, institutionally determining framework, emphasis within the SCP is on the positive sum consequences of cooperation between classes as opposed to the relations between capital and the state. For the SCP, the goal is to avoid the dysfunctions attached to excessive pursuit of class interests through conflict and so share the reasonable, less excessive gains of collaboration and avoid negative sum outcomes. More specifically, a virtuous circle of success as opposed to a vicious circle of failure will arise out of mutually supportive commitment to investment, productivity gains, correspondingly moderate wage increases, full employment and increasing, broadening and universal health, education and welfare provision.[25]

Fourth, not surprisingly given how extensive is the middle ground, the SCP and the DSP occupy different locations within it. In some respects, the SCP penetrates more deeply beneath state-market relations to those that underpin them, especially capital-labour relations. At the same time, its focus is also narrower in more or less explicitly acknowledging its own comparative and historical limitations – that it is concerned with late capitalism alone (in which both capital and labour are fully formed and central agencies) and with advanced economies only. Nonetheless, as described by Molina and Rhodes (2002, p. 306):

> Since it first entered the academic lexicon and debate, the term corporatism has been characterized by ambiguity, imprecision, and a liberal, rather undisciplined usage. This has been because of its initial ideological connotations (connected to twentieth-century fascism), its gradual

25 But see Siegel (2005) and Brandl and Traxler (2005) for doubts over whether social compacts lead to positive outcomes for welfare state reform.

> (and at times fashion-driven) adoption to explain diverse phenomena, and its application to very different time periods and countries. Despite great attempts to clarify the term … corporatism became a multipurpose concept. Its elasticity has ensured its popularity; but simultaneously its power to explain or even characterize political systems and processes has been diluted.

In addition, as with all middle-range theory, there is an issue of how causation and explanation are to be discerned. For Siegel (2005, p. 106):

> Inevitably, under circumstances of complex causality, it is a risky undertaking to assess the real net effects of social pacts. Hence *careful* inferences to establish causal relations are a major challenge in the search for robust conclusions about the effects of social pacts on policy outcomes.

Subject to the vicious/virtuous circle syndrome, are social compacts the cause or the consequence of enhanced performance, in what domains of activity, by what mechanisms and over what time periods and circumstances?

Fifth, the DSP and the SCP have different histories in content and timing, with the former lagging the other in some respects (if perhaps inevitably, given that each experiences rises and falls in popularity). The SCP comes of age with the post-war boom and the idea that (Molina and Rhodes, 2002, p. 307, drawing on Shonfield, 1965):

> in order to attain a high level of macroeconomic performance within the Keynesian framework, modern economies had promoted processes, including state planning, in which the major interest groups are brought together and encouraged to conclude a series of bargains about their future behavior, which will have the effect of moving economic events along the desired path. The plan indicates the general direction in which the interest groups, including the state in its various guises, have agreed that they want to go.

But the collapse of the post-war boom initially leads to attempts to sustain the SCP by reference to what had made Keynesianism/welfarism successful. As a result, for Molina and Rhodes (2002, p. 307), "During the 1970s, corporatism acquired the status of a social science model", and in citing Wiarda (1997, p. 23), an "approach, an intellectual framework, a way of examining and analyzing corporatist political phenomena across countries and time periods". Indeed (Molina and Rhodes, 2002, p. 307):

> Corporatism, it seemed, would offer an overarching and coherent method for understanding the working of economies and societies. At the same time, there occurred a shift in the locus of corporatist literature from political theory to political economy.

As we now know in retrospect, such neo-corporatism failed as it was presumed to have been overtaken or swamped by neoliberalism and globalisation. It suffered a death, not least with, "the demise of Swedish centralized wage bargaining in the 1980s [that] heralded the end of corporatism everywhere (if it could not survive post-industrial pressures in its 'homeland', how could it be feasible elsewhere?)" (Molina and Rhodes, 2002, pp. 312–313).[26]

Neo-corporatism has, however, since experienced something of a revival, with claims that its death has been exaggerated (Molina and Rhodes, 2002, p. 306). However, its rebirth is marked by a substantial degree of change, not least in accommodating to neoliberalism. Molina and Rhodes, if not seeing it explicitly in these terms, point to a number of shifts: away from a focus on redistribution to participation in macroeconomic and microeconomic management; away from incomes policy (wage restraint) in return for social wages to a commitment to fuller employment (as opposed to taking relatively full employment for granted); to pragmatism in policy that extinguishes differences in political programmes; to more or less decentralised forms of wage-bargaining that allow for labour market flexibility; to greater scope in the range of policies incorporated as bargaining ploys; and to more frequent renegotiation of compacts in light of greater volatility and uncertainty, pp. 317/8.

There is, then, a watershed in the SCP in the early 1990s as its energies in preserving presumed post-war models of success are eventually strangulated by neoliberalism. Indeed, the last heave in favour of neo-corporatism was at least implicitly embodied in the Varieties of Capitalism (VoC) approach. It offered a mix of (market imperfection) microeconomics, macroeconomics and institutionalism, building upon the following "five spheres" that are taken as the building blocs of capitalism's national varieties: industrial relations, vocational

---

26 See Blyth (2001) for an account with some emphasis on ideational factors, p. 11, "In sum, the huge financing at its disposal allowed SAF [employers] to mount a sustained attack on the Swedish model. Initially however, business began this revolution rather traditionally [with lockouts]. Aiming at defeating labor itself, business did not yet realize the importance of defeating labor's ideas first." See also Öberg et al. (2011) for an account of the decline of Scandinavian corporatism in view of a mix of factors such as decline of strength of labour movement, dilution and fragmentation of interests, devolution to higher and lower levels than national government, and growing strength of employer organisations.

training and education, corporate governance, inter-firm relations, and intra firm-employee relations. Even if each sphere could only take on binary values, admittedly independently of one another, this would allow for 32 varieties of capitalism! Nonetheless, these are initially reduced to the two ideal types of liberal as opposed to coordinated market economies.

However, as observed by Ashman and Fine (2013a), there is peculiar tension in the VoC approach in relation to its treatment of finance. It does not appear in the five building blocs, and yet it is frequently and increasingly referenced as a major factor in economic performance (with a predisposition to favour coordination between this sixth sphere and the other five). In retrospect, irrespective of the other criticisms that might be levelled at the VoC approach, this is a major deficiency. For it seriously distorts how varieties of capitalism are understood and what the prospects are for one or other variety to emerge and prosper.

In other words, as with the DSP, there is an issue of how the SCP confronts financialisation. In many respects, the answer is similar, with an equally oxymoronic neoliberal neo-corporatism[27] (if not in name) to parallel the neoliberal developmental state.[28] This can be seen in two different, possibly overlapping, ways. One is to acknowledge that neoliberalism has shifted the form and content of neo-corporatism but that it tends to remain stronger where it previously had a more significant presence. The second is to disaggregate and broaden the conception of neo-corporatism to discover social compacting in specific instances across a wider range of applications and constituencies (as opposed to economy- or society-wide compacting primarily involving capital and labour). In a sense, this is the way in which it is acknowledged that financialisation (and neoliberalism), especially in the wake of the global crisis, have hollowed out the prospects for social compacting. Unless finance and financialisation are addressed, it is liable to be confined and fragmented, and this is reflected in a declining and piecemeal literature on the topic.

Indeed, it is apparent that the SCP has come to offer little more than a commitment to examine how interest groups are formed and represented in the policymaking process and with what consequences. Whatever the paradigm's purchase on the past, it inherits traditions that are marked by two sore deficiencies for the present – one is neglect of the power of finance (and

---

27 Possibly "competitive corporatism" serves as a moniker and allows escape from being an oxymoron (Rhodes, 2001).

28 Indeed, "corporatism" is probably now used more to express commercialisation and/or the influence of corporations than, to some extent, its opposite as the negotiated settlement between capital and (influence of) labour.

financialisation) and the other is the heterogeneity of how interests are formed and represented across different countries and issues. Such is, for example, obvious from the deficiencies of the various attempts to draw out ideal types of welfare provision which, equally, differ across and within countries and by, and even within, programmes – see Fine (2012c and 2014) and Powell and Barrientos (2011), for example.

In short, there is the prospect for social compacting to become a buzzword, as for the DSP. The attraction of this derives from the promise of positive sum outcomes, the predominance of cooperation over conflict, the nostalgia for sources of success within the post-war boom, an anti-neoliberal ethos, and even more modest aspirations to ride the impact of the global crisis. The appeal of the SCP in the context of developing countries is even more prone to such buzz as has been implicitly highlighted by Mkandawire (2012). For, as the SCP has become both more wide-ranging and potentially selective, so it can be deployed to serve a number of different purposes. One is to use it to rebuild the state capacity that has been hollowed out by neoliberalism (and structural adjustment). Indeed, (Mkandawire, 2012, p. 5):

> this led to what Peter Evans terms "Institutional Monocropping" which pushed for a "one-size-fits-all" model. In the case of Africa, the institutional policy reform encouraged "institutional monotasking", where institutions that elsewhere performed many tasks were suddenly reduced to one task. Thus central banks that had elsewhere assumed many responsibilities other than monetary stability by taking on such tasks as facilitating housing loans, credit rationing in favour of strategic sectors, supporting employment creating policies etc., were assigned one mission, that of stabilisation. More significantly the new institutional landscape was to be filled by restraining rather than transformative institutions.

This is to exaggerate the reduced as opposed to the redirected role of the state (especially in favour of finance), but the point remains that social compacting is seen as necessary to create the democratic and the stable (let alone the developmental) state, together with its preconditions. In transition economies of whatever sort, such pacts have been deemed necessary "to make concessions in order to avoid chaos" (Mkandawire, 2012, p. 39, and, following, p. 40):

> Many of these new democracies tended to adopt neoliberal policies partly as a consequence of the compromises that had produced them, partly as a consequence of the ideological predispositions of the leaders

> of the main parties, and partly as a reflection of the limitations of the tools available to them for addressing the inherited economic problems.

Mkandawire (2012, p. 41) then immediately proceeds to discuss the "The Case of South Africa", highlighting that "the usual uncertainty that de-racialisation of any racial order is likely to create a large dose of confusion among capitalists used to doing things under one order and no longer sure about their long-term interests in the new South Africa" and concluding that "Social concertation and dialogue can provide for the disentangling of the maze of suspicion, confusion and uncertainty that seem to characterise South Africa's political economy", p. 42. I intend to probe these factors a little deeper in the context of whether concertation and dialogue, especially around the DSP, has been a source of confusion rather than its elimination.

Before doing so, it is germane to pinpoint the relationship between financialisation and neoliberalism,[29] especially as the latter is often ill-defined and liberally, and inconsistently, used as a pejorative explanation of negative outcomes in contemporary conditions. It is, however, no accident that financialisation and neoliberalism should coincide with one another over the period of the last thirty years. This is certainly true at the ideological level, as the imperative of freeing markets has been applied first and foremost to those supposedly pure markets associated with finance. But, as already suggested, finance has also been associated with the emergence, strengthening and influence of financial elites at both national and international levels.

As a result, I do not see financialisation as a simple associate of neoliberalism, but rather as its defining or underlying aspect, with a reach that goes far beyond financial markets themselves. This is not to reduce neoliberalism to financialisation, but rather to see the latter as its central or distinctive aspect. To make sense and even to defend this posture, two further points need to be made. The first is to highlight significant connections but also inconsistencies across the ideologies, the scholarship and policies in practice of neoliberalism. These have a shifting relationship to one another across time, place and topic. I have argued this at great length elsewhere, particularly in the context of development (Fine, 2001 and 2010a; Fine, Lapavitsas and Pincus, eds, 2001; and Bayliss, Fine and Van Waeyenberge, eds, 2011). Crucial, for example, is that, despite its scholarship and rhetoric, neoliberalism has always been heavily associated with state intervention. This has, however, been intervention

29 See Bayliss et al. (2015).

to promote (global) private capital in general and finance in particular. The response to the current crisis is no exception, and has seen the crisis within, and not of, neoliberalism associated with extraordinary measures of support to finance both in levels of state financial support and even in nationalisation of failing financial institutions. Indeed, so powerful has been finance's influence over policy in the wake of the crisis that it has jokingly been described as "socialism for the bankers" and as not a case of government Treasuries nationalising the banks but of the banks nationalising the Treasuries!

This is all indicative of a further feature of the relationship between financialisation and neoliberalism that can be characterised, very roughly, in terms of two phases of neoliberalism divided by the early 1990s. The first phase is aptly characterised as shock therapy in which, most strikingly – first in Latin America and, subsequently, in the former Soviet bloc – the promotion of private capital proceeded without regard to the consequences. The second phase has been, if only in part, a reaction to the consequences of the first phase in terms of the dysfunctions created, not least in social welfare provision, but it is also more marked by explicit intervention by the state to sustain the processes of, and to underpin, financialisation, as is again starkly demonstrated by responses to the crisis in terms of support to banks as the top priority over everything else.

5 South African DSP and SCP: 'Twixt a Rock and a Hard Place?

At the time that South Africa entered the post-apartheid era, it was uniquely situated in relation to the considerations raised by the DSP and the SCP. Although the DSP was about to enter into a period of decline in its classic form in the latter half of the 1990s, it was before that at its height of influence. The Washington Consensus had increasingly lost its legitimacy and appeal, in light of lost decades of development, and the DSP had played a major role in this (alongside adjustment with a human face) by appeal to the counter-evidence attached to the East Asian NICs. Indeed, this was so much so that the World Bank sought, somewhat unsuccessfully, to answer associated criticism through its *East Asian Miracle* (World Bank, 1993).[30] Over the period bridging the transition from apartheid, there was a plethora of options on offer and, certainly, South Africa as a prospective developmental state was one of them.

30 See Wade (1996).

In my own work, for example, the developmental state option was carefully considered and rejected if primarily on analytical grounds in light of the unsatisfactory dual dichotomies of state versus market, and of economic and political schools (Fine and Rustomjee, 1996).[31] Instead, South Africa was characterised as being based upon its Minerals-Energy Complex. The MEC signified not only heavy dependence on highly capital-intensive mining and energy sectors but also: a highly concentrated conglomerate structure; close collaboration between the state (and state-owned enterprises) and large-scale capital; a highly developed financial system incorporated into the conglomerate structure; for different reasons at different times, a failure to have diversified out of the mineral-energy core into capital and intermediate goods, with a correspondingly weak and protected consumer goods industries; and, despite a history of piecemeal resolution between the economic power of 'English' capital and political power of Afrikaner capital, an increasing rapprochement and integration between the two under the increasing hegemony of an incorporated, and relatively newly-formed, large-scale Afrikaner capital. Consequently, and perversely, as observed in retrospect once the developmental state did come on to the agenda for South Africa (see below), it could be claimed that such a status was more characteristic of the past than the present (Freund, 2012).

The situation with respect to the SCP was very different. Paradoxically, just as it was at its lowest ebb under the assault of neoliberalism, the defeat of apartheid was based upon a heady mix of social forces and organisations, almost a dream ticket for neo-corporatism if not socialist revolution. It comprised the following elements: majority support for democratisation against a white minority; anti-racism more generally; international solidarity; a powerful trade union movement, in alliance with the Communist Party and a popular political party, the ANC; as well as a mass democratic movement for change.

Nonetheless, progressive policies for the post-apartheid economy were very rapidly abandoned, and neo-corporatism was subject to a heavy assault once GEAR, generally (and correctly) acknowledged as neoliberal, was adopted in 1996 and claimed to be non-negotiable. For some, this represented the necessary subordination of domestic constituencies to the realities of global forces. Thus, for those disappointed in the neoliberal turn from the more radical Reconstruction and Development Programme (RDP) to GEAR, this was predominantly seen in terms of undue compromise with the old Afrikaner/white order and international capital. With the benefit of hindsight, and a broader

31 For subsequent contributions, see Fine (2010b and c) and Ashman et al. (2010a).

and deeper perspective, things look slightly different. In particular, it is important to recognise that, because of international sanctions, South Africa could only fully become incorporated into the previously elaborated processes of financialisation after they had already been underway for a decade or more elsewhere. This, then, points to the particular form taken in South Africa by financialisation, especially in a global context, for which there was a need for South Africans conglomerates to play catch up. Consequently, the South African financial sector has been the fastest growing in the economy. On a broad definition, it now makes up twenty per cent of GDP even though forty per cent of South Africans benefit from no financial services at all beyond stressed credit. Nonetheless, if the role of such financial services is to mobilise and allocate resources, South Africa has failed miserably. The level of investment in the South Africa economy has been at historically low levels; scarcely exceeding 15 per cent of GDP or half of what is necessary for developmental state status. Further, a major reason for this has been capital flight at unprecedented levels in post-apartheid South Africa peaking at 23 per cent of GDP in 2007. This has not been rectified, remedied nor even addressed by Treasury or the South African Reserve Bank.

Indeed, in effect, the opposite has been the case, with macroeconomic policy almost apparently unwittingly designed to support long-term (illegal) capital flight. Thus, an overvalued exchange rate has been highly advantageous to those taking capital out of the country as they earn more in foreign exchange for their rand-denominated assets. On the other hand, high domestic interest rates have provided for short-run capital inflows to balance long-term outflows. Both high exchange and interest rates are harmful to macroeconomic performance. In addition, rather than implement prevailing capital controls, these have been subject to creeping erosion, both rendering legal what has been previously done illegally, and always placing the economy on the verge of instability.

Further, even with the limited overall levels of investment generated within South Africa, there has been more concern to create and redistribute shareholder value through restructuring for domestic monopolies with capitalisation and short-run financial gains at the expense of long-run productivity, industrial development and promotion of employment. This has been accompanied by internationalisation of South African capital, not only through financialisation but also through both domestic and foreign integration into globalised networks of ownership, production, distribution and trade, not least with a permissive stance on allowing South African companies to list abroad.

But do things look different in the realm of social policy, something that had been marginalised in the DSP before it became a buzzword but has often, if not always, been central to the SCP as a bargaining chip on offer to labour in return for wage moderation? As has often been observed, South Africa has particularly generous levels of social security for a country at its level of per capita income. But this has to be set against the post-apartheid context of addressing the dysfunctions of the second phase of neoliberalism and, of obvious and more important significance, the inheritance of apartheid and its associated inequalities across each and every aspect of economic and social life. These have, if anything, been compounded in the post-apartheid period, not only in worsening inequality of income but also through the increasing levels of unemployment. It is far too simplistic to see such developments in social policy as a means of social control. But as capital goes about its business of financialisation and internationalisation, this certainly offers more purchase than viewing such policies as creating the foundations for a developmental state and/or reflecting social compacting.

Instead, it is more appropriate to focus upon a rather different element in post-apartheid compacting. This concerns the emergence of a new black elite in ways which have some parallels with the incorporation of Afrikaner capital, not least in terms of how black enrichment has depended upon trading political for economic power and privilege.[32] This has included patronage of the state in contracts and redistribution, for example, of mineral rights.[33] But, if not more important, there has been participation in, and promotion of, the processes of financialisation. But here there is the major difference with the earlier transformation of boundaries within and across the South African capitalist class. For, whilst each relates to the continuing dynamic of the MEC, for the earlier instance of incorporating Afrikanerdom, this was marked by a state-coordinated expansion of core mineral and energy activities. In the current restructuring of the MEC, through financialisation and globalisation, associated with the low levels of domestic investment, the appropriation of existing assets and surplus in place of its use for economic and social development has been even more significant than the failure to maintain adequate levels of real investment.

Accordingly, at a general level with much complexity and diversity as more detailed issues and outcomes are addressed, post-apartheid South Africa has suffered an almost perfect, destructive storm as far as strengthening its prospects for developmental state or social compacting are concerned. For traditional large-scale capital has been engaged in internationalisation and

32 For a wide-ranging comparison between the two elite redistributions of wealth, see Chatterjee et al. (2025).

33 See Pitcher (2012) for some account of this.

financialisation, including huge haemorrhaging of resources through (illegal) capital flight, incorporating a new black elite and, thereby, subordinating or precluding the forces and capacities for social compacting that are required to underpin the realisation of developmental policies. In short, post-apartheid restructuring in these terms has even been at the expense of policies that would benefit the collective interests of new and old elites as individual ministries, let alone their coordination, have been subordinated to that of finance. There has simply been lack of coherence and commitment to long-term developmental planning (as opposed to short-term macroeconomic policy properly understood), most notably in the shambolic plans for privatisation in general and the emergence of electricity power shortages in particular (neither of which would figure in a neo-corporatist developmental state). In this light, what is remarkable of the post-apartheid period is how rapidly the prospects for, and influence of, social compacting have been eroded and its scope reduced whilst rather different forms of compacting have emerged and consolidated around the financialisation and internationalisation of capital.

It is against such perspectives that we can assess the National Development Plan (NDP). But, initially, it has to be put into political context. First and foremost, it is a reflection of the regime shift from Mbeki to Zuma, following the ANC's Polokwane Conference of 2007, itself marking mounting dissatisfaction with government as a result of social and economic outcomes over the past decade. Though the regime shift is appropriately seen as a watershed,[34] it still remains bound by a combination of continuity and change. One element in this is the 'richness' (read incoherence and chaos) of policy postures – within a couple of decades, we have been offered the Freedom Charter, the RDP, GEAR, AsgiSA, the developmental state, the NGP (the New Growth Path),[35] the NDP (the National Development Plan)[36] and, most recently, the Second Transition. These policy initiatives and discourses have increasingly represented compromises, usually unresolved. Significantly, for example, the developmental state was introduced by the outgoing Mbeki regime in a desperate rhetorical attempt to regain legitimacy but was appropriated as the means for framing more interventionist and progressive policies. This reflects the casual buzz by which the

34 Followed by another "Watershed Conference", in 2012 (ANC, 2012).

35 "The New Growth Path: The Framework", Economic Development Department, South Africa, 2010, http://www.info.gov.za/view/DownloadFileAction?id=135748. For critical assessment of the NGP, see Fine (2011b).

36 *The National Development Plan: Vision for 2030*, issued in late 2011 by the National Planning Commission, http://www.npconline.co.za/medialib/downloads/home/NPC%20National %20Development%20Plan%20Vision%202030%20-lo-res.pdf. For critical assessment, see Fine (2012b) and, on agriculture and rural development, Sender (2012).

DSP can be deployed.[37] Also the NGP and the NDP, attached to the two newly formed, but functionally vaguely distinguishable Economic Development Department and National Planning Commission, respectively, represent the new and the old guard in terms of Ebrahim Patel (formerly trade unionist) and Trevor Manuel (Minister of Finance from 1966 to 2008). The watershed also allows for an ideological compromise in which the new path or change in direction is seen as building upon the old (and the stability it is deemed to have provided) or as departing it as unduly austere and neoliberal (or possibly both simultaneously).

Such complexities and incoherence in political discourse is to be expected even if it seems to take extreme form in South Africa. In addition, it has effectively thrown up a smokescreen around the underlying realities and dynamics of the post-apartheid economy. The result has been a peculiar mix of both loose and strong connections between scholarship, ideology and policy in practice. For example, whilst the post-apartheid economy could not have moved much further away from being a developmental state in the post-apartheid period,[38] its declaration as (prospectively) being such by the outgoing Mbeki regime, and accepted by the incoming regime, witnessed an explosion of academic research on the (South African) developmental state. In case of the NDP, however, what stands out is the extent to which it is detached both from policy and scholarship and primarily serves an ideological function.

For, whilst the NDP is itself a presentationally polished and lengthy document, it is far from inspiring and it is hard (or not rewarding) to read beyond a few pages at a time. Justification for, details of, and connections between its various stances are notable for their absence. It has at most a scattering of footnotes and references. Two of the most revealing (next to one another on

37 Although most extreme in South Africa, the buzz is not confined to it. As observed by Shaw (2012), in distancing itself from neoliberalism, the United Nations Economic Commission for Africa (UNECA) declared itself in favour of a "developmental state approach", p 838. Indeed, he quotes, p. 840, "Developmental states in Africa should be inclusive and operate through a democratic governance framework. Five major elements are crucial … purposeful leadership and a developmentalist coalition; transformative institutions; focused industrial policy; investment in research; and enhanced social policy."

38 Thus, in relatively empty substance by reference to the DSP, in the Second Transition Discussion Document, we are informed, p. 15, para 65, "The uniquely South African developmental state is defined … as a state: with capacity to intervene in the economy in the interest of higher rates of growth and sustainable development; with effective and sustainable programmes that address challenges of unemployment, poverty and underdevelopment with requisite emphasis on vulnerable groups; and that mobilises the people as a whole, especially the poor, to act as their own liberators through participatory and representative democracy."

page 55 in footnotes 8 and 9) are to Lin (2011) and Rodrik (2009), each of whom are leading exponents of some but not too much state intervention and fully committed to mainstream neoclassical economics, albeit mindful of empirical circumstances.[39] But once we scratch deeper, the hollowness of the NDP's public justification is revealed in what can only be described as being in bizarre ways. At the time of writing, on its website there are a number of background diagnostic reports for various areas of economic and social development. These themselves have little or no references or background papers.[40] But they have scattered web links to what are presumably background papers or readings which bear uncertain relationships to the content of the Plan itself. These range, for example, across a book published in 1990 on patriarchy, through a London School of Economics MSc dissertation on South Africa as a "brand" (actually how its rainbow nation tag is used to conceal rather than reveal its extensive problems), to an excellent piece on how minimum wages are more observed in the breach (the implications of which are certainly not taken up in the Plan).[41]

What the Plan does offer is a "Vision" for 2030, one that breaks with the past (as it must in legitimating itself as a break with apartheid and as a watershed within post-apartheid) but builds upon the stability that was created in the earlier post-apartheid period. The continuing challenges are acknowledged and addressed with the commitment to create eleven million new jobs, eliminate poverty across the majority, reduce inequality and corruption, create a national health service and major expansion in basic needs, and progressing towards a green economy. But, in doing so, there is little or no explanation for why these goals remained unaddressed in the previous twenty years and how they can be put right in the future. From my perspective, there is a notable lack of account of the MEC, its internationalised and financialised restructuring,

39 Chief Economist at the World Bank and Harvard academic, respectively. For critical commentary on Lin and Rodrik, see Fine (2011a and 2012b) and Fine and Van Waeyenberge (2013). Of course, paying attention to context as opposed to neoclassical deductive reasoning does not mean it is correctly assessed. See Fine (2009b and c) in debate with Hausmann and Andrews (2009) as members of the Harvard Team that advised Treasury and for which Rodrik is a leading participant. As was pointed out, the Team proceeded as if neither the MEC nor (illegal) capital flight exists even after this deficiency is revealed to them.

40 Details of location and links to these references across the Diagnostics, many of which take you to options to purchase on Amazon or otherwise, can be obtained from the author – now laid out, but no longer available in Fine (2025e, Ch. 12, Appendix).

41 Another interesting piece shows, with whatever validity, that *returns* to education between whites and blacks have become unequal having been equal under apartheid (if, of course, at very different levels of earnings). Again, this is not taken up in the Plan itself.

and of capital flight. Instead of addressing such issues, as I put it elsewhere (Fine, 2012b, p. 129):

> It reports with some satisfaction that the finance sector in South Africa had experienced a tripling of its output from 1994, compared to 67% for the rest of the economy, that it was responsible for between 300,000 to 400,000 jobs either directly or indirectly and that it should have expanded, and had the potential to expand, employment even more especially in bringing financial services to the 40% of the population that had been deprived of them.

So, far from bringing finance under control, the NDP sees it as expanding and providing an opportunity to become a financial hub for the rest of Africa (presumably spreading its financialised malaise there also).

Significantly, despite the prominence of the developmental state in defining the watershed (and its early use by Manuel whilst still under Mbeki, as evidenced in his budget speech of February, 2008), the term was notable for being almost entirely absent in the first draft of the NDP. This is indicative of casual disregard of the NDP's own context as well as of the debates that had preceded it and why these have taken the form and content they have (for example, around the shifts in policy from RDP, which is seen not to have met its goals when it was in fact abandoned, to GEAR, which is not even mentioned). It is as if these elements of context do not exist. Remarkably, however, they can be restored or inserted to suit, with the final draft of the NDP replete with references to the developmental state (in response to protests at its absence in earlier drafts) without any substantive difference in its content!

On the other hand, the role of social compacting is much more prominent. But it is given a particular set of twists. For, first, the vision is one in which all South Africans can benefit together in a virtuous circle of change in which the most disadvantaged, especially blacks, women and youth, are highest on the agenda. But this presumes a unity of purpose and identity that simply does not, and increasingly so, exist. The shadowy minority that exercises economic power, internationalised and financialised capital, has no necessary commitment to South Africa, as most obviously symbolised by capital flight. Similarly, the new black elite organised around such conglomerate capital and/or state largesse is not simply to be made more functional through elimination of corruption – its very functions themselves have to be changed. All of this more or less falls outside the social compacting up for consideration.

Second, though, the same neglect cannot be said to exist for the traditional position of labour, trade unions and the impoverished, who are required to grasp a new ethos. For example, on the NDP's very first page we are told of the need to abandon a "passive citizenry receiving services from the state" (NPC, 2012, p. 1). This is followed by the requirement of "shifting from a paradigm of entitlement", p. 5, and, whilst the treatment of finance only merits a couple of pages in the NDP (NPC, 2012, pp. 129–30), the contrast with labour could not be more striking. Almost as much attention is given to the details of the relatively minor but highly controversial and symbolic issue of regulating how employees may be dismissed in order to improve the functioning of the labour markets, pp. 113–14. Such labour market flexibility might be thought to be the exact antithesis of social compacting![42]

6 Concluding Remarks

To a large degree, the DSP and the SCP have persistently occupied a place where they can be used to identify both alternative policies to neoliberalism and alternative social arrangements that are more conducive to such alternative policies. Neoliberalism is not, after all, just a set of policies or ideologies but the contemporary phase of capitalism that conditions how the DSP and the SCP are conceived and what impact they do, or do not, have in practice. The two paradigms inevitably shed some light on policies and how they are made. However, both paradigms have evolved over time in terms of their substantive content and depth and breadth of appeal, as have the material and intellectual environments to which they have responded. The thrust of this Chapter has been to demonstrate that both intellectual and material trajectories have been particularly unkind to the DSP and to the SCP as the basis for posing development policy, as each has become an ideological construct of diverse meanings and neoliberalism has undermined their scope for meaningful application.

This does not necessarily mean that the paradigms should be abandoned for lack of potential progressive purpose, although each can serve specific, possibly elite, interests whilst obscuring such and presenting them ideologically as the general interest. But if these paradigms are to gain any effective purchase over policymaking, they will need to get to grips with financialisation; the ways in which it has underpinned neoliberalism; how this has hollowed

42 Note that the NGP (2010) is much clearer about the sort of social compacting it has in mind, p. 29: "it requires some sacrifice from union members … the New Growth Path must ensure that economic and social policies demonstrably reward any sacrifice by members with real gains for the working class as a whole."

out the processes of making policy and in the interests that can be expressed, and given a particular character to how compacting can be achieved and for what ends; how it has conditioned the forms and content taken by conflict, and institutional capacity to formulate, deliver and monitor policy; and how corruption and dysfunction have emerged and been enabled in the pursuit of conflicting interests. These are precisely what needs to be addressed in a South African context but it is far from clear whether the DSP and the SCP represent conduits or chains for these purposes.

CHAPTER 11

Vishnu Padayachee as Engaged Political Economist: A Personal Journey

Postscript as Personal Preamble

In May, 2021, Vishnu Padayachee unexpectedly and tragically died. His passing was marked by numerous friends, colleagues and collaborators from across his many activities and collaborations. A conference was organised to mark his achievements under the title, "Heterodox Economics and Social Change in Bleak Times: Challenges Confronting the Engaged Scholar in the Academy Leading to Appreciation of Vishnu Padayachee". I was asked to contribute in a panel on, "Challenging the hegemony of neo-classical economics: insights gained on social change by aligning heterodox economic thought with the Humanities (and vice versa)". I set about the task with gusto to temper my sadness and grief, and the results of my endeavours follow, bringing together longstanding work on both economics imperialism and the political economy of South Africa. The paper bordered on being close to three times too long for the conference volume that followed. It was reduced by the simple expedient of deleting footnotes, references and the first five sections of what follows (Fine, 2025d).[1]

1 Introduction[2]

I have written so often and for so long on mainstream and heterodox economics, and their relationships to interdisciplinarity, that I offer a sort of formulaic summary of my current position in Sections 3 and 4. Before that, in Section 2, for similar reasons, I contextualise this account of economics by doing the same for neoliberalism as the current phase of contemporary capitalism. These three opening Sections prepare the framing for two corresponding understandings of South African political economy. The first of these, Section 5, reviews

1 Thanks to University of KwaZulu-Natal Press for permission to reproduce the sections that were published in the tribute volume.

2 Thanks for comments on various versions from Robbie van Niekerk, John Sender and Bruno Tinel.

 | DOI:10.1163/9789004748330_012

the post-apartheid trajectory of the economy, once again something on which I have dedicated some efforts over the years and so amenable to drastic summary. The second, Section 6, is more novel, addressing the nature and role of mainstream and heterodox economics in the post-apartheid period drawing upon my own experiences. This is not so much because they are representative, nor sufficiently weighty, let alone important, but because, without having undertaken the necessary, and extensive, primary research, I have very little else on which to go. Others will be able to comment on their own experiences, how representative are my own, and how they relate to the broader issues of the relationship between scholarship and social change (to what extent does the latter reflect and/or steer the former) and whether the same applies to economics as for other disciplines, or different and in different ways, especially in the South African context.

Much of the text in these five sections is an exercise in self-indulgence, rehashing and, unduly at the expense of others, citing my own previous work and experiences. It was also an indulgence for a very different reason which I only realised as the drafting took place. I was going through these exercises not merely nor even primarily to contextualise what was to follow but in order psychologically and emotionally to put off, if not to avoid, arriving at the conclusion that was more or less inevitably derived from them. In Section 7, I consider the role of Vishnu as an engaged scholar across heterodox economics and interdisciplinarity. My instinct at the outset was to have designated him as an engaged scholar, par excellence, and without peer. But I could not do so as the thrust of my earlier sections is to see post-apartheid heterodox scholarship as systemically disengaged and disengaging, especially for economics and, possibly, of broader (inter)disciplinary scope. Consequently, Vishnu's contributions and roles are all the more remarkable and invaluable for having sustained interdisciplinary heterodoxy in an era when their policy and, to some degree, activist engagement have been at risk of being marginalised if not entirely eroded.

2 Neoliberalism Is as Neoliberalism Does

Whilst, in retrospect, we can date neoliberalism as originating from at least the early 1970s, I was uncomfortable with the term and declined numbers of opportunities to make contributions on neoliberal this or that (although at least tolerant with the use by others). The reason for my reluctance was that I did not consider I had a sufficient handle on how neoliberalism marked a distinct stage of capitalism (presumably as successor to Keynesianism on which I had, and continue to have, reservations as moniker for the period of the post-war boom, see below). Certainly, I was aware of what others might take as defining characteristics of neoliberalism such as ideology favouring the market over the state, leading to policies of privatisation, macroeconomic austerity, free movement of capital and goods, labour market deregulation and hostility to trade unions, and so on. But none of these, nor even their combination, seemed sufficiently to mark out the contemporary period as such. And there were also dissonances in taking these aspects as markers of neoliberalism (NL), not least because there was no question that the ideology of non-interventionism veiled a continuing and extensive role for the state in promoting capital accumulation through these policies, just as had been the case in the past with rhythms and balances of their own.

My stance changed once I came across, and was drawn to, the concept of financialisation. Initially, and to some degree by chance, my introduction to financialisation coincided with reviewing literature on social policy (Fine, 2011a and 2012c). This inspired the ability to understand financialisation as the factor distinguishing NL as the contemporary stage of capitalism, both critically drawing upon and departing from, prevailing interpretations (Fine, 2010e; and Fine and Saad-Filho, 2016).

Explanation for this requires a brief excursion in how to address periodisation of capitalism into different stages. Traditionally, at an economic level, I have seen this as reflecting changes in the dominant ways in or through which surplus value is produced and accumulated or how economic reproduction is realised through the production, distribution and exchange of (surplus) value. In brief, earlier periods had sequentially: combined production of absolute value with competitive (international) trading in commodities including labour power; followed by production of relative surplus value, and the factory system, with monopolisation, and global trading in finance, itself the major lever of restructuring; and, for the post-war boom, the internationalisation of production (MNCs) complemented by extensive state intervention in the restructuring of capital. Further, economic reproduction is to be seen as embedded within, not side-by-side with, social reproduction with, respectively, crude exploitation of the working class, followed by reform to restrict exploitation through ASV rather than RSV, ultimately leading to extensive state intervention in social reproduction through health, education, and welfare measures.

In this light, what distinguishes NL as the contemporary stage of capitalism is the increasingly extensive (new) and intensive (deeper) role played by finance in economic and social reproduction; it has become unavoidably present in economic and, increasingly, social restructuring (Fine, 2020). Across what is now an extensive literature, this is especially marked in contributions around what has been termed the financialisation of everyday life[3] – in which monetary exchange, calculation and ethos (alongside commodification, most obviously with privatisation of public services) is investigated as both materially and culturally pervasive.[4] But, whilst empirically prescient, financialisation understood in these broad terms is too analytically amorphous, conflating all aspects of anything to do with more money in exchange, motive or institutionally – forming part and parcel of a putatively homogeneous set of phenomena which are transparently heterogeneous, especially with burgeoning case studies. Instead of this undue homogenising, financialisation can be more narrowly seen as deriving from the gargantuan expansion of trading in securitised revenues, not rising numbers of mortgages as such for example, but bundling mortgages together into tradeable assets, possibly with others, from which correspondingly speculative rewards can accrue (in what might be seen as interest, sometimes rent or rentiers, inappropriately in my view). Inevitably, such expansion of financialisation in these narrower terms underpins its presence in other forms but these have to be seen in their own right, not as one and the same.

As has been documented in great detail, at all tiers and sorts of economic and social activity, financialisation (however understood) is associated with dysfunction. This is hardly surprising from a progressive point of view within which the period of neoliberalism is seen as one of faltering growth (ultimately giving way to the Global Financial Crisis and covid pandemic, quite apart from environmental degradation) and pervasive inequalities and deprivations of provision. As financial assets, and associated monetary relations, have grown globally at three times the rate of GDP over the period of neoliberalism, there is inevitably going to be strong correlations between the growth of finance and the incidence of dysfunction even if specifying the varieties of (causal) mechanisms by which these occur is considerably more demanding and contested.

The leading theoretical explanation in these respects is the association of the presence of finance with (speculative) short-termism at the expense of the longer term, most obviously with investment levels, productivity and conditions of work including wages and levels of secure employment. Similar considerations are carried over into the realm of policy ranging from cost- and service-cutting privatisation through to policies of public austerity. Such

3 For a recent review of financialisation of everyday life, focusing on eastern Europe, see Bobek (2019).

4 For extensive overview of financialisation, see Mader et al. (eds) (2020) and, for my own most recent take, Fine (2022a).

postures, however, illegitimately overgeneralise from what have been dominant trends to the presumption that they are universal which, if it were the case, would lead, ad absurdum, to an economy entirely based on finance with no "real" activity at all on which it is able to be parasitic, unproductive, rentier, or whatever. To the contrary, given financialisation depends upon securitisation of more or less guaranteed revenues, these ultimately have to derive from productive activity. And there can even be excessive 'real' investments underpinning financialisation, as with housing and construction booms before a crash and, most notably, what has been termed the (neoliberal) political economy of excess, with energy (and dysfunctional environmental change) and food (and more now globally suffering from obesity than undernutrition) to the fore (Bayliss and Fine, 2021a and b). In short, there is an uncertain relationship between financialisation and economic (and social) activity even if it is associated in general with the growth of what Marx called (potentially speculative) fictitious at the expense of, but also underpinning, real capital accumulation.

Significantly, the financialisation literature, much heavier in empirical than theoretical analysis and progress, has increasingly begun to recognise that both the incidence of financialisation and impact of that incidence, within and across countries (by sectors) and globally, is highly heterogeneous. As a result, financialisation has variously been described as variegated. Such variegation is itself intensified by the ever-increasing range and scope of financialisation and its effects. Accordingly, financialisation is appropriately deemed to underpin both economic *and* social reproduction under neoliberalism, with the former embedded within, not dualistic or in parallel with, the latter (Fine, 2020 and 2022a).

In part, to some degree independently of financialisation, if intensified and extended by it, related conceptualisations of NL and its fellow travellers, such as globalisation, privatisation, austerity, inequality and commodification, are equally highly variegated and in need of situating in relation to economic and social reproduction. Specifically, in case of commodification, (and correspondingly, decommodification and recommodification) three different aspects have commonly been conflated with one another. One is privatisation as such, when public provision is turned over to private capital as most obviously with denationalisation. Denote this by C. Another is the adoption of the commodity form without necessarily going as far as full-scale dependence upon private capitalist provision – a leading example of this, CF for short, would be imposition of non-commercial user charges where previously provision was free. And, third, is commodity calculation, CC, where a monetary ethos is present, most notably in the new public management, but 'transactions' as such are not monetised although they may be quantified and assessed by commercial logics of one sort or another.

These distinctions, collectively making up CCFCC, are far from rigid in practice for which they are also fluid. Securitisation, and financialisation in the narrow sense, depends upon at least a stream of revenue and so is confined to C and CF. But, with financialisation, there tends to be a trajectory from CC to CF to C, for example from NPM through more or less nominal user charges to full privatisation. But this is not unilinear with, for example, privatisation of what are deemed to be essential public services potentially depending upon corresponding expansion of continuing public support for those who are hard to serve (through the market) – thus, burgeoning financialisation of housing across Europe has depended upon an equally extensive expansion of housing benefit to those hard to house.

Such considerations dovetail with the embedding of economic within social reproduction. Across economic and social sectors, not only is financialisation variegated in its incidences and impacts, so is the extent to which provisioning for production, consumption or reproduction straddles the CCFCC divides. Within each sector, provisioning is uniquely tied to integral and sector-specific connections between production and consumption, in what has been termed systems of provision, SoPs,[5] as is popularly acknowledged in reference to distinct food, clothing, education, health, energy and transport systems, for example. Further, in the context of consumption and social reproduction more generally, each SoP is associated with (1) particular norms of provisioning, who (by socioeconomic strata) gets what and how (public or private provision, with or without charges, with or without dependence on credit, etc., quite apart from the links from production through distribution to consumption); and (2) increasing variegation, vulnerability and volatility, V^3, in these norms due to increasing economic and social instabilities and policies of austerity.

Further, each of these SoPs is integrally attached to material cultures, MCs, by which provisioning is not so much understood as taken for granted, or subject to unquestioned, but also possibly contested, meanings, as with water as a commodity or as a right, the deserving versus the undeserving poor, the primacy of owner-occupation over rental housing, or private over public medicine, and curative over primary and preventative, etc. Such MCs have been characterised as subject to the 10Cs – they are Constructed, Construed,

5 For a full account, see Bayliss and Fine (2021a) but dating back at least to Fine and Leopold (1992) and even informing the MERG approach to social and economic infrastructure (Fine, 1996).

Conforming, Commodified, Contextual, Contradictory, Closed, Contested, Collective and Chaotic.[6]

Material cultures are crucial as reflections, supports and in the making of NL and why it is able to be reproduced despite its unavoidable dysfunctions. But nor is NL (and its cultures) homogeneous and unchanging. In particular, three logically sequential phases of NL can be identified, although their incidences and rhythms are variable across time and place (just as, for example, sweated labour can be coterminous with, and even complementary to, more secure and better rewarded, capital-intensive employment).

The first phase of NL can be associated with 'shock therapy', not so much the rolling back of the state as the marginalisation of progressive forms of policy determination and influence upon it. Privatisation, austerity and deregulation of markets, especially finance, labour and international trade, are to the fore. State intervention is not reduced other than in ideological postures. Rather, it is geared to the promotion of immediate conditions conducive to private capital accumulation, especially of finance. The second phase of NL, associated with Third Wayism, combines continuing the financialisation of economic and social reproduction with selective amelioration of its dysfunctional and contested implications. The third phase, preceding the Global Financial Crisis, GFC, but intensified by it and, subsequently, the covid pandemic, involves increasing collaboration between the state and large-scale private capital, with finance to the fore, to renew accumulation, not least through 'new' or renewed but diluted industrial policy and promotion of economic and social infrastructure.

Whilst it has been commonplace to view the first phase of NL as rolling back the state, as opposed to rolling back the progressive influences upon it, and the subsequent phases as rolling that state out once again in more neoliberal-friendly forms, it is more appropriate to emphasise the significance of the state, and its interventions, at all stages of NL. However, unevenly and contextually, the NL state has tended to be subject to growing authoritarian centralism even if ideologically claiming decentralisation to lower levels (if without the resources as opposed to the responsibilities for rendering such devolution achievable). At the same time, such centralisation has witnessed closer integration of elite powers across politics, the media and policy advice and implementation (marked by 'revolving doors'), correspondingly increasing potential degradation of governance, and the rise of political populism and personalities, as electoralism comes to dominate politics in place of

6 For these in detail with applications, see Bayliss and Fine (2021a) and, for the material cultures of financialisation, Bayliss et al. (eds) (2017).

organisationally-grounded activism, with the extreme right gaining leverage far more readily than the left.[7]

With the exception of the last points on periodisation and authoritarian centralism, the analysis presented so far can be summarised by a sequence of acronyms/shorthands – GLOB, NL, FINN, ER/SR, SoPs, Norms, V^3, MC, 10Cs. How have these predominantly material developments related to the role of economics and its interdisciplinarity?

3 From Mainstream to …[8]

The beginnings of my mature understanding of the nature of mainstream economics, and its putative interdisciplinarity, date from Fine (1997f).[9] This paper was inspired by trying to bring together and locate the information-theoretic revolution in economics, with Stiglitz as a leading pioneer, the shift from Washington to Post-Washington Consensus, and the paradox that both rational choice and radical sociologists, James Coleman and Pierre Bourdieu, respectively, should each be deploying the term social capital from entirely different perspectives and for entirely different purposes.[10]

The thread running through my understanding of mainstream economics and its continuing evolution, is that it is dominated at its core, by what I have on occasion called a fortress, by its technical apparatus, TA1, and its technical architecture, TA2, forming TA^2 when taken together.[11] TA1 put simply is the use of production and utility functions, familiar to every student of economics at almost every level. TA2 is to deploy TA1 to focus upon

7 This and the previous paragraph are drastic summaries across numbers of complex issues. See Fine and Saad-Filho (2016), Boffo et al. (2018) and Fine (2020, 2021b and 2022a).

8 This term, as well as heterodoxy, is heavily contested, in meaning and use, with neoclassical and pluralist often used as terminological alternatives, respectively, equally contested and with shades of different meanings and, generally, each with narrower and broader content, respectively. For some of my own discussion, see Fine (2015 and 2022b).

9 For this situated in context of other continuing contributions to political economy, see Fine (2019a).

10 On all of this, see Fine (1999a, 2001 and 2010a). In the event, despite providing space for social capital at the World Bank, a meteoric rise and fall even in the decade straddling the millennium, Stiglitz primarily avoided using it until he spoiled himself in a bizarre attempt to promote micro-credit long after it had been discredited even in mainstream channels (Fine, 2025c for an account).

11 This terminology was suggested to me by Al-Jazaeri (2008).

optimisation, equilibrium and efficiency.[12] Significantly, the rise of TA^2 dates from the marginalist revolution of the 1870s but it is only fully established immediately after the second world war. For TA1, the formal implications of optimising on the basis of utility and production functions were only fully derived with the Hicks-Slutsky-Samuelson conditions for (individual) supply and demand curves in the 1930s. And TA2 had to wait upon general equilibrium and Arrow and Debreu in the 1950s.

What is more important in many respects than the results of TA^2 is the way and the context in which they were obtained. Essentially, this involved what I have called an implosion with whatever conceptual and even technical assumptions to be made as long as they are essential for deriving what was wanted. This is the source of the popular, and essentially correct, view of economists as being totally unrealistic (I look for my key under the lamppost not because I lost it there but because it is the only place I can see). So we assume that preferences are fixed over goods with fixed properties, that they are subject to diminishing returns, as are fixed technologies, for which there are no economies of scale and scope, nor externalities, and everyone is a competitive price taker.

Over the period during which TA^2 was being established, the Keynesian revolution occurred within macro, and what is now called the old institutional economics (with its empirically-grounded, inductive and systemic methods) was strong especially in the United States.[13] This created a tripartite division of the discipline into macro, micro and a wealth or umbrella of mixed applied fields. Micro was very much in a junior role given the issues associated with the Great Depression and the rise of corporate capitalism, with the USA to the fore. But its derivation by implosion was attached to a paradoxical historical logic. For, historically, it had been based upon what was presumed to be a single-minded focus upon teasing out the implications of individual optimisation in response to *market* prices, defining and confining the economy to the market insulated from other economic, let alone from social, political and ideological considerations altogether. However, logically, once these results had been obtained, TA^2 could be seen to be entirely free of the historical origins that gave rise to it. There is nothing about utility and production functions, nor optimisation, equilibrium and efficiency, that confines their application to the market alone. Indeed, these concepts are completely ahistorical and asocial – they could apply to anything and everything given imagination and licence.

12 For full account of what follows, see Milonakis and Fine (2009) and Fine and Milonakis (2009) and, most recently, Fine (2019a).

13 For fascinating vignettes around this, see Chirat (2021a and b).

This is exactly what happened in the post-war period, giving rise to what was initially a slow burn, and then an explosion of microeconomics, not only across economics but also other social sciences too, reversing the previous implosion (at least confinement to the market) and, ultimately, squeezing out applied fields and methods and subordinating macro to micro. This is what is termed economics imperialism (EI). Initially, within the context of the Keynesian era, the first phase of EI was confined within the discipline and, otherwise, only ranged over a few fields, most notably the new economic history (cliometrics, alongside the early versions of Douglass North's new institutional economics), human capital theory, and the public choice paradigm.

However, with the collapse of the post-war boom, the discrediting of Keynesianism and the rise of monetarism, the internal colonisation of the mainstream took on a new lease of life. It was most symbolically marked by the subordination of macro to micro through the extremes taken by the New Classical Economics (with representative individuals, perfectly clearing markets, rational expectations and state-ineffectiveness). As its leading proponent Robert Lucas (1987, p. 108), wrongly if arrogantly, put it, "the term 'macroeconomic' will simply disappear from use and the modifier 'micro' will be superfluous". By implication, the death of applied economics in general, or of (the old or classic) development economics in particular, was equally strongly signalled by Anne Krueger (1986, p. 62) in celebrating the Washington Consensus:

> Once it is recognised that individuals respond to incentives, and that 'market failure' is the result of inappropriate incentives rather than non-responsiveness, the separateness of development economics as a field largely disappears.

The mantle for EI in this vein was vigorously taken up by Gary Becker (following George Stigler); he was to microeconomics at Chicago what Friedman was to macroeconomics. In his pioneering contributions to the first phase, or to old EI, the starting point was to treat as many economic and social phenomena as if subject to optimising individuals in contexts of perfectly working markets. With the rarest of exceptions, it is striking that Becker rarely acknowledges the presence of unemployment nor money/finance in his analyses.

Unsurprisingly, there was a mainstream reaction against the NCE and its microfoundations but it is more marked by what it accepted than offering a radical alternative or even restoring the status quo ex ante. In particular, as well as accepting rational expectations (a logical consequence of extending individual optimising to information as data), the approach remained rooted in TA^2. The only break was to emphasise that information held by individuals is asymmetric as a result of which markets will work imperfectly in the sense of being inefficient, failing to clear and/or be absent altogether.[14] Not only could all microeconomics and macroeconomics be redone on this basis but also the second or new phase of EI was both more extensive and palatable given abandonment of the as if perfectly working market model of both economy and society. Instead, the non-economic becomes perceived as the optimising, individual responses to the presence of market failures. Apparently irrational behaviour as with customs, habits, norms, formation of institutions and so on, are the result of the rational response to market imperfections. With Akerlof's market for "lemons" the classic exemplar, honest second-hand car dealers might collectively institutionalise a warranty system is symptomatic and symbolic of all non-market forms and factors, from the mundane warranty to the nature and role of the state.

On this basis, as indicated, quite apart from rejuvenating microeconomics (often at the expense of more inductive approaches) and (diluted) Keynesianism, the new phase of EI both renewed its assault upon the other social sciences but also extended it to many new areas, often with 'new' as the operative word – such as the new welfare economics, the new(er) institutional economics, the new(er) economic sociology, and the newer development economics (in case of the Post-Washington Consensus, as opposed to the new development economics attached to the Washington Consensus).

Of particular interest is the new growth theory because it reflected some factors not already considered alongside those others of long standing. It did, if implicitly, rely, if partially, upon the technical apparatus, essentially deploying growth as an output and any potential contributor to growth as an input in a Cobb-Douglas production function for economic performance.[15] Secondly, in an explosion of interdisciplinarity on the narrowest of conceptual terms, any variable could be incorporated into statistical regressions and the numbers of them ran into the hundreds. Third is the flight from theory with a far from subtle change in the meaning of model for many, if not all, economists[16] and increasingly so for new students and practitioners. Instead of being underlying

14 A major exception is the work of Paul Krugman on economies of scale as the breach with perfectly working markets, this allowing for colonisation of trade theory and the new economic geography (Fine, 2010d for a critique).

15 As simply brought home by Rodriguez (2006) but transparent from Barro-style regressions in which estimated coefficients are growth elasticities of their corresponding variables.

16 See Boland (2014). Angus Deaton has been at the forefront of insisting upon theory as the basis for econometrics, especially in his critique of Randomised Control Trials in much practice. See Bédécarrats et al. (eds) (2020).

theory from which (systems of) equations could be formed to be statistically estimated, the theory part could be leap-frogged and the model becomes the equations for estimation directly without regard to theory other than through some sort of (usually mainstream) disposition that variables are related to one another quantitatively. Fourth, such empirical methods have expanded enormously in scale, scope and technique, alongside the mathematisation of the discipline and the ready availability of large data sets and cheap and readily available computer power. Fifth, policy variables are readily incorporated and trade-offs made between them in terms of their cost-growth effectiveness.[17]

Although the old growth theory was deeply embedded in the old EI – treating an economy as if it could be reduced to a given aggregate production function – the new growth theory anticipates the current phase of (newer) EI. In this, there is even more scope for colonising and appropriating the subject matter of other disciplines and, on occasion, to establish a stronger presence within, and not just alongside, them. For it involves not just the application but also what I have termed the "suspension" of TA^2. Paradoxically, if not perversely, and certainly inconsistently, so confident is the mainstream in the validity of TA^2 that it feels enabled both to hold on to it and to reject it at the same time, most obviously in supplementing it with whatever variables (to explain or to be explained), concepts and/or theoretical fragments, it cares to plunder from other social sciences (with social capital, alongside a plethora of other capitals as leading examples).[18]

Logical consistency, strenuous claims to the contrary through the endless, unexamined, justificatory appeal to mathematical rigour, has never been the strong point of the mainstream. It all began with the invention of the fictional Walrasian auctioneer so that all could be competitive price-takers. Never let realism get in the way of either TA^2 or its application. And this applies not only conceptually but also in the intra-disciplinary domain of theory itself, ranging over the conditions necessary for the existence, uniqueness and stability of general equilibrium, aggregation problems (both for Cambridge capital theory and for demand curves other than essentially for single individuals), trade theory (two sectors and no capital reversals), absence of increasing returns, the theory of the second best, etc. In short, where mathematical rigour suggests that the mainstream should walk away from its preferred results, it comes out second best. First best is to adopt what I call a unicorn approach – take

17 For all this, see Fine and Dimakou (2016).

18 My current, and most recent, favourite is, "Recovery capital ... the resources people can call upon to initiate and sustain alcohol and drug problem resolution" (Burns and Yates, 2022).

standard assumptions and results as the basis on which to judge select deviations from them in the real world – let us understand the anatomy of the horse by reference to the (invented) anatomy of the unicorn. And, where the empirical evidence is contrary, the analytical acrobatics is equally impenetrable. One of my favourite examples is the World Bank's response to the East Asian miracles, and the developmental state paradigm; yes, there was state intervention but it only did what the market would have done if it had been working perfectly. Another favourite is the ultra-mainstream response to the impact of minimum wages on employment; nett out all the factors that might make the relationship positive and, lo and behold, increasing minimum wages does decrease employment.

For the current phase of EI, logical incoherence derives from the predisposition to believe in the rational individual whose utility function depends upon fixed preferences over (culturally) fixed goods. But then analyses set about using such utility functions to explain why they are not fixed, or how variation in factors that have been taken to be fixed to construct utility functions in the first place, can also be explained by the very use of those utility functions.[19] No wonder, we now enter a world of mainstream economics self-designating itself as ranging from freakonomics through the economics of (almost) everything to the logic of life (Levitt, 2005; Harford, 2009; and Leigh, 2014).

The unworldliness, lack of realism, reductionisms, interdisciplinary parasitism, ignorances and arrogances of mainstream economics raise the issue of the relationship of its scholarship to both ideology and policy in practice (and how these all fit together to give rise to a world vision) (Fourcade et al. 2015; and Fine, 2013c and 2019b). Especially in the context of the World Bank, but of more general applicability, it is important to recognise that scholarship, ideology and policy in practice are rarely consistent with one another in their origins, content and use.[20] This does not mean they are not connected at all as they do mutually condition one another but in ways and to an extent, qualitatively and quantitatively, that varies across time, place and issue – and not least across different periods of capitalism, and phases within those periods.

For neoliberalism, we can acknowledge how its three phases have correspondences with the three phases of economics imperialism (and Keynesianism/ modernisation with the prior period). What is striking for scholarship for the current period is that the self-confidence of the mainstream in the form of monetarism has first at most been marginally eroded by the new

19 For the acrobatics around identity economics, see Fine (2009d).

20 See especially Bayliss and Fine (eds) (2008), Bayliss et al. (eds) (2011), and discussion of these issues in Fine (2001 and 2010a).

information-theoretic economics, and only further marginally disturbed by the GFC despite the failure either to predict or to remedy it. This compounds pre-existing weaknesses in the arena of ideology and policy, giving rise to a lack of theoretically-informed world vision (unlike Keynesianism for example). For ideology (and corresponding politics), neoliberalism has always drawn much more heavily upon the neo-Austrian antipathy to the state drawing as it does on the notions of inventiveness and spontaneous order which are simply absent from mainstream economics for which von Hayek and the Austrian school is as radically to be dismissed as Marxism. For policy, in contrast with ordo-liberalism and social market to the fore (we have ways of making the free market work and we will not hesitate to use them), mainstream economics has at best the piecemeal to offer in correcting market (and institutional) imperfections. So, once again, the mainstream is trumped by neo-Austrianism which, within the hands of neoliberal politicians, has an extremely flexible border between what the state must do (and how it does it) to guarantee individual (market) freedoms even across the economic domain.

The lack of any coherence within and across each of scholarship, ideology, policy in practice and corresponding overall world vision is a major source of weakness in the current position of mainstream economics although this is heavily outweighed from within by its extraordinarily monolithic and reductionist, if occasionally suspended, adherence to TA^2, its institutional command of the discipline (especially through the global reach of a few leading locations within the United States), and its intolerance for alternatives in teaching, appointments and research. Lacking the means by which to explain major economic developments by reference to its own theory, mainstream economics has sought to rely upon selective, suspended dependence upon other disciplines. But, by doing so, it more fully exposes its inner weaknesses to the alternative methodologies, methods, theories and conceptualisations from across the other social sciences relative to which it is extreme and outdated by most criteria and, in particular, incapable of either genuine, grounded systemic analyses (in light of its extreme form of methodological individualism) or critical scrutiny of conceptualisations (blissfully unaware of postmodernism and its aftermaths).

4 ... Heterodoxy

For most non-economists, the foregoing will be too detailed and technical an account of the dismal science which can be much more readily dismissed from a distance of the details involved. But the account is justified to the extent that, unsurprisingly, what might be a more acceptable interdisciplinary heterodox economic has itself to be situated in what is often a close if, at least to some degree, critical relationship to orthodoxy. Foremost is to observe how heterogeneous is heterodox economics, in taking orthodoxy as its critical point of departure. So extreme and narrow, and intolerant, is the orthodoxy that the only quality that heterodoxy need have in common is that it deviates in one, other, or any of the massive number of fallacious presumptions underpinning TA^2. In the wake of the GFC, with general (if predominantly intra-disciplinary) ineffective dissatisfaction with the mainstream, it is hardly surprising that there has been a wide-ranging and popular call for greater pluralism within economics, especially but not exclusively from students – that alternative approaches should at least be allowed a place at the curriculum table (Batifoulier et al. 2015, for example).

The substance of such pluralism (and demand for mainstream plus) and its relationship to heterodoxy can be looked at in a number of ways, often overlapping in emphasis and/or substance, reflecting absences, weaknesses and fallacies in the mainstream. These are so extensive that I do little more than provide lists in what follows.[21] First is the philosophy, methodology and ethics of economics, none of which would even tend to be mentioned other than in passing in mainstream teaching with most specialist journals primarily being populated by heterodox approaches.

Second is the history of economic thought which is equally more or less absent from standard teaching so that the classics – Smith, Ricardo, Marx, etc – do not warrant a mention, let alone from where current wisdom has derived because its origins do not matter from a perspective in which economics just got better and better. The so-called marginalist revolution of the 1870s is more or less unknown to many students, and so lacking in intra-disciplinary respect from their colleagues are historians of economic thought that they have more or less collectively determined to ally themselves to the history of science in order to secure any academic presence and prestige. The contrast with other social sciences, in which the classics of the disciplines remain prominent and continue to be influential and contested, could not be more marked.

Third, then, heterodoxy is spread to some degree across different schools of thought and approaches, ranging from Marxist political economy at one extreme to neo-Austrianism at the other, reflecting nothing in common other than rejection of (some) mainstream foundations. Such different schools of thought can derive to a greater or lesser extent from particular scholars, most

21 For the one-dimensioning of economics, `a la Marcuse, alongside a rather different one-dimensioning of economies (by money/commodification), see Fine (2017).

notably Keynes, Schumpeter, Veblen (if more as evolutionary economics) apart from those already mentioned. Or they are inspired by the mainstream neglect of particular topics or their unsatisfactory treatment as with technological change (and national systems of innovation), institutions, the social and the individual, development, monopolisation, and so on.[22]

And, fourth, across these different schools and otherwise, heterodoxy has been drawn to analyse topics that tend to be neglected by the mainstream other than in passing or as inappropriate applications of underlying principles and their suspension. This includes inequality,[23] distribution more generally, globalisation (and imperialism), neoliberalisation, periodisation of capitalism, long waves and crisis theory, labour relations and processes (beyond labour as a mere physical factor of production like others), economic and social reproduction, class relations and hierarchies, uncertainty as opposed to risk, gender, race and, most recently, financialisation which has been notably absent from the mainstream, perversely in contrast to its burgeoning presence in other disciplines over the last decade.

Fifth, then, heterodoxy's relationship to interdisciplinarity is complex and shifting. There is a strong case for arguing that the capitalist economy can be constituted as an object of analysis in its own right (Fine, 2022b). Such is the nature of mainstream economics, on the basis of TA^2 and beyond, and even of the interdisciplinarian par excellence, Karl Marx, given his (critique of the) political economy of capitalism. This raises the issue of what are the boundaries of the economy and the economic (as with EI for the mainstream) and how are these boundaries to be related to analytically co-constituting the economic and the non-economic or the social (a misnomer in light of acknowledging the economy is also social), with Marxism recently drawn to examining economic and social reproduction (Fine, 2021b), treating economic as embedded within rather than alongside social reproduction. Whether as a response to the mainstream's galloping EI or otherwise, heterodoxy has increasingly acknowledged the need to move beyond being a purely economic theory and to embrace interdisciplinary approaches and insights having been muted in this respect from the post-war period onwards, not least with the erosion of applied economics across both the Keynesian and especially the neoliberal periods.

Sixth, this points to the evolution of heterodox economics. But, although linked with it, it is considerably messier than for the mainstream, and is much

22 For an overview of heterodoxy, see Stilwell et al. (2022) noting that its chapters cover thirty or more different approaches to "Alternative Theories of Political Economy".

23 Until recently in light of the Piketty phenomenon that is the exception that proves the rule, see Fine (2021a).

less open to periodisation as such, as it is (re)constructed out of a number of influences: drawing upon history of thought; taking the (shifting) mainstream as critical point of departure; grounding analysis in contemporary developments; and drawing influences from other social sciences which have had their own evolutions. For the latter, in particular, a general trend across the social sciences has been the concerted and collective attempt to address the contemporary realities arising out of globalisation and neoliberalism, with a corresponding retreat from the excesses of postmodernism (which never touched mainstream economics and barely heterodoxy either). The result has inevitably been to promote the degree of economic analysis, generally through political economy of one or another variety, across the social sciences. Accordingly, the scope for interdisciplinary political economy has been enriched, especially where it involves the systemic (for which heterodoxy can be strong, most notably and recently with financialisation) and, if much less so, cultural and discursive content.[24] On the other hand, what were previously accepted orthodoxies – not least left Keynesianism (and its stronghold at Cambridge, UK)[25] – have been 'relegated' to heterodoxy.

Finally, the disparate spread and heterogeneity of heterodoxy is a consequence of the varieties of strategies and opportunities by which it seeks to prosper, or even survive, in the wake of the hostile dominance of the mainstream. Strategic survival for, and promotion of, heterodoxy, in teaching and research, depends upon taking contextually-grounded opportunities, trading off compromises with orthodoxy to gain a toehold for alternatives (Fine, 2018). A precondition for presence of heterodoxy within the discipline is the need for its practitioners to command the mainstream's demanding technical requirements and their consequences (whereas the reverse is not true with mainstream knowledge of alternatives more or less non-existent and unnecessary). The mainstream has an ethos of mathematical theory and modelling, with corresponding, increasingly sophisticated, statistical methods, as the only marker of scientific rigour and worth. This is so much so that, as an indication, in the research publication assessments in the UK, only a small minority of economics departments submitted to the economics panel, preferring to

24 This is particularly marked in the treatment of consumption where the majority of social science, other than all strands of economics including heterodoxy, witnessed an explosion of attention around the rise and fall of postmodernism. This is despite my best efforts (Fine and Leopold, 1993; Fine, 2002; and Bayliss and Fine, 2021a).

25 And more rounded institutionalists, such as J K Galbraith, with conceptualisations such as the military-industrial complex and affluent society, might just as well have never existed, whilst industrial relations has been transformed into human resource management and incorporated into business schools.

have their contributions to economics to be considered by other disciplines in anticipation of more favourable treatment than would be received from within their own discipline. More generally, reinforcing the two-way interdisciplinarity attached to economics, as observed, heterodoxy is liable to find more scope in other disciplines. This is even so for business and management studies in the UK, where large increases in student numbers have, alongside other factors, allowed for considerably more intellectual licence across research and teaching. Significantly, though, the biggest boost to heterodoxy derived from the student radicalism of the 1960s, and with renewal of activism around the GFC, the environment and the pandemic currently furnishing critiques of, and alternatives to, the mainstream.

5 The Post-apartheid Context

Early in my career, I undertook considerable research on the (history of the) British coal industry, in part as a case study of state intervention in industrial restructuring, including nationalisation and privatisation. A common conventional wisdom was that you could not understand the coal industry unless you had experience of being underground. For a young academic, without this qualification, it was both a put down and a challenge, inducing me to respond provocatively that, once you had been down a mine, you would never be able to understand coal.[26]

Both of these points of view are correct. You do need close knowledge and even experience as far as possible of your object of study but you also need to look at it from a distance, in the broader context, with critical appreciation of preconceptions. In some respects, I consider that my work on South Africa benefitted considerably from an initial ignorance, other than abhorrence for the apartheid system. I was also lucky in my first two readings, one by Duncan Innes on Anglo-American and the other a government report on Eskom. Although antagonistic to the notion of the United States as being driven by a military-industrial complex, these readings did inspire me to characterise South Africa as a Minerals-Energy Complex (MEC) in light of the close and coordinated relations between South African mining capital and its associated

26 Eventually, I did go underground and it did, indeed, add to my understanding of the labour process and the hostility to it. In part, my engagement with British coal was a reason for my being asked to be involved in South Africa, with some presumption of spillover knowledge.

conglomerates and the state and state enterprises.[27] In some respects, this specification was more easily recognised if setting aside the role of apartheid as such.

Indeed, the wisdom of not having been down the mine applies equally by analogy to the post-apartheid period. For it allows what is already a passage of almost thirty years to be seen as the neoliberalisation of South Africa, all the more clearly and better understood for not being designated primarily as post-apartheid, and so burdened by considerations of how apartheid is a lingering, even leading, burdensome determinant as opposed to a conditioning factor. Where the apartheid/post-apartheid division is particularly germane, however, is the extent to which the apartheid economy, despite its global connections as a major mineral producer and exporter, was at least partially insulated initially from the early phases of neoliberalism. As a result, the post-apartheid economy is readily seen as complex in both having combined, or overlain, the different phases of neoliberalism and to have done so, or to have caught up with elsewhere, particularly, even astonishingly, rapidly.[28]

How it did so, and what it did, is heavily marked by the heritage of the apartheid economy, and the central role of the MEC within it. By the time apartheid was entering its transitional phase to formal democracy, the MEC was already marked by a number of key features.

First, as already remarked, there was a close, integral relationship between a small number of conglomerate mining houses and the state and its nationalised industries, constituting the core of the MEC. Privately-owned coal mines produced fuel for state-owned power stations at guaranteed profits, with the electricity used to extract and process ore for privately run gold mines.

---

27 See Fine and Rustomjee (1996) although earlier work came in the form of papers for the ANC's Department of Economic Policy, between 1987 and 1992 on gold, coal, electricity, privatisation, employee share ownership plans, and the South African military-industrial complex. This was part of a pre-MERG, ANC-solicited research programme dubbed EROSA, Economic Research on South Africa. It was set up after but in parallel to Research on Education on South Africa, RESA, led by Harold Wolpe. The two programmes suffered similar fates in many respects if through different trajectories. My own contributions to EROSA included "The Gold Industry: Policy and Prospects", "The Coal Industry: Policy and Prospects", "The Electricity Industry: Policy and Prospects", "Privatisation in South Africa: An Assessment", "ESOPs in the South African Context" and "The South African Military-Industrial Complex".

28 It is worth recalling that Harold Wolpe intervened in the post-apartheid debate to question whether the appeal of social democratic policymaking was blinding the movement to the pitfalls of failing to challenge capitalist state power. Yet, social democracy was soon wiped from the policy agenda (Reynolds et al. eds, 2019). In passing, note that Wolpe is a leading example of a (dis)engaged scholar, as discussed in the final section.

And, similarly across coal exports with quotas allocated by the state, transported by state-owned rail to state-owned ports for sale at premium prices. Comparable observations can be made of steel, and of South Africa's (unique, sanction-busting) coal-to-oil facility, SASOL, itself the basis for petro-chemicals, and so on. In addition, though, especially in light of restrictions on the export of capital and informal or formal sanctions impeding inward investment, but more longstanding, was the extensive spread of conglomerate ownership across sectors not necessarily attached or linked to the core of the MEC.

Second, historically, most sharply revealed by the formal adoption of apartheid in the post-war period by the National Party government, was the disjuncture between the economic power held within the MEC, variously caricatured as English or foreign, and the political power that lay with Afrikanerdom. Uneasy compromises over the economy were reached, particularly through the growth of nationalised industries that served the MEC and beyond. However, long before the apartheid period was drawing to a close, two major political developments had been realised: on the one hand, while competitive conflicts still remained, large-scale conglomerate capital, both English and Afrikaner, had been closely integrated, across the MEC core and beyond; on the other hand, the representation of small-scale Afrikaner capital had been subordinated to large-scale capital. As a result, for example, the 1970s witnessed a major expansion of the MEC core, strongly coordinated by the state, in response both to the oil crisis and the unprecedented increase in the price of gold following the breakdown of Bretton Woods.

Third, a major mechanism underpinning these economic and political developments was the use of finance to promote Afrikaner capital, with English capital having long been integrated into (global) financial markets in light of the need for funding of large scale mining operations. As a result, the South African economy was marked by a particularly well-developed (internationalised) financial sector as apartheid was drawing to a close.

Fourth, an enduring feature of the South African economy, with a few exceptions, has been the failure to have diversified out of the core strengths of the MEC along value chains involving capital, intermediate and consumption goods. Initially, this was due to the disjuncture between economic and political power and the tentative, if growing, collaboration across political divides as the economic power of large-scale Afrikaner capital, its integration with English capital, and its dominance over small-scale capital strengthened. By the time, the strategy became politically feasible in the 1970s, the opportunity was taken to further consolidate the MEC core in light of oil and gold price increases. Traditionally, but totally wrongly, the failure to progress in consumption goods has been seen as a failure of import-substituting industrialisation as if South

Africa's industrialisation depended upon its consumer goods as opposed to its mineral-related sectors. But, in practice, ISI was never attempted in South Africa. Instead, if mistaken for ISI in retrospect, tariff protection to consumer industries was offered more or less on demand as a concession to small-scale (Afrikaner) industry (and agriculture) – as opposed to ISI proper, in which policy targets coordinated and integrated expansion of consumption goods not just market relief. Significantly, as the apartheid period was winding down, government reports were clearly aware that continuing with tariff protection was counterproductive, and the only appropriate choices were to abandon it altogether or to supplement it with more extensive measures, a decision essentially postponed under the crisis of the apartheid economy in the 1980s.

Such were the conditions, alongside gross social and economic inequalities, with which South Africa entered the post-apartheid period, or should we say its catch up period of neoliberalisation as can be seen to have been realised in retrospect, leading to the crunching together of NL's three phases. First and foremost, particularly on the basis of its well-developed financial markets, the South African economy entered an intensive and extensive period of financialisation or, more exactly, economic and social restructuring heavily compromised by financialisation. It might even be considered a classic case, albeit with its own peculiar features.

In brief, over a few following paragraphs, financialisation involves the securitization of streams of revenue that are then subject to speculative financial trading to make profits without producing which can only be at the expense of the rest of the economy. South Africa's growth of financial assets over the post-apartheid period has, much like the global average, exceeded that of its national income by roughly three times, indicating a heavy role of finance in appropriating from, as opposed to underpinning, growth. Correspondingly, in South Africa, over the post-apartheid period, the fastest growing sector has been finance, now contributing 20% to GDP as well as relatively few jobs and more inequality. Essentially this means, as finance itself produces nothing, that finance has stolen 25% of real GDP, claimed it has contributed this to GDP (20% is 25% of 125%), whilst actually only leaving 80% of GDP for other purposes. It is as if thieves claim to have added to GDP by their own activities and all of those deployed to prevent, catch, sentence and imprison them as well as for the remedial works done due to damages caused.

As South African financialisation has gathered pace, the majority of its citizens have seen it drawn into their everyday lives through increasing, often stressed, indebtedness (whereas, previously, 40% or so were free of any financial services at all – proportionally and certainly absolutely, the most indebted and the most advantaged by financialisation are always the wealthiest). But the abiding impact has been for the financial sector to have been totally deficient in what mainstream economics designates as its major function, to mobilise and allocate investment (as opposed to speculation). Over the post-apartheid period, despite its burgeoning financial sector, the overall level of real investment in the economy has rarely exceeded 20% of GDP, something in the region of 10% or more too little to meet the needs for economic and social development.

As a result, the South African economy is best characterised by the five lows. It suffers low investment, low productivity, low employment, low wages, and low social provision. These lows can only be managed, not addressed nor even substantially ameliorated, until low levels of financialised investment are remedied. In the post-apartheid period, however, the financialised, neoliberalised globalisation of the economy has been geared towards the unbundling of conglomerates and their integration, especially the MEC core, into multinational corporation activity (not least with offshoring), the outflow of capital (much of it illegally through transfer pricing on minerals, and, on occasion, even exceeding the domestic investment deficiency), and the holding of financial reserves for potential speculative purposes. In addition, the various machinations around Black Economic Empowerment have primarily created a new black elite with (the connections for) the purpose of facilitating these developments through political influence or power, with corresponding parasitic rewards for integration into such restructuring.

In general, the neoliberalisation of the South African economy has been most prominently signalled by what is perceived to be austere macroeconomic policy, alongside trade liberalisation and other similar market-friendly policies. The description of such policies as neoliberal is appropriate but they are as much the consequence as the cause of South Africa's neoliberalism. Most obviously, if you ignore or are complicit with capital flight, then it makes sense to raise interest rates and constrain government expenditure so that (potentially volatile) short-term inflows of capital can be used to balance long-term outflows. Turning a blind eye to the realities of economic restructuring inevitably leads to a logic of compensating for their effects by whatever means necessary.

However, the leap into NL also has to be managed politically and ideologically. Understandably, much attention has been focused upon the "Faustian Pact" and the discrete steps involving the abandonment of MERG and the RDP (after its marginalisation), and the adoption of (the non-negotiable) GEAR.[29] These were accompanied by correspondingly typical neoliberal political

29 For best account, see Padayachee and van Niekerk (2019).

developments around centralised authority – power to decide and coordinate rapidly devolved to Ministry of Finance (and, subsequently, also Presidency) and, initially, paving the way for what was to follow, key ministries (finance and minerals and energy) and the Reserve Bank remained with the National Party under the Government of National Unity. The MDM was effectively demobilised and the CPSA and COSATU were effectively incorporated as more or less willing partners in 'crime'.

All of this is well-known, and the various explanatory factors involved, from international conspiracy and coercion through to lack of professional economists and knowledge of economics by leadership, have been well rehearsed so that emphasising one or another has some but limited merit. In general, these factors generally reinforced one another and ran together.[30] Instead, what stands out, and yet is more readily missed, is just how rapidly and fully earlier aspirations evaporated alongside resistance to defend, let alone promote, them.

Here the material culture of South African politics comes to the fore. Entering the post-apartheid period, political cultures and organisations ranged across the entire spectrum, not only from left to right, but also from those of the Keynesian period (including both social democracy and Soviet communism albeit increasingly in disrepute) and across the three phases of neoliberalism. Initially, with the ANC in the lead and without denying the presence of some internal oppositions and conflicts, the Tripartite Alliance easily held these cultures together, drawing upon a single purpose, liberation and the prospective undoing the inequities of apartheid, and an unprecedented degree of trust and loyalty to the goals, to the organisations, and to the leadership.

In this light, once a determined faction within the leadership, presumed to be led by Thabo Mbeki, successfully determined to adopt a neoliberal strategy in all but name, bringing Mandela on board, a further aspect of material culture came into play, revolving around the processes of (individual) positioning in the outcomes to come, going far beyond, if heavily present, the self-enrichment and the climbing of this or that greasy pole. For access to position, power, wealth and/or influence depended upon unquestioned acceptance of trust and loyalty to the neoliberal turn and its leadership. Fail to support, and you were out, bringing root and branch leadership momentum behind the shift and, further, requiring contempt, stigma and marginalisation for those who failed to fall into line.

30 Unsurprisingly, I take the emphasis on lack of alternatives or knowledge to be nonsensical in light of choices that were rejected as well as those made. An economic strategy was deliberately chosen and imposed (Fine, 2025d).

Just imagine for a moment, that alternative world in which MERG was adopted and aggressively pursued by the leadership. Is there any doubt that those who turned against it would have been fully supportive? And even spirited opposition from the ANC's opponents (the white and international establishment) in that alternative world could well have been more muted than was experienced from the ANC itself in reality, given MERG's own emphasis upon state intervention to promote private through public investment as opposed to redistribution of, and assault upon, private ownership as such. Wherever it might have led, the MERG proposals were at most radical social democratic and entirely compatible, if with some detail and rationale attached, with the ANC intentions that had prevailed previously. The shift in posture during negotiations may have reflected a fear that they could fail at the expense of formal democratisation and liberation but they also seemed to reflect a pre-emptive strike on who was going to hold political (and economic) power and how.

Deference to leadership, and the reasons and motives for it, explains how the neoliberal turn should be so rapid and full, with limited contestation.[31] No more than symbolically, it speaks to my own experience of meteoric rise and fall. From nowhere, I was elevated to a position of engaging with, and drafting policy documents for, the ANC. This, no doubt, arose out of trusted connections, direct or indirect, with the CPGB, Joe Slovo, and the British NUM and, subsequently, with MERG, through Vella Pillay who was requested by Mandela to lead the project of providing an economic programme. Within a year or so of its being commissioned, Mandela was being instructed to disown the programme. At its presentation to the ANC, as show of solidarity, one after another of ministers or DGs in waiting showed themselves to be heavily opposed to its policies, often with ignorance of their content in equal measure, even though they had genuinely been constructed to meet the ANC's perceived aspirations and commissioned as such.[32]

But the aftermath of the abandonment of MERG is also symbolic of more general processes and prospects. Initially, though, bear in mind that my own involvement with South Africa remained as an outsider with another life in the UK, including an academic career that had come to include the South African economy but alongside a much broader portfolio of teaching and research

31 Once again, my own experience is that there was a golden moment for self-advancement over the period of transition, with erstwhile students experiencing meteoric rises in positions of power, influence and wealth across public and private sectors – the low hanging fruits for the qualified and the connected were bountiful.

32 Having drafted sections on education, health, housing and electrification, I was particularly at the rough end of harsh criticism.

interests. Nevertheless, I was committed to serve South African constituencies upon request, with no other motives as such other than to do so to the best of my available abilities and energies, willing to bend to what was perceived to be of need, even if with some regard for intellectual, personal and political integrity. As a result, the level and nature of my involvement in South Africa, post-MERG, is to some degree a weak weathervane for political and intellectual developments.

Following MERG, then, it was not just the rejection of a set of policy proposals but also those who were associated with them. My relations with the ANC and with the CPSA came to a more or less abrupt halt. Immediately afterwards, there remained at most lingering calls for support from the trade union movement and an (unexplained and anomalous) invitation to join the Presidential Labour Market Commission as one of four international expert advisors (Fine, 2025e, Ch. 1). Subsequently, I have been predominantly confined to a variety of teaching and training exercises alongside research initiatives prompted by my own interests and in response to requests from others outside the formal channels of policymaking.

I was sufficiently naïve not to question why this had happened until long after the event. Understandably, I had not been happy by the direction taken by policymaking, and the rejection of MERG, and in the way it was done in particular. But, until I was prompted much later to rethink, and more deeply, I saw this as the movement's choice and of no wider significance. It was only when MERG and more became an object of historical rather than contemporary history that I was forced to think about the processes involved and their role in what unfolded more generally. In short, left-wing economists, especially those associated with MERG and the like, were designated as persona non grata, treated contemptuously as unrealistic, buried in the past (of communism or even social democracy) and dismissed without serious consideration or debate. I felt this particularly for Vella Pillay who, apart from leading the MERG project, had an outstanding record as both activist and practising economist, and who reasonably became both bewildered and embittered by the way he was treated by his erstwhile comrades.[33] And, ultimately or long before that, even those committed to progressive change from within government found themselves thwarted by the structures and dynamics involved, voluntarily or forcibly leaving for the private sector to pursue their ambitions alongside those who had done so for less altruistic reasons.

33 See Padayachee and Sender (2017). Thus, Pillay also falls into the category of (dis)engaged scholar, see below, with a relatively rare movement from engaged to scholar rather than the more normal opposite direction and/or weight.

Such vignettes, writ large, tell us much about the evolution of neoliberalised South Africa. It is arguable that the direction taken by policy for the post-apartheid economy reflected a deep leadership distrust of the working class and its and other progressive organisations in terms of being incapable of being fiscally or otherwise responsible (as opposed to a prospective, idealised and idolised, black capitalist class). In addition, such postures may have given rise to antipathy to forms of provisioning that had the potential to create progressive organisations and demands – whether around economic or social provision. In short, the imperative was to command both policy and the policymaking process, the very antipathy of democracy and liberation. The corresponding centralised authoritarianism of the Mandela and Mbeki governments, together with their failure to deliver substantively for the majority, paved the way for neoliberalised politics par excellence in the form of Zuma and what has inappropriately been termed state capture (already captured but turned to more deeply entrenched corrupt practices). The loyalty and trust of the people for the ANC has been eroded through its abuse with the result that the political credit with which to neoliberalise has been spent and the Tripartite Alliance has correspondingly unravelled within and across its three components. Yet, nothing has yet emerged to offer alternatives other than more of the same with a new face in charge if hardly free of personal wealth and compromise. Such post-apartheid developments have heavily conditioned post-apartheid economics.

6 Post-apartheid Economics: From Unravelling to Disempowered

Under apartheid, with a few significant exceptions, academic economics and its offshoots can best be described as mainstream, weak, outdated and liable to be complicit with apartheid imperatives. As no doubt in many other fields, those who managed to rise above these confinements would be inclined to seek training and careers for themselves abroad. Such loss of talent was inevitably reinforced by choice or necessity in light of any compunctions about remaining and so being intellectually compromised by the ideologies and practices of apartheid. Even to the degree that there was some latitude in terms of academic freedom, heterodox economics would have been hard pressed to leverage a strong and stable position, with influence beyond academia, given the institutionalised pincer dominance of both apartheid and intra-disciplinary orthodoxy.

Unsurprisingly, then, home-grown heterodox economics was extremely limited within South Africa (other than a small, acceptable, idiosyncratic and accidental current of neo-Austrianism) although the 'liberal' mainstream could and did certainly display its antipathy in principle to apartheid as obstructing the free and efficient operation of markets as a starting point. Instead, then, heterodox political economy (and progressive social science more generally) drew upon a rich and eclectic combination of alternative overlapping influences, sources and themes. The first and foremost influence stemmed from the need to understand the nature and persistence of apartheid itself, and how it might best be contested. Second was the contributions of those individuals who had benefitted from overseas educations. Third was the role of progressive movements around the anti-apartheid movement and trade unions, and the protection allowed to some degree by academic freedom, with a mix of institutions and specific individuals tending to be to the fore.

As a result, as the apartheid period was drawing to a close, heterodox economics or, more exactly in terms of the terminology more likely to be deployed,[34] political economy was often left to economic historians but included heavily interdisciplinary contributions with the most significant and high quality of these contributions deriving from the outward reach of disciplines other than economics. The debate over the functionality of apartheid to capitalism between liberals and Marxists is a leading example, as are Wolpe's cheap labour power hypothesis (inspired by French anthropologists discussions of articulation of modes of production), the notion of apartheid's foundations upon the disjuncture between economic and political power (drawing upon Poulantzas), and the notion of South Africa as racial Fordism (imposing regulation theory on South African conditions). There was also very important studies in economic history, especially in relation to mining, agriculture, industrial and labour relations and migration. These contributions tended to straddle disciplinary boundaries in authorship and readership.

In the transition from apartheid, the situation changed dramatically and quickly in terms of balance of approaches, sources and subject matter. First and foremost was the switch from understanding the relationship between capitalism and apartheid to formulating policy proposals for post-apartheid South Africa with a general presumption, often implicit occasionally explicit, that this would be some form of non-racial capitalism seeking to redress the inherited inequities of apartheid to a greater or lesser extent at a greater or lesser speed. Second, there was a deluge of mainstream contributions, dovetailing with those deriving from (corporate) think-tanks, with sanctions and the stigma of apartheid no longer a barrier to the contribution of foreign

34 Nor pluralism in economics which is a more recent terminology to reflect antipathy to mainstream dominance of the discipline of economics.

participants, and the World Bank and the IMF to the fore, heavily in liaison (and personnel) with the old regime in the first instance and then with the new government especially once GEAR was adopted. Third, if more as a minority sport of temporary symbolic value was a flourishing of heterodox economics, not least with the preparation of the RDP, the role of MERG (in training black economists as its initial and prime task), and, particularly prominent, the Industrial Strategy Project.

The fate of the ISP offers some insight into the trajectory of post-apartheid heterodox economics. It was extraordinarily well-resourced in funds and personnel, and attracted some formal political support, not least through connections with Alec Erwin. Its intellectual inspiration was provided by one of its four co-directors, Raphie Kaplinsky, who hailed from IDS, the Institute of Development Studies, at the University of Sussex where Mbeki formed ideas about dependency theory and economics that later had a considerable influence on his policies. Paradoxically, the ISP was to some degree the descendant of the Economic Trends, ET, group, led by Stephen Gelb, which had dissolved with his disgruntled departure from it. But what ET and ISP had in common was a predilection for forcing the ill-fitting French regulation approach onto South Africa – racial Fordism for Gelb but, even more bizarrely (see below), post-fordism, the *filière* approach and flexible specialisation for ISP. Kaplinsky had presumably picked up flec-spec from his Sussex colleague Robin Murray who was its leading exponent in the UK.

By chance, Murray became Director-General of the Industry and Employment Branch of the Greater London Council,[35] where I also took a position, half-time on leave from academia, as a research editor responsible for bringing policy analysis to publication.[36] As a result, I was in a strong position to be extremely familiar both with the flec-spec approach and the unworldly appeal it exerted over its fanatical followers. In case of London, deindustrialisation had been driven by the rise of finance, its failure to promote industrial investment, and the global strategies of multinational corporations which had no intention of retaining, let alone siting, plant in the city with its high land, wage and transport costs. That this might be turned around or compensated for by supporting a few flec-spec, small-scale clothing and furniture firms, on the margins of survival, was simply laughable.[37]

35 On the left, under Ken Livingstone and, accordingly, along with other major metropolitan local government authorities, abolished by Mrs Thatcher in 1985.

36 See especially GLC (1985 and 1986).

37 Tellingly, the progressive criteria on which supported firms were supposed to operate were inevitably eroded by commercial pressures even if pursued in practice in the first

The ISP's application of the flec-spec approach to South Africa was totally inappropriate as the core of a strategy for the post-apartheid economy in general and for industry in particular. It simply failed to acknowledge the overwhelming roles of the MEC and finance, not least because they did not even begin to fit readily into the flec-spec framing. As a result, there was little or false diagnosis of the nature of the South African economy and, in particular, of the need to remedy the continuing historical failure to diversify out of the MEC core as a strategy for industrial development. Training, support to niche sectors to upgrade and the virtues of increased competitiveness were unduly exaggerated at the expense of dealing with levels of investment and economies of scale and scope across the major sectors of the economy (Fine, 1995b).

In the event, whatever its merits, the ISP has disappeared more or less without trace (despite the efforts of Mike Morris and Justin Barnes). The point of recalling it is not so much to settle scores over differences within heterodoxy which have now been rendered redundant, not least as flec-spec/post-fordism, if not appropriately (global) value chain analysis, has long since lost its lustre.[38] Rather, it is to highlight how the ISP engaged what much of what heterodox resources and influences there were in the immediate post-apartheid period, arguably at some expense to other approaches and influences, and with little or no impact upon building a broader constituency of heterodoxy in substance and personnel.

However, the ISP did have considerable purchase over (paper) policymaking at the DTI, especially in promoting a sectoral approach and in misplaced efforts to focus on increasing trade with other African countries.[39] Whatever the DTI's success in the first, and easier, step of formulating a scatter gun of policies, the second step of seeing these policies implemented has been hamstrung by lack of resources and political clout to implement its programmes other than piecemeal and ineffectively, with an overwhelming deadweight of

---

instance; and the Greater London Enterprise Board, GLEB, which was responsible for supporting firms to implement the London Industrial Strategy, made its money out of the appreciation of its property portfolio rather than from the businesses for which it was formed. Interestingly, Vella Pillay served on the GLEB board and so had first-hand experience of its futility, often mumbling under his breath at its folly as a measured form of loyalty and commitment.

38 Note the inconsistent approach to industrial policy in MERG, with the MEC and ISP stances uncomfortably set side by side (as a result of insistent lobbying for its inclusion by the ISP on grounds of democratic participation).

39 Although such an approach is not unique to flec-spec, is trumped by global commodity/value/chain/network analysis, and see my own sectoral approach, Fine (1997c) prepared for COSATU.

being hemmed in by the absence of any strategy to exert power over South Africa's major MEC sectors and industries.[40]

As a result, the ISP is the one early exception that proves the rule that heterodox economics in toto, let alone its interdisciplinarity, was entirely disempowered in the post-apartheid period. The fate of MERG is indicative, recalling that it was set up to train black economists until it was ceremoniously dumped in light of its policy proposals.[41] Continuing training and research projects, originating from SOAS (which had already trained many black economists through its separate distance learning programmes), with funding committed by international donors, failed to materialise simply because they could not be approved by ANC leadership as a stamp of support. This sheds some light on the we had no economists on our side explanation for the "Faustian pact". If so, the natural reaction would have been to seek to make up the shortfall, not to stand in the way (subject to the path-dependent rationale that, once pacted, antipathy to heterodoxy was set in stone – which, of course, is what happened).

Sadly, post-apartheid economic policy has not only been abysmal but has also shifted from one bewildering approach to another, from GEAR as the early marker of what was to come through to the NDP as an extraordinarily ill-researched and argued set of proposals. Along the way, other policy initiatives have also been aired with greater or lesser attachment to each of reality and, hence of necessity and in implementation, policy in practice.[42] Retrospective assessment of what policies have achieved, or not, let alone why and how with whatever lessons to be garnered, are notable for their absence as one posture gives way to another, see below on the developmental state.

---

40 Sadly, the failure to renew the contract of Zavareh Rustomjee as DG of DTI set aside a force for taking MEC considerations into account both in formulating policy and in potentially providing a bridgehead for a more rounded and realistic heterodox economics for post-apartheid South Africa. As Zav put it himself on policy in personal communication, "the locus of (and any coordinating mechanism for) Industrial Policy increasingly fragmented from the early 1990s onwards ... a trajectory that ... ties up with the power of the MEC/finance interests to minimise cross-cutting coordination by, amongst other factors, exacerbating policy fragmentation and segmentation, co-opting individuals and shaping emerging classes".

41 It continued, admirably spearheaded by Jaya Josie and then Asghar Adelzadeh as the National Institute for Economic Policy, NIEP, but was entirely marginalised.

42 For my own takes on some of these shenanigans, see Fine (2009b and c, and 2012a and b) covering the putative radical chic of the Harvard Group (responsible for the Treasury-commissioned Accelerated and Shared Growth Initiative (ASGI-SA), available at https://growthlab.cid.harvard.edu/publications/final-recommendations-international-panel-asgisa, the New Growth Path and the NDP.

Presentationally, policy postures have rarely diverged far from those proposed by the IMF and the World Bank but for occasional rogue and casual interventions. How can policy statements reflect realities if this means saying explicitly that we are globalising, financialising and neoliberalising the economy (and social provision), with the restructuring of the MEC at its core, through heavy levels of (illegal) capital flight, whilst serving the interests of existing white and newly-emerged black elites, with at most a lingering commitment to redress the five lows in response to ill-coordinated and sporadic if extensive protest.

In this light, engaged heterodoxy has only managed to survive at the margins, thanks to the dedication of (at most small groups of) individuals in fragmented locations. With African economics, and training, dominated by the World Bank and its Oxford offshoot (CSAE), the Economic Society of South Africa remains mainstream, and the discipline has been more or less untouched despite (a) the main source of the mainstream within academia, and beyond in media, think-tanks and the like, deriving from apartheid origins (b) the explosion of the demand for pluralism worldwide, especially after the GFC, and its institutionalisation in many heterodox movements and organisation (c) the increasing demand for decolonisation of academia (d) the variety of demands deriving from South African student movements (e) the unavoidable failings of South African economy and polity.

One further characteristic of South African academia, common in many developing (and "small society") countries, is the undue prominence if not necessarily influence of its scholars[43] – as evidenced, for example, by my own participation with the high and mighty from a standing start if, equally rapidly, subject to decline and fall. Politicians and government can still pick and choose from their advisors to suit. A striking example of this close relationship is the sudden, opportunistic adoption of South Africa as a developmental state, defying all analytical and empirical logic, in the death throes of the Mbeki regime. The post-apartheid economy had nothing at all by way of resembling a developmental state up to that point, and it was certainly rejected for framing economic (and especially industrial policy) in light of GEAR. Yet, the academic response to its being embraced by the ANC leadership, as a symbolic token recognition of its failings to deliver on economic and social development, was an immediate outpouring on South Africa as a developmental state, a minor turbulence in the otherwise marginalisation of heterodoxy (and more taken up by non-economists than economists).[44]

43 Although, also think Keynes, Friedman and Mont Pelèrin more generally.

44 For my own take on South Africa as a developmental state, not, see Ashman et al. (2013) and Fine (2010b and c, 2013d and 2016a). That its characteristics, albeit with a racialised

This fashion, like policies and the NDP to which it became attached, passed almost as rapidly as it arose. Much more promising, a late exception that also proves the rule around disempowered heterodoxy in the post-apartheid period, has been the successful campaign for a national minimum wage. It was sustained by a combination of outstanding academic research, communication, networking and campaigning, drawing strong if not uniform support from trade unions and political organisations, striking popular consciousness in times of low wages and high poverty and unemployment, and the benefits of high-level intervention from government (Ramaphosa himself being brought on board).[45]

Significantly, this rare, even unique, example of success has been closely associated with the late but welcome institutional breathing of life into heterodox economics in a South African context. Much of this has been spearheaded by the newly-formed Institute for Economic Justice, founded by the leading personnel in the academic campaign, and more, for the national minimum wage. The IEJ has a wide programme of academic research informing an equally wide-ranging set of policy issues. It has also been instrumental in promoting Rethinking Economics for Africa, REFA, a latecomer and broader counterpart to APORDE which for more than a decade has attempted to fan the few sparks of heterodox economics into life in South Africa, campaigning for pluralism and alternatives in (the teaching of) economics.

7 Locating Vishnu

As much as these new initiatives are most welcome and important, and, hopefully, the shape of things to come, what still stands out in the South African context, is just how much there has been a syndrome of 'so little, so late', a moniker that applies equally to economic and social development in the post-apartheid period. To some degree, all that has gone before points to the connections between these dual deficits, in their context not only of South Africa (and its MEC corporate restructuring with incorporation of BEE more generally) but also of globalised, neoliberalised, financialised contemporary

core, could better be found in the apartheid era, around the MEC, is argued in detail by Freund (2013 and 2018).

45 Minimum wages are not simple as such, going far beyond the traditional debate over whether they affect employment or not, but also depending upon whom they cover, at what level(s), how these are determined and changed, and how they are policed (or realised or not in practice). For an overview with South Africa as a case study, see Konopelko (2023).

capitalism into which the formally democratically-liberated society was both released and, for the main part, bewildered. To put it bluntly, compared to the successful initiative on minimum wages, and the current endeavours of the IEJ and others that have gone before, where are those for health, education, housing, agriculture, etc. This is not to say that nothing has occurred across these and other sectors from engaged, committed and conscientious scholars, but that the results in terms of impact have been weak, ineffectual and marked by a lack of strong, organised presence around home-grown (or any other) heterodox economics.[46]

This is despite the concerted efforts of a few, isolated institutional bases and a few dedicated scholars of ability, integrity and conscientiousness in research and teaching, of whom Vishnu is a leading example. It is surely telling that someone with his stature and experience should have been more or less forced out of his longstanding academic base in Durban and ended up at Wits where heterodoxy has only just begun to find a degree of security again thanks to those who kept it alive in the past, against mainstream hostility, and those who have promoted it in the present (as was Vishnu's own mission upon arriving and until his tragic, early death).

When asked to prepare this piece for this occasion, I felt that it was both an honour and that it would be a simple task of reviewing Vishnu's published work and cv more generally, picking all the low-hanging fruit to offer the flavour of an astonishing record of an engaged scholar, standing astride if not shattering the boundaries of interdisciplinarity. Whilst as a heterodox economist, it would be easy to label Vishnu as a post-Keynesian, this is at least slightly misleading if not wrong. First, within that school, it is important to see his approach to be more informal and discursive than attached to formal model-building and statistical methods (although empirical as well as other primary and secondary historical material was vital to his research). But, second, post-Keynesianism does not cover his much broader approach and contributions which straddle what I have previously described as falling under the umbrella rubric of applied fields – historically, institutionally and empirically informed, extending far beyond the methods and scope of (post-Keynesian) economics and political economy. At least partially, in this respect, Vishnu had some partial overlap, convergence even, with Bill Freund, the major difference

46 As elsewhere, it may be that the environment is an issue where this perspective is more complex, displaying a greater degree of both progressive momentum and establishment inertia. It also demonstrates that heterodoxy-informed political economy is at most a necessary condition for correspondingly fully effective policy activism.

being their initial starting points, from economics and economic history, respectively, with each comfortable where the two are inclined to meet.

So, no question, Vishnu ticks all the boxes of the scholarly part of the engaged scholar. But the engaged is more problematic raising, in the first instance, what it is to be an engaged scholar, potentially ranging in conceptualisation from some sort of organic intellectual through intellectual agitator-activist to policy advisor. Certainly, Vishnu was engaged, not least in having served on the Board of the Reserve Bank. But why was it that he was not even more engaged, especially given his much broader range of talents than those of a scholar, incorporating management, administrative, practical and personal skills.

Some might seek an answer in Vishnu's own personality and character – his dedication to scholarship and his broader interests and activities that were so dear to him and made his lifestyle what it was. This is to suggest that lesser engagement was a consequence of his own choices. I consider this to be a case of blaming the victim. Vishnu's 'leisure' activities and leisurely manner to a large extent concealed an extraordinarily high level of hard, effective, dedicated and conscientious work. More fundamentally, the thrust of what I have argued previously is that heterodox economists in post-apartheid South Africa were deeply structurally disengaged by much more general processes of disempowerment that rendered them neither wanted nor able to prosper. To paraphrase Marx, the engaged scholar can only be made in circumstances that are not self-chosen.

Paradoxically, then, Vishnu's own personality (try never to let disappointment get in the way of enjoyment for yourself or others), his capacities for collaboration and cooperation, and the breadth and depth of his contributions, can give the impression of satisfaction rather than frustration with the levels and directions of his engagements as a scholar and otherwise. His experience and deep disappointment, deriving initially from being an editor for MERG, gave him a head start in active antipathy to ANC economic policymaking (from a post-Keynesian perspective of inequality and inadequate effective demand and beyond). This placed him from the outset, anomalous appointment to Reserve Bank apart, on the margins of policymaking engagement but he remained dedicated to engagement where he could be both useful and retain his integrity. From this, so many of us benefitted in joint work or simply amiable, informative discussions in light of a calm, determined persona, openness to the views and contributions of others, and apparent lack of bitterness.

Others, at all levels, have responded to the context of (scholarly) disengagement and disempowerment in a variety of ways, displaying one or more in mixed combinations, open to shifting over time. The options are and have been of being (over-)active, inactive, resentful, frustrated, envious or, to the extent of being in a position to do so, pursuing self-interest by becoming incorporated into the mainstream and establishment through combinations of political position, government or public sector appointment, or private sector pursuit of enrichment and/or, possibly more worthy, doing stuff, with various degrees of dishonesty and/or rationalisation/self-justification through appeal to pragmatism and realism.

In short, Vishnu's position derived not simply from his talents, integrity, conscientiousness, collegiality, and hard work. He also finessed, with considerable aplomb, the personal, practical and intellectual tensions of being an engaged scholar in an age of scholarly disengagement. He was fully engaged but not so much that he fell victim to greasy pole or slippery slope. Hopefully, what he has left us in our memories and in his body of work will inspire more of the same and contribute to renewal of an age of scholarly engagement in which it can prosper for the benefit of one and all.

References

Abiad, A., E. Detragiache and T. Tressel (2008) "A New Database of Financial Reforms", IMF Working Paper WP/08/266, www.imf.org/external/pubs/ft/wp/2008/wp08266.pdf.

Adelzadeh, A. (2023) "Why Is the South African Economy Stuck in Chronic Crises?", in Mohamed et al. (eds) (2023), pp. 86–134.

Akerlof, G. (1970) "The Market for 'Lemons': Quality Uncertainty and the Market Mechanism", *Quarterly Journal of Economics*, vol 84, no 3, pp. 488–500.

Akerlof, G. and R. Kranton (2000) "Economics and Identity", *Quarterly Journal of Economics*, vol 115, no 3, pp. 715–53.

Al-Jazaeri, H. (2008) *Interrogating Technical Change through the History of Economic Thought in the Context of Latecomers' Industrial Development: the Case of the South Korean Microelectronics, Auto and Steel Industries*, SOAS, University of London, unpublished Phd Thesis.

Amphlett, G. (1914) *History of the Standard Bank of South Africa Ltd.*, 1862–1913, Glasgow: R. Maclehose and Co. Ltd.

Amsden, A. (ed.) (1994) "The World Bank's The East Asian Miracle: Economic Growth and Public Policy", special section, *World Development*, vol 22, no 4.

ANC (2012) "The Second Transition?: Building a National Democratic Society and the Balance of Forces in 2012", Discussion Document towards the National Policy Conference, Version 6.0 as amended by the Special NEC, February 27th, 2012, http://us-cdn.creamermedia.co.za/assets/articles/attachments/38020_anc_strategyq.pdf.

Andreoni, A., L. Kaziboni and S. Roberts (2021a) "Metals, Machinery, and Mining Equipment Industries in South Africa: the Relationship between Power, Governance, and Technological Capabilities", in Andreoni et al. (eds) (2021), pp. 53–77.

Andreoni, A., P. Mondliwa, S. Roberts and F. Tregenna (2021b) "Towards a New Industrial Policy for Structural Transformation", in Andreoni et al. (eds) (2021), pp. 337–62.

Andreoni, A., P. Mondliwa, S. Roberts, and F. Tregenna (eds) (2021) *Structural Transformation in South Africa: the Challenges of Inclusive Industrial Development in a Middle-Income Country*, Oxford: Oxford University Press.

Andreoni, A., N. Robb, and S. van Huellen (2021c) "Profitability without Investment: How Financialization Undermines Structural Transformation in South Africa", in Andreoni et al. (eds) (2021), pp. 213–36.

Andreoni, A. and S. Roberts (2024) "Minerals, Energy-Intensive Industries and Development: Green Transition and Employment in Southern Africa", Working Paper, no 3, Centre for Sustainable Structural Transformation, SOAS, https://www.soas.ac.uk/sites/default/files/2024-12/CSST_Working%20Paper_No_3%20Antonio%5E0Simon_Final.pdf.

Andreoni, A. and F. Tregenna (2021) "The Middle-Income Trap and Premature Deindustrialization in South Africa", in Andreoni et al. (eds) (2021), pp. 237–60.

Andrews, D. (2005) *Political Economy of the Growth and Ascendancy of the Finance Sector in Post-Apartheid South Africa*, MA Dissertation, Institute of Social Studies, The Hague.

Arrighi, G. (1994) *The Long Twentieth Century*, London: Verso.

Aryeetey, E., J. Harrigan and M. Nissanke (eds) (2000) *Economic Reforms in Ghana: the Miracle and the Mirage*, Oxford: James Currey.

Ashman, S. and B. Fine (2013a) "Neo-Liberalism, Varieties of Capitalism, and the Shifting Contours of South Africa's Financial System", *Transformation*, no 81/82, pp. 145–78. See Chapter 8.

Ashman, S. and B. Fine (2013b) "The Meaning of Marikana", *Global Labour Column*, no 128, https://www.global-labour-university.org/wp-content/uploads/fileadmin/GLU_Column/papers/no_128_Ashman_Fine.pdf. See Chapter 9.

Ashman, S. and B. Fine (2013c) "The Meaning of Marikana", *New Agenda*, no 51, pp. 27–30. See Chapter 9.

Ashman, S., B. Fine and S. Newman (2010a) "The Developmental State and Post-Liberation South Africa", in Misra-Dexter and February (eds) (2010), pp. 23–45.

Ashman, S., B. Fine and S. Newman (2010b) "The Crisis in South Africa: Neoliberalism, Financialization and Uneven and Combined Development", in Panitch et al. (eds) (2010), pp. 174–95.

Ashman, S., B. Fine and S. Newman (2011) "Amnesty International? The Scale and Impact of Capital Flight from South Africa", *Journal of Southern African Studies*, vol 37, no 1, pp. 7–25. See Chapter 7.

Ashman, S., B. Fine and S. Newman (2013) "Systems of Accumulation and the Evolving MEC", in Fine et al. (eds) (2013), pp. 245–67.

Atkinson, A. (1999) "Is Rising Inequality Inevitable? A Critique of the Transatlantic Consensus", third WIDER Annual Lecture, Helsinki.

Ault, D. and G. Rutman (1992) "The Effects of Social, Political, and Economic Constraints on the Black African's Allocation of Time: Evidence from Oscillating Migrants in the Republic of South Africa", *Oxford Economic Papers*, vol 44, no 1, pp. 135–55.

Aybar S. and C. Lapavitsas (2001) "Financial System Design and the Post-Washington Consensus", in Fine et al. (eds) (2001), pp. 28–51.

Batifoulier, P., B. Chavance, O. Favereau, S. Jallais, A. Labrousse, et al. (2015) "What Good Are Economists If They All Say the Same Thing?", Manifesto for Pluralist Economics, Association Française d'Economie Politique, AFEP, https://halshs.archives-ouvertes.fr/halshs-02885420/file/AFEP-Manifesto-for-pluralist-economics.pdf.

Bankscope (2012) "Database of Banks' Financial Statements, Ratings and Intelligence", http://www.bvdinfo.com/Products/Company-Information/International/.

Barker, F. (1992) *The South African Labour Market*, Pretoria: Sigma Press.

Barnes, J., A. Black and L. Monaco (2021) "Government Policy in Multinational-Dominated Global Value Chains: Structural Transformation within the South African Automotive Industry", in Andreoni et al. (eds) (2021), pp. 100–119.

Bayliss, K. and B. Fine (1998) "Beyond *Bureaucrats in Business*: a Critical Review of the World Bank Approach to Privatization and Public Sector Reform", *Journal of International Development*, vol 10, no 4, pp. 841–55.

Bayliss, K. and B. Fine (2021a) *A Guide to the Systems of Provision Approach: Who Gets What, How and Why*, Basingstoke: Palgrave.

Bayliss, K. and B. Fine (2021b) "Food, Diet and the Pandemic", *Theory and Struggle*, vol 122, no 1, pp. 46–57.

Bayliss, K. and B. Fine (eds) (2008) *Whither the Privatisation Experiment?: Electricity and Water Sector Reform in Sub-Saharan Africa*, Basingstoke: Palgrave MacMillan.

Bayliss, K., B. Fine and M. Robertson (2017) "Introduction to Special Issue on the Material Cultures of Financialisation", *New Political Economy*, vol 22, no 4, pp. 355–70, reproduced in Bayliss et al. (eds) (2018) together with special issue.

Bayliss, K., B. Fine and M. Robertson (eds) (2018) *Material Cultures of Financialisation*, London: Routledge.

Bayliss, K., B. Fine and E. Van Waeyenberge (eds) (2011) *The Political Economy of Development: the World Bank, Neo-Liberalism and Development Research*, London: Pluto Press.

Bayliss, K., B. Fine, M. Robertson and A. Saad-Filho (2015) "Thirteen Things You Need to Know about Neoliberalism", Thematic Paper, submitted to FESSUD for Deliverable D8.27, reproduced in Fine (2024, Ch. 2).

Bédécarrats, F., I. Guérin and F. Roubaud (eds) (2020) *Randomized Control Trials in the Field of Development, a Critical Perspective*, Oxford: Oxford University Press.

Beja, E. (2010) "Balance of Payments-Consistent Unreported Flows", IDEAs Working Paper Series, no 01/2010.

Bell, T. (1993) "The Impact of Sanctions on South Africa", *Journal of Contemporary African Studies*, vol 12, no 1, pp. 1–28.

Bell, T. (1995) "Improving Manufacturing Performance in South Africa: a Contrary View", *Transformation*, no 28, pp. 1–34.

Bell, T. (1996) "Improving Manufacturing Performance in South Africa: a Rejoinder", *Transformation*, no 31, pp. 43–56.

Bell, T. (1997) "Trade Policy", in Michie and Padayachee (eds) (1997), pp. 71–90.

Bell, T. and G. Farrell (1997) "The Minerals-Energy Complex and South African Industrialisation", *Development Southern Africa*, vol 14, no 4, pp. 591–613.

Bell, T. and G. Farrell (1998) "The Minerals-Energy Complex and South African Industrialisation: a Rejoinder", *Development Southern Africa*, vol 15, no 4, pp. 703–14.

Bell, T. and N. Cattaneo (1997) "Foreign Trade and Employment in South African Manufacturing Industry", Employment and Training Department, Occasional Report, no 4, ILO: Geneva.

Bezuidenhout, A. and S. Buhlungu (2010) "From Compounded to Fragmented Labour: Mineworkers and the Demise of Compounds in South Africa", *Antipode*, vol 43, no 2, pp. 237–63.

Bezuidenhout, A. and E. Webster (2008) "Trajectories of Manufacturing: White Goods Manufacturing in Australia, South Africa and South Korea", Paper for Workshop at University of KwaZulu-Natal, June.

Blanchard, O., G. Dell'Ariccia, and P. Mauro (2010) "Rethinking Macroeconomic Policy", IMF Staff Position Note, 12th February, SPN/10/03, http://www.imf.org/external/pubs/ft/spn/2010/spn1003.pdf.

Blyth, M. (2001) "The Transformation of the Swedish Model: Economic Ideas, Distributional Conflict, and Institutional Change", *World Politics*, vol 54, no 1, pp. 1–26.

Boateng, K. and B. Fine (2000) "The Labour Market", in Aryeetey et al. (eds) (2000), pp. 227–45.

Bobek, A. (2019) "Financialisation of Households: a Preliminary Literature Review", GEOFIN Working Paper, no 2, Trinity College, Dublin, https://geofinresearch.eu/wp-content/uploads/Bobek-2019-GEOFIN-WP-2-final.pdf.

Boffo, M., B. Fine and A. Saad-Filho (2018) "Neoliberal Capitalism: the Authoritarian Turn", in Panitch and Albo (eds) (2018), pp. 247–70.

Boland, L. (2014) *Model Building in Economics. Its Purposes and Limitations*, Cambridge: Cambridge University Press.

Bond, P. (2003) *Against Global Apartheid: South Africa Meets the World Bank, IMF and International Finance*, Cape Town: University of Cape Town Press.

Bookbinder, R. (2024) "Politicising Energy Transitions: the Political Economy of Reducing Dependence on Coal in South Africa's Minerals Energy Complex", *Environmental Politics*, vol 34, no 6, pp. 1000–1021.

Bowman, A. (2019) "Black Economic Empowerment Policy and State – Business Relations in South Africa: the Case of Mining", *Review of African Political Economy*, vol 46, no 160, pp. 223–45.

Boyce, J. and L. Ndikumana (2001) "Is Africa a Net Debtor? New Estimates of Capital Flight from Severely Indebted Sub-Saharan African Countries, 1970–98", *Journal of Development Studies*, vol 38, no 2, pp. 27–56.

Brandl, B. and F. Traxler (2005) "Industrial Relations, Social Pacts and Welfare Expenditures: a Cross-National Comparison", *British Journal of Industrial Relations*, vol 43, no 4, pp. 635–58.

Brenner, R. (1998) "The Economics of Global Turbulence", *New Left Review*, no 229, pp. 1–264.

Breznitz, D. (2012) "Ideas, Structure, State Action and Economic Growth: Rethinking the Irish Miracle", *Review of International Political Economy*, vol 19, no 1, pp. 87–111.

Bruff, I. (2011) "What about the Elephant in the Room? Varieties of Capitalism, Varieties in Capitalism", *New Political Economy*, vol 16, no 4, pp. 481–500.

Buhlungu, S., J. Daniel, R. Southall and J. Lutchman (eds) (2007) *State of the Nation: South Africa 2007*, Cape Town: HSRC Press.

Burns, J. and R. Yates (2022) "An Examination of the Reliability and Validity of the Recovery Capital Questionnaire (RCQ)", *Drug and Alcohol Dependence*, doi: 10.1016/j.drugalcdep.2022.109329.

Cable, J. (1985) "Capital Market Information and Industrial Performance: the Role of West German Banks", *Economic Journal*, vol 95(March), pp. 118–32.

Carmody, P. (2002) "Between Globalisation and (Post) Apartheid: the Political Economy of Restructuring in South Africa", *Journal of Southern African Studies*, vol 28, no 2, pp. 255–275.

Capps, G. (2012a) "Victim of Its Own Success? The Platinum Mining Industry and the Apartheid Mineral Property System in South Africa's Political Transition", *Review of African Political Economy*, vol 39, no 131, pp. 63–84.

Capps, G. (2012b) "A Bourgeois Reform with Social Justice? The Contradictions of the Minerals Development Bill and Black Economic Empowerment in the South African Platinum Mining Industry", *Review of African Political Economy*, vol 39, no 132, pp. 315–33.

Cassim, F. (1982) "Labour Market Segmentation: the Theoretical Case", *South African Journal of Economics*, vol 50, no 4, pp. 362–74.

Cassim, F. (1983a) "Reply to Truu", *South African Journal of Economics*, vol 51, no 4, pp. 574–78.

Cassim, F. (1983b) "Rejoinder to Truu", *South African Journal of Economics*, vol 51, 4, p. 580.

Castree, N. (2006) "Commentary", *Environment and Planning A*, vol 38, no 1, pp. 1–6.

Chabane, N., A. Goldstein and S. Roberts (2006) "The Changing Face and Strategies of Big Business in South Africa: More than a Decade of Political Democracy", *Industrial and Corporate Change*, vol 15, no 3, pp. 549–77.

Chamber of Mines (1984) "Structure of the Mining Industry in South Africa", *Mining Survey*, no 3/4.

Chambers, R. (2005) "Critical Reflections of a Development Nomad", in Kothari (ed.) (2005), pp. 67–87.

Chang, H.-J. (1994) *The Political Economy of Industrial Policy*, Basingstoke: Macmillan.

Chang, H.-J. (2002) *Kicking Away the Ladder – Development Strategy in Historical Perspective*, London: Anthem Press.

Chang, H.-J. (2007) *Bad Samaritans – Rich Nations, Poor Policies, and the Threat to the Developing World*, London: Random House.

Chang, H.-J. (2010) *23 Things They Don't Tell You About Capitalism*, London: Allen Lane (Penguin).

Chatterjee, A., I. Valodia and B. Siwisa (2025) "Empowerment versus (Re)Distribution in South Africa: the Political Economy of Assets in Elite Transitions", *Canadian Journal of Development Studies*, vol 46, no 2, pp. 355–80.

Chester, L. and T.-H. Jo (eds) (2022) *Heterodox Economics: Legacy and Prospects*, Bristol: World Economics Association.

Chirat, A. (2021a) "When Berle and Galbraith Brought Political Economy back to Life: Study of a Cross-Fertilization (1933–1967)", *EconomiX Working Papers*, 2021–27, University of Paris Nanterre, https://ideas.repec.org/p/drm/wpaper/2021-27.html.

Chirat, A. (2021b) "The Correspondence between Baumol and Galbraith (1957–1958): an Unsuspected Source of Managerial Theories of the Firm", *EconomiX Working Papers, 2021–35*, University of Paris Nanterre, https://ideas.repec.org/p/drm/wpaper/2021-35.html.

Chisholm, L. and B. Fine (1994) "Context and Contest in South African Education Policy: Comment on Curtin", *African Affairs*, vol 93, 1994, pp. 233–48.

Clark, N. (1987) *From Dependence to Defiance: State Intervention in a Capitalist Economy: the South African State Corporations*, PhD thesis, University of Yale.

Clark, N. (1994) *Manufacturing Apartheid: State Corporations in South Africa*, New Haven: Yale University Press.

Clarke, G., B. Eiffert, J. Haby, M. Ingram, W. Kapery, D. Kaplan, M. Schwartz and V. Ramachandran (2007) *South Africa: an Assessment of the Investment Climate*, Africa Private Sector Group, World Bank, DTI South Africa, and Citizen Surveys.

Coetzee, J., J. Graaf, F. Hendricks and G. Wood (eds) (2001) *Development: Theory, Policy and Practice*, Oxford: Oxford University Press.

Collier, P., A. Hoeffler and C. Pattillo (2001) "Flight Capital as a Portfolio Choice", *World Bank Economic Review*, vol 15, no 1, pp. 55–80.

Competition Commission South Africa (2008) *Banking Enquiry: Report to the Competition Commissioner by the Enquiry Panel, Executive Overview*, http://www.compcom.co.za/assets/Banking/Executive-overview.pdf.

Connell, R. (1987) *Gender and Power: Society, the Person and Sexual Politics*, London: Polity.

Corbett, J. (1987) "International Perspectives on Financing: Evidence from Japan", *Oxford Review of Economic Policy*, vol 3, no 4, pp. 30–55.

Cornwall, A. and D. Eade (eds) (2010) *Deconstructing Development Discourse: Buzzwords and Fuzzwords*, Oxfam and Rugby: Practical Action Publishing.

COSATU and IEJ (2023) "Joint Submission on the draft South African Renewable Energy Masterplan", August 18th, https://iej.org.za/submission-south-african-renewable-energy-masterplan/.

Cowling, K. (1982) *Monopoly Capitalism*, London: Macmillan.

Cross, T. (1993) *The Political Economy of a Public Enterprise: the South African Iron and Steel Corporation, 1928–1989*, unpublished DPhil thesis, University of Oxford.

Cross, T. (1994) "Afrikaner Nationalism, Anglo American and Iscor: the Formation of the Highveld Steel and Vanadium Corporation, 1960–70", *Business History*, vol 36, no 3, pp. 81–99.

Crotty, J. (2009) "Structural Causes of the Global Financial Crisis: a Critical Assessment of the 'New Financial Architecture'", *Cambridge Journal of Economics*, vol 33, no 4, pp. 563–80.

Crush, J. (1989) "Migrancy and Militance: the Case of the National Union of Mineworkers of South Africa", *African Affairs*, vol 88, no 1, pp. 5–23.

Crush, J. (1993) "'The Long-Averted Clash': Farm Labour Competition in the South African Countryside", *Canadian Journal of African Studies*, vol 27, no 3, pp. 404–23.

Crush, J., A. Jeeves and D. Yudelman (1991) *South Africa's Labor Empire: a History of Black Migrancy to the Gold Mines*, Cape Town: David Philip.

Damodaran, S., S. Gupta, S. Mitra and D. Sinha (eds) (2025) *Development, Transformations and the Human Condition: Volume in Honour of Professor Jayati Ghosh*, London: Routledge.

Daniel, J., P. Naidoo, D. Pillay and R. Southall (eds) (2010) *New South African Review 2010: Development or Decline?*, Johannesburg: Wits University Press.

de Villiers, W. (1984) *Report of the Commission of Inquiry into the Supply of Electricity in the Republic of South Africa*, Pretoria: Government Printer.

Decker, S., W. Elsner and S. Flechtner (eds) (2018) *Advancing Pluralism in Teaching Economics*, London: Routledge.

Deraniyagala, S. and B. Fine (2001) "New Trade Theory Versus Old Trade Policy: a Continuing Enigma", *Cambridge Journal of Economics*, vol 25, no 6, pp. 809–25.

Deraniyagala, S. and B. Fine (2006) "Kicking Away the Logic: Free Trade is neither the Question nor the Answer for Development", in Jomo and Fine (eds) (2006), pp. 46–67.

DMEA (1980) *Annual Report*, Department of Mineral and Energy Affairs.

dos Santos, P. (2009) "On the Content of Banking in Contemporary Capitalism", Research on Money and Finance, Discussion Paper, no 3, Department of Economics, School of Oriental and African Studies, www.soas.ac.uk/rmf/papers/47509.pdf, *Historical Materialism*, vol 17, no 2, pp. 180–213.

dos Santos, P. (2011) "A Policy Wrapped in 'Analysis': the World Bank's Case for Foreign Banks", Bayliss et al. (eds) (2011), pp. 188–214.

Du Boff, R. (2011) "Who Controls Capital? What Does Capital Control?", http://mrzine.monthlyreview.org/2011/db261111.html.

Edigheji, O. (ed.) (2010) *Constructing a Democratic Developmental State in South Africa: Potentials and Challenges*, Cape Town: Human Sciences Research Council Press.

EIU (1982 fwd) *Quarterly Energy Review of Africa*, Annual Supplement and various issues, London: Economist Intelligence Unit.

EIU (1985) "Steam Coal in Southern Africa", Special Report no 122, London: Economist Intelligence Unit.

EIU (2007) *South Africa*, Annual Report, London: Economist Intelligence Unit.

Epstein, G. (ed.) (2005) *Capital Flight and Capital Controls in Developing Countries*, Cheltenham: Edward Elgar.

Epstein, G. (2005) "Capital Flight and Capital Controls in Developing Countries: an Introduction", in Epstein (ed.) (2005), pp. 3–14.

EROSA (1987a) "South Africa's Electricity Industry and Policy", Erosa Economic Assessment Paper, no 3, June.

EROSA (1987b) "South Africa's Coal Industry and Policy", Erosa Economic Assessment Paper, no 4, June.

EROSA (1988) "South Africa's Gold Industry", Erosa Economic Assessment Paper, no 8, December.

EROSA (1992) "Defence Expenditure and the Post-Apartheid Economy: a Briefing Paper for the ANC", mimeo, see Fine (2025d, Ch. 3).

ESCOM (1985) *Report of the Commission of Inquiry into the Supply of Electricity in the Republic of South Africa*, Pretoria: Government Printer.

Evans, P. (2008) "In Search of the 21st Century Developmental State", Centre for Global Political Economy, Working Paper, no 4, University of Sussex, http://www.sussex.ac.uk/cgpe/research/publications/workingpapers.

Falkena, H. and eight others (2004) "Competition in South African Banking: Task Group Report for The National Treasury and the South African Reserve Bank", http://www.compcom.co.za/banking/Documents/task.pdf.

Fallon, P. (1992) "An Analysis of Employment and Wage Behaviour in South Africa", Washington DC: World Bank.

Fasenfest, D. (ed.) (2022) *Marx Matters*, Leiden: Brill.

Ferguson, J. (2007) "Formalities of Poverty: Thinking about Social Assistance in Neoliberal South Africa", *African Studies Review*, vol 50, no 2, pp. 71–86.

Ffrench-Davis, R. (ed.) (2005) *Seeking Growth under Financial Volatitilty*, London: Palgrave Macmillan.

Financial Mail (1985) "Mining: a Surrey", October.

Fine, B. (1980) *Economic Theory and Ideology*, London: Edward Arnold.

Fine, B. (1982) *Theories of the Capitalist Economy*, London: Edward Arnold.

Fine, B. (1987) "Segmented Labour Market Theory: a Critical Assessment", Birkbeck Discussion Paper in Economics, no 87/12, reproduced in shortened form as Thames Papers in Political Economy, Spring, 1990.

Fine, B. (1988) "The British Coal Industry's Contribution to the Political Economy of Paul Sweezy", *History of Political Economy*, vol 20, no 2, pp. 235–50.

Fine, B. (1990a) *The Coal Question: Political Economy and Industrial Change from the Nineteenth Century to the Present Day*, London: Routledge, reprinted as Routledge Revival, 2013.

Fine, B. (1990b) "Defence Expenditure and the Post-Apartheid Economy", paper prepared for the Conference on the Future of the Military and Defence in South Africa, mimeo, but see Fine (2025d, Ch. 3).

Fine, B. (1992a) "Total Factor Productivity versus Realism: the South African Coal Mining Industry", *South African Journal of Economics*, vol 60, no 3, pp. 277–92. See Chapter 2.

Fine, B. (1992b) *Women's Employment and the Capitalist Family*, London: Routledge.

Fine, B. (1992c) "Linkage and the State: the Case of South Korea", SOAS Department of Economics Working Paper, no 2.

Fine, B. (1993a) "Economic Development and Technological Change: From Linkage to Agency", in Liodakis (ed.) (1993), (in Greek) but see SOAS Department of Economics Working Paper, no 14, March 1992.

Fine, B. (1993b) "The Military-Industrial Complex: an Analytical Assessment", *Cyprus Journal of Economics*, vol 6, no 1, pp. 26–51.

Fine, B. (1994a) "Coal, Diamonds and Oil: towards a Comparative Theory of Mining", *Review of Political Economy*, vol 6, no 3, pp. 279–302.

Fine, B. (1994b) "'Politics and Economics in ANC Economic Policy': an Alternative Assessment", *Transformation*, no 25, pp. 19–33.

Fine, B. (1994c) "Towards a Political Economy of Food", *Review of International Political Economy*, vol 1, no 3, pp. 519–45.

Fine, B. (1994d) "'The Rise in African Wages: 1975–1985' – a Dissenting and Wide-Ranging Commentary", mimeo. See Chapter 3.

Fine, B. (1995a) "Privatisation and the RDP: a Critical Assessment", *Transformation*, no 27, pp. 1–23.

Fine, B. (1995b) "Flexible Production and Flexible Theory: the Case of South Africa", *Geoforum*, vol 26, no 2, pp. 107–19.

Fine, B. (1996a) "A Formal Note on New Theories of International Trade and Development", *Journal of International Development*, vol 8, no 6, pp. 805–11.

Fine, B. (1996b) "Some Perspectives on the Provision of Social and Economic Infrastructure", June, 1996, prepared for but not presented at Workshop for South African Policy Makers, available at https://eprints.soas.ac.uk/32961/1/MERGINTR.docx.

Fine, B. (1997a) "Interrogating the Financial System: with an Application to South Africa", mimeo.

Fine, B. (1997b) "Industrial and Energy Policy", in Michie and Padayachee (eds) (1997), pp. 125–53, incorporated into Fine (1997c).

Fine, B. (1997c) "Industrial Policy and South Africa: a Strategic View", NIEP Occasional Paper Series, no 5, Johannesburg: National Institute for Economic Policy.

Fine, B. (1997d) "Privatisation and the Restructuring of State Assets in South Africa: a Strategic View", NIEP Occasional Paper Series, no 7, Johannesburg, National Institute for Economic Policy.

Fine, B. (1997e) "Privatisation: Theory and Lessons from the UK and South Africa", *Seoul Journal of Economics*, vol 10, no 4, pp. 373–414.

Fine, B. (1997f) "The New Revolution in Economics", *Capital and Class*, no 61, pp. 143–48.

Fine, B. (1998a) *Labour Market Theory: a Constructive Reassessment*, London: Routledge.

Fine, B. (1998b) "Industrial Policy Revisited – an Exercise in Self-Indulgence", TIPS Conference, September, mimeo.

Fine, B. (1998c) "Vertical Relations in the South African Steel Industry", NIEP Occasional Paper Series, no 13, Johannesburg: National Institute for Economic Policy, originally a report for NUMSA Investment Company, December, 1997.

Fine, B. (1998d) *The Political Economy of Diet, Health and Food Policy*, London: Routledge, reprinted as Routledge Revival, 2013.

Fine, B. (1999a) "The Developmental State Is Dead – Long Live Social Capital?", *Development and Change*, vol 30, no 1, pp. 1–19, reproduced with afterword, in Moore (ed.) (2007), pp. 121–44.

Fine, B. (1999b) "Transition and the Political Economy of South Africa", revised version of paper presented to African Studies Association of Australasia & the Pacific, Perth, Australia, November.

Fine, B. (1999c) "The Political Economist's Tale: or, If Globalisation, (Welfare) State versus Market and Social Capital Are the Answers, Do We Have the Right Questions?", paper presented to conference, "Civilising the State: Civil Society, Policy and State Transformation", Deakin University, Melbourne, December.

Fine, B. (2000a) "Globalisation in Light of the Political Economy of Finance and the Political Economy of the Welfare State", paper presented to METU Annual Economics Conference, Ankara, September.

Fine, B. (2000b) "Whither the Welfare State: Public versus Private Consumption?", SOAS Working Paper in Economics, no 92.

Fine, B. (2000c) "ESOP's Fable: Golden Egg or Sour Grapes?", NIEP Occasional Paper Series, no 9, April, 1997, Johannesburg, National Institute for Economic Policy, reproduced in Toporowski (ed.) (2000), pp. 179–93.

Fine, B. (2001) *Social Capital versus Social Theory: Political Economy and Social Science at the Turn of the Millennium*, London: Routledge.

Fine, B. (2002) *The World of Consumption: the Material and Cultural Revisited*, London: Routledge,

Fine, B. (2004) "Beyond the Developmental State: towards a Political Economy of Development", in Hirakawa et al. (eds) (2004), (in Japanese), pp. 2–43, with English version in Lapavitsas and Noguchi (eds) (2005), pp. 17–33.

Fine, B. (2005) "Addressing the Consumer", in Trentmann (ed.) (2005), pp. 291–311.

Fine, B. (2006) "The Developmental State and the Political Economy of Development", in Jomo and Fine (eds) (2006), pp. 101–22.

Fine, B. (2007a) "Financialisation, Poverty, and Marxist Political Economy", Poverty and Capital Conference, 2–4 July 2007, University of Manchester.

Fine, B. (2007b) "State, Development and Inequality: the Curious Incidence of the Developmental State in the Night-Time", paper presented to Sanpad Conference, Durban, June 26–30.

Fine, B. (2007c) "Rethinking Critical Realism: Labour Markets or Capitalism?", *Capital and Class*, no 91, pp. 125–29.

Fine, B. (2008a) "Can South Africa Be a Developmental State?", paper presented to APORDE workshop, Pretoria, June.

Fine, B. (2008b) "Engaging the MEC: Or a Lot of My Views on a Lot of Things", paper for MEC workshop at University of KwaZulu-Natal, Durban, June. See Chapter 5.

Fine, B. (2008c) "Development as Zombieconomics in the Age of Neo-Liberalism", paper in preparation for 35th anniversary of the Center for International Development Issues, CIDIN, Radboud University, Nijmegen, Netherlands, September.

Fine, B. (2008d) "The Minerals-Energy Complex is Dead: Long Live the MEC?", Amandla Colloquium, http://www.amandlapublishers.co.za/component/option,com_docman/task,cat_view/gid,100/Itemid,163/.

Fine, B. (2008e) "Zombieconomics: the Living Death of the Dismal Science in the Age of Neo-Liberalism", paper for ESRC Neoliberalism Seminar, 1st April, http://www.cppr.ac.uk/centres/cppr/esrcneoliberalismseminar/.

Fine, B. (2008f) "Debating Lebowitz: Is Class Conflict the Moral and Historical Element in the Value of Labour Power?", *Historical Materialism*, vol 16, no 3, pp. 105–14.

Fine, B. (2009a) "Social Policy and the Crisis of Neo-liberalism", prepared for Conference on "The Crisis of Neo-Liberalism in India: Challenges and Alternatives", Tata Institute of Social Sciences (TISS) Mumbai, and International Development Economics Associates (IDEAs), March 13th–15th.

Fine, B. (2009b) "Submission to the COSATU Panel of Economists on 'The Final Recommendations of the International Panel on Growth' (The Harvard Panel)", *Transformation*, no 69, pp. 5–30.

Fine, B. (2009c) "A Rejoinder to 'A Response to Fine's "Harvard Group Shores up Shoddy Governance"'", *Transformation*, no 69, pp. 66–79.

Fine, B. (2009d) "The Economics of Identity and the Identity of Economics?", *Cambridge Journal of Economics*, vol 33, no 2, pp. 175–91.

Fine, B. (2009e) "Looking at the Crisis through Marx", *International Socialist Review*, Issue 64, March–April, pp. 40–47.

Fine, B. (2009f) "Engaging the MEC: or a Few of My Views on a Few Things", *Transformation*, no 71, pp. 26–49.

Fine, B. (2009g) "Financialisation, the Value of Labour Power, the Degree of Separation, and Exploitation by Banking", Research Students, Summer Seminar Series, April 30th.

Fine, B. (2009h) "Political Economy for the Rainbow Nation: Dividing the Spectrum?", prepared for "Making Sense of Borders: Identity, Citizenship and Power in South Africa", South African Sociological Association, Annual Conference, June/July, Johannesburg, available at http://eprints.soas.ac.uk/7972/ See Chapter 6.

Fine, B. (2009i) "Enigma in the Origins of Paul Sweezy's Political Economy", *Review of Political Economy*, vol 21, no 1, pp. 157–161.

Fine, B. (2010a) *Theories of Social Capital: Researchers Behaving Badly*, London: Pluto Press.

Fine, B. (2010b) "The Developmental State?", in Maharaj et al. (eds) (2010), pp. 101–124.

Fine, B. (2010c) "Can South Africa Be a Developmental State?", in Edigheji (ed.) (2010), pp. 169–82.

Fine, B. (2010d) "Flattening Economic Geography: Locating the World Development Report for 2009", *Journal of Economic Analysis*, vol 1, no 1, pp. 15–33.

Fine, B. (2010e) "Neo-Liberalism as Financialisation", in Saad-Filho and Yalman (eds) (2010), pp. 11–23.

Fine, B. (2011a) "Locating the Developmental State and Industrial and Social Policy after the Crisis", UNCTAD, *The Least Developed Countries Report 2011: the Potential Role of South-South Cooperation for Inclusive and Sustainable Development*, Background Paper, no 3, 2011, http://www.unctad.org/Sections/ldc_dir/docs/ldcr2011_Fine_en.pdf.

Fine, B. (2011b) "New Growth Path – Elephant in the Room", *The Shopsteward*, vol 20, no 4, pp. 16–25, http://www.cosatu.org.za/docs/shopsteward/2011/aug-sept.pdf, see Fine (2012a).

Fine, B. (2012a) "Assessing South Africa's New Growth Path: Framework for Change?", *Review of African Political Economy*, vol 39, no 134, pp. 551–68, revised from Fine (2011b).

Fine, B. (2012b) "Chronicle of a Developmental Transformation Foretold: South Africa's National Development Plan in Hindsight", *Transformation*, no 78, pp. 115–32.

Fine, B. (2012c) "Financialisation and Social Policy", in Utting et al. (eds) (2012), pp. 103–22.

Fine, B. (2013a) "Beyond the Developmental State: an Introduction", in Fine et al. (eds) (2013), pp. 1–32.

Fine, B. (2013b) "Consumption Matters", *Ephemera*, vol 13, no 2, pp. 217–48, https://ephemerajournal.org/contribution/consumption-matters.

Fine, B. (2013c) "Economics: Unfit for Purpose", *Review of Social Economy*, vol LXXI, no 3, pp. 373–89, shortened version of "Economics – Unfit for Purpose: The Director's Cut", SOAS Department of Economics Working Paper Series, no 176.

Fine, B. (2013d) "Beyond the Developmental State", *African Communist*, vol 186, pp. 40–54.

Fine, B. (2014) "The Continuing Enigmas of Social Policy", prepared for the UNRISD project on Towards Universal Social Security in Emerging Economies, UNRISD Working Paper 2014-10, June, http://www.unrisd.org/Fine.

Fine, B. (2015) "Neoclassical Economics: an Elephant is not a Chimera but Is a Chimera Real?", in Morgan (ed.) (2015), pp. 180–99.

Fine, B. (2016a) "Across Developmental State and Social Compacting: the Peculiar Case of South Africa", ISER Working Paper no. 2016/1. Grahamstown: Institute of Social and Economic Research, Rhodes University, https://eprints.soas.ac.uk/34148/1/iserwp.pdf See Chapter 10.

Fine, B. (2016b) *Microeconomics: A Critical Companion*, London: Pluto.

Fine, B. (2017) "From One-Dimensional Man to One-Dimensions Economy and Economics", *Radical Philosophy Review*, vol 20, no 1, pp. 49–74.

Fine, B. (2018) "In and Against Orthodoxy: Teaching Economics in the Neoliberal Era", in Decker et al. (eds) (2018), pp. 78–94.

Fine, B. (2019a) "Economics and Interdisciplinarity: One Step Forward, N Steps Back?", *Revista Crítica de Ciências Sociais*, no 119, pp. 131–48.

Fine, B. (2019b) "Post-Truth: An Alumni Economist's Perspective", *International Review of Applied Economics*, vol 33, no 4, pp. 542–67, revised and shortened version of similarly entitled, SOAS Department of Economics Working Paper No. 219, 2019, https://www.soas.ac.uk/economics/research/workingpapers/file139489.pdf.

Fine, B. (2020) "Framing Social Reproduction in the Age of Financialisation", in Santos and Teles (eds) (2020), pp. 257–72.

Fine, B. (2021a) "Contesting Piketty: an Extended Review", *Theory & Struggle*, vol 122, no 1, 208–217.

Fine, B. (2021b) "Situating PPPs", in Gideon and Unterhalter (eds), pp. 26–38.

Fine, B. (2022a) "From Marxist Political Economy to Financialisation or Is It the Other Way about?", in Fasenfest (ed.) (2022), pp. 43–66.

Fine, B. (2022b) "Towards Interdisciplinarity as Instinctive", in Chester and Jo (eds) (2022), pp. 290–325.

Fine, B. (2023) "Discrimination through Bargaining Structures: Gender Bias in the National Coal Board and British Coal", *Historical Studies in Industrial Relations*, vol 44, no 1, pp. 63–74.

Fine, B. (2024a) *Economics Imperialism and Interdisciplinarity: before the Watershed; Critical Reconstructions of Political Economy*, Volume 1, Leiden: Brill, and Chicago: Haymarket.

Fine, B. (2024b) *Economics Imperialism and Interdisciplinarity: the Watershed and After; Critical Reconstructions of Political Economy*, Volume 2, Leiden: Brill, and Chicago: Haymarket.

Fine, B. (2024c) *Cliometrics as Economics Imperialism: across the Watershed; Critical Reconstructions of Political Economy*, Volume 3, Leiden: Brill, and Chicago: Haymarket.

Fine, B. (2024d) *The Financialisation of Social Reproduction in the Age of Neoliberalism: from Theory to Case Studies: Critical Reconstructions of Political Economy*, Volume 4, with Kate Bayliss, Mary Robertson and Alfredo Saad-Filho, Leiden: Brill.

Fine, B. (2024e) "Financialisation and Illegal Capital Flight", in Wiegratz (ed.) (2024), pp. 169–77.

Fine, B. (2025a) *In and against Development: from New to Newest Development Economics; Critical Reconstructions of Political Economy*, Volume 5, Leiden: Brill, and Chicago: Haymarket.

Fine, B. (2025b) *In and against Development: the World Bank behind the Looking Glass: Critical Reconstructions of Political Economy*, Volume 6, Leiden: Brill.

Fine, B. (2025c) "Social Capital: the Indian Connection", in Damodaran et al. (eds) (2025), pp. 545–67.

Fine, B. (2025d) "Locating Vishnu as Engaged Political Economist, A Personal Journey" in Mesthrie et al. (eds) (2025), pp. 198–216. See Chapter 11.

Fine, B. (2025d) *The Political Economy of South Africa's Post-Apartheid Transition: the Rejection of Alternatives to Neoliberalism: Critical Reconstructions of Political Economy*, Volume 7, Leiden: Brill.

Fine, B. (2025e) *Debating Economic Policy for South Africa's Post-Apartheid Transition: from Scholarship and Ideology to Policy in Practice: Critical Reconstructions of Political Economy*, Volume 8, Leiden: Brill.

Fine, B. and O. Dimakou (2016) *Macroeconomics: A Critical Companion*, London: Pluto.

Fine, B. and L. Harris (1979) *Rereading Capital*, London: Macmillan.

Fine, B. and L. Harris (1985) *The Peculiarities of the British Economy*, London: Lawrence and Wishart.

Fine, B., L. Harris, A. Mason, M. Mayo and E. Wilson (n.d.) *Class Politics: an Answer to Its Critics*, pamphlet.

Fine, B., M. Heasman, and J. Wright (1996) *Consumption in the Age of Affluence: the World of Food*, London: Routledge.

Fine, B., C. Lapavitsas and D. Milonakis (1999) "Addressing the World Economy: Two Steps Back", *Capital and Class*, no 67, pp. 47–90.

Fine, B., C. Lapavitsas and J. Pincus (eds) (2001) *Development Policy in the Twenty-First Century: Beyond the Post-Washington Consensus*, London: Routledge.

Fine, B. and E. Leopold (1993) *The World of Consumption*, London: Routledge.

Fine, B. and D. Milonakis (2000) "From New to Newest: The Economic History of Douglass North", mimeo, eventually appearing as Fine and Milonakis (2003) but see also Fine (2024d).

Fine, B. and D. Milonakis (2003) "From Principle of Pricing to Pricing of Principle: Rationality and Irrationality in the Economic History of Douglass North", *Comparative Studies in Society and History*, vol 45, no 3, pp. 120–44.

Fine, B. and Milonakis, D. (2009) *From Economics Imperialism to Freakonomics: the Shifting Boundaries Between Economics and Other Social Sciences*, London: Routledge.

Fine, B. and A. Murfin (1984) *Macroeconomics and Monopoly Capitalism*, Brighton: Wheatsheaf.

Fine, B. and V. Padayachee (2000) "A Sustainable Growth Path?", drafted to appear in Friedman (ed.) (2000) but never published other than as Fine and Padayachee (2001).

Fine, B. and V. Padayachee (2001) "A Sustainable Macroeconomic Growth Path for South Africa?", in Coetzee et al(eds) (2001), pp. 269–81.

Fine, B., A. Petropoulos and H. Sato (2005) "Beyond Brenner's Investment Overhang Hypothesis: the Case of the Steel Industry", *New Political Economy*, vol 10, no 1, pp. 43–64.

Fine, B. and Z. Rustomjee (1992) "The Political Economy of South Africa in the Interwar Period", *Social Dynamics*, vol 18, no 2, pp. 26–54.

Fine, B. and Z. Rustomjee (1995) "'Afrikaner Nationalism, Anglo American and Iscor: the Formation of the Highveld Steel And Vanadium Corporation, 1960–70' – a Comment", *Business History*, vol 37, no 3, pp. 111–14.

Fine, B. and Z. Rustomjee (1996) *South Africa's Political Economy: From Minerals-Energy Complex to Industrialisation*, Johannesburg: Wits University Press.

Fine, B. and Z. Rustomjee (1998) "Debating the South African Minerals-Energy Complex", *Development Southern Africa*, vol 15, no 4, pp. 689–70. See Chapter 4.

Fine, B. and A. Saad-Filho (2016) "Thirteen Things You Need to Know about Neoliberalism", *Critical Sociology*, vol 43, no 4–5, pp. 685–706.

Fine, B., J. Saraswati and D. Tavasci (eds) (2013) *Beyond the Developmental State: Industrial Policy into the 21st Century*, London: Pluto.

Fine, B. and C. Stoneman (1996) "Introduction: State and Development", *Journal of Southern African Studies*, vol 22, no 1, pp. 5–26.

Fine, B. and E. Van Waeyenberge (2013) "A Paradigm Shift that Never Was: Justin Lin's New Structural Economics", *Competition and Change*, vol 17, no 4, pp. 355–71, with longer revised version as "A Paradigm Shift that Never Will Be?: Justin Lin's New Structural Economics", SOAS Department of Economics Working Paper Series, no 179, http://www.soas.ac.uk/economics/research/workingpapers/file81928.pdf.

Finscope South Africa (2011) http://www.finscope.co.za/new/pages/default.aspx.

Fleetwood, S. (2006) "Rethinking Labour Markets: a Critical-Realist-Socioeconomic Perspective", *Capital and Class*, no 89, pp. 59–89.

Fofack, H. and L. Ndikumana (2010) "Capital Flight Repatriation: Investigation of Its Potential Gains for Sub-Saharn African Countries", *African Development Review*, vol 22, no 1, pp.4–22.

Fourcade, M., E. Ollion and Y. Algan (2015) "The Superiority of Economists", *Journal of Economic Perspectives*, vol 29, no 1, pp. 89–114.

Frangie, S. (2011) "Post-Development, Developmental State and Genealogy: Condemned to Develop?", *Third World Quarterly*, vol 32, no 7, pp. 1183–198.

Freund, B. (1991) "South African Gold Mining in Transformation", in Gelb (ed.) (1991), pp. 110–28.

Freund, B. (2010) "The Significance of the Minerals-Energy Complex in the Light of South African Economic Historiography", *Transformation*, no 71, pp. 3–25.

Freund, B. (2011) "A Ghost from the Past: the South African Developmental State of the 1940s", http://www.nai.uu.se/ecas-4/panels/41-60/panel-57/Bill-Freund-Full-paper .pdf, but see Freund (2013).

Freund, B. (2013) "A Ghost from the Past: the South African Developmental State of the 1940s", *Transformation*, no 81–82, pp. 86–114.

Freund, B. (2018) *Twentieth Century South Africa: a Developmental History*, Cambridge: Cambridge University Press.

Freund, B. and V. Padayachee (1998) "Post-Apartheid South Africa: the Key Patterns Emerge", *Economic and Political Weekly*, vol 33, no 20, pp. 1173–180.

Friedman, S. (2000) (ed.) *South African Review*, vol 8, Pretoria: HSRC. SAR8 never materialised, with the seventh being the last volume. The *New South African Review* first appeared in 2010, with blurb, "the editors seek to follow that tradition of critical scholarship established so firmly by the seven volumes of the South African Review which appeared in the 1980s and 1990s".

Galbraith, J. (1967) *The New Industrial Estate*, London: Hamilton.

Gelb, S. (2005) "Macroeconomics in Post-Apartheid South Africa: Real Economic Growth versus Financial Stability", in Ffrench-Davis (ed.) (2005), pp. 184–218.

Gelb, S. (2006) "The RDP, GEAR and All That: Reflections Ten Years Later", *Transformation*, no 62, pp. 1–8.

Gelb, S. (ed.) (1991) *South Africa's Economic Crisis*, Cape Town: David Philip.

Ghosh, J. (2005) "The Economic and Social Effects of Financial Liberalization: a Primer for Developing Countries", DESA Working Paper, no 4, https://digitallibrary.un.org/record/570310?ln=en&v=pdf.

Gideon, J. and E. Unterhalter (eds) (2020) *Critical Reflections on Public Private Partnerships*, London: Routledge.

Giliomee, H. (2003) *The Afrikaners: Biography of a People*, Cape Town: Tafelberg Publishers and Charlottesville: University of Virginia Press.

GLC (1985) *The London Industrial Strategy*, London: Greater London Council.

GLC (1986) *The London Labour Plan*, London: Greater London Council.

Glyn, A. (1984) *The Economic Case against Pit Closures*, Sheffield: NUM.

Goga, S. and P. Mondliwa (2021) "Structural Transformation, Economic Power, and Inequality in South Africa", in Andreoni et al. (eds) (2021), pp. 165–88.

Goldstein, J. (2009) "Introduction: the Political Economy of Financialization", *Review of Radical Political Economics*, vol 41, no 4, pp. 453–57.

Gough, I. (1979) *The Political Economy of the Welfare State*, London: MacMillan.

Gray, K. (2011a) "The Social and Geopolitical Origins of State Transformation: the Case of South Korea", *New Political Economy*, vol 16, no 3, pp. 303–22.

Gray, K. (2011b) "Taiwan and the Geopolitics of Late Development", *The Pacific Review*, vol 24, no 5, pp. 577–99.

Guerrien, B. and O. Gun (2011) "Efficient Markets Hypothesis: What Are We Talking about?", *Real-World Economics Review*, no 56, pp. 19–30, http://www.paecon.net/PAEReview/issue56/GuerrienGun56.pdf.

Hall, D. (2008) "Economic Crisis and Public Services", Public Services International Research Unit, note 1, December, http://www.psiru.org/reports/2008-12-crisis-1.doc.

Hall, P. and D. Soskice (2001) "An Introduction to Varieties of Capitalism", in Hall and Soskice (eds) (2001), pp. 1–68.

Hall, P. and D. Soskice (eds) (2001) *Varieties of Capitalism: the Institutional Foundations of Comparative Advantage*, Oxford: Oxford University Press.

Hamman, R. et al (2008) "South Africa's Charter Approach to Post-Apartheid Economic Transformation: Collaborative Governance or Hardball Bargaining", *Journal of Southern African* Studies, vol 34, no 1, pp. 21–37.

Harcourt, G. (1972) *Some Cambridge Controversies in the Theory of Capital*, Cambridge: Cambridge University Press.

Hardman, D. and J. Oberholzer (1987) "The Performance of Continuous Miners in South African Collieries", *Journal of the South African Institute of Mining and Metallurgy*, vol 87, no 1, pp. 7–13.

Harford, T. (2009) *The Logic Of Life: Uncovering the New Economics of Everything*, London: Little, Brown Book Group.

Hart, G. (2002) *Disabling Globalization: Places of Power in Post-Apartheid South Africa*, Durban: University of Natal Press.

Hart, G. (2008) "The 2007 *Antipode* AAG Lecture – the Provocations of Neoliberalism: Contesting the Nation and Liberation after Apartheid", *Antipode*, vol 40, no 4, pp. 678–705.

Hart, G. (2014) *Rethinking the South African Crisis: Nationalism, Populism, Hegemony*, Athens, GA: University of Georgia Press.

Hart, G. (2015) "Political Society and Its Discontents: Translating Passive Revolution in India and South Africa Today", *Economic and Political Weekly*, vol 50, no 43, pp. 43–51.

Hartford, G. (2012) "The Mining Industry Strike Wave: What Are the Causes and What Are the Solutions?", was available at http://www.miningweekly.com/article/migrant-labour-system-lies-at-heart-of-mine-unrest-hartford-2012-10-08.

Hausmann, R. and M. Andrews (2009) "Why We Still Believe Exports for Jobs Will Lead to Shared Growth: a Response to Fine's 'Harvard Group Shores up Shoddy Governance'", *Transformation*, no 69, pp. 31–65.

Hawkins, P. (2003) *South Africa's Financial Sector Ten Years on: the Performance of the Financial Sector since Democracy*, Report prepared for Trade and Industrial Policy Strategies, www.tips.org.za/files/736.pdf.

Heintz, J. and D. Posel (2008) "Revisiting Informal Employment and Segmentation in the South African Labour Market", *South African Journal of Economics*, vol 76, no 1, pp. 26–44.

Heller, P. (1995) "From Class Struggle to Class Compromise: Redistribution and Growth in a South Indian State", *Journal of Development Studies*, vol 31, no 5, pp. 645–72.

Heller, P. (1996) "Social Capital as a Product of Class Mobilization and State Intervention: Industrial Workers in Kerala, India", *World Development*, vol 24, no 6, pp. 1055–72.

Heller, P. (1999) "Social Capital and the Developmental State: Industrial Workers in Kerala", in Parayil (ed.) (1999), pp. 66–87.

Hendricks, F. (2008) "The Private Affairs of Public Pensions in South Africa: Debt, Development and Corporatization", UNRISD, Social Policy and Development Programme, Paper no 38.

Herrera, R. (ed.) (2025) *Trajectories of Declining and Destructive Capitalism, Research in Political Economy*, vol 40, Leeds: Emerald Publishing Limited.

Hildyard, N. (1998) *The World Bank and the State: a Recipe for Change?*, London: Bretton Woods Project.

Hillbom, E. (2012) "Botswana: a Development-Oriented Gate-Keeping State", *African Affairs*, vol 111, no 442, pp. 67–89.

Hindson, D. (1987) *Pass Controls and the Urban African Proletariat*, Johannesburg: Ravan Press.

Hindson, D. (1991) "The Restructuring of Labour Markets in South Africa", in Gelb (ed.) (1991), pp. 228–43.

Hindson, D. and O. Crankshaw (1990) "New Jobs, New Skills, New Divisions – the Changing Structure of South Africa's Workforce", *South African Labour Bulletin*, vol 15, no 1, pp. 23–31.

Hirakawa, H., M. Noguchi and M. Sano (eds) (2004) *Beyond Market-Driven Development: a New Stream of Political Economy of Development*, Tokyo: Nihon Hyoron Sha, in Japanese.

Hodgson, G. (1996) "Varieties of Capitalism and Varieties of Economic Theory", *Review of International Political Economy*, vol 3, no 3, pp. 380–433.

Hofmeyr, J. (1990a) "Black Wages: the Post-War Experience", in Nattrass and Ardington (eds) (1990), pp. 129–47.

Hofmeyr, J. (1990b) "The Rise in African Wages in South Africa: 1975–1985", Economic Research Unit, University of Natal, Durban, Occasional Paper, no 22.

Hofmeyr, J. (1993) "African Wage Movements in the 1980s", *South African Journal of Economics*, vol 61, no 4, pp. 266–80.

Hofmeyr, J. (1994) "The Rise in African Wages: 1975–1985", *South African Journal of Economics*, vol 62, no 3, pp. 198–215.

Horner, D. and A. Kooy (1980) "Conflict on South African Mines, 1972–1979", *SALDRU Working Paper*, no 29.

Hosking, S. (1992a) "A Rent-Seeking Perspective on the Demand for Educational Expenditure in South Africa", *Journal of Studies in Economics and Econometrics*, vol 16, no 1, pp. 49–58.

Hosking, S. (1992b) "A Welfare Analysis of Government Expenditure on Education", *Journal of Studies in Economics and Econometrics*, vol 16, no 2, pp. 1–9.

Hosking, S. (1992c) "On Social Rates of Return to Investment in Education", *South African Journal of Economics*, vol 60, no 2, June, pp. 221–32.

Hosking, S. (1992d) "Social Rates of Return to Investment in Black Schooling", *Journal of Studies in Economics and Econometrics*, vol 16, no 1, pp. 93–95.

IEA (1986) *The Availability and Costs of Coal in South Africa*, London: International Energy Authority Coal Research.

IEJ and CliFT (2023) "Submission to the Presidential Climate Commission on South Africa's Just Energy Transition – Investment Plan", The Institute for Economic Justice and the Climate Finance for Equitable Transitions, March, https://iej.org.za/submission-to-the-presidential-climate-commission-on-south-africas-just-energy-transition-investment-plan/.

ILO (1996) *Restructuring the Labour Market: the South African Challenge – an ILO Country Review*, Geneva: ILO.

Ingham, G. (1988) "Commercial Capital and British Development – a Reply", *New Left Review*, no 172, pp. 45–65.

Innes, D. (1984/1983) *Anglo-American and the Rise of Modern South Africa*, Johannesburg: Ravan Press.

ISP (A. Joffe, D. Kaplan, R. Kaplinsky and D. Lewis) (1995) *Improving Manufacturing Performance in South Africa: Report of the Industrial Strategy Project*, Cape Town: UCT Press.

Itzikowitz, A. (1992) "The Deposit Taking Institutions Act no. 94 of 1990: Its History and Overview of Its Main Provisions", *South African Mercantile Law Journal*, vol 4, pp. 170–97.

James, W. (1992) *Our Precious Metal: African Labour in South Africa's Gold Industry, 1970–1990*, Cape Town: David Philip.

Jayachandran, S. and M. Kremer (2006) "Odious Debt", *American Economic Review*, vol 96, no 1, pp. 82–92.

Jeeves, A. (1985) *Migrant Labour in South Africa's Mining Economy: the Struggle for the Gold Mine's Labour Supply, 1890–1920*, Montreal: McGill-Queens University Press.

Jenkins, C. and N. Siwisa (1997) "Overview of Trade Policy in South Africa", Annual forum of the Trade and Industrial Policy Secretariat, Johannesburg.

Jomo, K. and B. Fine (eds) (2006) *The New Development Economics: after the Washington Consensus*, Delhi: Tulika, and London: Zed Press.

Jones, J. (1995) *Through Fortress and Rock: the Story of Gencor, 1895–1995*, Johannesburg: Jonathan Ball Publishers.

Jones, R. (1983) "Mechanization, Learning Periods, and Productivity Change in the South African Coal Mining Industry", *South African Journal of Economics*. vol 51, no 4, pp. 342–51.

Jones, S. (1994) "Origins, Growth and Concentration of Bank Capital in South Africa, 1860–92", *Business History*, vol 36, no 3, pp. 62–80.

Jones, S. (1996) *The Great Imperial Banks in South Africa: a Study of the Business of Standard Bank and Barclays Bank, 1861–1961*, Pretoria: University of South Africa.

Jones, S. (2009) "The Role of Banking Development: South African Economic Development during the Period of Functional Stability, 1850s–1970s", *South African Journal of Economic History*, vol 24, no 1, pp. 94–117.

Jones, S. (ed.) (1992) *Financial Enterprise in South Africa since 1950*, Basingstoke: Macmillan.

Kaplan, D. (1990) *The Crossed Line: the South African Telecommunications Industry in Transition*, Johannesburg: Witwatersrand University Press.

Kaplan, D. (2007) "The Constraints and Institutional Challenges Facing Industrial Policy in South Africa: a Way Forward", *Transformation*, no 64, pp. 91–111.

Kaplan, D. and D. Lewis (1996) "Improving Productivity Performance in South Africa: a Response to Trevor Bell", *Transformation*, no 30, pp. 115–28.

Kar, D. and D. Cartwright-Smith (2008) "Illicit Financial Flows from Developing Countries: 2002–2006", Global Financial Integrity, Washington DC.

Kessides, I., Z. Bogetic and L. Maurer (2007) "Current and Forthcoming Issues in the South African Eectricity Sector", World Bank, Policy Research Working Paper, no WPS 4197.

Khosa, M. (1990) "The Black Taxi Revolution", in Nattrass and Ardington (eds) (1990), pp. 207–16.

Kim, S.-Y. (2012) "Transitioning from Fast-Follower to Innovator: the Institutional Foundations of the Korean Telecommunications Sector", *Review of International Political Economy*, vol 19, no 1, pp. 140–68.

Kindleberger, C. (1937) *International Short-Term Capital Movements*, New York: Augustus Kelley.

King, N. (2021) *Non-financial Firms in South Africa: a Comparative Analysis of the Variegated Forms of Financialisation in Minerals, Beverages, and Retail*, unpublished DPhil, University of Johannesburg, https://hdl.handle.net/10210/485216.

King, P. (1985) "Costs of Production and Forecast Price of South African Steam Coal", *South African Mining World*, June.

Knight, J. and M. McGrath (1987) *The Erosion of Apartheid in the South African Labour Market: Measures and Mechanisms*, Oxford Institute of Economics and Statistics, Applied Economics Discussion Paper, no 35.

Konopelko, E. (2023) *Factors behind National Minimum Wage Introduction and Design: With an Application to South Africa*, SOAS, University of London, Phd thesis.

Kothari, U. (ed.) (2005) *A Radical History of Development Studies: Individuals, Institutions and Ideologies*, London: Zed Books.

Kraak, A. (1991) *Beyond the Market: Comprehensive Institutional Restructuring of South African Labour Markets, Education, Training and Work*, Johannesburg: University of Witwatersrand Education Policy Unit.

Kraak, G. (1993) *Breaking the Chains: Labour in South Africa in the '70s and '80s*, London: Pluto Press.

Krueger, A. (1986) "Aid in the Development Process", *World Bank Research Observer*, vol 1, no 1, pp. 57–78.

Krugman, P. (1994) "The Myth of Asia's Miracle", *Foreign Affairs*, vol 73, no 6, pp. 62–68.

Lachman, D. and K. Bercuson (1992) "Economic Policies for a New South Africa", IMF Occasional Paper no 91, Washington DC.

LaMagdeleine, D. (1986) "US Catholic Church-Related Jobs as Dual Labour Markets: a Speculative Enquiry", *Review of Religious Research*, vol 27, no 4, pp. 315–27.

Lambert, R. (2000) "Globalization and the Erosion of Class Compromise in Contemporary Australia", *Politics and Society*, vol 28, no 1, pp. 93–118.

Lapavitsas, C. (2009) "Financialised Capitalism: Crisis and Financial Expropriation", Research on Money and Finance, Discussion Paper no 1, Department of Economics, School of Oriental and African Studies, www.soas.ac.uk/rmf/papers/47508.pdf, *Historical Materialism*, vol 17, no 2, 114–48.

Lapavitsas, C. and M. Noguchi (eds) (2005) *Beyond Market-Driven Development: Drawing on the Experience of Asia and Latin America*, London: Routledge.

Lee, K. (2002) *Industrial Policy and Industrialisation in South Korea – the Case of the Car Industry*, SOAS, University of London, PhD thesis.

Leftwich, A. (2010) "Beyond Institutions: Rethinking the Role of Leaders, Elites and Coalitions in the Institutional Formation of Developmental States and Strategies", *Forum for Development Studies*, vol 37, no 1, pp. 93–111.

Leigh, A. (2014) *The Economics of Just About Everything: the Hidden Reasons for Our Curious Choices and Surprising Successes in Life*, Sydney: Allen and Unwin.

Levenson, Z. and M. Paret (2025) "Absorbed in Struggle: South Africa's Passive Revolution from Below", *Critical Sociology*, https://doi.org/10.1177/08969205251330900, forthcoming.

Levitt, S. with S. Dubner (2005) *Freakonomics: a Rogue Economist Explores the Hidden Side of Everything*, New York: William Morrow.

Lewis, D. (1991) "Unemployment and the Current Crisis", in Gelb (ed.) (1991), pp. 244–66.

Lewis, D., K. Reed and E. Teljeur (2004) "South Africa: Economic Policy-Making and Implementation in Africa: a Study of Strategic Trade and Selective Industrial Policies", in Soludo et al. (eds) (2004), pp. 151–78.

Lewis, J. (1984) *Industrialisation and Trade Union Organisation in South Africa: the Rise and Fall of the South African Trades and Labour Council*, Cambridge: Cambridge University Press.

Lin, J. (2011) "From Flying Geese to Leading Dragons: New Opportunities and Strategies for Structural Transformation in Developing Countries", WIDER Annual Lecture, no 15, http://www.wider.unu.edu/publications/annual-lectures/en_GB/AL15/.

Lin, J. (2012) *New Structural Economics: a Framework for Rethinking Development and Policy*, Washington: World Bank, http://siteresources.worldbank.org/DEC/Resources/84797-1104785060319/598886-1104951889260/NSE-Book.pdf.

Liodakis, G. (ed.) (1993) *Society, Technology and Restructuring of Production*, Athens: V. Papazissis.

Liow, E. (2012) "The Neoliberal-Developmental State: Singapore as Case Study", *Critical Sociology*, vol 38, no 2, pp. 241–64.

LMC (1996) *Restructuring the South African Labour Market Report of the Presidential Commission to Investigate Labour Market Policy*, June 1996, available at, www.polity.org.za/polity/govdocs/commissions/fintoc.html.

London CSE Group (1979) "Crisis, Labour Movement and the Alternative Economic Strategy", *Capital and Class*, no 8, pp. 68–95.

Lucas, R. (1987) *Models of Business Cycles*, Oxford: Blackwell.

Lundahl, M. (1989) "Apartheid: *Cui Bono?*", *World Development*, vol 17, no 6, pp. 825–37.

Lundahl, M. (1992) *Apartheid in Theory and Practice: an Economic Analysis*, London: Routledge.

Lundahl, M. and L. Petersson (1991) *The Dependent Economy: Lesotho and the Southern African Customs Union*, Boulder: Westview Press.

Lütz, S. (1998) "The Revival of the Nation-State?: Stock Exchange Regulation in an Era of Globalized Financial Markets", *Journal of European Public Policy*, vol 5, no 1, pp. 153–68.

MacIntosh, M. and H. Wainwright (eds) (1987) *The Politics of Local Economics*, London: Verso.

Machaka, J. and S. Roberts (2003) "The DTI's New 'Integrated Manufacturing Strategy': Comparative Industrial Performance, Linkages and Technology", *South African Journal of Economics*, vol 71, no 4, pp. 679–704.

Mader, P., D. Mertens and N. van der Zwan (eds) (2020) *International Handbook of Financialization*, London: Routledge.

Maharaj, B. A. Desai and P. Bond (eds) (2010) *Zuma's Own Goal: Losing South Africa's "War on Poverty"*, Trenton, NJ: Africa World Press.

Makgetla, N. (2007) "Local Government Budgets and Development: a Tale of Two Towns", in Buhlungu et al. (eds) (2007), pp. 146–70.

Malan, T. (1985) "Migrant Labour in Southern Africa", *Africa Insight*, vol 15. no 2, pp. 103–14.

Martin, W. and M. Beittel (1987) "The Hidden Agenda of Reproduction: Conceptualising Households in Southern Africa", *Development and Change*, vol 18, no 2, April, pp. 215–34.

Marx, K. (1978) *Capital: Volume Two*, translated by D. Fernbach and introduced by E. Mandel, London: Pelican/New Left Books.

Matthews, R., C. Feinstein and J. Odling-Smee (1982) *British Economic Growth, 1856–1973*, Oxford: Clarendon Press.

May, J. (1990) "The Migrant Labour System: Changing Dynamics in Rural Survival", in Nattrass and Ardington (eds) (1990), pp. 175–86.

Mazzucato, M. and S. Gasperin (2023) "Transforming the System of SoEs in South Africa: towards a Mission-Oriented State Holding Company", IIPP Policy Brief, no 27, Institute for Innovation and Public Purpose, University College, London, https://www.ucl.ac.uk/bartlett/public-purpose/publications/2023/nov/transforming-system-soes-south-africa-towards-mission-oriented-state-holding.

Mbeki, T. (2024) "How Our Democracy Went off Track", https://www.politicsweb.co.za/documents/how-our-democracy-went-off-track--thabo-mbekigoogle, May 5th.

McDonald, D. (ed.) (2008) *Electric Capitalism: Recolonizing Africa on the Power Grid*, Cape Town: HSRC.

McGrath, M. (1990) "Economic Growth, Income Distribution and Social Change", in Nattrass and Ardington (eds) (1990), pp. 88–106.

McKinnon, R. (1973) *Money and Capital in Economic Development*, Washington DC: Brookings Institution.

MERG (Macroeconomic Research Group) (1993) *Making Democracy Work: a Framework for Macroeconomic Policy in South Africa*, Cape Town: CDS.

Mesthrie, R., R. van Niekerk and I. Valodia (eds) (2025) *Political Economy and Critical Engagement in South Africa: Essays in Honour of Vishnu Padayachee*, Pietermaritzburg: University of KwaZulu-Natal Press.

Michie, J. and V. Padayachee (eds) (1997) *The Political Economy of South Africa's Transition – Policy Perspectives in the Late 1990s*, London: Dryden Press.

Milonakis, D. and B. Fine (2009) *From Political Economy to Economics: Method, the Social and the Historical in the Evolution of Economic Theory*, London: Routledge.

Misra-Dexter, N. and J. February (eds) (2010) *Testing Democracy: Which Way Is South Africa Going?*, Institute for a Democratic South Africa, Cape Town: ABC Press.

Mkandawire. T. (2012) "Building the African State in the Age of Globalisation: the Role of Social Compacts and Lessons for South Africa", Mapungubwe Institute for Strategic Reflection, Inaugural Annual Lecture, MISTRA, http://www.mistra.org.za/Media Docs/The%20role%20of%20social%20compacts.pdf.

Mohamed, S. (2010) "The State of the South African Economy", in Daniel et al. (eds), (2010), pp. 39–64.

Mohamed, S. and B. Fine (2025) "Post-Apartheid South Africa: a Neoliberal Disaster Made and in the Making", in Herrera (ed.) (2025), pp. 141–67.

Mohamed, S. and K. Finnoff (2004/2005) "Capital Flight from South Africa, 1980 to 2000", African Development and Poverty Reduction: the Macro-Micro Linkage, Forum Paper, October 11th–15th, Somerset West, South Africa, also in Epstein (ed.) (2005), pp. 85–115.

Mohamed, S., A. Ngoma and B. Baloyi (eds) (2023) *The Evolving Structure of South Africa's Economy: Faultlines and Futures*, Johannesburg: Mistra.

Molina, O. and M. Rhodes (2002) "Corporatism: the Past, Present, and Future of a Concept", *Annual Review of Political Science*, vol 5, pp. 305–31.

Moll, P. (1992) "The Decline of Discrimination against Colored People in South Africa, 1970 to 1980", *Journal of Development Economics*, vol 37, no 1/2, Nov, pp. 289–307.

Moll, P. (1993) "Black South African Unions: Relative Wage Effects in International Perspective", *Industrial and Labor Relations Review*, vol 46, no 2, January, pp. 245–61.

Molyneux, M. (2008) "The 'Neoliberal Turn' and the New Social Policy in Latin America: How Neoliberal, How New?", *Development and Change*, vol 39, no 5, pp. 775–97.

Mondliwa, P. and S. Roberts (2021) "The Political Economy of Structural Transformation: Political Settlements and Industrial Policy in South Africa", in Andreoni et al. (eds) (2021), pp. 312–36.

Montmasson-Clair, G. (2024) "Bridging the Gap between Aspiration and Reality: What Would It Take to Localise the Renewable Energy Value Chain in South Africa", TIPS Policy Brief, no 3/2024, https://www.tips.org.za/images/TIPS_Policy_Brief_Bridging_the_gap_between_aspiration_and_reality_What_would_it_take_to_localise_the_renewable_energy_value_chain_in_South_Africa__April_2024.pdf.

Moore, D. (ed.) (2007) *The World Bank: Development, Poverty, Hegemony*, Scotsville: University of KwaZulu-Natal Press.

Morgan, J. (ed.) (2015) *What Is This 'School' Called Neoclassical Economics?: Debating the Origins, Meaning and Significance*, London: Routledge.

Morrell, R. (1988) "The Disintegration of the Gold and Maize Alliance in South Africa in the 1920s", *International Journal of African Historical Studies*, vol 21, no 4, pp. 619–35.

Morris, M., G. Robbins, J. Barnes (2006) "The Role of Government in Fostering Clusters: the South African Automotive Sector", in Padayachee (ed.) (2006), pp. 201–23.

Morris, M., G. Robbins, U. Hansen and I. Nygard (2022) "The Wind Energy Global Value Chain Localisation and Industrial Policy Failure in South Africa", *Journal of International Business Policy*, vol 5, pp. 490–511, https://doi.org/10.1057/s42214-021-00123-8.

Murray, C. (1989) "Class, Gender and the Household: the Developmental Cycle in Southern Africa", *Development and Change*, vol 18, no 2, pp. 235–49.

Murray, N. and A. Granville (1982) "Coal Mining in the Republic of South Africa", *Glückauf*, vol 118, no 4, pp. 66–68 & 186–189.

Nattrass, N. (1990) "The Small Black Enterprise Sector – a Brief Note of Caution", in Nattrass and Ardington (eds) (1990), pp. 217–28.

Nattrass, N. (1995) "A Reply to Ben Fine", *Transformation*, no 26, pp. 91–92.

Nattrass, N. and E. Ardington (eds) (1990) *The Political Economy of South Africa*, Cape Town: MacMillan.

Nattrass, N. and J. Seekings (2010) "State, Business and Growth in Post-apartheid South Africa", IPPG Discussion Paper, no 34. http://www.ippg.org.uk/papers/dp34a.pdf.

Naudé, W. (2009) "After the G-20 Summit: What Prospects for Global Development?", www.wider.unu.edu/publications/newsletter/articles/en_GB/09-04-09-g20/.

Ndikumana, L. and J. Boyce (2008) "New Estimates of Capital Flight from Sub-Saharan African Countries: Linkages with External Borrowing and Policy Options", PERI Working Paper, no 166, University of Amherst.

Netshitenze, J. (2023) "Lifting the Colony While Improving the Metropolis: Addressing Duality in Economic Development", in Mohamed et al. (eds) (2023), pp. 328–60.

Newman, S. (2009) "Systematised Capital Flight in South Africa", paper presented at the Third International Research Workshop of the International Initiative for Promoting Political Economy, METU, Ankara, 14–15 September.

Newman, S. (2019) "The Minerals-Energy-Complex and Structural Inequality in South Africa", Briefing paper for Oxfam South Africa, May, https://oro.open.ac.uk/73184/4/Oxfam_MEC_final-converted.pdf.

NGP (2010) *The New Growth Path: the Framework*, Economic Development Department, South Africa, https://www.gov.za/sites/default/files/gcis_document/201409/ngp-framework-public-release-final15.pdf.

Nolan, P. (1993/94) "The Past Strikes Back: Industrial Relations and UK Competitiveness: an Inaugural Lecture", *Review*, University of Leeds, vol 36, pp. 195–210.

Noman, A., J. Stiglitz, H. Stein and K. Botchwey (eds) (2012) *Good Growth and Governance in Africa: Rethinking Development Strategies*, Oxford: Oxford University Press.

NPC (2011) *National Development Plan: Vision for 2030*, National Planning Commission, https://www.gov.za/sites/default/files/gcis_document/201409/devplan2.pdf.

NPC (2012) *National Development Plan 2030: Our Future – Make It Work*, Pretoria: the Presidency.

O'Meara, D. (1983) *Volkscapitalisme: Class, Capitalism and Ideology in the Development of Afrikaner Nationalism*, Cambridge: Cambridge University Press.

O'Meara, D. (1996) *Forty Lost Years: the Apartheid State and the Politics of the National Party, 1948–1994*, Randburg: Ravan Press.

Öberg, P., T. Svensson, P. Christiansen, A. Nørgaard, H. Rommetvedt and G. Thesen (2011) "Disrupted Exchange and Declining Corporatism: Government Authority and Interest Group Capability in Scandinavia", *Government and Opposition*, vol 46, no 3, pp. 365–91.

O'Donnell, K. (2023) "Canteen Workers' Wages and Collective Bargaining Arrangementsin British Coal", *Historical Studies in Industrial Relations*, vol 44, no 1, pp. 75–89.

Orhangazi, O. (2011) "'Financial' vs. 'Real': an Overview of the Contradictory Role of Finance", PERI Working Paper Series, no 274, http://www.peri.umass.edu/fileadmin/pdf/working_papers/working_papers_251-300/WP274.pdf.

Ostry, J., A. Ghosh, K. Habermeier, M. Chamon, M. Qureshi and D. Reinhardt (2010) "Capital Inflows: the Role of Controls", IMF Staff Position Note, February 19th, SPN/10/04.

Padayachee, V. (2006) "Obituary Tribute to Trevor Bell", *Transformation*, no 60, pp. 6–7.

Padayachee, V. (ed.) (2006) *The Development Decade?: Economic and Social Change in South Africa, 1994–2004*, Pretoria: HSRC.

Padayachee, V. and R. van Niekerk (2019) *"Shadows of Liberation": ANC Economic and Social Policy from African Claims (1943) to GEAR (1996)*, Johannesburg: Wits University Press.

Padayachee, V. and J. Sender (2017) "Vella Pillay: Revolutionary Activism and Economic Policy Analysis", *Social Scientist*, March–April, Vol. 45, no 3/4, pp. 17–40.

Panitch, L. and G. Albo (eds) (2018) *A World Turned Upside Down?, Socialist Register, 2019*, vol 55, London: Merlin Press.

Panitch, L., G. Albo and V. Chibber (eds) (2010) *The Crisis and the Left, Socialist Register, 2011*, vol 47, London: Merlin Press.

Parayil, G. (ed.) (2000) *Kerala: The Development Experience, Reflections on Sustainability and Replicability*, London: Zed Books.

Pardoe, D. and E. Pedroncelli (1982) "Winning Methods in South African Coal Mining", *Glückauf*, vol 118, no 4, pp. 68–70 & 190–194.

Parsons, R. (ed.) (2004) *Manuel, Markets and Money*, Cape Town: Juta.

Peck, J. and N. Theodore (2007) "Variegated Capitalism", *Progress in Human Geography*, vol 31, no 6, pp. 731–72.

Petropoulos, S. (2011) "The 2008 Global Crisis and the East Asian Developmental States Shifts of Export-Driven Strategies", *European Journal of East Asian Studies*, vol 10, no 2, pp. 181–202.

Pierson, P. (ed.) (2001) *The New Politics of the Welfare State*, Oxford: Oxford University Press.

Pilling, G. (1980) *Marx's 'Capital': Philosophy and Political Economy*, Routledge and Kegan Paul: London.

Piore, M. and C. Sabel (1984) *The Second Industrial Divide: Possibilities for Prosperity*, New York: Basic Books.

Pitcher, A. (2012) "Was Privatisation Necessary and Did It Work? The Case of South Africa", *Review of African Political Economy*, vol 39, no 132, pp. 243–60.

Posel, D. (1991) *The Making of Apartheid, 1948–1961: Conflict and Compromise*, Oxford: Clarendon Press.

Powell, M. and A. Barrientos (2011) "An Audit of the Welfare Modelling Business", *Social Policy and Administration*, vol 45, no 1, pp. 69–84.

Pradella, L. (2014) "New Developmentalism and the Origins of Methodological Nationalism", *Competition and Change*, vol 18, no 2, pp. 180–93.

Rebitzer, J. (1993) "Radical Political Economy and the Economics of Labor Markets", *Journal of Economic Literature*, vol XXXI, Sept, pp. 1394–1434.

Reboredo, R. and P. Carmody (2024) Between Energy and Politics: Ruin, Renewal, and the Contours of State Power in Post-apartheid South Africa", *Environment and Planning D: Society and Space*, vol 43, no 4, pp. 598–616.

Reinert, E. (2012) "Neo-classical Economics: a Trail of Economic Destruction since the 1970s", *Real-World Economics Review*, no 60, pp. 2–17, http://www.paecon.net/PAERevview/issue60/Reinert60.pdf.

Rethel, L. (2010) "The New Financial Development Paradigm and Asian Bond Markets", *New Political Economy*, vol 15, no 4, pp. 493–517.

Reynolds, J., B. Fine and R. van Niekerk (eds) (2019) *Race, Class and the Post-Apartheid Democratic State*, Pietermaritzburg: University of KwaZulu-Natal Press.

Rhodes, M. (2001) "The Political Economy of Social Pacts: 'Competitive Corporatism' and European Welfare Reform", in Pierson (ed.) (2001), pp. 165–94.

Roberts, S. (2004) "Investment in South Africa – a Comment on Recent Contributions", *Development Southern Africa*, vol 23, no 4, pp. 743–56.

Roberts, S. and Z. Rustomjee (2009) "Industrial Policy under Democracy: Apartheid's Grown-up Infant Industries? Iscor and Sasol", *Transformation*, no 71, pp. 50–75.

Rodriguez, F. (2006) 'Cleaning Up the Kitchen Sink: Growth Empirics When the World Is Not Simple', Wesleyan Economics Working Papers 2006–4, Wesleyan University, Department of Economics.

Rodrik, D. (2009) "One Economics, Many Recipes", Sir Arthur Lewis Distinguished Lecture, March 26th, http://www.youtube.com/watch?v=fBAF5sGtPPY.

Rodrik, D. (2010) "The End of an Era in Finance", http://rodrik.typepad.com/dani_rodriks_weblog/2010/03/the-end-of-an-era-in-finance.html.

Rustomjee, Z. (1990) *Regulating South Africa's Corporate Oligopoly*, Unpublished MPhil dissertation, Institute of Development Studies, University of Sussex.

Rustomjee, Z. (1991) "Capital Flight from South Africa – 1970–1988", *Transformation*, no 15, pp. 89–103.

Rustomjee, Z. (1993) *The Engineering Sector in South Africa*, Report prepared for the Cosatu/Economic Trends Industrial Strategy Project, March.

Rustomjee, Z. (1994) *The Political Economy of South African Industrialisation – the Role of the Minerals-Energy Complex*, SOAS, University of London, unpublished PhD thesis.

Rustomjee, Z., L. Kaziboni, and I. Steuart (2018) "Structural Transformation along Metals, Machinery and Equipment Value Chain – Developing Capabilities in the Metals and Machinery Segments", CCRED Working Paper, no 7/2018, Johannesburg, CCRED.

Saad-Filho, A. and G. Yalman (eds) (2010) *Transitions to Neoliberalism in Middle-Income Countries: Policy Dilemmas, Economic Crises, Forms of Resistance*, London: Routledge.

Sabel, C. and J. Zeitlin (1985) "Historical Alternatives to Mass Production: Politics, Markets and Technology in Nineteenth-Century Industrialisation", *Past and Present*, no 108, pp. 133–76.

Sachs, M. (2024) "Strategic Reflections on South Africa's Economy", *South African Journal of Science*, vol 120, no 7/8, 10.17159/sajs.2024/18034.

Santos, A. and N. Teles (eds) (2020) *Financialisation in the European Periphery: Work and Social Reproduction in Portugal*, London: Routledge.

Saraswati, J. (2007) *The Development of the Indian IT Industry: a Linkage-Agency Approach*, SOAS, University of London, PhD thesis.

SARB (2011) "Bank Supervision Department Annual Report, 2011", South African Reserve Bank, http://www.resbank.co.za/Lists/News%20and%20Publications/Attachments/5048/01%20Annual%20Report%202011.pdf.

Schindler, M. (2009) "Measuring Financial Integration: a New Data Set", *IMF Staff Papers*, vol 56, no 1, pp. 222–38.

Schneider, B. (2003) 'Measuring Capital Flight: Estimates and Interpretations', ODI Working Paper Series, no 194.

Schneider, H., P. Barren and S. Fonn (2007) "The Promise and the Practice of Transformation in South Africa's Health System", in Buhlungu et al. (eds) (2007), 289–311.

Sender, J. (2012) "Fictions and Elephants in the Rondawel: a Response to a Brief Chapter in South Africa's National Development Plan", *Transformation*, no 78, pp. 98–114.

Soer, E. (2025) "Neoliberalism's True Heirs: What Late-apartheid South Africa Can Teach Us about the Contemporary Far Right", MPIfG Discussion Paper, no 25/2, Max Planck Institute for the Study of Societies, Cologne, https://hdl.handle.net/21.11116/0000-0010-FD2B-2.

Shaw, E. (1973) *Financial Deepening in Economic Development*, New York: Oxford University Press.

Shaw, T. (2012) "Africa's Quest for Developmental States: 'Renaissance' for Whom?", *Third World Quarterly*, vol 33, no 5, pp. 837–51.

Shonfield, A. (1965) *Modern Capitalism: the Changing Balance of Public and Private Power*, Oxford: Oxford University Press.

Siegel, N. (2005) "Social Pacts Revisited: 'Competitive Concertation' and Complex Causality in Negotiated Welfare State Reforms", *European Journal of Industrial* Relations, vol 11, no 1, pp 107–26.

Simkins, C. (1990) "Economic and Political Aspects of Urbanisation and Housing Policy", in Nattrass and Ardington (eds) (1990), pp. 187–206.

Singleton, J. and G. Verhoef (2010) "Regulation, Deregulation, and Internationalisation in South African and New Zealand Banking", *Business History*, vol 52, no 4, pp. 536–63.

Soludo, C., M. Ogbu and H.-J. Chang (eds) (2004) *The Politics of Trade and Industrial Policy in Africa*, Ottawa: IDRC.

Song, H.-Y. (2011) "Theorising the Korean State beyond Institutionalism: Class Content and Form of 'National' Development", *New Political Economy*, vol 16, no 3, pp. 281–302.

Spandau, A. (1980a) "A Note on Black Employment Conditions on South African Mines", *South African Journal of Economics*, vol 48, no 2, pp. 214–17.

Spandau, A. (1980b) "Mechanization and Labour Policies on South African Mines", *South African Journal of Economics*, vol 48, no 2, pp. 167–82.

Steyn, G. (2004) "Taming the Rand", in Parsons (ed.) (2004), pp. 109–30.

Stiglitz, J. (1985) "Credit Markets and the Control of Capital", *Journal of Money, Credit, and Banking*, vol 17, no 2, pp. 133–52.

Stiglitz, J. (1998) "More Instruments and Broader Goals: Moving Toward the Post Washington Consensus", the 1998 WIDER Annual Lecture, January 7th, Helsinki.

Stiglitz, J. and A. Weiss (1981) "Credit Rationing in Markets with Imperfect Information", *American Economic* Review, vol 71, no 3, pp. 393–410.

Stilwell, F., D. Primrose and T. Thornton (eds) *Handbook of Alternative Theories of Political Economy*, Cheltenham: Edward Elgar.

Streeck, W. (2010) "E Pluribus Unum? Varieties and Commonalities of Capitalism", Max Planck Institute for the Study of Societies, Discussion Paper, no 10/12. http://www.mpifg.de/pu/mpifg_dp/dp10-12.pdf.

Summers, L. and V. Summers (1989) "When Financial Markets Work Too Well: a Cautious Case for a Securities Transactions Tax", *Journal of Financial Services*, vol 3, pp. 163–88.

Toporowski, J. (ed.) (2000), *Political Economy and the New Capitalism: Essays in Honour of Sam Aaronovitch*, London: Routledge.

Törnquist, O. (1999) "The New Popular Politics of Development: Kerala's Experience", in Parayil (ed.) (1999), pp. 116–38.

Trentmann, F. (ed.) (2005) *The Making of the Consumer: Knowledge, Power and Identity in the Modern World*, Oxford: Berg.

Truu, M. (1983a) "Comment on Cassim (1982)", *South African Journal of Economics*, vol 51, no 4, pp. 567–73.

Truu, M. (1983b) "Final Comment on Cassim (1982)", *South African Journal of Economics*, vol 51, no 4, p. 579.

Tsukamoto, T. (2012) "Neoliberalization of the Developmental State: Tokyo's Bottom-Up Politics and State Rescaling in Japan", *International Journal of Urban and Regional Research*, vol 36, no 1, pp. 71–89.

UBS (2008) "The Impact of South Africa's Power Crisis", Global Equity Research, South Africa Strategy, March 3rd.

UN (2009) *Report of the Commission of Experts of the President of the United Nations General Assembly on Reforms of the International Monetary and Financial System*, New York: United Nations.

UNECA (1999) *Economic Report on Africa: the Challenges of Poverty Reduction and Sustainability*, UNECA, Addis Ababa, Ethiopia.

Utting, P., S. Razavi and R. Buchholz (eds) (2012) *Global Crisis and Transformative Social Change*, London: Palgrave MacMillan.

Valodia, I., R. Davies, M. Altman and J. Thurlow (2007) "Exploring Economic Behaviour in South Africa's Informal Economy, Especially in Relationship to the Formal Economy", Report to the Conflict and Governance Facility (CAGE), October.

van Garderen, D. (1982) "Bosjesspruit", *Glückauf*, vol 118, no 4, pp. 76–77 & 202–204.

Van Waeyenberge, E. (2007) *Exploring the Emergence of a New Aid Regime: Selectivity, Knowledge and the World Bank*, PhD thesis, SOAS, University of London.

Van Wyk, K., Z. Botha and I. Goodspeed (eds) (2012) *Understanding South African Financial Markets*, fourth edition, Pretoria: Van Shaik Publishers.

Verhoef, G. (1992a) "Afrikaner Nationalism in South African Banking: the Case of Volkskas and Trust Bank", in Jones (ed.), (1992), pp. 115–53.

Verhoef, G. (1992b) "Nedbank 1945–89: the Continental Approach to Banking in South Africa", in Jones (ed.), (1992), pp. 80–114,

Verhoef, G. (2009a) "Concentration and Competition: the Changing Landscape of the Banking Sector in South Africa, 1970–2007", *South African Journal of Economic History*, vol 24, no 2, pp. 157–97.

Verhoef, G. (2009b) "Savings for Life to Build the Economy for the People: the Emergence of Afrikaner Corporate Conglomerates in South Africa, 1918–2000", *South African Journal of Economic History*, vol 24, no 1, pp. 118–163.

Vilakazi, T. and T. Bosiu (2021) "Black Economic Empowerment, Barriers to Entry, and Economic Transformation in South Africa", in Andreoni et al. (eds) (2021), pp. 189–213.

Vilakazi, T. and T. Bosiu (2023) "The Evolution of South Africa's Economic Structure: Key Trends amongst the Top 100 Firms on the JSE", in Mohamed et al. (eds) (2023), pp. 168–98.

Viljoen, D. (1991) *Labour and Employment in South Africa: a Regional Profile, 1980–1990*, Halfway House: DBSA.

Vitali, S., J. Glattfelder and S. Battiston (2011) "The Network of Global Corporate Control", http://arxiv.org/pdf/1107.5728v2.pdf.

Wade, R. (1996) "Japan, the World Bank, and the Art of Paradigm Maintenance: *the East Asian Miracle* in Political Perspective", *New Left Review*, no 217, pp. 3–37.

Wade, R. (2012) "Return of Industrial Policy?", *International Review of Applied Economics*, vol 26, no 2, pp. 223–39.

Webster, E. (1985) *Cast in a Racial Mould: Labour Process and Trade Unionism in the Foundries*, Johannesburg: Ravan Press.

Webster, E. and G. Adler (1999) "Toward a Class Compromise in South Africa's 'Double Transition': Bargained Liberalization and the Consolidation of Democracy", *Politics and Society*, vol 27, no 3, pp. 347–85.

Webster, E. and K. von Holdt (eds) (2005) *Beyond the Apartheid Workplace*, Pietermaritzburg: University of KwaZulu-Natal Press.

Wesso, G. (2001) "The Dynamic of Capital Flows in South Africa: an Empirical Investigation", *South African Reserve Bank Quarterly Bulletin*, June, no 220, pp. 59–77.

Wiarda H. (1997) *Corporatism and Comparative Politics: the Other Great Ism*, New York: Sharpe.

Wiegratz, J. (ed.) (2024) *Capitalism and Crime in Africa: the Neoliberal Period*, London: Routledge.

Wichahn, N. (1979/80) *Report of the Commission of Inquiry into Labour Legislation*, Pretoria: Government Printer.

Williams, M. (ed.) (2014) *The End of the Developmental State?*, London: Routledge.

Wilson, F. (1972a) *Migrant Labour in South African Gold Mines, 1911–1969*, Cambridge: Cambridge University Press.

Wilson, F. (1972b) *Migrant Labour in South Africa*, Johannesburg: Christian Institute of South Africa.

Wilson, F. and M. Ramphele (1989) *Uprooting Poverty: the South African Challenge*, Cape Town: David Philip.

Wolpe, H. (1972) "Capitalism and Cheap Labour-power in South Africa: from Segregation to Apartheid", *Economy and Society*, vol 1, no 4, pp. 425–56.

World Bank (1993) *The East Asian Miracle: Economic Growth and Public Policy, A World Bank Policy Research Report*, Oxford: Oxford University Press.

World Bank (1997) *The State in a Changing World*, World Development Report, Washington DC: World Bank.

World Bank (2006) *Global Development Finance: the Globalization of Corporate Finance in Developing Countries*, Washington DC: World Bank.

World Bank (2007) "Stolen Asset Recovery Initiative: Challenges, Opportunities and Action Plan", Washington DC, World Bank.

World Bank (2011) *World Development Indicators*, http://data.worldbank.org/data-catalog/world-development-indicators.

Xirinachs, J., I. Nübler and R. Kozul-Wright (eds) (2014) *Transforming Economies: Making Industrial Policy Work for Growth, Jobs and Development*, Geneva: ILO.

Zalk, N. (2012) "South African Post-apartheid Policies towards Industrialization: Tentative Implications for Other African Countries", in Noman et al. (eds) (2012), pp. 345–71.

Zalk, N. (2014) "Industrial Policy in a Harsh Climate: the Case of South Africa", in Xirinachs et al. (eds) (2014), pp. 327–54.

Zalk, N. (2017) The Things We Lost in the Fire: the Political Economy of Post-Apartheid Restructuring of the South African Steel and Engineering Sectors, SOAS University of London, PhD thesis, http://eprints.soas.ac.uk/26166.

Zalk, N. (2021) "Structural Change in South Africa: a Historical Sectoral Perspective", in Andreoni et al. (eds) (2021), pp. 28–52.

Zysman, J. (1983) *Governments, Markets and Growth: Financial Systems and the Politics of Industrial Change*, New York: Cornell University Press.

Index

Abiad, A. 200, 287
ABSA (Amalgamated Banks of South Africa Limited) 201–202, 204
abstraction 6 74–75, 81
academia 47, 81, 125–26, 275, 277, 279, 282–83
accumulation 3, 21, 72–73, 75, 82–84, 87–88, 96–97, 102, 106, 115, 128, 141, 159, 161, 164–65, 172, 174, 181, 195, 199, 208–209, 223, 226, 254, 256, 258
  system of 19, 21, 82–84, 87–88, 96–97, 141, 161, 182
activism 1, 3, 143, 259, 269, 284–285
Adelzadeh, Asghar 7, 281, 287
adjustment (structural) 9, 65, 105, 155, 164, 168, 173, 177–78, 224, 240, 242
Adler, G. 95, 98, 111, Ch. 5, Appendix 317
Advanced Manufacturing Technology Strategy 11
AES (Alternative Economic Strategy) 102–103
Africa(n) 40, 45, 47, 53, 68–69, 115, 160, 166, 175, 182, 195, 201–202, 206, 209, 240, 247, 249, 272, 280, 282–83
  wages Ch. 3
African National Congress. *See* ANC
Afrikaners. *See also* capital 89, 104, 116, 162, 196, 243, 245, 271–72
agriculture. *See also* farming 39, 44, 62–64, 66–67, 71, 76, 109, 122, 156, 171, 195–96, 204, 223, 272, 278, 284
  bantustan 71 72, 76
AIG (American International Group) 147
Akerlof, G. 140, 189, 262, 287
Albaraka 202
Albo, G. 290, 312
Algan, Y. 302
Al-Jazaeri, H. 223, 259, 287
Althusserian 105
Altman, M. 316
Amalgamated Banks of South Africa 201
AMCU (Association of Mineworkers and Construction Union) 211
Amphlett, G. 195, 287
Amplats 213, 216
Amsden, A. 92, 224, 235, 287
ANC (African National Congress) 7–8, 16, 18, 20, 22, 78, 80, 90, 95–96, 98, 102, 104–105, 107, 116, 126, 133–35, 137, 210, 212, 214, 217, 219, 221, 243, 246, 270, 274–77, 281–82, 285, 287, 294–95, 312
  leadership 8, 80, 219, 281–82
Andreoni, A. 9–11, 13, 19–20, 287–89, 303, 310, 316, 318
Andrews, D. 110, 288
Andrews, M. 148, 160, 248, 304
Anglo American Platinum Corporation 211, 213
Anglo American 12–13, 163, 197–99, 211, 213–14, 218, 233
Anglo Plats 215
Anglo-Vaal 33, 197
anti-apartheid 102, 139, 278
apartheid 8, 19, 22, 36–37, 41–42, 44–46, 55, 60, 62–64, 68–69, 71, 76–77, 88–89, 117, 126–27, 142, 149–50, 154–55, 158, 160, 162–64, 174–76, 182, 194–95, 200, 210–11, 214, 242–43, 248, 269–72, 277–78, 282–83
APORDE (African Programme on Rethinking Development Economics) 283
appropriation 14–15, 125, 245, 263, 272
Ardington, E. 305–306, 309, 311, 315
Arrighi, G. 193, 288
Arrow, K. 260
articulation 70–71, 76, 102, 181, 278
Aryeetey, E. 288, 290
ASGI-SA (Accelerated and Shared Growth Initiative) 148, 246, 281
Ashman, S. 39, 154, 156, 160, 163, 181, 185, 204, 206, 210, 239, 243, 282, 288
Asia 47, 78, 167, 233
assets 10, 12, 44, 110, 114, 117, 155–57, 161–63, 166, 174–75, 188, 190, 192–93, 197–98, 200–206, 212–13, 232, 245, 255
Atkinson, A. 129, 288
Ault, D. 44, 63, 288
austerity 164, 256–58, 255
Australia 33, 98
Austrian school 265

authoritarianism 5, 20, 258–59, 277
autonomy 225–26, 228–29, 234
Aybar, S. 114, 195, 288

Babha, Homi 141
Bafokeng 212
balance of payments 94, 101, 112, 117, 157, 168, 177
Baloyi, B. 310
Bank of Athens 202
Bank of Baroda 202
Bank of China 202
Bank of England 150, 203
Bank of Taiwan 202
banking systems 114, 191–93
banks and banking 100–101, 104, 112–14, 116, 145–47, 150–51, 166–67, 181–82, 187, 189–92, 195–206, 209–10, 216, 230, 233, 235, 240, 242
Bankscope 201, 288
bantustans 63, 66–67, 70–71, 79, 212, 214, 238
Barclays 195–96, 198–99, 201
Barker, F. 40, 289
Barnes, J. 11, 280, 289, 310
Barren, P. 314
Barrientos, A. 240, 313
Barro-style regressions 262
BASA (Banking Association South Africa) 202–203, 205
Basel accord 200
Basic Income Grant 144
Batifoulier, P. 266, 288
Battiston, S. 317
Bayliss, K. 5, 75, 92, 100, 116, 132, 137, 142, 241, 256–58, 264, 268, 289, 293, 300
Becker, G. 261
Bédécarrats, F. 262, 289
BEE (black economic empowerment) 7, 12–15, 17, 20, 97, 108, 117–18, 120, 138, 155, 162, 164, 211, 221, 273, 282
Beittel, M. 61, 309
Beja, E. 167, 289
Bell, T. 78–80, 82–90, 92, 106, 289–90, 306, 312
Bercuson, K. 45, 307
Bezuidenhout, A. 124, 215, 290
BHP (Billiton) 33, 163
Bidvest Bank 202
Birkbeck College 23, 79, 97–98, 104, 179
Bizana 214
black elite/capital. *See also* BEE 14, 18–20, 65, 77, 91, 95, 136, 149, 164–65, 211–13, 217, 219, 221–22, 228, 245–46, 249, 273, 277, 281, 286
black 12, 14, 19, 35–36, 44, 47, 52–53, 60, 62–67, 91, 108, 117–18, 149, 161–62, 164, 213, 219, 222, 245, 248–49, 273, 282
  workers 36–37, 45, 52, 57, 59–60, 63–64, 161
Black, A. 7, 59, 108, 117, 138, 155, 164, 213, 222, 273, 288–91, 293, 305–6, 310–11, 315–16
Blanchard, O. 173, 290
Bloemfontein 196
Blyth, M. 238, 290
Boateng, K. 109, 290
Bobek, A. 255, 290
Boffo, M. 259, 290
Bogetic, Z. 306
Boland, L. 262, 290
Bond, P. 106, 110, 290, 309, 313
bonds 110, 112, 143, 215
Bonuskor 197
Bookbinder, R. 9, 290
borders 137, 139–41, 143, 148, 151, 153
Bosiu, T. 12, 14, 316–17
Bosjesspruit colliery 27, 29, 33
Botchwey, K. 311
Botha, Z. 316
Botswana 228
Bourdieu, Pierre 259
Bowman, A. 14, 290
Boyce, J. 109, 166, 177, 290, 311
Boyle, B. 156
Brait Merchant Bank 201
Brandl, B. 236, 290
Brenner, R. 115, 128, 290, 301
Bretton Woods 162, 271
Breznitz, D. 228–29, 291
BRICS countries 200, 217
Britain 37, 85, 94, 96, 99–101, 103, 105, 125, 134, 150, 161, 182, 186, 195, 198, 269, 275
Bruff, I. 208, 291
Buchholz, R. 316
Buhlungu, S. 215, 290–91, 309, 314
Burawoy, Michael 141

Burns, J. 263, 291
Bush, President 144
Bushveld Ignateous Complex (BIC) 211–12, 215
Business Day 117, 154
Business Times 156
business 7, 9, 14, 91, 116, 118–20, 133–34, 156, 211, 238, 245, 269, 280
buzzword 221, 230, 240, 244, 246–47

C, commodification 5, 145, 255–56
Cable, J. 191, 291
Cadiz Investment Bank and Corpcapital Bank 201
Cambridge Capital Controversy 22, 24, 31, 263
Cambridge 268
Cape Colony 195
Cape Town 119
capital and labour 26, 31, 43, 75, 128, 132, 143, 235–36, 239
capital controls 111–13, 148, 158–59, 172–73, 176, 200, 244
capital export/import 97, 109–111, 113–14, 118, 141, 156–57, 159–62, 166–73, 175, 177, 204, 213, 244, 271, 273
capital flight 7, 16–18, 21, 94, 111, 138, Ch. 7, 182, 199, 213, 206, 209, 244, 246, 248–49, 262
  repatriation 159, 166–67, 206
capital goods 28, 85–86, 107, 218, 243
capital 23–26, 30–32, 46, 65, 72–74, 82–85, 90–91, 95–98, 102, 105–107, 109, 111–12, 115, 117, 127–29, 131, 135–36, 144, 146, 155–60, 162–67, 170–72, 174 77, 180–82, 186, 188, 195–98, 200–201, 207–208, 212, 226, 213, 243–46, 249, 254, 263, 271, 273
  domestic 110, 160, 164, 182, 206, 218, 221, 227–28
  Afrikaner capital 14–16, 67, 85, 88–89, 162, 195–97, 199–200, 212, 243, 245, 271
    large-scale 14, 89, 199, 201, 243, 271
    small-scale 118, 271
    finance 182, 196, 198, 212
  English 85, 88–89, 196–97, 199, 243, 271
  large-scale 104, 133, 135–36, 161–62, 243, 245, 271
  small-scale 63, 99, 108, 118, 271
capital-intensity 25, 29, 43, 47–48, 50, 52, 58, 67, 121, 243
capitalism 4–5, 9, 41, 105, 125–27, 161–62, 165, 179–81, 194, 207–208, 235, 250, 253–54, 260, 267, 278
  contemporary 6, 127, 180, 193, 208, 232, 252
capitalist economies 41, 69, 130, 208, 225, 233, 235, 267
capitalists 43, 45–46, 63–64, 73, 131, 196, 226, 229, 235, 241
Capitec Bank 202
Capps, G. 211, 291
Capulets 138, 143
Carmody, P. 18, 182, 291, 313
cars 7, 10–11
Cartwright-Smith, D. 159, 306
Cassim, F. 56, 291, 316
Castree, N. 144, 291
Cattaneo, N. 90, 290
Caylon Corporate and Investment Bank 202
CC, commodity calculation 5, 256–57
CCFCC 5, 17, 257
centralisation 5, 8, 19–20, 76, 99, 119, 130, 198, 258, 274
Centre for the Study of African Economies (CSAE) 282
CEPSA (Centre for Economic Policy for Southern Africa) 79–80
CF, commodity form 5, 74, 256–57
Chabane, N. 111–12, 164, 291
Chamber of Mines 29, 34–35, 37, 139–40, 142, 161, 291
Chambers, R. 95, 291
Chamon, M. 312
Chang, Ha-Joon 222, 232, 291–92, 315
Chaotic 5, 141, 143, 258
Chase Manhattan 199
Chatterjee, A. 14, 245, 292
Chavance, B. 288
chemicals 10, 30–31, 150, 171, 196
Chester, L. 292, 299
Chibber, V. 312
Chicago 261
childcare 55, 62
Chile 167
China Construction Bank 202

China 104, 165, 201–202, 217, 227, 229, 234
Chirat, A. 260, 292
Chisholm, L. 69, 292
Christiansen, P. 312
chromium 211
Citibank 202
cities 99, 119, 183, 279, 147
Citigroup Report 211
citizenship 137–41, 148, 151–53, 230, 272
Clark, N. 65, 196, 292
Clarke, G. 110, 292
class interests 7, 180–82, 194, 225–26, 228, 236
classes 14, 18–19, 59, 75, 120, 127–30, 132, 136, 143, 151, 179, 200, 208, 221, 226–28, 236, 245, 267
CliFT 9, 305
cliometrics 3, 261
clothing 77
clusters 87, 161
coal 9, 18, 21, Ch. 2, 37–38, 101–102, 117, 161, 197, 218, 269–71
Coetzee, J. 292, 301
Cold War 231, 233
Coleman, J. 259
Collier, P. 159, 166, 292
commercialisation 146, 152, 163, 194, 232, 239
commodities 14–15, 24, 30–32, 42, 64, 74, 76, 105, 135, 142, 204, 212, 218, 254, 257, 280
communism 147, 151, 235, 274, 276
Communist Party (of South Africa, CPSA) 101–103, 147, 243, 274, 276
companies 13, 19, 33–34, 37, 65, 111–12, 114, 125, 144, 147, 150, 156–58, 163, 186, 191–92, 196–98, 201, 213, 215–17, 223, 244
Competition Commission South Africa 108, 204, 292
competition 22–23, 26, 32–35, 50, 52, 56, 60, 62, 68, 82, 85, 121, 128–29, 173, 185, 191, 200, 203, 206, 260, 263, 280
compounds 35, 37, 66, 206, 214–15, 265
concentration. *See also* monopolisation 50, 161, 164, 195, 198, 200, 203–204, 206, 212, 243
Conference of Socialist Economists (CSE) 99
conflicts 14, 45–46, 64–65, 67, 88, 106, 130, 143, 146, 149, 172, 181, 196, 207, 224, 227, 236, 240, 271, 275
conglomerate(s) 11–12, 15, 18, 23, 84, 90, 94, 97–98, 110–15, 117, 119–20, 124, 136, 141, 155, 158–59, 161–65, 174, 182, 195–96, 198–99, 201, 206–207, 221, 243, 249, 270–71, 273
  houses 161, 182, 195–96, 213
  unbundling 7, 12, 17–18, 79, 112, 138, 164, 201, 212–13, 273
Congress of South African Trade Unions. *See* COSATU
Connell, R. 55, 292
construction 36, 115, 142–43, 197, 256
Consumer Association 151
consumption goods 39, 63, 85–86, 97, 108, 119, 174, 271–72
consumption 3–5, 13, 30, 32–35, 42–45, 73, 75–76, 79, 86–87, 108, 122, 137, 141–42, 151–556, 193–95, 204, 216, 227, 232–33, 257, 272
  norms of 76–77, 122
contracting 34, 117, 186, 189, 191–92, 214, 245, 281
converters, catalytic 216–17
cooperation 9, 34, 118, 193, 197, 217, 236, 240, 285
coordination 19, 35, 37, 114, 117, 173, 181, 186, 193, 224, 239, 246, 281
Corbett, J. 191, 292
Cornwall, A. 230, 292
Corpcapital Bank 201
Corporate Strategy and Industrial Development (CSID) 157, 171
corporate 18, 84, 103, 108–109, 138, 164, 186, 195, 198, 204, 206–207, 211, 213, 234, 239
corporations 13, 18, 34, 66, 71, 84, 88, 91, 102, 111–12, 138, 155, 163–64, 175, 182–83, 201, 206, 239
  multinational (MNCs) 99–100, 183, 201, 213–229, 254, 273, 279
corporatism 220, 227, 235–39, 246
corruption 8, 20, 110, 172, 185, 220, 230, 248–49, 251, 277

COSATU (Congress of South African Trade Unions) 9, 78, 210, 221, 274, 280, 292, 297
costs 26–27, 30, 65, 101, 110, 115, 117, 139, 147, 150, 166, 175, 178, 184, 186, 190, 204, 206, 216
Cowling, K. 30, 292
cows 108, 119–20
CPGB 275
Crankshaw, O. 40, 304
credit 13, 76, 193, 200, 204, 216, 232, 240, 244, 257, 259, 277
crime 110, 119, 159, 210, 214, 274
crises. *See also* global 5, 63, 78, 109, 144, 146, 162, 170, 173, 176, 184, 193–95, 199, 219–11, 216–18, 228, 232–34, 242, 267
  current 144–45, 173, 232, 234, 242
Cross, T. 65, 88, 290, 292–93
Crotty, J. 163, 293
Crush, J. 65–67, 293
Cs 141–43, 148, 151
cultures 43, 75–76, 135, 137, 141–42, 193, 258, 274

Dahmén, Erik 235
Damodaran, S. 293, 300
Daniel, J. 291, 293, 310
Davies, R. 316
DCCS (Duty Credit Certificate Scheme) 11
de Beers 163, 197
de Kock Commission 200
de Villiers, W. 102, 293
Deaton, A. 262
Debreu, G. 260
debt 38, 70, 76, 109, 147 49, 166–68, 170, 172, 174, 176–77, 199, 204, 216
Decker, S. 293, 299
deindustrialisation 10, 155, 159, 279
Dell'Ariccia, G. 290
demand 10, 24, 33, 46, 49, 51, 56, 58, 113, 129, 185, 191, 204, 229, 260, 263
democracy 19–20, 46, 116, 118, 127, 130, 144, 148, 165, 224, 228, 240, 243, 247, 270, 275, 277
  social 270, 274, 276, 280
denationalisation 256
Department for International Development (DFID) 80
Department of Economic Planning 102
Department of Economic Policy (DEP) 90, 102, 134, 270
Department of Mineral and Energy Affairs (DMEA) 35, 37, 293
Department of Trade and Industry (DTI) 10, 20, 79, 90, 118, 172, 280–81
Department of Trade, Industry, and Competition (DTIC) 11
Deraniyagala, S. 118, 293
deregulation 142, 164, 173, 187, 190, 199–200, 204, 258
derivatives 145, 193, 222, 232
Desai, A. 309
Detragiache, E. 287
Deutsche Bank 202
development economics 3, 261
  classical/old 222
  new 230, 262
  newer 185, 262
development 2, 6–8, 10, 16–17, 20, 37, 63, 85, 87–90, 119, 127–28, 132–33, 135–36, 147–48, 157–58, 161, 164–67, 181, 196–98, 208, 212–13, 215, 217, 219–20, 223–28, 230–32, 234, 241–42, 244, 246–47, 250, 265, 273–74, 277, 280
  economic and social 131–32, 155, 228, 245, 248, 273, 282–83
Developmental State Paradigm (DSP) 16, 78, 20–21, 92, 94–96, 103, 105, 125, 150, 165, 179, 185, 219–51, 264, 281–82
  economic school 92, 224–25, 235, 228, 243
  political school 92, 225, 228, 234–35, 243
developmentalism 15, 19, 97, 155, 157, 159–60, 165, 173, 220, 222, 225, 227–2, 234–35, 240–246, 247, 231
devolution 238, 258
diamonds 161, 197
Dimakou, O. 4, 263, 300
discourses 4, 15, 106, 108, 144, 152, 230, 246–47, 284
discrimination 21, 44–48, 57–59, 69, 121
disinvestment 111, 113, 162, 174
distribution 24, 37, 48, 116, 128, 152, 161, 165, 244, 254, 257, 267
diversification 10–11, 20, 86–89, 116, 162, 204, 211, 213, 217–18

domestic servants 40, 52, 64, 74, 122
dos Santos, P. 145, 182, 293
dotcom bubble 194, 232
DSP. *See* Developmental State Paradigm
DTI. *See* Department of Trade and Industry
Du Boff, R. 201, 293
Dubner, S. 308
Durban 66, 217, 284
Duty Credit Certificate Scheme (DCCS) 11
dynamics 6, 9, 106, 108, 120, 125–26, 128, 181, 192–93, 199, 208, 212, 221, 247, 276
dysfunctions 8, 146, 152, 162, 16, 18, 75, 187, 236, 242, 245, 251, 255–56, 258

Eade, D. 230, 292
Eagle Life Assurance and Western Bank 198
earnings. *See also* wages 44, 109, 157, 163, 191, 216, 248
East Asia 23, 92, 165, 173, 219, 221–24, 227–31, 233, 242, 264
  NICS 23, 221–22, 224, 227–29, 242
Eastern Cape 214
econometrics 2, 24, 39–40, 47, 54, 57, 80, 101, 187, 262–63
economic and social reproduction 5, 7, 17, 70–71, 74–76, 124, 128–29, 163, 179, 254, 256, 258–59, 267
Economic and Social Research Council (ESRC) 23, 40, 81, 104
Economic Development Department 172, 246–47
economic empowerment 7, 12, 14–15, 108, 117, 138, 155, 162, 164, 273
economic history 3, 94, 99, 278, 285
  new 261
Economic Research on South Africa. *See* EROSA
Economic Society of South Africa 282
economics imperialism (EI) 2–4, 40, 78, 137, 140–41, 184, 252, 261–64, 267
  new phase of 2, 262
economics, mainstream/neoclassical/orthodox 1–4, 19, 21–23, 30, 39–42, 44–47, 54, 56–58, 60–61, 68–69, 73, 82, 96, 107, 110, 114, 118, 121–22, 126, 130, 140, 180, 183, 188–89, 206, 248, 252–53, 259, 261, 263–69, 273, 277–78, 282, 284, 286
  heterodox 1–2, 140, 184, 232, 252–53, 265–69, 277–79, 280–85
    marginalisation 5, 8, 19, 102, 184, 258, 273–74, 282
economists 99, 129, 133, 135, 148, 260, 262, 274, 276, 281–82
  black 133, 279, 281
Edigheji, O. 293, 298
education 46, 48–50, 53, 55, 57–59, 61–64, 68–69, 71, 110, 121, 151–52, 232, 254, 257, 270
Efficient Markets Hypothesis (EMH) 163, 180–82, 188–89, 193
Eiffert, B. 292
Eire 228
Eisenhower, President 106
EIU (Economist Intelligence Unit) 32–34, 112, 294
electricity 6–7, 11, 32–35, 37, 48, 101–102, 115–17, 119, 152, 162, 196, 217, 246, 270
electrification 17, 77, 104, 116, 125, 275
elites. *See also* BEE 5, 7, 14–15, 139, 143, 204, 221, 231, 233–34, 241, 245–46, 250, 258
Eloff Mining 33
Elsner, W. 293
employee share ownership plans 270
employees 35, 52, 121, 140, 215, 250
employers 34, 36, 43, 47, 49–50, 64, 67, 101, 121, 124, 211, 216, 218, 238
employment 10–11, 30, 41–43, 47, 51–54, 56, 58–59, 62–64, 66–67, 85, 103, 121, 123–24, 142–43, 156, 164, 172, 186, 207, 211, 213, 215, 218, 230, 238, 258, 264, 273, 279
energy 9–10, 18, 32, 34–35, 37, 52, 77, 79, 81, 96–97, 102, 117, 133, 161–62, 165, 170, 196, 206, 212, 243, 245, 256–57
enterprises 13–14, 19, 23, 110, 117, 123, 190, 192, 197, 243
environment 9–10, 151–52, 156, 215, 217, 230, 247, 255, 256, 269, 284
EPC (Energy Policy Committee) 35
Epstein, G. 168, 294, 310
equality 68–69, 77, 143, 152
equilibrium 3, 35, 42–43, 57, 68, 110, 183–84, 187–88, 260, 263
equity 70, 157, 176, 192, 204

EROSA (Economic Research on South Africa) 81, 102–103, 105–106, 270, 294
Erwin, Alec 107–108, 117, 279
Eskom 32–35, 53, 78, 88, 108, 116–17, 120, 139, 196, 213, 269–70, 294
Esping-Andersen, G. 128–29
establishments 22, 28, 88, 165, 172, 196, 212, 275, 284, 286
ethics 4, 151, 266
ethnic 98, 227
ethos 131, 150, 230, 235, 240, 250, 255, 268
Eurocommunism 101
Europe 115, 147, 198, 257
 eastern 146–47, 255
Evans Peter 228, 231, 240, 294
everyday life 3, 77, 143, 255
excess capacity 22, 34, 37, 48, 52
exchange controls 91, 109, 111, 113, 156–59, 162, 164, 170, 172, 174–76, 212
exchange, foreign 13, 32, 101, 109–110, 112–13, 152, 166, 176, 200, 204, 244, 254–55
 overvalued 94, 174, 244
exploitation 37, 73, 96, 161, 212, 254
exports 10–11, 27, 31–33, 35, 37, 85–86, 98, 115, 117, 160, 163, 173, 176–78

Falkena, H. 203–204, 294
Fallon, P. 45, 47–48, 121, 294
Farlam Commission 214, 217
farming. *See also* agriculture 45, 60, 62–63, 66–67, 136, 227
Farrell, G. 78–80, 82–89, 92, 106, 289
Fasenfest, D. 294, 299
Faustian Pact 273, 281
Favereau, O. 288
February, J. 155, 157, 173, 249, 287–88, 290, 309, 312
Federal Chemical Investments 197
Federal Industries 197
Federal Mining Limited 197, 204
Federal People's Investments 196
Federal Telectra 197
Federale Mynbou 197
Federale Volksbeleggings 196
Fedfood 197
Fedservices 197
Feinstein, C. 309
female 39–40, 64, 67, 122
Ferguson, J. 144–45, 294
ferrochrome 211, 213
Ffrench-Davis, R. 294, 302
filières 87, 279
finance 3, 18, 32, 38, 100–101, 109–10, 114, 128–29, 141, 145–47, 151–52, 162–63, 165–66, 173–74, 180–82, 184, 186–94, 197–200, 204, 206–208, 212–13, 224, 226, 231–35, 238–42, 246–47, 249–50, 254–56, 258, 271–72, 274, 279–81
Financial Mail 33, 294
financial 13, 23, 77, 89, 104, 109, 115, 118, 135, 145–46, 162–63, 166–67, 173, 180, 182, 190–91, 193–95, 198–201, 204, 206–209, 212, 216, 232–33, 241, 244, 271, 273
 assets 115, 163–64, 174, 188, 191, 193, 200, 207, 232, 255, 272
 crisis 110, 146, 173, 194, 232, 234
 institutions 46, 159, 163, 206, 226, 208, 242, 249
 liberalisation 189–91, 200, 207
 markets 13, 145, 162–64, 173, 186–89, 191, 206, 228, 241, 271–72
 services 52, 109, 112, 145, 162, 174, 200–201, 204, 206, 244, 249, 272
 systems 110, 114, 144, 146, 179–83, 187, 189–92, 194–95, 199–201, 204, 206–209, 243
financialisation 4–5, 12–15, 17–19, 77, 97–98, 109–12, 114–15, 117, 130, 141, 145–46, 148–50, 152, 155, 160, 162–65, 174, 180, 182, 193–94, 199–200, 206, 208, 220–22, 231–34, 239–42, 244–46, 249, 254–58, 272–73, 282
Finnoff, K. 110–11, 158, 170, 310
Finscope South Africa 301
firms 9, 11–13, 15, 30, 73, 99–100, 119, 186, 189, 191, 201, 207, 211, 214, 279–80
First National Bank 199, 201
First Rand Limited 199, 201–202
FirstRand Bank 202
FirstRand Group 199
fiscal 8, 164, 172, 194, 232
five lows 7, 13, 15, 20, 273, 282
Flagstaff 214
Flechtner, S. 293

Fleetwood, S. 74, 301
flexible-specialisation (flec-spec) 82, 99–100, 107–108, 121, 279–80
Fofack, H. 158, 166, 302
Fonn, S. 314
food 3, 10, 75, 77, 87, 142, 171, 194, 232, 256–57
Fordism 82, 235
  racial 81, 107, 125, 278–79
foreign 11, 13, 33, 35, 65–67, 101, 105, 109, 111, 161–62, 166, 168, 174, 176–77, 182, 196, 199–200, 206, 213, 244
  direct investment (FDI) 13, 97, 111, 113, 115, 154, 164, 173–74, 176, 204
Fourcade, M. 264, 302
France 9
Frangie, S. 223, 302
Franszen Commission 199
freakonomics 264
Freedom Charter 246
Freund, B. 16, 65, 81, 93–94, 165, 243, 283–84, 302
Friedman, S. 261, 282, 301–302
fringe benefits 61
frontline states 65
fruits 235, 275
fuels 32, 171, 196, 270
FVB (Federale Volks-Beleggings) 196–98

G-20 Summit 146
Galbraith, J. K. 106, 268, 292, 302
game theory 127, 132, 186
garnishee orders 216
Gasperin, S. 19, 309
Gauteng 211
GBS Mutual Bank (Grahamstown Building Society) 202
GEAR 16, 19, 101–102, 104, 111, 114–15, 148–49, 154, 164, 182, 243, 246, 249, 279, 281–82
Gelb, Stephen 17, 81, 107, 110–12, 279, 302, 304, 308
Gencor 197, 213
gender 41, 48–51, 55–57, 59, 64, 68–69, 121, 123, 143, 151, 267
Germany 9, 100, 128–29, 183, 191, 223
Ghana 109
Ghosh, A. 312
Ghosh, J. 173, 293, 302
Gideon, J. 299, 302
Giliomee, H. 195, 302
Glass-Steagall Act 182
Glattfelder, J. 317
GLC (Greater London Council) 98–100, 103, 106, 108, 125, 279, 302–303
GLEB (Greater London Enterprise Board) 100, 280
Global Value/Commodity Chain approach (GVC/GVC) 9–10, 12–13, 107, 137, 280
  upstream/downstream 9–12, 89, 211, 213, 217–18
global 5, 7, 9–10, 13, 78, 99–100, 107, 117, 127, 148, 155, 159, 161–62, 164, 166, 168, 173–74, 180–82, 184, 187, 201, 204, 217, 219, 226, 229, 243–44, 254, 279
  crisis 173, 184, 187, 194, 231, 239–40
  Financial Crisis (GFC) 255, 258, 265–66, 269, 282
globalisation 5, 7, 9–10, 12, 14, 17–18, 42, 44, 54, 57, 59, 71, 78, 90, 95, 109–111, 114–15, 117, 121, 127, 129–30, 141, 145, 148, 155, 159–66, 168, 174, 180–82, 184, 217, 228, 231, 244–46, 254, 259, 267–68, 270, 280, 282
Glyn, Andrew 101, 303
GNU (Government of National Unity) 8
Godsell, Bobby 139–40
Goga, S. 12, 303
gold 34–35, 37, 48, 52, 66, 79, 83–84, 101–102, 107, 112, 133, 161–62, 171, 191, 195–98, 214–15, 257, 270–71
Goldstein, A. 291
Goldstein, J. 193, 303
Goodspeed, I. 316
Gordhan, Pravin 156, 161
Gough, I. 128, 303
governance 9, 21, 109, 127, 143, 164, 167, 186, 230, 233–34, 239, 247, 258
government 7–8, 18–19, 32, 34–35, 45, 52, 44–46, 69, 97, 101, 104, 117, 119, 125–26, 129, 132–33, 135, 149, 152, 155–58, 160, 164, 167, 172–73, 176, 198, 207, 214–15, 217–19, 238, 242, 269, 273, 279, 282–83
Graaf, J. 292
Granville, A. 30–31, 33, 311
Gray, K. 226–27, 303
greasy pole 80, 274, 286

Great Britain 102–103
Great Depression 260
Grinrod Bank 202
Grootgeluk colliery 31
growth theory
  new 231, 262–63
  old 263
growth 10, 15, 24–26, 28, 37, 45, 47, 63, 66, 85, 94, 110, 156, 163, 165–67, 173, 198, 206, 211–12, 216–17, 220, 227, 229, 231, 233, 235, 255–56, 262, 271–72
Guerrien, B. 188, 303
Guérin, I. 289
Gun, O. 188, 303
Gupta, S. 293

Habermeier, K. 312
Habib Overseas Bank 202
Haby, J. 292
Hall, D. 146, 303
Hall, P. 179, 181, 185–86, 192, 207, 303
Hamman, R. 117, 303
Hansen, U. 311
Harcourt, G. 24, 303
Hardman, D. 29, 303
Harford, T. 264, 303
Harrigan, J. 288
Harris, Laurence 80, 100, 102–103, 105, 183, 300
Hart, G. 18, 148–49, 303
Hartford, G. 215, 304
Harvard Group 148, 281
Harvard Panel 160, 248
Hausmann, Ricardo 148, 160, 248, 304
Hawkins, P. 203–204, 304
Hayek, Friedrich 265
Hayter, Teresa 98
HBZ Bank 202
health 6, 71, 77, 104, 110, 125, 146, 149, 151–52, 223, 232, 236, 254, 257
Heasman, M. 300
Heintz, J. 123, 304
Heller, P. 130–32, 304
Hendricks, F. 149, 292, 304
Herrera, R. 304, 310
Hicks-Slutsky-Samuelson conditions 260
hierarchies 13, 64, 67, 73, 123, 186, 267
Hildyard, N. 90, 304
Hillbom, E. 229, 304
Hindson, D. 40, 63, 304
Hirakawa, H. 296, 304
Historical Materialism 128
historiography 16–17, 108, 119, 124
history of economic thought 1, 4, 266, 268
history 2, 41, 69–70, 72, 75–77, 81, 85, 87, 93, 95, 97–98, 120–21, 138–39, 161, 180, 194–95, 199, 216, 223, 243, 266, 276, 269, 280
HIV/AIDS epidemics 234
Hodgson, G. 208, 304
Hoeffler, A. 292
Hofmeyr, J. 39–42, 45, 49–55, 60–61, 66, 68–69, 121, 305
homelands. *See* bantustans
Hong Kong 202
Horner, D. 66, 305
Hosking, S. 305
hostels 50, 214–15
households 49, 76, 97, 147, 204, 233
housing 17, 38, 46, 55, 59, 62–63, 66, 68, 71, 76–77, 101, 104, 125–28, 142, 151, 207, 212–15, 225, 227, 237, 240, 256–57, 262
human capital 44, 49–51, 53, 58, 60, 69, 261

I&E (GLC Industry and Employment) 98–99
IDA (International Development Assistance) 229
IDC (Industrial Development Corporation) 11, 115, 196, 198, 212
identity 4, 21, 137, 139–44, 148, 150–51, 153, 227, 249, 264
ideology 3, 5, 8–9, 14, 19, 21, 63–64, 91–92, 96, 99–100, 126, 129, 140, 144, 149–50, 193, 222, 228, 236, 240, 247, 250, 254, 258, 264–65
IDRC (International Development Research Centre) 133
IEA (International Energy Authority) 24
IEJ (Institute for Economic Justice) 9, 283–84
IEMH (Inefficient Market Hypothesis) 182, 186, 188, 190, 192–93
ILO 105, 135

IMF 81, 90–91, 109, 134, 159, 173, 176–77, 279, 282
Impala Platinum 211–13
Imperial Bank 195–96, 201–202
imperialism 2–3, 195, 267
imports 9, 12, 32, 86–87, 94, 176–78, 204
import-substituting industrialisation. *See* ISI
incentives 11, 112, 154, 164, 175, 190, 261
incomes 14, 55, 86, 129, 161, 165, 167, 193, 200, 206, 216, 229, 232, 245, 272
Independent Coal Producers Association 34
India 97, 131, 202, 217
Industrial Development Corporation. *See* IDC
Industrial Policy Action Plans (IPAPS) 11
industrial policy 7, 9–11, 20–21, 85, 87–89, 90, 100, 108, 118–20, 126, 172, 222–24, 229–31, 233, 258, 280–82
industrial 10, 12, 16, 50, 84–86, 89, 99–100, 119, 121, 123, 131, 159, 164–65, 173, 181–82, 190–92, 195–98, 200, 206, 213, 217–18, 226, 229, 235, 243–44, 280
  relations. *See also* trade unions 47, 52–53, 56–57, 66, 70, 73, 123, 183, 186, 211, 238, 268
industrialisation 10, 79–80, 82, 85–88, 93, 99, 108, 119–20, 198, 212, 218, 223–25, 227–28, 230–31, 235, 272
industry 10–14, 30–38, 64, 78, 80, 85, 87–88, 97–98, 100–101, 108, 114, 117–18, 120–21, 161–62, 191–92, 195, 197–98, 203–204, 208, 210–13, 215, 217–19, 229, 270–72, 279–81
Inefficient Market Hypothesis. *See* IEMH
inequality 7, 14, 18–19, 20, 55–56 58, 76–77, 151–52, 155, 163, 165, 172, 176, 193, 232, 245, 255–56, 267, 272, 274, 278
inflation 32, 41, 110, 164, 173, 206–207
inflows of capital 109–11, 154, 161, 166, 173–74, 273
information 29, 184, 186–88, 261
  asymmetric 40, 114, 180–81, 184, 187, 189, 193, 259
infrastructure 18, 156
  economic 76, 97, 115, 125, 257
  social 7, 194, 213, 232, 258
Ingham, G. 183, 305
Ingram, M. 292
Innes, Duncan 195, 198–99, 102, 269, 305
innovation 125, 192, 267
input-output 18, 101, 105
inputs 22, 24–27, 28, 30–32, 36, 52, 63, 86, 190, 204, 218, 262
instability 33, 159, 174, 244, 257
  economic 159, 170
  financial 113, 163, 194, 232
  political 234
institutional economics 185, 231, 260–61
institutional 8, 12–14, 19, 32, 41, 45, 51–54, 61, 69, 81, 114, 116, 118–19, 130, 149, 161– 62, 180–81, 183, 185, 187, 208, 223, 227, 229, 234, 238, 240, 251, 261–62, 265, 268, 277, 282–83
institutions 5, 7, 11, 19, 50, 53, 60–61, 132–33, 162, 172–73, 180–81, 183, 187, 192, 196, 200, 204, 208, 212, 226, 231, 234, 236, 240, 247
insurance 196, 112, 125, 144, 147, 178, 196, 198–201
interdisciplinary 4, 61, 70, 252–53, 259, 262, 264, 266–69, 278, 281, 284
interest rates 166, 174, 176, 191, 200, 206, 244
interests. *See also* classes. 1, 9, 88–89, 100, 135–36, 157, 165, 194–95, 221, 232, 235–36, 250–51, 276, 281
  economic and political 68, 87–88, 92, 101, 108, 120
  vested 9, 93, 188, 212
intermediate goods 85, 107, 243
international 4, 11–12, 24, 33, 37, 92, 113, 128–29, 132–33, 135–36, 140, 154–57, 159–60, 165, 173–74, 176, 182, 199–200, 206, 221, 226, 228–29, 233, 241, 243–45, 258, 274–76, 281
internationalisation 12, 103, 105–106, 129, 136, 163–64, 174, 182, 199–200, 206, 208, 213, 221–22, 244–46, 254
intervention 3, 5–7, 11, 53, 88, 99–100, 108, 119, 133, 144, 158, 147, 149, 156, 162, 183–85, 192, 207, 221–22, 224, 226–27, 229–31, 235, 241–42, 246, 254, 258, 264, 275, 282–83

Investec Bank 202
investment. *See also* foreign 7, 11–12, 15, 31, 38, 44, 48, 104, 110–12, 114–17, 131–33, 135, 156, 161, 163–64, 166, 168, 174, 186, 188, 190–92, 196, 199, 201, 206–207, 209, 227, 224, 233–34, 244, 273, 256, 279
  domestic 155, 157–59, 161, 164, 166–68, 273
  public 48, 52, 97, 114, 159, 167, 275
Ireland 228–29, 234
iron 33, 161, 171, 218
IS/LM interpretation of Keynesianism 2
ISCOR 12, 33, 35, 53, 65, 88, 108, 196
ISI (import-substituting industrialisation) 79, 82, 85–87, 108, 223, 227, 271–72
ISP (Industrial Strategy Project) 80–81, 85–87, 90, 99, 104, 107–8, 118, 279–81, 305
Itzikowitz, A. 199, 305

Jallais, S. 288
James, W. 66, 259, 288, 305
Japan 97, 128, 183, 191, 217, 227, 229, 231
Jayachandran, S. 172, 306
JCI Ltd (Johannesburg Consolidated Investment) 213
Jeeves, A. 214, 293, 306
Jenkins, C. 85, 306
JET-IP (Just Energy Transition Investment Plan) 9
Jo, T.-H. 292, 299
jobs 36, 43, 45, 49–50, 53–56, 64, 112, 115, 121, 123, 126, 134, 139, 156, 214, 217, 248, 272
  creation 172, 176, 228
  losses 133–34, 216 18
  reservation 36, 54, 59, 61–62, 64, 66, 67
Joffe, A. 305
Johannesburg Stock Exchange 14, 197, 212
Johannesburg 98, 195
Johnnic 213
Johnson Matthey 217
Johnson, Boris 98, 235
Jomo, K. 125, 293, 297, 306
Jones, J. 197, 306
Jones, R. Ch. 2, 306
Jones, S. 195, 306, 316
Josie, Jaya 281
JP Morgan Chase 202
Juliet 138–39, 143

Kahn, Brian 158
Kanbur, Ravi 132–33
Kapery, W. 292
Kaplan, Dave 64, 80, 85, 118–19, 292, 305–306
Kaplinsky, R. 107–108, 279, 305
Kar, D. 159, 306
Kaziboni, L. 287, 314
Kerala 130–32
Kessides, I. 116, 306
Keynes, J. M. 190, 267, 282
Khan, Sadiq 98
Khosa, M. 64, 306
Kim, S.-Y. 223, 306
Kimberley 195
Kindleberger, C. 159, 306
King, N. 13, 307
King, P. 33, 307
Knight, J. 45, 307
Kock Commission 200
Konopelko, E. 283, 307
Kooy, A. 66, 305
Korea 223, 226
Kothari, U. 291, 307
Kozul-Wright, R. 318
Kraak, A. 56, 307
Kraak, G. 51, 62, 307
Kranton, R. 140, 287
Kremer, M. 172, 306
Krueger, Anne 261, 307
Krugman, Paul 184, 227, 262, 307
KwaZulu-Natal 93
KwaZulu-Natal Press 252

labour brokers 214
labour economics 21, 40–41, 57, 70
Labour Market Commission (LMC) 101, 105, 120, 134–35, 139, 141–42, 308
labour markets 21, Ch. 3, 121–24, 133, 135, 151, 214, 238, 250, 254
  segmentation. *See also* segregation 42, 50–51, 54, 56–63, 68, 73–74, 76, 121–24, 281
Labour Party 102–103

labour power (cheap) 70–77, 122, 128, 254
Labrousse, A. 288
Lachman, D. 45, 307
laissez-faire 34, 100, 102, 105
LaMagdeleine, D. 55, 307
Lambert, R. 130, 307
land 43–45, 62, 67, 131, 136, 140, 215–16, 227, 279
Lapavitsas, C. 114, 145, 195, 241, 288, 296, 300, 307
latecomer 41, 145, 223, 225, 228, 235, 283
Latin America 223, 227–29, 242
leadership 5, 7–8, 19–20, 105, 134, 153, 160, 210, 240, 247, 274–75, 277
learning 25–26, 28–29
Lebowitz, M. 70, 72–74
Lee, K. 97, 307
Leftwich, A. 234, 307
Leigh, A. 264, 307
lending 100, 189, 191, 197, 204, 206, 216
Leopold, E. 61, 122, 141, 257, 268, 300
Lesotho 64, 215
Levenson, Z. 20, 308
Leverhulme 39
Levitt, S. 264, 308
Lewis, D. 67, 80, 108, 305–3066, 308
Lewis, J. 64, 308
Lewis, W. A. 43
liberalisation 20, 41, 89–90, 110, 113, 127, 133, 136, 148, 158–60, 173, 182, 192, 200, 206–207, 233, 273
liberation 65, 142, 148, 212, 274–75, 277
Liberty Holdings 201
Liberty Life Insurance 201
Liberty 163
Limpopo Provinces 211, 215
Lin, Justin 230–31, 248, 301, 308
linkagencies 82, 84, 103
linkages 10, 23, 81–82, 84, 86–89, 97, 101, 124, 212
Liodakis, G. 295, 308
Liow, E. 229, 308
List, Friedrich 223
Livingstone, Ken 98–99, 279
loans 134, 189, 192, 204, 216
London CSE Group 102–103, 308
London Financial Strategy 99
London Industrial Strategy (LIS) 99, 280
London Labour Plan (LLP) 99
London School of Economics 248
London Stock Exchange 163
London 98–99, 104, 163, 201
Lonhro 213
Lonmin 210–11, 213–14, 218
Louw, Tienie 196
loyalty 8, 100, 126, 135, 274, 277, 280
Lucas, Robert 261, 308
Lundahl, M. 45–46, 64, 308
Lusikisiki 214
Lutchman, J. 291
Lütz, S. 129, 308

Machaka, J. 11, 308
machinery 10, 12, 28–29, 171
MacIntosh, M. 100, 308
Macroeconomic Research Group. *See* MERG
macroeconomics 4, 13, 20, 47, 85, 90–91, 101, 109–10, 112, 114, 118, 146, 148, 155–56, 164–65, 183–84, 186, 207, 237–38, 244, 246, 254, 260–62, 273
Mader, P. 255, 309
Maharaj, B. 298, 309
maize 79, 83
Makgetla, N. 149, 309
Malan, T. 35, 309
male 40, 58, 64, 74
management 20, 45, 62, 64, 69, 116, 123, 129, 140, 150, 164, 173, 189–90, 201, 214–15, 238, 256, 268, 285
Mandel, E. 309
Mandela, Nelson 8, 274–75, 277
Manuel, Trevor 79–80, 111, 113–14, 134, 247, 249
manufacturing 11, 13, 15, 36, 62, 65, 67, 82, 86–87, 90, 99, 101, 119, 124, 131, 156, 197–98, 204, 229, 231
Mao 142
Marcuse, H. 266
marginal productivities 24, 29, 35–36, 43, 45
Marikana 21, 210–17
market and institutional imperfections 130, 161, 185
market forces 32–33, 43, 45, 47, 53, 115, 191
market imperfections (economics) 2, 40, 46, 58, 121, 140, 180–81, 184–88, 192, 223, 225, 236, 238, 261–62

Martin, W. 61, 309
Marx, Karl 72–73, 82, 181, 256, 266–67, 285, 294, 297, 309, 313
Marxism 1, 4, 68, 72–73, 82, 105, 115, 140, 265–67, 278
Marxist value theory 71, 74, 82, 96, 103
Mason, A. 300
Mass Democratic Movement. *See* MDM
material culture 3, 5, 137, 257–58, 274
Matthews, R. 37, 309
Maurer, L. 306
Mauro, P. 290
May, J. 66, 98, 117, 252, 309, 311
Mayo, M. 300
Mazzucato, M. 19, 309
Mbeki governments 8, 277
Mbeki, Thabo 19–20, 95, 148, 219, 246–47, 249, 274, 277, 279, 282, 309
Mboweni, Tito 105, 134
McCarthy Bank 201
McDonald, D. 119, 309
McGrath, M. 45, 307, 309
McKinnon, R. 163, 309
MDM (Mass Democratic Movement) 20, 133–34, 274
mechanisation 65–66, 218
media 5, 7, 156, 211, 258, 282
Medium Term Budget Policy Statement 156, 161
MEFC (Minerals-Energy and Financial Complex) 15, 17–18, 27, 20
Mercantile Bank 202
Mercantile Lisbon and McCarthy Bank 201
MERG (Macroeconomic Research Group) 8, 16–17, 39–40, 76–77, 80, 90, 97, 102, 104, 116, 124, 133–35, 137, 257, 273, 275–76, 279–81, 285, 309
mergers 12, 112, 164, 195, 198, 201, 212–13
Mertens, D. 309
Merton, Robert K. 222
Mesthrie, R. 300, 309
metals 10, 161, 170–71, 213
methodological nationalism 181, 185, 207, 226, 233, 235
Mexico 173
MIC. *See* military-industrial complex
Michie, J. 289, 295, 309
microeconomics 4, 101, 183–86, 193, 207, 238, 260–62
Middle East and North Africa 229
MIDP (Motor Industry Development Programme) 11
migrant labour 35–36, 43–44, 46, 55, 60, 62–67, 122, 131, 138–39, 161, 211, 214–15, 217, 278
  system 23, 161, 212, 214
military-industrial complex (MIC) 81, 103, 106, 268–70
Millennium Development Goals 166
Milonakis, D. 141, 260, 300–301, 309
Minerals and Petroleum Resources Development Act 211
minerals 10, 34–35, 37, 80–81, 117, 120, 161, 170, 174, 195–96, 206, 211–13, 217–18, 245, 270, 272–74
mines 26–29, 33–35, 37, 44, 65–67, 101, 115, 122, 138–40, 142, 161, 212, 215–16
mineworkers 40, 44, 74, 101, 103, 125, 214–18
minimum wages 3, 7, 39, 248, 264, 283–84
mining 12, 14, 25, 27–29, 30–31, 34, 36–37, 44–45, 52–53, 60, 65–67, 79, 81, 83–84, 102, 134, 155–56, 159, 161–65, 174, 195–97, 210–11, 213, 215, 218, 243, 270–711
  houses 23, 34, 88, 104, 162, 165, 195–98, 212, 214
Minister of Finance 113, 117, 134, 235, 247, 274
Mirrlees, Jim 179
Mis-invoicing. *See* trade
Misra-Dexter, N. 288, 309
Mitra, S. 293
Mkandawire, T. 228, 234, 240–41, 310
modernisation 90, 127, 222, 264
Modigliani-Miller hypothesis 188
Mohamed, S. 7, 9, 15, 110–11, 158, 164, 170, 287, 310–11, 317
Molina, O. 235–38, 310
Moll, P. 45, 53, 310
Molyneux, M. 145, 310
Momentum Insurance 201
Monaco, L. 289
Mondliwa, P. 12, 19, 287, 303, 310
monetarism 2, 183, 185, 261, 264
monetary policy 110, 173, 192, 200

Moneyweb 216
Monitor Group 87
monopolisation. *See also* concentration 12, 29–30, 41, 43, 45, 56, 58, 103, 105, 195, 204, 206, 211, 213, 217, 244, 254, 267
Mont Pelèrin 282
Montagues 138, 143
Montmasson-Clair, G. 9, 310
Moore, D. 296, 310
Morgan, Alan 116
Morgan, J. 299, 310
Morrell, R. 79, 83, 310
Morris, Mike 9, 108, 118, 280, 310–11
Motor Industry Development Programme (MIDP) 11
Mozambique 80, 215
MPRDA (Mineral and Petroleum Resources Development Act) 212, 215
municipalities 35, 149, 215–16, 279
Murfin, A. 30, 301
Murray, C. 61 311
Murray, N. 30–31, 33, 311
Murray, Robin 99, 107, 279

Naidoo, P. 293
National Bank of China 104
National Credit Act 216
National Credit Regulator 216
National Development Plan. *See* NDP
National Finance Corporation (NFC) 197–98
National Party 196, 198, 212, 271, 274
National Planning Commission (NPC) 172, 246–47, 250, 311
nationalisation 101, 144, 242, 269–71
Nattrass, N. 63, 90, 182, 305–306, 309, 311, 315
Naudé, W. 146, 311
NCE (New Classical Economics) 184, 261
Ndikumana, L. 109, 158, 166, 177, 290, 302, 311
NDP (National Development Plan) 217–19, 222, 246–50, 281, 283
Nedbank 196, 198, 201–204
Nedsual 198–99
negotiation 117, 133, 153, 275
  secretive 134
neo-Austrianism 22, 265–66, 278
neo-corporatism 220, 235, 238–39, 243
neoliberal 2–3, 7–8, 20, 77, 90, 94–95, 105, 110, 113, 115, 125, 144–46, 148–49, 159, 162–64, 174, 187, 194, 219–20, 226, 228–30, 232–33, 239–40, 242–43, 247, 253, 256, 265, 267, 273–74
neoliberalism (NL) 2–6, 8, 17–20, 95, 125, 130, 141, 143–49, 152, 179–85, 160, 193–209, 219–21, 228, 235, 238–43, 250, 252–56, 258–59, 264–65, 268, 270, 272–73
Netshitenzhe, J. 15, 17
new economic, geography 184–85, 262
New Financial Economics 180–81, 185, 187–89
New Growth Path (NGP) 156, 158, 172, 176, 219, 246–47, 250, 281, 311
Newman, Susan 10, 18, 154, 158, 185, 204, 206, 288, 311
NFI (net foreign investment) 37, 168–70, 176–77
Ngoma, A. 310
nickel 211, 218
NIEP (National Institute for Economic Policy) 78, 134, 281
Nigeria 97, 167
Nissanke, M. 288
Nobel Prize in Economics 140, 222
Noguchi, M. 296, 304, 307
Nolan, P. 70, 311
Noman, A. 311, 318
Nordic countries 235
norms 5, 17, 27, 68, 75–77, 229, 257, 259, 262
North Africa 229
North West Province 211, 215
North, Douglass 261
Northern Rock 147
NPM (New Public Management) 257
Nübler, I. 318
NUM (National Union of Mineworkers) 39, 101, 103, 134, 210, 214, 275
NUM (South Africa) 66, 214–15
NUMSA (National Union of Metalworkers) 107–108, 215
Nygard, I. 311

O'Donnell, K. 39, 312
O'Meara, D. 89, 195–97, 312
Öberg, P. 238, 312
Oberholzer, J. 29, 303
ODA (Overseas Development Assistance) 80
Odling-Smee, J. 309
OECD 160
Ogbu, M. 315
oil conversion plants 27, 30, 32, 37, 271
Old Mutual 163, 198–99, 201
Ollion, E. 302
OPEC 217
Oppenheimer, Harry 197
optimisation 3, 184, 186, 193, 260–62
Orange Free State Goldfields 197
ordo-liberalism 265
ore 270
organisations 29, 34, 37, 56–57, 73, 101, 120, 122–23, 131, 151, 153, 214, 228, 238, 243, 274, 277, 282–83
Orhangazi, O. 181, 312
Ostry, J. 173–74, 312
outflows 110–11, 135, 155–56, 159, 161, 164, 166–68, 173–74, 176–77, 204, 206, 244, 273
output 22, 24–27, 29–33, 36, 78, 86, 89, 94, 101, 103–104, 109, 130, 206, 212–13, 262
ownership 13, 44, 84, 89, 91, 104, 124, 138, 161–62, 165, 197, 199, 213, 244
Oxbridge 179
Oxfam 147
Oxford Institute for Economics and Statistics 179

Padayachee, Vishnu V. 21, 79, 93, 95, 105, 165, Ch. 11, 289, 295, 301–202, 309–10, 312
pandemic 255, 258, 269
Panitch, L. 288, 290, 312
Parayil, G. 304, 312, 315
Pardoe, D. 27, 312
Paret, M. 20, 308
Parsons, R. 312, 315
participation 5, 99, 107, 116, 153, 196, 201, 230–31, 238, 245, 247, 280, 282
parties 7, 18, 46, 112, 132, 136, 191, 193, 241, 243
Patel, Ebrahim 247
Pattillo, C. 292
Peck, J. 181, 208, 312
Pedroncelli, E. 27, 312
pensions 149, 193, 232
periodisation 70, 103, 105, 181, 254, 259, 264, 267–68
Perth Conference 94–95, 98, 126
Petersson, L. 64, 308
petro-chemicals 271
Petroleum Resources Development Act 211
Petropoulos, A. 229, 301, 312
PFI 147
Phakisa 218
Philip Hill Acceptance Co 198
Pierson, P. 312–13
Piketty, T. 267
Pilger, John 136
Pillay, D. 293
Pillay, Vella 100, 104, 275–76, 280
Pilling, G. 82, 313
Pincus, J. 241, 300
Piore, M. 99, 121, 313
Pitcher, A. 245, 313
platinum group metals (PGMs) 17, 79, 161, 211, 213, 215, 217–18
pluralism 266, 278, 282–83
policies 1–4, 6–10, 12, 15–17, 19–21, 34–35, 52, 63, 68, 78–81, 87–89, 90–92, 97–99, 106–10, 114, 118–19, 134, 146–49, 151, 160, 163–65, 167, 172–75, 183, 207, 212, 221–23, 225–26, 233–3, 235–38, 245–47, 250–51, 253–55, 257, 264–65, 279–81
policy 7, 9, 13, 15–16, 21, 58–59, 78, 90, 92, 96, 99, 104, 106, 114, 119–20, 126, 133–34, 137, 145, 148, 152, 156, 158, 160–61, 164, 170, 173, 168, 182, 185, 191, 194, 197, 219, 237, 246, 250, 263, 270, 272, 279, 282, 285
  economic 100, 102, 104, 126, 133–35, 154, 156–58, 164, 172, 176, 228, 281
  industrial 9–11, 20–21, 85, 87–88, 90, 100, 108, 118–20, 126, 172, 222–24, 229–31, 280–82
  macroeconomic 13, 20, 90, 109, 112, 114, 146, 206, 244
  social 4, 8, 125, 144–46, 163, 165, 194, 219, 224, 232, 244–45, 254

policymaking 3, 5, 9, 48, 91, 98, 126, 183, 220, 239, 250, 270, 276–77, 280, 285
political economy 4, 6, 17, 72–73, 81, 93–95, 125–26, 137–53, 157, 160, 174, 184, 186, 208, 211, 238, 252, 266–68, 278, 284
politics 5, 17–18, 87–88, 91, 130, 133, 141, 150–53, 162, 164, 207, 226, 258, 265, 277
Polokwane Conference 246
popularity 8, 20, 128, 237
population 46, 53, 76, 112, 120, 149, 157, 174, 204, 209, 249
populism 5, 258
POSCO 224–25
Posel, D. 41, 123, 304, 313
post-apartheid 6–8, 15, 17, 19, 76–77, 80, 94, 97, 102, 118, 120–21, 138, 152, 155, 160, 162, 165, 174–75, 180, 194, 210, 212, 217, 221, 242, 244–48, 253, 269–70, 272–74, 277–81, 283, 285
  economy 21, 108–109, 141, 160, 194, 211, 213, 222, 244, 247, 253, 277, 280, 282
post/neo-fordism 81, 107, 279
post-Keynesian 284–85
postmodernism 152, 265, 268
post-war boom 2, 128, 162, 165, 179, 183, 188, 219–20, 235, 237, 240, 254, 261
Post-Washington Consensus (PWC) 3, 78, 90–92, 98, 114, 125, 127, 130–32, 147, 185, 227–28, 259, 262
Poulantzas, N. 71, 278
poverty 132, 147, 149, 155, 157, 165, 172, 247–48
Powell, M. 240, 313
power 7–9, 12–14, 19–20, 68, 88–90, 99–100, 125–26, 137, 143–44, 150, 163, 193, 207, 213, 217, 226, 228, 234, 243, 245, 249, 258, 271, 273–75, 278, 281
  economic and political 88–89, 125–26, 271, 278
  economic 14, 243, 245, 249, 271
  political 88–90, 162, 243, 271, 278
power, electric 27, 30, 33, 37, 115, 117, 119, 218, 270
Pradella, L. 226, 313
Presidency 7, 20, 95, 117, 274
Presidential Labour Market Commission 39, 105, 276
Primrose, D. 315
privatisation 2, 7, 78, 100–101, 115–17, 125, 145–47, 200, 215, 246, 254–58, 269–70
procurement, public 10–12
production functions 23–24, 26–27, 30, 48, 260, 263
production 11, 24, 26, 30, 32, 37, 42–43, 56, 70–75, 83, 86–87, 89, 99, 105–106, 124, 128, 161, 190, 211, 213, 217, 226, 254, 257
productive 12–13, 21, 71, 155, 159, 164, 174, 256
productivity 7, 22–23, 25–29, 31, 41–42, 63, 72–73, 75–76, 100, 109, 128–29, 131, 165, 189–90, 236, 244, 255
profitability 13, 33, 43, 52, 56, 65, 72, 128, 186, 204, 207, 217–18
profits 23, 26–27, 41, 82, 128, 145, 163, 190, 196, 206, 213, 270, 272
protection 10, 67, 79, 85–87, 90–91, 108, 118–19, 207, 229, 278 272
protests 15, 18, 117, 249, 282
public sector systems of provision 75
public sector 5, 48, 75, 77, 104, 133, 149, 159, 183, 286
PWC. *See* Post-Washington Consensus

quality 30–31, 62, 75, 126, 151, 189, 266, 278
Qureshi, M. 312

race 41, 46–47, 55–57, 59, 67–69, 71, 74, 76, 82, 120–21, 123, 126, 143, 151, 241, 243, 267
railways 31, 37
Rainbow Nation 21, 137–53, 248
Ramachandran, V. 292
Ramaphosa, Cyril 20, 214, 283
Ramphele, M. 64, 66, 317
Rand (Barlow) 48, 110, 112–13, 161, 174, 198, 204
Rand Merchant Bank and Remgro 201
Randomised Control Trials 262
rational choice 141, 259
rational expectations 184, 261
Razavi, S. 316
Rebitzer, J. 57, 313
Reboredo, R. 18, 313
recession 30, 47, 144, 183
Reconstruction and Development Programme (RDP) 102, 104, 134, 148, 243, 246, 249, 273, 279

redistribution 14–15, 117, 130–32, 213, 238, 245, 275
Reed, K. 308
regulation 10, 81, 105, 107, 110, 113, 129, 154, 189, 192, 204, 207, 216, 229, 278
Reinert, E. 235, 313
Reinhardt, D. 312
relations 17–18, 30, 40, 43, 47–48, 50–51, 71, 73–74, 89, 103, 117, 123–24, 135, 160, 162, 185–8, 1897, 192–93, 199, 226, 236–37, 239, 255, 269, 278
relationships 30, 39–41, 74, 84, 122, 126, 165, 167, 180–81, 186–187, 226, 228, 241–42, 252–53, 256, 264, 266–67, 270, 282
Remgro 201
remittances 63–66, 131, 140, 214
renationalisations 147
rents 13, 19, 41, 255
reproduction
  economic and social 6–7, 40, 70–71, 74–76, 124, 128–29, 163, 179, 254, 256, 258, 267
  social 4–7, 17 62, 70–71, 74–76, 124, 128–29, 145, 179, 254, 256–58, 267
RESA 102, 270
research 3, 10, 23, 40, 78, 80–81, 89, 94–95, 97, 100, 102–104, 107, 115, 126, 133, 137, 157, 172, 180, 247, 253, 265, 268–70, 276, 279, 281, 283–84
Reserve Bank 101, 134, 139, 274, 285
reserves 33, 112, 116, 168, 176–77, 273
resistance 69, 76, 104, 120, 274
retail 10, 13, 204
Rethel, L. 233, 313
Rethinking Economics for Africa (REFA) 283
Reynolds, J. 270, 313
Rhodes University 220
Rhodes, M. 220, 235–39, 299, 310, 313
Ricardo, David 82, 266
Richards Bay 31, 33
Riekert Commissions 65
Robb, N. 287
Robbins, G. 310–11
Roberts, S. 9, 11, 19, 93, 115, 287, 291, 308, 310, 313
Robertson, M. 289, 300
Robinson, Joan 24
Rodriguez, F. 262, 313
Rodrik, Dani 129,173, 248, 313
Romeo 138–39, 143
Rommetvedt, H. 312
Roubaud, F. 289
Royal Bafokeng Holdings 212
Royal Bank of Scotland 202
rural 43–44, 48, 63, 71, 165, 215, 246
Russia 173, 217
Rustenberg 216
Rustomjee, Zavareh 11–12, 16, 52, 78–81, 84, 88, 90, 93, 96, 98, 104, 106, 109, 120, 124, 158, 160–61, 182, 196–97, 212, 224, 243, 270, 281, 301, 313–14
Rutman, G. 44, 63, 288

SA Bank of Athens 202
Saad-Filho, A. 254, 259, 289–90, 298, 300–301, 314
SAAMBOU (Saambou Nasionale Bouvereniging) 201
Sabel, C. 99, 313–14
SACEEC (South African Capital Equipment Export Council) 11
Sachs, Michael 15–17, 314
SADC (Southern African Development Community) 112
San Luis Rey 139
sanctions 22, 32, 37, 87, 162–63, 174, 180, 182, 199–200, 244, 271, 278
Sanlam 195–98, 201
Sano, M. 304
Santam 195–96
Santos, A. 299, 314
Saraswati, J. 97, 301, 314
SARB. *See* South African Reserve Bank
SARS (South African Revenue Service) 155
Sasfin 202
Sasol 12–13, 27, 29, 32–33, 87, 108, 163, 196, 271
Sato, H. 23, 301
Savoy Hotel 116
Scandinavia 235, 238
Schindler, M. 200, 314
Schlesinger 198
Schneider, B. 168, 314
Schneider, H. 149, 314
Scholes, Myron S. 222

School of Oriental and African Studies. *See* SOAS
schools 58, 77, 79, 104, 224, 266–67, 284
Schumpeter, Joseph 267
Schwartz, M. 292
Scotland 202
SCP. *See* Social Compacting Paradigm
second world 66, 94, 195, 235, 260
Secunda 27
securitisation 255–57, 272
Seekings, J. 17, 182, 311
segregation 64, 70, 77
  occupational 54–55, 59, 61, 69, 121, 123
Sender, J. 40, 105, 135, 246, 252, 276, 312, 314
services 11, 13, 17, 62, 67, 76–77, 79, 89, 91, 109, 112, 144, 155, 231, 250
  public 152, 255, 257
sexism 56
Shanghai Banking Corporation 202
shareholders 12–13, 146, 163, 189, 194, 196, 232, 244
Sharpeville massacre 199, 210
Shaw, E. 163, 247, 314
Shaw, T. 247, 315
shipbuilding 88
shock therapy 115, 222, 242, 258
Shonfield, A. 237, 315
Shoprite 13
Siegel, N. 236–37, 315
Sigma 33
Simkins, C. 62, 315
Singapore 228–29
Singleton 199
Singleton, J. 199, 315
Sinha, D. 293
Siwisa, B. 292
Siwisa, N. 85, 306
skills 11, 36, 38, 45, 48, 58–59, 64–66, 69, 73, 80, 110, 122, 224, 285
slavery 150–51
Slovo, Joe 275
Smith, Adam 266
SOAS (School of Oriental and African Studies) 10, 15, 79–80, 97, 105, 281
Social Compacting Paradigm (SCP) 21, 179, Ch. 10
social development. *See also* development 131–32, 155, 228, 245, 248, 273, 282–83
social sciences 2–3, 137, 141, 261–63, 265–66, 268, 278
social security 6, 77, 245
socialism 219
Societe Generale 202
sociology 40, 57, 73, 107, 123, 137–38, 141, 143, 186, 224, 259, 262
Soer, E. 19, 314
Soludo, C. 308, 315
Song, H.-Y. 226, 315
Sorec Ltd 198
Soskice, D. 179, 181, 185–86, 192, 207, 303
South African Breweries 13, 163
South African Capital Equipment Export Council (SACEEC) 11
South African Communist Party (SACP) 210, 221
South African Institute of Race Relations 40
South African Journal of Economics 22, 39
South African Military-Industrial Complex 270
South African Mutual Life Association Society 198, 201
South African National Life Assurance Company 196
South African Presidential Labour Market Commission 139
South African Reserve Bank (SARB). *See also* Reserve Bank 41, 48–51, 55–57, 59, 68–69, 112, 121, 123, 143, 151, 154–58, 175–76, 204, 267, 314
South African Sociological Association 137
South African Transport Services (SATS) 35, 53
South Asia 229
South Indian states 131
South Korea 23, 82, 87–88, 96–97, 224, 226–27
Southall, R. 291, 293
Southern Africa 10, 214
Southern Centre for Inequality Studies (SCIS) 16
Soviet Union 135, 219, 242, 274
Soweto uprising 210
Spandau, A. 36, 65, 315
specialisation 189
  flexible 81, 125, 279

speculation 20, 85, 91, 110, 113, 145, 163, 199, 255, 272–73
stability 8, 90–91, 110, 214–15, 235, 240, 247–48, 263
stagflation 179, 183
stagnation 48, 52, 206
Stals, Chris 101, 139
Stamp, Sir Josiah 150
Standard Bank 195, 199, 201–202, 204
Standard Chartered Bank 199, 202
Standard/Liberty Life 198
Standing, Guy 135
Stanlib 201
state capture 8, 20, 79, 95, 155
Stein, Gertrude 30
Stein, H. 311
Steuart, I. 314
Steyn, G. 113–14, 315
Stigler, George 261
Stiglitz, Joe 90, 92, 114, 132, 184–85, 187, 189–90, 193, 259, 311, 315
Stilwell, F. 267, 315
stock market 129, 186, 190, 201
Stockholms Enskilda Bank 235
Stoneman, C. 92, 301
stop-go 85, 94
Sträng, Gunnar 235
Streeck, W. 181, 315
strikes 210, 275
sub-Saharan Africa 100, 109, 158, 166, 229
subsistence 63, 66, 71, 76
Summers Larry 132, 188, 315
Summers, V. 188, 315
supply 22, 32–33, 42, 47, 49–51, 56, 58, 69, 115, 117, 190, 217, 260
surplus value 72, 73, 75, 254
surplus 15, 75, 109, 115, 154, 188, 196, 198, 245, 254
Sussex 99, 107, 279
Svensson, T. 312
Swaziland 215
Sweden 235, 238
Sweezy, Paul 106
Swiss canton 116, 167
Syfrets Trust Co 198
Syfrets-UAL Holdings 198
systems of provision (SoPs) 4–5, 17, 74–75, 77, 142, 152, 257, 259
Taiwan 202, 226–27
takeover 186, 190, 200
tariffs 32, 118, 135, 164, 212
Tavasci, D. 301
tax(es) 11, 101, 151, 155, 158–59, 164, 166, 170, 172
taxi 64
Teba Bank 202
technical apparatus (TA1) 259–60, 262
technical architecture (TA2) 259–60
technology 10–12, 22, 27, 30–31, 48, 56, 64, 97, 106, 139, 192, 194, 217, 223, 226, 233, 260, 267
telecommunications 64
Teles, N. 299, 314
Teljeur, E. 308
textiles 7, 11
TFP (total factor productivity) 21–38, 52
Thatcher, Margaret 98, 100–101, 103, 135, 142, 279
Thatcherism 96, 99, 105, 135
Theodore, N. 181, 208, 312
Thesen, G. 312
think-tanks 278, 282
Third Wayism 2, 130, 235, 258
Thornton, T. 315
Thurlow, J. 316
Tinel, Bruno 252
TIPS Conference 98, 119
Todaro, M. 43
Tomas Barlow 198
Toporowski, J. 296, 315
Törnquist, O. 131, 315
total factor productivity. *See* TFP
trade unions 20, 36, 38, 41, 43–44, 50, 52–53, 55–59, 61, 64–65, 68–69, 100, 102, 105, 131, 144, 152, 210–11, 214, 219, 228, 243, 247, 250, 254, 276, 278, 283
trade 11–12, 33, 85–86, 90, 102, 109, 117–19, 135, 164, 167, 170, 172, 176–78, 184, 188, 194, 206–207, 226, 232, 244–45, 254–55, 258, 262–63, 268, 273, 280
  mis-invoicing 158, 168, 170–72, 174, 177
training 35–36, 42, 64, 66, 80, 94, 104, 239, 276–77, 279–80, 281–82
transaction costs 80, 166, 184, 186
transfer pricing 155, 175, 273

transformation 10, 13–14, 26, 37, 40, 65, 75–76, 93, 112, 124, 179, 200, 219, 225–27, 230, 233, 245
transition 9–10, 20, 41, 77, 98, 107, 126–27, 130, 132, 136, 219, 223, 225–26, 229, 240, 242, 278
Transkei 214
TRANSNET 53
transparency 113, 175, 230
transport 30–31, 37, 46, 55, 62, 64–65, 68, 75, 77, 97–98, 171, 257, 279
Transvaal 195
Traxler, F. 236, 290
Treasury 7, 15, 148, 172, 197, 242, 244, 248, 281
Tregenna, F. 10, 287–88
Trentmann, F. 296, 316
Tressel, T. 287
Tripartite Alliance 7–8, 14, 20, 133, 210, 220–21, 274, 277
Trust Bank 198, 201
Truu, M. 56, 291, 316
Tsukamoto, T. 229, 316

UA (Union Acceptances Limited) 198
UBS (Union Bank of Switzerland) 117, 316
UDF (United Democratic Front) 20
UK 3, 39–40, 81, 97, 99–100, 105, 109, 147, 150–51, 183, 191–92, 194, 232, 268–69, 279
UN 167, 187, 316
UNCTAD 166, 171
underdevelopment 165, 247
UNECA (United Nations Economic Commission for Africa) 166, 247, 316
unemployment 41, 48, 54, 66, 69, 123–24, 139, 157, 159, 165, 245
uneven development 182, 185, 198
Union Corporation Company 197
United Nations Economic Commission for Africa (UNECA) 166, 247
Unterhalter, E. 299, 302
urban 43–44, 48, 60–66, 68, 72, 139, 147, 195
USA 54, 56, 106, 128, 132, 194, 223, 227, 232, 260, 265, 269,
user charges 146, 256–57
Usury Act 216
Utah International 33
utility functions 2, 42, 140, 259, 260, 264
Utting, P. 298, 316

Valodia, I. 124, 292, 309, 316
van der Zwan, N. 309
van Garderen, D. 29, 316
van Huellen, S. 287
van Niekerk, Robbie 252, 273, 309, 312–13
Van Waeyenberge, Elisa 147, 223, 230, 241, 248, 289, 301, 316
Van Wyk, K. 206, 316
vanadium 211
Varieties of Capitalism (VoC) 21, 179–209, 219, 238–39
VBS Mutual Bank 202
Veblen, Thorstein 267
Verhoef, G. 195–99, 315–16
Vilakazi, T. 12, 14, 316–17
Viljoen, D. 40, 317
violence 19, 21, 68, 139, 234
Vitali, S. 201, 317
volatility 5, 14, 110–11, 163, 174, 194, 204, 232, 238, 257, 273
Volkskas Bank 196–98, 201
Voluntary Disclosure Programme (VDP) 155, 157–60, 175
von Holdt, K. 12, 317

Wade, R. 92, 224, 229–30, 235, 242, 317
wages. *See also* discrimination and minimum wages Ch. 3
  differentials 41–42, 50, 54–55, 57, 69, 74, 121
Wainwright, H. 100, 308
Wallenberg, Marcus 235
Washington Consensus 3, 90–91, 127, 147, 221–25, 242, 261–62
Washington 125, 222, 227, 259
water 6, 101, 147, 152, 257
wealth 14–15, 68, 76, 99, 117, 158–59, 165, 167–68, 175, 187, 211, 213, 245, 260, 274–75, 277
  personal
Webster, Eddie 65, 95, 98, 111, 123–24, Ch. 5 Appendix 290, 317
Weeks, John 105, 135
Weiss, A. 187, 315

Welfare Regimes Approach (WRA) 128, 179, 219
welfare state 129, 132, 145, 152, 236
welfare 68, 71, 110, 128–30, 146, 167, 179, 207, 223, 228, 235
welfarism 90, 129, 219, 227, 236–37, 240, 242, 254, 262
Wesbank 201
Wesgro 119
Wesso, G. 111, 317
Western Bank 198
Western Cape Investment and Trade Promotion Agency 119
Western Cape 119
whites 35–36, 38, 44–47, 52–53, 56–57, 59–60, 62–64, 66, 69, 85, 102, 136, 149, 195–96, 212, 217, 243, 248
Wiarda, H. 237, 317
Wiegratz, J. 300, 317
Wiehahn, N. 36, 65, 317
Williams, M. 231, 317
Wilson, E. 300,
Wilson, F. 64–66, 317
Wolpe, Harold 70–72, 77, 102, 270, 278, 317
women 42, 48, 50, 54–56, 59–60, 62, 64, 95, 98, 121–22, 227, 249
Wood, G. 292
work 1–4, 39–40, 42–44, 49, 55–56, 59, 61–62, 64–65, 73, 80, 82, 94–95, 102–103, 105–108, 115, 122–23, 128, 137, 140–41, 151–52, 172, 252–53, 262, 269–70, 285
workers 36–37, 39, 41–43, 45, 49–50, 52–53, 55, 57, 59–60, 64–65, 67, 73, 115, 121, 131, 211, 214–17, 227
workforce 28, 35–37, 42, 44, 47–48, 53, 57, 59, 62–63, 65–67, 74, 98, 100–101, 122, 145, 214–15
working class 5, 43, 45, 70, 73, 75, 130, 250, 254, 277
working conditions 38, 40, 54–56, 59, 62, 64, 67, 122–23, 140, 151
World Bank Commission on Growth and Development 160
World Bank 4, 47, 81, 88, 90–92, 104, 109–10, 116, 121, 126, 132–35, 148, 160, 166–68, 177, 182, 206, 224, 229–30, 242, 248, 259, 264, 279, 282, 287, 289–90, 292–94, 300, 304, 306–308, 310, 316–18
world systems theory 226
Wright, J. 300
WTO 118, 135

Xirinachs, J. 318
Xstrata 213

Yalman, G. 298, 314
Yates, R. 263, 291
youth 48, 249
Yudelman, D. 293

Zalk, N. 10–12, 15, 20, 318
Zeitlin, J. 99, 314
Zimbabwe 22, 136
Zuma, Jacob 8, 16–17, 20, 95, 172, 219, 246, 277
Zysman, J. 207, 318

www.ingramcontent.com/pod-product-compliance
Lightning Source LLC
LaVergne TN
LVHW020653300926
849161LV00004B/928
9789004748323